"Terrific...A boon for beginners and a bible for professionals. This book will become as indispensable to anyone in the graphic arts industry as a set of magic markers and a layout pad."

Steve Alburty, MIS Director
Chiat/Day Inc. Advertising

"This book should be a fundamental part of any computer artist's library. It covers all the essential ins and outs of Photoshop more succinctly and vividly than other books of its kind."

Sally Face, Manager of Computer Systems
BBDO New York

"Photoshop is one of the most powerful programs available to desktop publishers today, with a daunting array of features geared to varying areas of professional publishing. *Fundamental Photoshop* presents the features of the program in logically organized chapters and provides examples each step of the way. It is a well-organized, easy-to-follow guide to this sometimes difficult program."

Wendy Allen, Director of Electronic Publishing Systems
New York Times Women's Magazines

"Oh, no—not another Photoshop book! Oh, YES! If you only have time for one Photoshop book, *Fundamental Photoshop*, with its clarity, information, and pertinent examples, is the one to get."

Donald Gambino, Chairman of the Computer Art Department
School of Visual Arts, New York City

"*Fundamental Photoshop* is an unusually informative and highly readable introduction to the magic of Adobe Photoshop. It is of value to newcomers as well as experienced users in learning to effectively use Photoshop's power for image processing, photo retouching, and electronic painting. Particularly helpful are the clear illustrations, easy-to-understand explanations, and detailed step-by-step exercises. This is a truly comprehensive, single-source reference to Photoshop that will be of long-time value."

Burton Holmes, President of Burton Holmes Associates
Corporate Marketing Communications

FUNDAMENTAL

PHOTOSHOP

CENTENNIAL COLLEGE
COMMUNICATIONS DEPARTMENT
P.O. Box 631, Station A
Scarborough, Ontario
M1K 5E9

FUNDAMENTAL

PHOTOSHOP

Adele Droblas Greenberg
Seth Greenberg

Osborne **McGraw-Hill**

Berkeley   New York   St. Louis   San Francisco
Auckland   Bogotá   Hamburg   London   Madrid
Mexico City   Milan   Montreal   New Delhi   Panama City
Paris   São Paulo   Singapore   Sydney
Tokyo   Toronto

Osborne **McGraw-Hill**
2600 Tenth Street
Berkeley, California 94710
U.S.A.

For information on software, translations, or book distributors outside of the U.S.A., please write to Osborne McGraw-Hill at the above address.

FUNDAMENTAL PHOTOSHOP

1234567890 DOC 9987654

ISBN 0-07-881994-6

To Beatriz, Ben, Gloria, Max, Ginger, Steven, Gary, Joshua, and Stacy for their love and support

CENTENNIAL COLLEGE
COMMUNICATIONS DEPARTMENT
P.O. Box 631, Station A
Scarborough, Ontario
M1K 5E9

CONTENTS AT A GLANCE

A book as extensive as *Fundamental Photoshop* could not have been written without the help of numerous people.

Above all we'd like to thank the editorial and production staff at Osborne/McGraw-Hill, particularly Publisher Larry Levitsky, Editor-in-Chief Jeff Pepper, and Acquisitions Editor Scott Rogers. We owe a debt of gratitude to Scott for his dedication, perseverance, help and enthusiasm during the writing, editing, and production stages of *Fundamental Photoshop*. We also would like to express our sincere appreciation to Project Editor Janet Walden, Associate Editor Emily Rader, Editorial Assistant Sherith Pankratz, Copyeditor Carol Henry, Proofreader Charlotte Bagby, Graphic Designer Mason Fong, and Illustrators Marla Shelasky and Lance Ravella. In addition, special thanks go to Computer Designer Mickey Galicia who not only created the look of the book, but also went above and beyond the call of duty in order to make sure it shipped on time. All of these people spent many long hours helping us ensure that *Fundamental Photoshop* would be the clear, concise, and attractive book that it is.

We'd also like to thank the many artists whose excellent work appears in the color insert and the "Photoshop in Action" sections in this book.

Thanks to everyone at Adobe systems, especially Steve Guttman, Senior Product Manager of Macintosh applications, for his support and help. We are especially grateful to Eric Thomas, Senior Support Specialist for Photoshop Windows, for graciously hunting down answers to our questions. We'd also like to thank Adobe Product Managers Jeff Parker, Bryan Lampkin, and Jerry Granucci. Above all, we thank the Photoshop programmers who created and developed such an outstanding product. Their hard work makes our work look like magic.

We'd also like to express our thanks to Martha Wells, Peter Faucetta, Maureen Beirne, Anthony Cozzolino, Joseph Burke, Ernie Migliaccil, Steve Kelsall, and the computer operators at Applied Graphics Technology who helped create the beautiful color insert in this book.

We're grateful to our friends, clients, and students who kept asking us to put our consulting and training skills down on paper and provide a book for them. Special thanks are due to Mitch Rose, Richard Lombard, Ethan Ernest, Jurgen Wolff, David Peters, Paul and Pam Einarsen, Richard

Berenson, Dave Trooper, Ken Chaya, Bianca McGibny, Barbara Rietschel, Dolores Calafati, Joseph LaRezza, Dottie Gettelson, Won Chung, Emily Singer, Bill Lyon, Suzanne Arden, Richard DiLorenzo, Bill Glass, Dennis Green, Mary Kelly, Bruce Stark, James Dowlen, Craig Mullins, Carol Chen, Steve Sardo, Miles Perkins, Paul Lasaine, Michael Curtis, Barry Hyton, Lynda Freeman, Marian Powers, Jim Hamilton, Alisa Hill, Joseph Favale, Phil Rose, and Ken Echevarria. We'd also like to thank everyone else who helped along the way.

We're grateful to Gary Stone of Lebanon Valley Offset for his assistance in tracking down the image we needed and sending it so quickly.

We thank the many corporations who graciously provided assistance: Agfa, Apple Computer, ColorBytes, Corel, D'pix, Daystar, EFI, IBM, ImSpace, HSC Software, Iris Graphics, Ken Hansen Photography, Kodak, LetraSet, Light Source, Linotype-Hell, Logitech, PANTONE, PixelCraft, QMS, Radius, Scitex, Strata, SuperMac, Tektronix, Toshiba, TRUMATCH, and Wacom.

In the late 1980s, Thomas Knoll, a University of Michigan graduate student, created a computer program whose primary purpose was to open and display different graphics files on a Macintosh Plus. This was the humble beginning of the program that was eventually to become Photoshop.

Thankfully for Photoshop users, Tom found that working on a computer program proved to be much more fun than writing a thesis paper. With the encouragement of his brother John Knoll, a special effects supervisor at George Lucas' Industrial Light and Magic Company, Tom began adding image-editing capabilities to his program.

Adobe took Tom's creation under its wings. Soon Tom's brother John was creating filters for the program, and through the collaborative efforts of the Knoll brothers, Adobe's programmers, and the program's original project manager, Steve Guttman, Photoshop evolved into a software package that began revolutionizing the color publishing world.

As Photoshop grew in power and popularity, its users sought help. As consultants, trainers and Photoshop users, we were encouraged to write an easy-to-understand book that would cover the program's fundamentals, yet go well beyond the basics. The result is *Fundamental Photoshop*.

ABOUT THIS BOOK

Whether you are a Photoshop beginner or an experienced user, we're sure you'll find *Fundamental Photoshop* to be both a unique instruction and reference book.

We not only cover virtually every command and dialog box in the program, but we also have you try them out. The book is filled with features, hints, tips, step-by-step tutorials, and full-fledged Photoshop projects that you can create with your own images or those provided by Adobe with the Photoshop package. As you read through the book, you'll learn how magazine and book covers, advertisements, and television series and film backgrounds were created by some of the top Photoshop artists in the country.

Disk Offer

Even though we've carefully designed the book so that you can easily re-create the sample projects using Photoshop Tutorial files or your own images, you may wish to practice with some of the images used in the book.

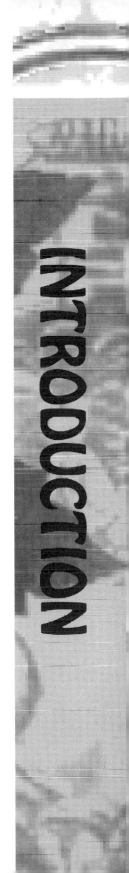

INTRODUCTION

If so, you can send for a high-density disk containing 12 images. The cost of the disk is $12.95. Make your check or money order to "AD. Design" and send to the address listed at the end of Chapter 14 (page 513). Make sure you specify whether you would like a Mac or PC disk.

HOW THIS BOOK IS ORGANIZED

Chapters 1 through 6 are introductory chapters that guide you through the fundamental tools and basic features of the program.

- Chapter 1 begins with an overview of the entire Photoshop design process, from digitizing images to outputting them at a prepress house. The chapter concludes with a guide to calibrating your monitor to ensure that you start your Photoshop work with the colors on your screen displayed as accurately as possible.

- In Chapter 2, we enter the world of Photoshop by introducing you to the basics with a tour of the program's menus, tools, and palettes. The first tutorial emphasizes the importance of thinking like a painter and understanding the concepts and capabilities of a pixel-based program.

- Chapter 3 provides an introduction to the selection tools. You may be surprised to see that even with the program's basic selection tools, you can create interesting and attractive montages, collages, and vignettes.

- Chapter 4 provides an introduction to color theory. Understanding color theory is one of the prerequisites to successfully using Photoshop for color publishing. We'll take a look at the difference between the RGB (red/green/blue), CMYK (cyan/magenta/yellow/black), HSB (hue/saturation/brightness), and Lab color models.

- Chapter 5 covers Photoshop's painting tools.

- Chapter 6, which concludes the first section of this book, is an introductory look at image-editing techniques.

Chapters 7 through 11 bring you to an intermediate level.

Chapter 7 covers digitizing images, image cropping and rotating, and changing brightness and contrast. We round out the chapter by covering image-editing commands, such as Perspective and Distort, so that you not only learn the basics of scanning, but can create a design project with the images you scan.

Chapter 8 teaches you how to apply various filters such as Unsharp Mask, Gaussian Blur, Motion Blur, Emboss, and Spherize. If you like special effects, you'll especially enjoy this chapter.

Chapter 9 provides an in-depth discussion on switching modes; in particular, converting an RGB Color file to a CMYK Color file. This chapter will also lead you step-by-step through the process of creating a duotone and a mezzotint.

Chapter 10 introduces you to Photoshop's powerful Pen tool. Here you'll be able to try your hand at creating paths and Bézier curves. You'll also learn how to create a clipping path, which is used to silhouette images that you place in other programs.

Chapter 11 completes the intermediate section of the book with a look at creating special effects with Photoshop's Composite Controls and Paste commands.

Chapters 12 through 14 lead you to more advanced levels.

Chapter 12 provides an in-depth discussion of creating masks and using channels. You'll also learn how to save and load selections. The chapter ends with an overview of each of Photoshop's Calculate commands.

Chapter 13 takes you step-by-step through the retouching and color-correcting processes. We'll explore Photoshop's Rubber Stamp, Airbrush, and Dodge/Burn tools when we show how to correct old and damaged photographs. For many readers, this chapter may be one of the most interesting in the book.

Chapter 14 explains the printing process and includes instructions for calibrating your system to a proof.

Appendix A concludes *Fundamental Photoshop* with a discussion of file formats and techniques for exporting and importing Photoshop and other application files.

Although this book concentrates on the Mac and PC versions of Photoshop, users with Silicon Graphics and Sun Computers can also take advantage of this book. The keyboard shortcuts for both of these computers are similar to those for the PC. Note, however, one exception: the Sun computer has a META key which is similar to the ALT key. See your Quick Reference card for more details on keyboard shortcuts.

THE PHOTOSHOP STUDIO

Photoshop is truly magical. It can pluck a pyramid from the sands of Egypt and gently drop it down on the Champs-Elysées, looking so real that even a Parisian might not think anything is out of place. Photoshop can make the wrinkles of age vanish magically—or create them where they haven't yet appeared. It can transform a scan of a torn and discolored photograph so that it looks like a flawless image taken by a master photographer. And Photoshop can turn your blank computer screen into an artistic masterpiece—a blaze of fantastic designs, patterns, and colors.

As you'll see in the many professional art and design samples throughout this book, especially in the color insert, the Photoshop design process can take many forms and can lead in a multitude of directions. Photoshop is an electronic passport to high-end color desktop publishing as well as prepress, multimedia, animation, digital photography, and painting.

Photoshop transports you to these ports of call in many different ways. Once an image is input into Photoshop from a scanner, digital or video camera, video recorder, or Photo CD image, it can be retouched, painted, color-corrected, sharpened, rippled, or distorted. An image can be cut apart, juxtaposed, or blended into another. It can then be output to a slide recorder, a video recorder, a black-and-white or color printer, or an imagesetter to create the final film, which is used to make plates for a printing press. Figure 1-1 illustrates the various input and output devices that cooperate in the Photoshop design and production process.

Although you undoubtedly are anxious to jump right in and start turning your artistic visions into reality, take some time first to get acquainted with the Photoshop design process and the digital technology involved in computer image editing. This chapter provides a brief overview of the entire process—inputting, editing, and outputting images—and covers the basics of computers, storage devices, monitors, video display and accelerator cards, scanners, Photo CDs, digital and video cameras, and color printers.

You may want to consider purchasing much of the equipment reviewed in this chapter, but keep in mind that some of it is best left to the professional prepress houses, service bureaus, and electronic imaging centers that can afford state-of-the-art, high-end technology. For a fee, these electronic production companies will digitize your photos, slides, and artwork on drum scanners,

The
Photoshop
design and
production
process

FIGURE 1-1

providing you with high-quality images without your having to spend a fortune. A service bureau can also output your work to a color printer or imagesetter in preparation for the project's final destination, the printing press.

This chapter's overview of studio equipment begins with a discussion of computers and computer peripherals, and then branches out to input and output devices. Then you'll find a brief discussion of installing Photoshop and calibrating your monitor. Understanding Photoshop's equipment requirements will help guarantee that the program is running at optimum speed, so that you will be able to complete your design work efficiently.

MACINTOSH AND PERSONAL COMPUTER SYSTEMS

The focal point of the Photoshop studio is your computer. To a significant degree, Photoshop's performance depends upon the speed and power of your computer.

The minimum system requirements recommended by Adobe for running Photoshop are

- On the Macintosh, a 68030 microprocessor with 5MB of RAM (random access memory) and at least an 80MB hard drive.

- On the PC, an 80386 machine with at least 4MB of RAM and at least an 80MB hard drive.

If your computer meets these minimum requirements, you'll be able to run Photoshop and perform the exercises in this book. However, if your computer system barely squeaks by, be warned: Photoshop is a very enticing program. The more you learn about it, the more potential you'll see for its use. As you master Photoshop, you'll probably want to enhance your system to accelerate its performance and increase its ability to utilize Photoshop's power. And if you are buying a new computer just for Photoshop work, by all means consider purchasing the most powerful system you can afford, with the most amount of memory.

You might wonder why Photoshop is so demanding. The answer is that a large, high-quality color image can easily consume over 20 million bytes, or 20MB, of storage space. When such a large file needs to be loaded, color-corrected, and edited, a computer that typically is adequate for other tasks may bog down under the stress of working with Photoshop.

The CPU

To evaluate Photoshop's performance on your system, or to decide what system to buy, you should have a basic knowledge of what controls a computer's operating speed. Perhaps the most important component is the computer's *microprocessor,* or *CPU* (central processing unit). The microprocessor is a chip that is often called the "brains" of a computer. Its job is to process the steps of a computer program and send instructions along the various data highways connected to its circuitry. In any microprocessor, regardless of whether it is driving a Macintosh or a PC, two main factors determine performance: the speed of the chip and the amount of data the chip can process.

Available CPUs run at various speeds and process various amounts of data. The primary CPUs for the Mac are the 68030 and the 68040, both manufactured by Motorola. The Mac LCIIIs, IIcis, and IIFXs all are powered by 68030 chips. The 68030 can send information over 16 data channels at once—the equivalent of a 16-lane highway, with carloads of information running through the CPU. This highway is called a *16-bit data bus.* The bigger the data bus, the better the performance. The 68040 CPUs in the Mac Quadra and Centris can process *twice* as much data as computers with a 68030 chip. The 32-bit data bus of the 68040 allows it to process more instructions simultaneously and handle the data more efficiently than the 68030. Among PC-compatible computers, the 80386 (known as the 386) is equipped with a 16-bit bus. The 80486 (or 486) features a 32-bit bus.

The speed of the microprocessor measures how fast it handles a computer program's instructions. The speed of the microprocessor, usually called its *clock speed,* is measured in megahertz (MHz, which equals one million clock cycles). A 33MHz 68040 is faster than a 25MHz 68040. But a 25MHz 68040 will generally run programs faster than a 40MHz 68030. Again, this is because the 68040 is a more sophisticated chip and can handle more instructions per second. The same is true of 386 and 486 chips in PCs: a 50MHz 386 will not run faster than a 25MHz 486.

If you already own a computer, there are sometimes ways of improving the clock speed of your machine. Apple has traditionally provided motherboard upgrades (which should be installed by authorized Apple dealers) so that many of its older computers can be improved to function like the faster models. Apple's 040 line of computers will be upgradable to its new line of Power PCs, which will feature a faster and more sophisticated chip. Many PCs sold today come outfitted with an empty microprocessor socket to allow an upgrade to the Pentium chip, the successor to the 486. If you are interested in investigating upgrades, contact an authorized Apple or PC vendor.

If you can't wait for an upgrade, or if none is available, a variety of manufacturers sell *accelerator cards* that take over the processing chores for slower computers. Many vendors and mail-order suppliers sell these cards (circuit boards), which generally are easily installed in a slot on your computer's motherboard.

AUTION: *Before buying any accelerator equipment, be sure to verify that it will run with Photoshop and any of the other peripherals connected to your system.*

Frequently, however, when you want to speed up your computer, you do not have to do anything as drastic as replacing its CPU. Instead, adding memory will often provide a noticeable increase in Photoshop performance.

RAM

Much of Photoshop's speed is based upon how much work it can accomplish directly in your computer's RAM (random access memory). RAM is the area of memory your computer uses when you are first working on a file, before you store the data on your hard disk or on a floppy disk. Once a file is saved, when you reload it Photoshop will keep as much of the file in RAM as it can.

If you do not have enough RAM available for Photoshop's operations, it turns to your hard disk and grabs as much free space as it can to complete its chores. Memory accessed from the hard disk when RAM is insufficient is called *virtual memory*. Operations that take place purely in RAM are always going to be faster than those using virtual memory. The computer can interact faster with data it accesses from electronic chips than from a spinning mechanical disk.

As a rule of thumb for estimating RAM requirements, Adobe suggests having three to five times your file size available in RAM or on your hard disk. The more RAM available, the less often Photoshop will need to rely on virtual memory. Despite the safety net of virtual memory, you should be aware that certain Photoshop special effects will not operate at all unless sufficient RAM is available.

When upgrading your system's memory or purchasing a new computer, remember that not all computers are expandable to the same degree. The less expensive Macs and PCs generally will not allow as much memory expansion as the more expensive models. If you can't add any more RAM to your system, your hard disk becomes a crucial element in the Photoshop studio.

Hard Disks

Since Photoshop must work with your hard disk when RAM is insufficient, the disk's speed and size have a direct effect on Photoshop productivity.

When Photoshop uses your hard disk in place of RAM, the speed of operations is directly related to the speed of your hard disk. In Photoshop, a hard disk used for virtual memory is called a *scratch disk*. If you don't have enough room on your hard disk, Photoshop may not be able to complete the command you are trying to execute. You will receive a screen alert with the message "Scratch Disk Full." It is imperative that you have sufficient hard disk space, or you may not have room to save the file you are working with.

If you are planning to add a hard disk to your system, purchase the largest and fastest one that you can afford. Usually, the larger the hard disk, the faster its access speed. Hard disk access speed is measured in milliseconds (ms). A 10ms hard disk is faster than a 20ms hard disk. Many new 100MB drives have access times of 17ms or less. The 500MB drives will often have access times of 10ms and faster.

Removable Hard Disks

Before you add another hard disk to your system, you might consider offloading data to a *removable hard disk* to free up space on your system's internal hard disk. Removable hard disks are not only valuable for backing up data but have become essential to many Photoshop users because graphics files are often too large to fit on a floppy disk. When graphic designers need to send a large file out to a service bureau or deliver it to a client, they usually save it on a removable hard-disk cartridge. These cartridges slide in and out of a drive mechanism much as video cassettes do in a VCR, and thus are easily transported from computer to computer.

The most popular removable hard drives for Macs are manufactured by Syquest and store 44MB of data, though larger format drives holding 88MB will probably be the new standard.

Iomega's Bernoulli drives and cartridges are another well-known family of removable hard disks. Bernoulli cartridges are often considered sturdier than Syquest's, but, up until recently, the Bernoulli drive mechanism and its cartridges were more expensive than those manufactured by Syquest. Syquest and Bernoulli removable drives are available for PCs as well as Macs.

Bernoulli sells a 150MB model that is quite fast for a removable hard drive. You might find that the 150MB model is not only convenient for large files but works adequately as a scratch disk. When working with large color files, we place a blank 150MB disk in our Bernoulli drive. This gives Photoshop 150MB of contiguous free space to churn through.

Optical and DAT Drives

When you need to store many large files for archival purposes, you may wish to purchase an *optical drive.* Although much slower than hard disks, optical drives often store between 500MB and 1,000MB (1 gigabyte). The chief appeal of opticals is that the cost per gigabyte is much lower than that of hard disks or removable hard disks.

Another economical choice for storing large amounts of data is a *digital audio tape (DAT) drive.* These tape drives store several gigabytes of data on tapes that cost approximately $10.00 each. Many DAT drives are available for under $2,000. Unlike hard drives, which can quickly access data anywhere on a spinning platter, the DAT has to wind and unwind to read and record data. This makes DAT drives inappropriate for most operations except archiving files.

File Compression

If you are short on hard disk or archival storage space, one scheme for managing large files is to save them in *compressed format.* Various types of data compression exist. Some compression methods result in data loss; others compress without sacrificing picture quality. If you plan to compress your files, you should know whether your compression software will remove picture information during the compression process.

On the Mac, programs such as Stuffit Deluxe and Disk Doubler can compress files without losing data. On the PC, PKZIP and Stacker are two popular programs that offer compression without data loss. PKZIP, a shareware program, is available on many computer bulletin boards, and Stacker is a commercially available program that automatically compresses *every* file on a hard disk, as opposed to individual files that you select for compression.

Photoshop can save files using JPEG and LZW compression formats. JPEG results in data loss; LZW does not. These options are discussed in more detail in Appendix A.

COLOR VIDEO MONITORS

As you create and edit images, your window into the color digital world is your video monitor. Your monitor's screen size, sharpness, and color accuracy are all critical factors when working with Photoshop.

Although using a full- or two-page monitor is not a necessity in Photoshop, the larger your monitor, the more efficiently you'll be able to work. Even if you are working on small images, you're sure to want to magnify them. You will often want a palette of colors or brushes to be open while you paint or edit, or to have several images open at the same time. You may even wish to view the same image at various sizes in separate windows. All of these factors make screen real estate an important commodity.

If you think that 19- or 21-inch color monitors are beyond your budget, consider purchasing a 16- or 17-inch model. Many 17-inch monitors cost about half the price of 19-inch monitors and will probably pay for themselves in convenience and ease of use. The difference between 13- and 17-inch monitors may not seem like much, but because monitor size is measured diagonally, a 17-inch monitor actually provides approximately 85 percent more viewing area than a 13-inch one.

If you are planning to buy a new monitor, you'll find that many of the major desktop publishing vendors, such as Apple, NEC, SuperMac, Radius, RasterOps, and Sony, offer models that will suit your needs.

All good graphics monitors have a resolution of approximately 72 pixels per inch (ppi). A *pixel* is the smallest element visible on screen. At 72 pixels per inch, the resolution on a 13-inch monitor is 640 by 480 pixels. On a 20-inch monitor, the resolution can be 1,024 by 768 pixels. Some monitors, such as SuperMac 17T (a 17-inch monitor), allow you to switch resolution modes to match the resolution of larger monitors. This produces more pixels and thus increases the viewing area of the file on screen.

A good monitor should not flicker. Most high-end monitors refresh the screen fast enough so that flicker is not a problem. When you look at monitor specifications, look for vertical scan rates (the *refresh rate*) at around 72 hertz (Hz, cycles per second). This means the screen is scanned from top to bottom 72 times a second. Rates lower than 65Hz often cause flickering.

When analyzing an image on a monitor, study the uniformity of the colors displayed. Different areas of the screen should generally appear at the same levels of brightness. Images should look sharp, not blurry. A straight line that traverses the screen should look straight, not bent. Circles should look like perfect circles.

Any new color monitor you buy should be capable of displaying over 16 million colors. The number of colors a monitor displays is closely tied to the video display card inside your computer, as explained next.

VIDEO DISPLAY CARDS

The video display card, one of the circuit boards found in a computer, controls how many colors the monitor displays and often controls how fast the monitor redraws images on the screen. Some computers, including the newer models from Apple, have a video card built in, and no extra hardware is needed to drive the monitor.

The minimum number of colors displayed by Apple's color computers and most video display cards is 256. But for many Photoshop users, 256 colors just isn't enough. In order to view digitized images of color photographs on screen and see them as realistically as possible, millions of colors are needed. The reason so many colors are needed is simple: The human eye can discern millions of colors.

In order to view millions of colors, you will need a 24-bit video display color card. If you own one of Apple's high-end Quadras and a 13- or 16-inch color monitor, you can add chips called *video RAM* to get 24-bit color.

If you're wondering how 24-bit color translates into 16 million colors, you need to know something about computer technology. This knowledge will be helpful because you will see the term *bit* used in several Photoshop dialog boxes. A bit is the smallest element the computer uses to describe data. The bit has two states: on or off. The total possible combinations for 8 bits of data yield 256 colors ($2\times2\times2\times2\times2\times2\times2\times2=256$). A 16-bit system yields over 65,000 colors.

A 24-bit color system divides the 24 bits into 8 bits for red values, 8 bits for green values, and 8 bits for blue values. This produces 256 possible values of red, 256 of green, and 256 of blue. By making combinations of all the possible values of red, green, and blue, the computer can create over 16.7 million colors ($256\times256\times256=16,777,216$).

If you do need to buy a 24-bit card, make your purchase carefully. Not all 24-bit cards will work with all monitor sizes. One 24-bit card may produce millions of colors on a 13-inch monitor, but not on a 19-inch monitor. One reason for this is that video cards need more memory to address larger screens.

Accelerated Video Display Cards

If you decide you need a 24-bit video card, your next decision should be whether to buy an *accelerated video display card.* Acceleration is desirable because it takes a lot less time to update the thousands of pixels on a large color screen.

In addition to producing 16.7 million colors, accelerated 24-bit video cards speed up screen operations by adding an extra microprocessor, called a *coprocessor*, to your computer. This accelerates the entire procedure of working with graphic images. When your computer has a graphics coprocessor, its microprocessor can take a break from handling time-consuming screen processing operations.

Manufacturers of 24-bit cards for both PCs and Macs include Radius, RasterOps, SuperMac, TrueVision, and NEC.

*n*OTE: *If you do plan to purchase an accelerated video card, be aware that it's hard to predict how much these will speed up screen display when you are working with Photoshop. They will undoubtedly accelerate screen redraw and scrolling, but they may not affect specific Photoshop functions.*

Custom Photoshop Accelerator Cards

The demand for speed among Photoshop users has produced a market for cards whose sole purpose is to speed up various Photoshop operations.

Vendors such as Daystar, Mirror, Radius, SuperMac, and Spectral Innovations all manufacture Photoshop accelerator cards for the Macintosh. Storm Technology manufactures two Photoshop accelerator cards for the PC. Perhaps the best known of the custom cards is SuperMac's Thunderstorm. Thunderstorm and Daystar's Charger cards will work in most Macs that accept Nubus-specification cards. The Radius Photobooster will only work in Centris and Quadra models.

When you are shopping for a Photoshop accelerator card, you'll usually see the advertisement that the card is "Adobe Charged." This means that Adobe has approved the card for use with its products. If you purchased a card before the release of the current version of Photoshop, contact the card's manufacturer to ensure that you are using the most recent version of its software. The newer card software makes use of the open architecture introduced with Photoshop 2.5.

*n***OTE:** *Before you purchase a custom accelator card, be aware that they do not speed up every Photoshop function. Most of the cards will improve the speed of resizing, rotating, compression, and several of the filters that you will learn about in Chapter 8. If you are using these features, the increase in speed can be dramatic.*

GRAPHICS TABLET WITH STYLUS PEN

Often overlooked in the array of sophisticated graphic peripherals is the value of a graphics tablet and stylus pen. The stylus pen is a pressure-sensitive device that replaces the mouse. A stylus can simulate the pencil, pen, and paintbrush more accurately than the mouse, and thus many artists find it easier to use. The fine point of the stylus pen also enables you to more precisely retouch photographs in Photoshop. Figure 1-2 shows artist C. David Piña using a Wacom tablet and stylus pen with Photoshop to work on the main title design for the 63rd Annual Academy Awards show.

The stylus must be used in conjunction with a graphics tablet. Wacom manufactures a tablet that includes a plastic overlay. Art can be slid under the overlay so that it can be traced much more accurately than would be possible with a mouse. Other manufacturers of tablets with stylus pens include CalComp and Kurta.

INPUT DEVICES

Input devices digitize images so they can be edited and color-corrected in Photoshop. These devices include scanners, Photo CDs, digital cameras, and video cameras. Chapter 7 covers the digitizing process in detail.

Although the use of Photo CDs and digital photography is growing, the most common technique for digitizing images is with a scanner.

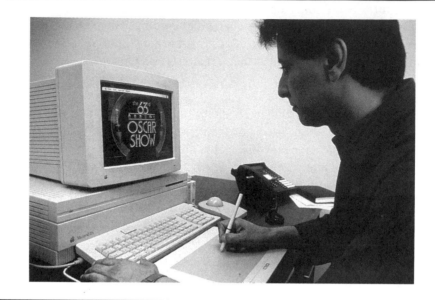

A Wacom tablet and stylus pen, courtesy of Wacom Technology Corp.

FIGURE 1-2

Scanners

Scanners are used primarily to digitize photographs, flat art, and slides. Although the price of many scanners fits the budget for many Photoshop studios, the quality of low-cost scanners may not suit your needs. Depending upon the type of work you do, you may find it necessary to send your files to a prepress house or service bureau to get the final quality you desire.

Even if you aren't going to purchase a scanner or actually do the scanning yourself, you should know the basics of how scanners work. This will give you an idea of what quality you can expect from various types of scanners.

Flatbed Scanners

Most scanners sold today are flatbed scanners. In many ways, a flatbed scanner resembles a copy machine. Art or a photograph is placed under the scanner's cover, and the digital reproduction process begins. Some of the better-known manufacturers of flatbed scanners are Agfa, Hewlett-Packard, Howtek, La Cie, Microtek, Sharp, and Umax.

Flatbed scanners are sometimes called *CCD*s. CCD stands for *charged coupled device*, a component in the scanner's head that sends thousands of beams of light across the object being scanned. Photoelectric cells on the head detect red, green, and blue components of light that are reflected back to the CCD. The reflected information produces high and low voltages depending upon the lightness and darkness of the image. This information is digitized so it can be saved to disk.

There are several factors to consider when evaluating what scanner to use or buy. The first is *resolution*, or how many pixels per inch (ppi) the scanner can create. The greater the number of pixels, the sharper the image. Many scanners in the $1,000 dollar range will scan at 600 ppi. Some use an *interpolation* to make the resolution appear as high as 1200 ppi. When a scanner interpolates, it's not really a sharper representation of the actual scanned image. It merely adds more pixels and then colors the new pixels with the average color of surrounding pixels. For more information about scanning resolution, see Chapter 7.

One of the primary factors that determines scanned image quality is *dynamic range*. A scanner's dynamic range measures its ability to capture gradations from the lightest to darkest parts of an image. The greater a scanner's dynamic range, the sharper the image. To provide better dynamic range, the scanner needs to utilize more bits to store the information. Most low-end scanners scan at 8 bits per each red, green, or blue component. Technically, this should produce over 16.7 million colors; however, 2 bits are needed to handle noise and calibration, so this decreases the dynamic range.

Mid-range scanners, such as Agfa's Arcus Plus shown in Figure 1-3, are 10-bit scanners. A high-end scanner such as the Scitex Smartscan is a 12-bit. This scanner,

Agfa's
Arcus Plus
scanner,
courtesy of
Agfa Corp.

FIGURE 1-3

which sells for about $80,000, not only has a better dynamic range than lower-bit scanners but also has its own image-processing system. The Smartscan operator can make color adjustments before and during the scanning process.

Slide Scanners

If you can obtain your image as slides, you're likely to improve the quality of your digital images. Slides are brighter than prints and have a higher dynamic range; thus the originating image for the scan is better than an opaque object.

In many slider scanners, the CCD is stationary, and light is redirected back to the photo sensors through a combination of mirrors and lenses. The optical system of slide scanners is often better than flatbeds; many slide scanners have resolutions in the 5,000-6,000 ppi range. Some of the better-known manufacturers of slide scanners are BarneyScan, Kodak, and Nikon.

Though slide scanners can be expensive, several models fall into the price range of flatbed scanners. Nikon's LS-10 Coolscan, shown in Figure 1-4, retails for about $2,000. The internal model will fit in a drive bay of various Macs and PCs.

Rotary Drum Scanners

For most color professionals, the best way to ensure the highest digital quality is to scan with a drum scanner, as shown in Figure 1-5. Instead of utilizing a CCD to emit

Nikon's
LS-10
Coolscan
slide
scanner,
courtesy of
Nikon.

FIGURE 1-4

Dupont
Crosfield
drum
scanner,
courtesy of
Dupont
Crosfield

FIGURE 1-5

light, the drum scanner uses a *photomultiplier tube,* often called a PMT. In PMT technology, the image being scanned rotates on a drum while a stationary source transmits light using photomultiplier tubes.

The rotary drum's sophisticated photoreceptors and advanced optics make the drum scanner much more sensitive to highlights and shadows than most CCD scanners. Service bureaus typically charge from $25 to $100 for images scanned on drum scanners. These scanners cost from $30,000 to several hundred thousand dollars and require trained operators to get the best scanning results.

If you need to digitize photographic images, you may be able to avoid scanning altogether and take advantage of the most recent and one of the more important developments in digitizing images: the Photo CD.

Photo CDs

Since Eastman Kodak developed the Photo CD in 1992, it has become a serious and high-quality alternative to scanning. For a nominal fee per photo, a Photo CD service bureau can digitize your photographic film directly to a Photo CD disc. Kodak's Photo CD Master discs can hold 100 high-resolution 35mm images. Kodak's Pro Photo CD format allows the following film formats to be digitized on a Photo CD: 120mm, 70mm, 35mm, and 4-by-5 inch. The Photo CD image can be opened directly into Photoshop for image editing and color correcting.

If you are in the market for a CD-ROM player and wish to use Photo CD images, you must purchase a CD-ROM XA (extended architecture). Prices for Photo CDs generally range from $300 to $900, with the fastest models generally being the most expensive. Some, such as Apple's PowerCD shown in Figure 1-6, can be connected to both Macs and PCs, allowing Photo CD images to be viewed on a television as well as on a computer screen.

Video and Digital Cameras

If your Photoshop work requires that you take your own photographs, you may want to investigate using a video or digital camera in order to digitize your images instantaneously. This eliminates delays caused by film processing, test shoots, and scanning prints or transparencies.

Many video cameras require that a video card be installed in your computer to digitize the video signal from the camera. There are also many systems that come with software that allows you to control the video digitizing process directly from within Photoshop.

Although capturing an image from video is convenient and quick, the resolution of images produced on most video digitizing systems is not better than 640 by 480 pixels (72 ppi). This is because they use the NTSC (National Television System Committee) standard. Sony's SEPS-1000, approximately $40,000, has proven to be

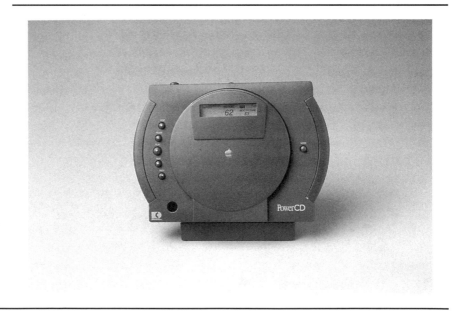

Apple's PowerCD, courtesy of Apple Computer, Inc.

FIGURE 1-6

an exception, however. Its still-video camera produces high-resolution images suitable for publishing.

The alternative to a video camera is a digital camera. Many of these cameras look like standard 35mm cameras, but they store images to the camera's memory or to a small attached hard disk. Besides providing higher resolution than a video camera, the digital camera is extremely portable. Kodak, for instance, has released several models of its DCS 200 digital camera, shown in Figure 1-7, which uses a 35mm Nikon body as the optical power behind its digital camera system. The price for this camera runs from about $8,500 to $10,000.

Leaf Systems, a Scitex company, has developed a digital camera back that attaches to high-end cameras such as the Mamiya RZ 67 and Hasselblad's 500 EL and 553 RLX. Images taken by these cameras can then be downloaded to a Macintosh IIfx or Quadra.

Video Capturing Cards

Another method for capturing video images is to use a video card, such as those manufactured by Syquest and TrueVision. These allow you to use your computer to directly input from and output to video tape. Most cards allow you to capture directly from a video camera as well.

Kodak Professional DCS 200 digital camera, courtesy of Eastman Kodak Company

FIGURE 1-7

OUTPUT DEVICES

Once you start working in Photoshop, you'll undoubtedly want to print your color images for final output or as a *proof*, a sample of your final printed version. Proofs created from the desktop before the film negative stage are often called *digital proofs*. To print a proof on paper, you can use either a black-and-white or color printer. Output devices generally used for producing color proofs include inkjet printers, thermal wax printers, dye-sublimation printers, color laser printers, and imagesetters. Most manufacturers of printers produce models that accept data from both Macs and PCs.

When outputting, its always important to consider the quality of the color and the sharpness of the output. Printer resolution is usually measured in *dots per inch (dpi)*. The greater the number of dots, the better the quality.

***n*OTE:** *If your final output will be slides, you'll need to buy a film recorder or send your files to a service bureau that can output to a film recorder. If your final output will be videotape, you may need a special video card to output to a VCR.*

Inkjet Printers

Low-end inkjet printers are the most inexpensive way of producing color files. These printers create colors by spraying ink from cartridges, using a process called *dithering*. The dithering process typically uses dot patterns of cyan, magenta, yellow, and often black inks (CMYK) to create the illusion of millions of colors. In many inkjet printers, the dot patterns are easy to see and the color is not always highly accurate. Cost per page for inkjet printers is usually less than thirty cents. Although many new inkjet printers output at 300 dpi, the dithering and color quality of most inexpensive inkjets is not precise enough to provide highly accurate representations of screen images.

On the high end of the scale for inkjet printers is the Scitex IRIS and IRIS Series 3000 printers. These printers cost from $40,000 to over $100,000 and are usually found at service bureaus and ad agencies. The IRIS produces near-photo-graphic-quality images by varying the dot size as it produces an image. In terms of color output, the IRIS provides higher quality than thermal wax and most dye-sublimation printers. The smallest printout from an IRIS printer is approximately 11 by 17 inches. The IRIS can also print poster-size images. The IRIS 3024 prints images as large as 24 by 24 inches; the 3047 prints images 34 by 44 inches.

Thermal Wax Printers

Thermal wax printers are a large step up in quality from low-end inkjet printers, and thus are a popular choice for producing samples for clients or internal evaluation of layout and design. In the thermal wax printing process, ribbons coated with cyan, magenta, yellow, and black waxes are heated and transferred to paper. During the printing process, heat from the printer's head fuses dots of color to the page. The dot combinations produce the color. The cost per page averages from fifty cents to a few dollars.

If you're interested in a thermal wax printer, you might want to investigate the Tektronix Phaser III PXI. This printer prints on plain paper instead of coated, and the cost per page is about twenty-five cents. The printer will print on paper as large as 12 by 18 inches, thus allowing bleeds for work on 11-by-17-inch paper. Other well-known manufacturers of thermal wax printers include QMS and Océ.

Dye-Sublimation Printers

Dye-sublimation printers produce photorealistic-quality images by printing colors created with dyes that *sublimate,* or turn into gas, when a heated printhead hits a colored ribbon. The gaseous colored inks are absorbed on special and expensive paper needed to output the print job. By properly controlling heat, the printhead applies pigments in specific amounts to produce many thousands of colors. Images are not created from a pattern of dots that produce an illusion of color; rather, the printer fills specific amounts of colored ink into each dot. The result is an image that is very detailed, with smooth transitions. Even though most dye-sublimation printers print at about 300 dpi, the quality resembles resolutions of 1,500 dpi.

Dupont, 3M, Kodak, SuperMac, and Tektronix all make dye-sublimation printers that cost in the neighborhood of $10,000. The cost to output a print is from $3.00 to $5.00 when all consumables are added together.

Apart from the high cost of each printed page, the main disadvantage of dye-sublimation printers is that text can appear a bit fuzzy.

Color Laser Printers

Perhaps the best-known color laser printer is the Canon ColorLaser copier, which doubles as a color copy machine. The laser technology uses toner colors of cyan, magenta, yellow, and black to create colored images.

Service bureaus and art departments that use the Canon often hook it up to a Fiery IPU (intelligence processing unit), allowing it to print PostScript images directly from the computer.

Imagesetters

One of the last stops for the Photoshop design project that is headed for a commercial printer is the imagesetter. An imagesetter is a high-end output device used by prepress houses to record images on paper or film at resolutions from approximately 1,200 to 3,500 dpi. From film, the prepress house can provide a proof, giving an accurate preview of the final color output. The imagesetter output is then delivered to a commercial printer who creates printing plates from the film. These plates are used on the press to produce the final product.

OTE: *Chapter 14 takes you step by step through the process of printing composite proofs and separations with Photoshop.*

INSTALLING AND OPTIMIZING PHOTOSHOP

Now that you've had a brief look at some of the important elements involved in the Photoshop design process, you're ready to start installing Photoshop. We won't repeat the thorough explanations provided by Adobe in the "Getting Started" manual included in the Photoshop package. Installation is simple and involves merely running the installation program from the installation disk.

If you haven't installed Photoshop, use the "Getting Started" booklet as a guide and begin the installation process. After you've completed the installation, read through the tips and reminders in the "Getting Started" booklet.

If you are running Photoshop on a Mac, you must be using System 6.07 or greater. On the PC, you must be using Windows 3.0 or greater. In order for both programs to display type without jagged edges, Adobe Type Manager must be installed. Both Mac and PC versions of Adobe Photoshop come with complete instructions for installing Adobe Type Manager. Mac users should open the Calibration folder and move the Gamma control panel into the Control Panels folder in your System folder. You will use the Gamma control panel to calibrate your monitor later in this chapter. (If you have a third-party calibration utility, do not drag the Gamma control panel icon into your System folder.) After you install the Gamma control panel, you should restart your Macintosh.

If you have a hardware and software monitor calibration system created by a company such as Kodak, SuperMac, or RasterOps, follow those instructions for calibrating your monitor. Figure 1-8 displays Kodak's ColorSense Calibrator unit, which includes a suction-cup calibrator for measuring the monitor's white, black, gray, and color levels.

Kodak's
ColorSense
Calibrator
unit,
courtesy of
Eastman
Kodak
Company

FIGURE 1-8

The Read Me File

Read Me

Before running Photoshop for the first time, double-click on the Read Me file that is installed along with the program. This file will explain any changes to the program that are not included in the Photoshop manual. If you are upgrading from Photoshop 2.5 to a more recent version, the Read Me file will detail the changes to be found in the latest version.

 OTE: *For PC users, the Read Me file explains several video card incompatibilities.*

Installing Plug-Ins

Your next step is to install any Photoshop plug-ins created by third-party software vendors. *Plug-ins* are programs that work within Photoshop, often created to run scanners or to output images to printers more efficiently. On both Mac and PC systems, all plug-ins that you wish to use in Photoshop should be copied to the Plug-ins folder (PC users: plugins).

Installing Dynamic Sliders on the Mac

An extremely helpful feature that is not installed automatically on the Mac is the Dynamic Sliders plug-in. This plug-in makes it easier to choose and mix colors when you are working in Photoshop's Colors palette. When the Dynamic Sliders feature is activated, the sliders in the Colors palette help you see a color before you create it. Using Dynamic Sliders is covered in Chapter 4.

Before installing Dynamic Sliders, be aware that this plug-in is recommended for use with faster computers. You may want to install this plug-in only before completing the exercises in Chapter 4.

Dynamic Sliders

On the Mac, the Dynamic Sliders plug-in is in the Optional Extensions folder. To activate the plug-in, drag it from the Optional Extensions folder to the Plug-ins folder. The next time you load Photoshop, Dynamic Sliders will be activated.

Installing Dynamic Sliders on the PC

To enable the Dynamic Sliders feature on the PC, open up the PHOTOSHP.INI file located in the WINDOWS directory. Probably the easiest way to do this is to run File Manager and double-click on the Windows folder, then on the PHOTOSHP.INI file. This opens PHOTOSHP.INI into the Notepad accessory.

Underneath "[Photoshop]", insert the following line exactly as shown, with no spaces and in capital letters:

L 1.1   `DYNAMICSLIDERS=1`

Save the file by choosing Save from the File menu.

The changes will be visible in the Colors palette when you load Photoshop.

Allocating Memory for Photoshop on the Mac Using System 7

System 7 Mac users should be aware that Photoshop will not necessarily access all free memory in your computer unless you allocate it to Photoshop. Just because 20MB of RAM is available on your Mac doesn't mean Photoshop will grab extra memory when it needs it. You need to allocate the amount of memory you want to reserve for Photoshop. On the Mac, allocating memory is handled from the Finder.

To allocate memory to Photoshop in System 7, first click on the Photoshop program icon, which is in the Adobe Photoshop folder. When you select Photoshop, the program's icon will turn darker. Then choose Get Info from the File menu. In the lower-right corner of the Adobe Photoshop Info window, you will see a number indicating the current size of memory allocated to Photoshop. The suggested size is 5,120K, which is a little over 5MB. You should allocate as much memory as you can afford, but be sure to leave about five percent free for the Mac's operating system.

After you've set the memory allocation, close the Adobe Photoshop Info window. The next time you use Photoshop, it will open into the memory partition size that you designated.

Later in this chapter, the section, "Resetting the Scratch Disk" describes another memory allocation adjustment that can aid Photoshop's performance.

Memory Control Panel Settings

System 7 users should turn off the disk cache in their System folder, because Photoshop does not take advantage of it. If you leave the disk cache on, you are only sealing off memory that Photoshop could use.

Access the disk cache by double-clicking on the Memory control panel in the Control Panels folder. In the Memory window that appears, as shown in the following illustration, make sure that the Off radio button for Virtual Memory is selected. Photoshop has its own virtual memory system. If you leave System 7's virtual memory on, the two systems may conflict.

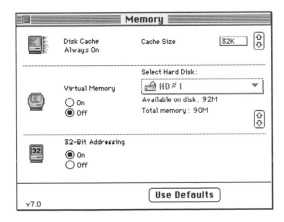

If you have more than 8MB of RAM, the 32-Bit Addressing On radio button should also be selected in this window to ensure that your Mac can access the extra memory beyond 8MB. If you have an older Mac, you may be able to use 32-bit addressing by installing a program called MODE 32. Contact your Apple dealer if you need a copy and for more details.

Allocating Memory for Photoshop on the PC

For PC users, memory allocation is handled automatically from within Photoshop. Load Photoshop now to check the memory allocation. First start Windows, if it is not already running. In the Program Manager, double-click to open the Adobe group window. There you will see the Adobe Photoshop program icon. To load Photoshop, double-click on the Adobe Photoshop icon.

When Photoshop first loads, it will allocate as much memory as possible to itself. If you wish to change this allocation, choose Preferences in the File menu. From the Preferences submenu, choose Memory.

OTE: *Photoshop version 2.5.1 for Windows will* not *automatically allocate as much memory as possible to itself. Set the desired memory allocation in the Memory Preferences dialog box.*

The Memory Preferences dialog box displays the currently allocated memory for Photoshop. If you think this will interfere with the operation of other programs, you can change the percentage of allocation by typing a number in the Used by Photoshop field or by clicking the down arrow to the right of the field.

Resetting the Scratch Disk

Your last installation step is to check the memory allocated to your scratch disk. In order to do this, you'll need to load Photoshop. To start Photoshop, double-click on the Adobe Photoshop icon in the Adobe Photoshop folder.

After the program loads, you may want to reset the scratch disk that Photoshop uses for virtual memory.

Adobe Photoshop™ 2.5.1   As mentioned earlier in this chapter, when Photoshop needs more memory than it can find in RAM, it will start using your hard disk as virtual memory. By default, Photoshop will use your startup drive as the scratch disk. If you have another hard disk connected to your computer that is faster or has more space available, you may want to set the scratch disk to this drive.

Mac users will need to enter a dialog box to set the scratch disks. If you wish to reset the scratch disk, choose Preferences from the File menu. From the Preferences submenu, choose Scratch Disks.

```
┌─────────────────── Scratch Disk Preferences ───────────────────┐
│                                                                 │
│   ┌─ Scratch Disks ──────────────────┐      ┌──────────┐        │
│   │                                  │      │    OK    │        │
│   │   Primary:   [ HD#1      ▼ ]     │      └──────────┘        │
│   │                                  │      ┌──────────┐        │
│   │   Secondary: [ Untitled  ▼ ]     │      │  Cancel  │        │
│   │                                  │      └──────────┘        │
│   └──────────────────────────────────┘                         │
│                                                                 │
│      ┌──┐   Note: Any changes will not take effect             │
│      │  │   until the next time Photoshop is opened.           │
│      └──┘                                                        │
└─────────────────────────────────────────────────────────────────┘
```

PC users will already be in the Memory dialog box if they checked Memory allocation in the procedure outlined in the previous section. If necessary, choose Preferences from the File menu, then choose Memory from the Preferences submenu.

In the Memory Preferences dialog box that appears, click on the Primary or Secondary pop-up menu and choose the desired drive. Your primary scratch disk should be the fastest and emptiest hard drive connected to your system.

If you wish to boost the performance of Photoshop, be sure that the free space on your hard disk is as contiguous as possible. If you've been accessing your hard disk frequently during your computer sessions, available free space may be spread over many different sectors. Packages such as Norton Utilities, PC Tools, and Mac Tools include optimization programs that will reallocate the files on your hard disk so the free space is as contiguous as possible.

IP: *If you are not going to be copying and pasting to other applications, you can free up a bit more memory if you turn off the Export Clipboard option. You can access this by selecting General Preferences in the File menu.*

MONITOR CALIBRATION

In order for the colors you see on screen to match as closely as possible those on the printed page, your system needs to be properly calibrated. The first step is to calibrate your monitor.

Every monitor has preset color intensity levels called gamma. *Gamma* is the relationship between the picture data input from your software and the color values that are output on screen. For example, if the stored color values saved to disk for an image are set for a light shade of yellow, the screen may display it darker despite the fact that the values are correct on disk. Adjusting a monitor's gamma can help you distinguish between light and dark shades in an image. Many color monitors also display *color casts* and *color shifts* toward red or blue. These color shifts can be corrected by calibrating your monitor.

Another variable that must be factored into the calibration equation is room lighting. Bright light, shifts in sunlight, and even color reflection from objects near a monitor can change the way color is perceived on screen.

Preparing for the Calibration Process

Before you begin to calibrate your monitor

1. Make sure that your computer's screen display has been turned on for a half hour or more. This stabilizes your monitor.

2. Adjust the room lighting, if necessary, so it is at the level you will maintain while working on the computer. Remember that if you are working near a window, colors may appear different depending upon the amount of sunlight entering your room.

3. Adjust your monitor's brightness and contrast controls to the desired levels. Once the brightness and contrast are set, you may wish to put tape across the monitor's knobs so they can't be changed.

4. Set your monitor's background color to gray. This will prevent background colors from altering your color perception while you are calibrating and while working in Photoshop. For instance, if the background color on your screen is blue, yellows might appear to have a greenish shade around them.

General Controls

Mac users: Use the General Controls control panel device to change your background screen to gray.

PC users: Double-click on the Color icon in the Control panel.

Gamma

5. Once your monitor's background color has been set to gray, you need to access the calibration program.

System 7 Mac users: Open the Control Panels folder by choosing Control Panels from the Apple menu, and then double-click on the Gamma icon to open the Gamma control panel. Make sure that the On button in the lower-left corner is selected. System 6 Mac users: Click on the Gamma icon after opening the Control Panel.

PC users: The calibration program is directly accessible from within Photoshop. Make sure Photoshop is loaded, and then choose Preferences from the File menu. In the Preferences submenu, choose Monitor Setup, and click on the Calibrate button.

6. Set the target gamma.

Mac users: In the Gamma dialog box, the 1.8 Target Gamma radio button should be selected (the default setting for Macintosh displays). This is your target gamma. If you are outputting to video or slides, Target Gamma should be set to 2.2. A lower gamma results in lower contrast and darker images; a higher gamma results in higher contrast and lighter images.

PC users: You don't need to set a target gamma in the Calibrate dialog box. (You will set it in the Monitor Setup dialog box.)

The Calibration Process

After you've followed all the preparatory steps outlined in the previous section, you're ready to begin the actual calibration process.

The first step will be to make an adjustment to help eliminate color casts that appear in most monitors. For instance, a bluish color cast is produced by many 13-inch monitors, and a reddish color cast often appears in larger monitors. To adjust for unwanted color casts, you need to match the white on your monitor to a sample of the paper stock you will be using when printing. Hold the paper up beside the screen. In the Gamma control panel (PC users: Calibrate dialog box), select the White Pt radio button. Then drag the red, green, and blue slider controls (just above the White Pt radio button) until the monitor matches the white paper as closely as possible.

Next, you'll adjust the gray levels of the monitor. To do this, click on the control for the Gamma Adjustment slider (located at the top of the dialog box). Drag the control left or right until the solid and patterned grays in the dialog box match one another as closely as possible. When you're done, the strip should look as much as possible like one tone of gray.

Monitor calibration can also help eliminate red, green, and blue color casts that result from one of your monitor's red, green, or blue color components being out of balance. To eliminate these types of color casts, click on the Balance button, then drag the red, green, and blue slider controls so that no color tints are visible in the gray strip at the bottom of the dialog box. If you notice that the Gamma setting has shifted, readjust it; then close the Gamma control panel. (PC users: Click on the Preview button to see the changes.)

If you are using a variety of paper stocks, it's advisable to save various calibration settings for the different papers. If you need to reuse a calibration setting, return to the Gamma control panel (PC users: Calibrate dialog box) and load the settings.

When you are finished adjusting the Gamma settings, close the Gamma control panel by clicking on the Close box (the small square located in the upper-left corner of the window). (PC users: Click OK.) Mac users will next need to load Photoshop to open the Monitor Setup dialog box. PC users will now be in the Monitor Setup dialog box, where you will continue calibrating your monitor.

The Monitor Setup Dialog Box

The final stage of monitor calibration is to set the options in Photoshop's Monitor Setup dialog box. The Monitor Setup dialog box allows Photoshop to set display output depending upon the type of monitor being used, the room lighting, and the gamma setting.

If Photoshop is not loaded, load it now by double-clicking on the Adobe Photoshop icon. Open the Monitor Setup dialog box by choosing Preferences in the

File menu. From the Preferences submenu, choose Monitor Setup. (PC users: You will already be in this dialog box if you just completed the previous calibration steps.)

```
┌─────────────────── Monitor Setup ───────────────────┐
│                                                      │
│  Monitor: [ Default                    ▼]  ┌──────┐  │
│  ┌─ Monitor Parameters ───────────────┐   │  OK  │  │
│  │                                     │   └──────┘  │
│  │     Gamma: [1.80]                   │  ┌────────┐ │
│  │                                     │  │ Cancel │ │
│  │  White Point: [ 6500°K    ▼]        │  └────────┘ │
│  │                                     │  ┌────────┐ │
│  │    Phosphors: [ Trinitron    ▼]     │  │ Load...│ │
│  │                                     │  └────────┘ │
│  └─────────────────────────────────────┘  ┌────────┐ │
│  ┌─ Room Parameters ──────────────────┐   │ Save...│ │
│  │                                     │  └────────┘ │
│  │  Ambient Light: [ Medium ▼]         │            │
│  └─────────────────────────────────────┘            │
│                                                      │
└──────────────────────────────────────────────────────┘
```

OTE: *The settings in the Monitor Setup dialog box are used by Photoshop during conversion between RGB and CMYK color modes. CMYK mode is used for printing four-color process separations. These subjects are covered extensively in Chapters 4 and 9. If you plan to convert from RGB to CMYK mode, it is vital that the settings in the Monitor Setup dialog box be correct.*

In the Monitor Setup dialog box, click on the Monitor pop-up menu and select your monitor from the list.

Enter a target gamma in the Gamma field. This gamma should be the same as that entered in the previous calibration settings procedure. PC users should enter 1.8 or 2.2 if outputting to slides or video. PC and Mac users who are sharing data files should keep their gammas set to identical values.

Leave White Point set at 6500°K (K stands for Kelvin, a temperature measurement scale). The white point is the color measure of white when the intensities of red, green, and blue are equal. The setting 6500°K is used because it is the color temperature of cool daylight. If you are using a third-party calibration device, use the setting recommended for it. If that setting is not in the pop-up menu list, choose Custom from the list and enter the appropriate value.

From the Phosphors pop-up menu, choose the listing that matches the phosphors arrangement in your monitor. (Note that many manufacturers, such as Apple, use Sony monitors that take the Trinitron setting.) If your monitor is not on the list, obtain

Photoshop in Action

The windows in the second floor needed to be removed

Some of the windows on the side needed to be removed

Artist: Yusei Uesugi   Client: Lucasfilm Ltd.

The images on these two pages will give you an idea of the image-editing power of Photoshop.

Yusei Uesugi of Industrial Light & Magic, a division of Lucasfilm, creates mattes (backgrounds) for films. Often he must take a dull vintage image, such as the one shown above used for a scene in the television program "Young Indiana Jones" and transform it into a lively background. This image was captured on film, transferred to video, and then digitized into Photoshop, where the image-editing process began.

Photoshop in Action

Photoshop was used to delete the windows and create the movie marquee and the awning.

The windows on the side were deleted. More light was added to the center of the image, and the movie posters were added.

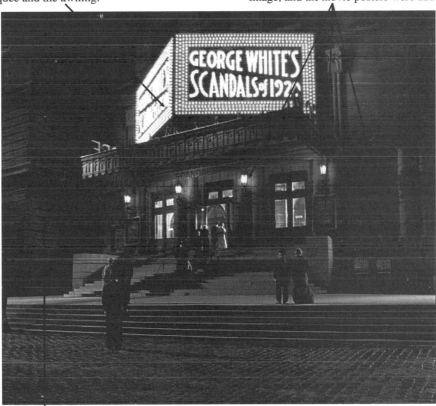

A new wall was painted in to separate the theater from its surroundings

In Photoshop, Yusei removed the windows on the side of building and on the second floor. He also created the marquee and movie posters near the entrance with Photoshop's painting tools.

After the editing was completed, a printout of the image was used by a model maker to create a model. Yusei then took photographs of the model, which provided him with various angles and light settings so that versions of the image could be created for different scenes.

The versions of the image were digitized into Photoshop for some touching up and so that more details could be added. The result shown above appears to be a photograph taken of an actual location.

the proper red, green, and blue chromacity coordinates from your monitor manu-facturer. These can be entered by choosing Custom in the Phosphors pop-up menu.

Next, choose a setting from the Ambient Light pop-up menu. Medium is the default, which means the monitor's brightness is about the same as the room lighting. Choose the High setting if the room lighting is brighter, or the Low setting if the room lighting is not as bright as the screen's.

If you will be using various levels of lighting or several different monitors, retain your settings by using the Save button. You then can access these settings with the Load button.

When you are finished entering the information in the Monitor Setup dialog box, click OK.

Now that you've completed the program's installation and calibrated your monitor, you're ready to proceed to the next chapter for your first tour of Photoshop.

GETTING STARTED IN THE
WORLD OF PHOTOSHOP

If you begin to use Photoshop, mouse in hand but without any "basic training," it won't take long for you to figure out how to fill your screen with assorted shapes, text, and rainbows of brilliant colors. But without a foundation of knowledge about Photoshop's simple tasks and operations, your creativity will soon give way to frustration: How do you move an object from one place to another? How do you edit a word on screen? How do you delete everything from the screen?

Although it's tempting to dive right into Photoshop and start grabbing every tool in sight, the best way to learn how to use this powerful program is to start with the basics. You need to get acquainted with the overall structure of the program and find out how the program works. That's the goal of this chapter. You'll begin with an introductory tour of the program's menus, windows, and palettes; then you'll create a new file and try out several of the tools in the Toolbox. By the end of the chapter, you'll have good idea of what's going on behind the scenes in Photoshop.

What's behind the scenes in Photoshop? Pixels. When you paint, retouch, cut, paste, or alter any image in Photoshop, you are changing individual pixels on the screen. A *pixel* is the smallest dot or picture element on your screen—in fact, the word was created from the two words picture and element. A pixel is approximately equivalent to a *point*, which is the unit of measurement used in typesetting (there are 72 pixels per inch and 72.27 points per inch). All Photoshop images and shapes are comprised of pixels.

Drawing programs such as Adobe Illustrator, Aldus Freehand, Claris MacDraw, and CorelDRAW utilize lines to create shapes; each shape you draw and each letter you type is an object, separate from other objects. In these programs, when you want to move or resize an object, you can often simply click on it and drag it with the mouse.

Not so in Photoshop. When you work in Photoshop, you have to think like a painter. When you draw a line, create a shape, or type text, you are filling in pixels on screen, painting on an electronic canvas. After you create an object or text, it "dries" on the canvas, almost as if it's imbedded on the screen. If you wish to move the object, you'll need to use the proper tool, which essentially cuts the object out of its background so it can be lifted and moved. To delete the object, you have to paint over it—usually with a white background color.

Once you begin to think like a painter, what once may have seemed to be a Photoshop peculiarity will begin to feel more natural. By the end of this chapter, we promise you'll be thinking like a painter.

TOURING PHOTOSHOP

When you are ready to begin your tour of Photoshop, launch the program by double-clicking the Photoshop icon.

Adobe Photoshop™ 2.5.1

After Photoshop is loaded, its menu bar, Toolbox, and a Brushes palette appear on the screen. Unlike many programs, Photoshop does not automatically open a new document for you to work in. You'll learn how to do this later in the chapter, in the section "Creating a New File."

Photoshop has seven pull-down menus available in the menu bar (PC users have an eighth, Help). The more familiar you are with how Photoshop divides up its power, the more likely you are to take the right path when you begin to work with the program.

A Tour of Photoshop Menus

Most of the commands in the File menu are for storing, loading, and printing files. The New, Open, Save, Save As, Page Setup, Print, and Quit (PC users: Exit) commands work very much as they do in other Macintosh and Windows applications. Revert is covered later in this chapter. The Acquire command allows you digitize images from scanners, digital cameras and video capture boards directly into Photoshop. Many of the File menu commands are covered in Appendix A.

The Edit menu is generally used for duplicating or moving parts of images to other areas of a document or to other files. The Edit menu also features an Undo command that allows you to void the action of your last command. Mac and Windows users will recognize standard Edit menu commands: Undo, Cut, Copy, and Paste.

Photoshop's Edit menu also allows you to create a custom pattern that can be used in place of a painting color. The Take Snapshot command allows a version of your file to be held in the computer's memory, so you can revert to it, if necessary, after making changes. The Composite Controls command provides a means of controlling how one image blends with another. The Take Snapshot and Define Pattern commands are discussed in Chapter 6. The Composite Controls command is covered in Chapter 11.

The Mode menu allows you to change a color image to grayscale and then from grayscale to black and white. The Mode menu also allows you to convert a file from RGB (red/green/blue), the standard computer color monitor display mode, to CMYK (cyan/magenta/yellow/black), the mode used for four-color process printing. Changing modes is covered in Chapter 9.

The Image menu is primarily used to manipulate the shape of an image, and analyze and correct its color. For example, you can rotate an image, distort it, change its size, and adjust its color balance, brightness, or contrast. Image menu commands are covered in Chapters 7, and 11 through 14.

The Filter menu creates effects similar to a photographer's filter that is placed in front of a lens to produce a special effect. By applying a Photoshop filter in one of the Filter submenus, you can sharpen, blur, distort, stylize, and add noise to an image or part of an image. Photoshop features over 40 different filters. The Filter menu is covered in Chapter 8.

The Select menu allows you to choose part of, or an entire image. (In Photoshop, before you can change any part of an image, you often need to isolate or *select* it.) Select Grow expands a selection, and Select Inverse reverses a selection so that everything that isn't selected will be selected. Select Border turns a selection into one that borders the previous selection. Select Feather blurs the edges of a selection. The Select commands are covered in Chapters 3, 11, and 12.

The Window menu allows you to move from one document on the screen to another, to zoom in/out, and to show or hide Photoshop's rulers. You can also create a new window to view the same image simultaneously at different magnifications; when an image is being edited, both windows get updated. The Window menu will also allow you to open and close Photoshop's various palettes. The Window menu will be discussed later in this chapter.

The Help menu is only available in the Windows version of Photoshop. From this menu you can quickly access information about Photoshop features and commands. In many respects, the Help menu is like having the Photoshop manual a few mouse clicks away.

CREATING A NEW FILE

In this section, you'll create a new file so that you can explore and get familiar with the Photoshop document window, and get started using the Toolbox. Without a document on screen, you won't be able to use Photoshop's palettes or any of its tools. You'll be creating a document 7 inches wide by 5 inches high, which will provide a comfortable working area on most monitors.

1. To create your new document, select New from the File menu. The New dialog box appears. The settings in the New dialog box will either be Photoshop's default settings or the settings that were last used. As you work

in Photoshop, you'll find that the program often retains the dialog box settings that were last used.

2. If the Width and Height measurement units are not set to inches, change them by selecting inches in the pop-up menus to the right of the Width and Height fields. Pop-up menus are represented by a box containing a down-pointing arrowhead and are outlined with a drop shadow. To access the pop-up menus, Mac users can click anywhere in the pop-up menu but must keep the mouse button pressed in order to drag down and select inches from the list. PC users must click on the down arrow in the pop-up menu and then choose inches.

3. If Width is not set to 7 and Height is not set to 5, enter these values now. Click in the Width field to select it, and type **7**. Press TAB to move to the Height field and type **5**. (Note that you can move among the fields in a dialog box by either clicking in the field you want or pressing the TAB key to move the cursor from one field to the next.) If you make a mistake, press DELETE (PC users: BACKSPACE) and then retype your entry.

Notice that the Resolution field is set to 72 pixels per inch. Photoshop uses 72 as the default ppi because most monitors display 72 pixels for every inch of screen area. In other words, you are setting the resolution of your document to be the same as the resolution of your monitor.

4. If necessary, change the Resolution setting to 72. Press TAB to move to the Resolution field, and type **72**. If you make the Resolution, Height, or Width settings larger, the size of your image file will grow. Try to avoid large images; they're cumbersome to work with and they slow down your computer.

OTE: *If a file has a resolution higher than your monitor's 72 pixels per inch, Photoshop will display the image larger than actual size, because it needs the extra screen area to display the extra pixels. For example, on a 72-ppi monitor Photoshop will display a 300-ppi file approximately four times larger than its actual size, because there are about four times as many pixels in the 300-ppi grid than on a 72-ppi grid. In other words, since your monitor can only display 72 dots per inch, Photoshop stretches the image across a wider screen area in order to display it.*

The Mode option should be set to RGB Color (red/green/blue). Photoshop uses RGB Color as the default display mode because RGB is the standard color model used by video monitors to display colors. In RGB mode, colors are created from red, green, and blue values. When Mode is set to RGB Color, all painting and editing features of Photoshop are available. For a full discussion of the different file modes in Photoshop, please refer to Chapter 9.

5. If necessary, set the Mode option to RGB Color by clicking on the Mode pop-up menu (PC users: click on the down arrow), and choosing RGB Color from the Mode list. (PC users can also choose the Mode by typing the first letter of the Mode name.)

6. To assure that the background of your new document is white, click on the radio button to the left of the White option. If you choose the Background Color option instead, the background color that was last used in Photoshop will be used for your new document.

7. Click OK to close the dialog box.

A new Untitled document window appears. If you wish to magnify the screen, select Zoom In from the Window menu or, on the keyboard press the key combination COMMAND-PLUS (PC users: CTRL-PLUS). To zoom out, select Zoom

Out from the Window, or press COMMAND-MINUS (PC users: CTRL-MINUS). You can press the PLUS and MINUS keys either on the keyboard or the numeric keypad (with NUM LOCK on).

THE PHOTOSHOP WINDOW

The Photoshop window shown in Figure 2-1, conforms to Mac and Windows conventions. You can scroll, zoom, resize, and close it as you would in most Windows or Mac applications. You can move the window by clicking and dragging in the title bar. In the window's title bar are the document's filename, mode, and magnification ratio. In the bottom-left corner of the window is the file size indicator that shows how large the document on screen is.

A magnification ratio of 1:1 indicates that you are viewing the file at its actual size; 2:1 means you are viewing the file at 200% magnification (two times actual size); and 1:2 is a 200% reduction, or half the size.

The Photoshop window

FIGURE 2-1

No matter what magnification ratio you're working in, it's generally a good idea to display Photoshop's horizontal and vertical rulers on screen. That way, you won't lose sight of how large or small your file's dimensions and images are. To make the rulers visible if they're not already onscreen, choose Show Rulers from the Window menu.

Horizontal mouse position

Vertical mouse position

The rulers continually indicate your position in the window with a mark that glides along each ruler as you move the mouse. If you haven't noticed the marks, focus on the either the horizontal or vertical ruler and move the mouse diagonally across the screen until you see each of them.

Along the left side of the window is Photoshop's Toolbox. The Toolbox contains the essential tools for painting, selecting, and altering graphics. Each tool is depicted by an icon. Understanding the purpose and power of each tool is the key to learning Photoshop. Just as an artisan must know the right tool to use for each job, so must the Photoshop user.

THE PHOTOSHOP TOOLBOX

There are 22 tools in the Photoshop Toolbox, shown in Figure 2-2, each providing a specific utility to aid you when you're creating, editing, and color correcting images. The first time you load Photoshop after it is installed, the Rectangular Marquee is the selected tool. Thereafter, when you load Photoshop or create a new file, the last tool used remains selected. When a tool is selected, its Toolbox location turns black and its icon turns white. This section introduces you to the tools as well as the other icons that share the Toolbox.

The Selection Tools

The first four tools in the Toolbox are the selection tools: Rectangular Marquee, Elliptical Marquee, Lasso, and Magic Wand. If you wish to make changes to an object, you'll usually need to select it with one of these tools first.

The Rectangular Marquee tool allows you to make square and rectangular selections. The Elliptical Marquee tool creates circular and elliptical selections. The Lasso tool can be used as a freehand tool; you use it to outline irregularly shaped selections. The Magic Wand selects according to similarity of colors.

Several of the selection tools also allow you to create shapes. You will learn how to do this in Chapter 3.

Rectangular Marquee →			← Elliptical Marquee
Lasso →			← Magic Wand
Cropping →			← Type
Hand →			← Zoom
Paint Bucket →			← Gradient
Line →			← Eyedropper
Eraser →			← Pencil
Airbrush →			← Paintbrush
Rubber Stamp →			← Smudge
Blur/Sharpen →			← Dodge/Burn
Foreground Color →			← Switch Colors
Default Colors →			← Background Color
Standard mode →			← Quick Mask mode

Standard window display — Full-screen display without menu

Full-screen display with menu

The
Photoshop
Toolbox

FIGURE 2-2

The Cropping Tool

The Cropping tool is used to select a portion of an image and remove the rest. It can also be used to resize an image. The Cropping tool is covered in Chapter 7.

The Type Tool

With the Type tool, you can add text to your document as well as choose different fonts and type sizes. You will use the Type tool in this chapter and in the exercises throughout this book.

The Hand Tool and Zoom Tool

The Hand and Zoom tools are often used in conjunction with each other. The Hand tool allows you to scroll through a document to view areas that don't fit in the

Photoshop window. It allows more control than the window's scroll bars because you can click in the document and scroll in any direction.

The Zoom tool increases or decreases the magnification of an image. After zooming, you may need to use the Hand tool to reposition the area you zoomed into. You will use the Hand and Zoom tools in this chapter and throughout the book.

The Painting Tools

The painting tools are the Paint Bucket, Gradient, Line, Eyedropper, Eraser, Pencil, Airbrush, and Paintbrush. In Photoshop the painting color is called the foreground color, and the background color (usually white) is the color used for erasing parts of an image or deleting an entire object.

The Paint Bucket, Line, Paintbrush, and Airbrush all paint with the foreground color. The Eraser paints with the background color. The Pencil tool simulates drawing with a pencil, in either the foreground or background color. The Gradient tool creates a blend with both the foreground and background colors. The Eyedropper picks up colors from your image and changes the foreground or background color to the Eyedropper color. The painting tools are covered in Chapter 5.

The Editing Tools

The editing tools are the Rubber Stamp, Smudge, Blur/Sharpen, and Dodge/Burn.

The Rubber Stamp is a cloning tool. With it you can sample an area and copy it elsewhere, pixel by pixel, by clicking and dragging the mouse. You'll use this tool frequently when retouching images or creating special effects.

The Smudge tool allows you to create a watercolor effect. It smudges a color to make it look as if water has been applied to it.

Blur and Sharpen are two tools that appear under one roof; the icon in the Toolbox changes to reflect which tool is selected. To choose between Blur and Sharpen, double-click on the Blur/Sharpen icon. The Blur/Sharpen Options dialog box will appear. The Tool pop-up menu in the dialog box allows you to choose between the two tools. Blur softens hard edges, and Sharpen brings out more detail.

Dodge and Burn, like Blur and Sharpen, also share a Toolbox location. As with Blur/Sharpen, you double-click on the Dodge/Burn icon in the Toolbox and choose between the tools from a pop-up menu in the dialog box that appears. The icon always displays the selected tool. Dodge and Burn are traditional darkroom tools that are used to correct exposure by lightening and darkening specific areas.

The Color-Control Icons

Just below the Blur/Sharpen and Dodge/Burn tools are several color-control icons that allow you to view and switch colors.

The Foreground Color or Background Color icons display the current foreground and background colors. If you click on either icon, Photoshop's Color Picker dialog box will appear, allowing you to change either the Foreground or Background Color. The Color Picker will be explored in Chapter 4.

The Switch Colors icon changes the color of the Foreground Color icon to the Background Color icon and vice versa.

The Default Colors icon restores the default colors for the Foreground Color (black) and the Background Color (white).

The Mode Icons

The right-hand icon represents the Quick Mask mode, which allows you to easily create, view, and edit a mask. This lets you view your work through a colored tint overlay and edit areas in a cutout (similar to a *rubylith*—a red film that is used to shield objects in print production). The area outside of the cutout is normally protected; the area inside is unprotected. If you're unfamiliar with the concept of a mask, think of a painter laying down masking tape so he or she can paint without ruining surrounding areas. In Photoshop, working in the cutout allows you to refine your work without affecting areas beyond the cutout.

Clicking on the Quick Mask mode icon turns the masking function on. Once you enter the Quick Mask mode, you can create and edit a mask's shape with the selection tools as well as the painting tools. The left-hand Standard mode icon, the default, takes you out of the Quick Mask mode. Creating Quick Masks will be discussed in Chapter 12.

The Screen Display Icons

The three Screen Display icons at the bottom of the Toolbox change the window display modes. The left-hand icon represents the standard window. Clicking on the middle icon zooms the window out to occupy all of the video screen. Clicking on the right-hand icon also zooms out to full-screen size and hides the menus, as well.

TOURING PHOTOSHOP'S FLOATING PALETTES

Now that you're familiar with the Toolbox, take a quick look at Photoshop's floating palettes. By choosing Show Brushes, Show Colors, Show Info, Show Paths, or Show Channels from the Window menu, you can open these palettes. Once a palette is open, the word "Show" in the Window menu will change to "Hide."

*n*OTE: *When you load Photoshop for the first time after installation, the Brushes palette will load automatically. If the palette isn't open on screen, open it by choosing Show Brushes in the Window menu.*

Photoshop's palettes were designed to provide quick and easy access to procedures that are used frequently. Each palette can be moved by clicking and dragging in its title bar. This lets you keep palettes handy at all times. Unlike other windows, palettes always float above your active window. This means that they will never drop behind any open document. (Windows that are not palettes can drop behind other documents.) When more than one document is open, clicking on a Photoshop window will cause it to jump in front of all other windows on the screen.

Certain features are common in all the palettes. In Figure 2-3a you can see the Close box, which closes the palette; the title bar, which you click to move the palette; and the Expand/Collapse box. The Expand/Collapse box allows you to shrink a palette so that it uses less room onscreen, thus letting you view more of your image. After a palette shrinks, you can expand it by clicking once again on the Expand/Collapse box. Below the Expand/Collapse box is the Options menu arrow. When clicked, it displays a menu of options for that palette, as shown in Figure 2-3b.

PC users can click on the Control menu button in the upper-left corner of the palette (see Figure 2-4a) to display the menu of options for each palette (Figure 2-4b). To close the Control menu, select Close from the list of options, or you can double-click on the Control menu button.

(a) The
Mac
Brushes
palette,
collapsed;
(b) the Mac
Brushes
palette,
expanded,
with its
Options
menu
displayed

FIGURE 2-3

> *n* **OTE:** *All of the palettes except the Info palette can be resized. To resize a palette on the Mac, click and drag on the Resize box in the lower-right corner of the palette. On the PC, click and drag on the palette's border.*

Let's start our examination of the palettes by looking at one of the most frequently used, the Brushes palette.

The Brushes Palette

You'll use the Brushes palette, shown in Figure 2-3a (PC users: Figure 2-4a), primarily to choose the size of a brush and whether it will be soft- or hard-edged.

The Brushes palette also provides control over how paint is applied to an image. The Opacity slider allows you to make your painting color more transparent. This

(a) The
Windows
Brushes
palette;
(b) the
Windows
Brushes
palette
options,
displayed
via the
Control
menu button

Control menu button

(a)

(b)

■ **FIGURE 2-4**

slider changes to a Pressure gauge when the Airbrush, Smudge, and Blur/Sharpen tools are used, and to an Exposure slider when the Dodge/Burn tool is activated.

The Brushes palette even allows you to switch painting Modes (by clicking on the Mode pop-up menu). The painting Modes are usually used to change the effect when one color is painted over another. For instance, if you switch from Normal to Lighten mode, Photoshop will lighten image areas by only painting over those areas that are darker than your painting color. The painting Modes in the Brushes palette are discussed in Chapters 5 and 11.

In the Options menu of the Brushes palette are commands for loading, saving, creating, and deleting brushes. To see these commands, click on the Options menu arrow in the Brushes palette. PC users should click on the Control menu in the upper-left corner of the palette. Using the commands in the Brushes palette's Options menu will be covered in Chapter 5.

The Colors Palette

In the Colors palette you can pick colors for the Foreground and Background selection boxes by clicking on color swatches (small color samples) or by using sliders based upon color models such as RGB and CMYK. The Colors palette Options menu can be used to switch to sliders based upon different color models. This topic is discussed in Chapter 4.

The large white square with a black frame in the Colors palette is the scratch pad, which is used for mixing colors, and previewing brush strokes and effects. The scratch pad is discussed in Chapter 5.

The Info Palette

The Info palette displays the x-coordinate (horizontal) and y-coordinate (vertical) of the mouse pointer. Move the mouse pointer across the screen, and you'll see the X and Y values in the palette change. If you wish to change the measurement units for the mouse coordinates displayed in the Info palette, access the Info palette's Options menu. The mouse coordinates can be displayed in inches, points, pixels, or centimeters.

If you move the mouse pointer over colored or gray areas, the Info palette will function as a *densitometer* (an instrument used by printers to measure color density), displaying color values as you move over them. For instance, if you position the pointer over an area painted with 60% magenta, the Info palette will display 60% in the M (for magenta) readout.

The Paths Palette

The Paths palette allows you to access Photoshop's Pen tool, which can be used to create Bézier curves and straight lines. The Paths palette contains its own set of tools that enable you to adjust and edit the shapes, called *paths*, that the Pen tool creates. The Selection pointer allows you to select paths so they can be moved and edited. The Pen+ and Pen- tools allow points to be added and subtracted from paths. The Corner tool can change a soft curve into a sharp corner or vice versa. The Paths palette's Options menu can be used to outline or fill paths with colors and change paths into selections. The Pen tool and Paths palette are covered in Chapter 10.

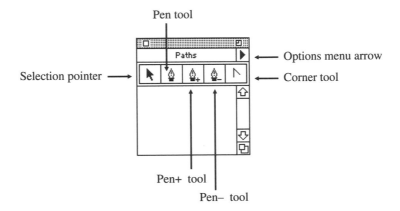

The Channels Palette

A *channel* is similar to a plate in commercial printing. The Channels palette allows you to easily view a channel or edit an image in a channel.

The Channels palette will display different channels depending upon the file Mode of the image. If you are working in an RGB Color file, the Channels palette will display the separate channels for each of the Red, Green, and Blue color components of the image along with the RGB composite. If you are viewing a CMYK Color file onscreen, the Channels palette will display the separate channels

for Cyan, Magenta, Yellow, and Black along with the CMYK composite. If you wanted to alter only the Yellow component of a CMYK image, you could choose Yellow in the Channels palette and then make your changes.

The Channels palette Options menu allows you to create and name channels to use as masks. See Chapter 12 for an in-depth discussion on using channels and masks.

IP: *To temporarily clear the screen of all palettes, press TAB. Press TAB again to redisplay the palettes.*

USING PHOTOSHOP TOOLS TO EXAMINE AND EDIT PIXELS

Now that you're familiar with the Photoshop window and have an understanding of how to use the palettes, you're ready to try out a few tools and start exploring the fundamentals of a pixel-based program. The following exercise demonstrates how to use the Type tool to enter text, the Zoom tool to examine pixels, and the Eraser tool to edit pixels. Let's start with the Type tool; this is a comfortable bridge to the Toolbox because many users are already familiar with the concept of placing text on a screen.

Entering Text with the Type Tool

Even though the Type tool is not complex, you may be surprised when you first try to enter text, because Photoshop (unlike many other programs) does not allow you to type directly on screen. Text must be typed into a dialog box. In the following exercises, you'll learn how to activate the Type Tool dialog box, enter text, and edit it with the Eraser tool.

OTE: *Before beginning this next series of exercises, check to see what colors are displayed in the Foreground Color and Background Color icons in the Toolbox. If black is not the Foreground Color and white is not the Background Color, click on the Default Colors icon. This will ensure that your text is black and the Eraser tool erases with white.*

T 1. Before you can create any text in Photoshop, you must first activate the Type tool in the Toolbox. To do this, simply point to and click on the Type tool.

2. Move the mouse pointer toward the document window. As you do, notice that the pointer changes. This pointer is called the *I-beam.*

3. To enter text in the upper-left corner of the window, move the I-beam to this part of the screen.

4. Click the mouse to open the Type Tool dialog box, shown in Figure 2-5.

   In the Type Tool dialog box, you can pick a font by choosing from a list in the Font pop-up menu. You can also change point size, *leading* (space between lines), *spacing* (space between the letters), text style, and

```
┌─────────────────────────────────────────────────────┐
│≣≣≣≣≣≣≣≣≣≣≣≣≣≣≣≣≣  Type Tool  ≣≣≣≣≣≣≣≣≣≣≣≣≣≣≣≣│
│                                                       │
│   Font: [ Times                      ▼ ]  (   OK   )  │
│                                                       │
│   Size: [100]  [ points ▼ ]               ( Cancel )  │
│                                                       │
│  Leading: [    ]                                      │
│                                                       │
│  Spacing: [    ]                                      │
│                                                       │
│  ┌─ Style ──────────────────────┐  ┌─ Alignment ──┐  │
│  │ ☐ Bold      ☐ Outline        │  │ ◉ Left       │  │
│  │ ☐ Italic    ☐ Shadow         │  │ ○ Center     │  │
│  │ ☐ Underline ☒ Anti-Aliased   │  │ ○ Right      │  │
│  └──────────────────────────────┘  └──────────────┘  │
│  ┌─────────────────────────────────────────────────┐ │
│  │ nancy                                           │ │
│  │                                                 │ │
│  │                                                 │ │
│  │                                                 │ │
│  │                                                 │ │
│  └─────────────────────────────────────────────────┘ │
└─────────────────────────────────────────────────────┘
```

The Type
Tool dialog
box with
entered text

FIGURE 2-5

alignment. For leading or alignment to take affect, you need at least two rows of text. Also, Photoshop does not allow you to choose more than one font or point size, or more than one leading or spacing setting for a text selection.

Before you begin to enter text, change the font and point size.

5. Click on the Font pop-up menu and choose Times or any other font from the list provided.

6. Click in the Size text box and type **100**. (Make sure points has been selected from the pop-up menu.) This sets your font size to 100 points, about 1.5 inches high.

7. Click in the text box at the bottom of the dialog box. A blinking cursor will appear; this is where you enter your text. Type **nancy** (or your own name) in the text box, as shown in Figure 2-5.

8. Check to make sure you haven't made any typos. If you made a mistake, this is your chance to fix it. The simplest way to replace a character is to position the cursor to the right of the character you want to change, and press DELETE (PC users: BACKSPACE). Then type the correct character.

9. When you're done, click the OK button. Your text appears in the document window surrounded with a marquee (represented by a series of dotted lines):

nancy

The marquee surrounding your text indicates the object is in *floating* mode. (Think of this as the text being suspended in air above the electronic canvas.) Only when the text is floating can it be deleted or moved around in the window. In a sense, floating mode gives you one last chance to delete the text and retype it before the paint has dried on the electronic canvas.

Moving and Locking Text into Position

To see floating mode in action, move your text to a new position on screen, using either the keyboard arrows or the mouse.

NOTE: *In order to perform the following exercise, you must keep the text selected. Don't click away from your text. If you do, the marquee will disappear and the text will no longer be floating. If this happens, immediately select Undo from the Edit menu.*

1. Press the UP ARROW on your keyboard two or three times. Each time you press it, your text will move up one pixel at a time.

2. To move the text by clicking and dragging the mouse, first position the I-beam over any letter. When the I-beam changes to a pointer, click and drag the text to a new position about an inch lower. (Do not move the text too far down because you're going to use the lower part of the screen later.) Notice that as you drag the mouse a skeleton version of the text is moved, though Photoshop still shows the text's original position on screen.

nancy

When you release the mouse, the skeleton version of the text turns black, and the text that was seen in the original position disappears.

3. When you're satisfied with the placement of your text, lock it into position to prevent it from being inadvertently moved or deleted. To do this, you must first exit floating mode. Click above, below, to the left, or to the right of your text. The marquee disappears, indicating that the text is no longer floating.

When text is not floating, it becomes locked down on the screen's grid of pixels, like dried paint on a canvas. The only way to change the locked text is to do what a painter would do—paint over it with white (the color of the canvas), and then re-create the text. In the next section, you'll examine the pixels that make up the text, to see what you'll eventually be painting over.

IP: *Floating text can be deleted from the screen by pressing DELETE (PC users: BACKSPACE). Even though the text is deleted from the screen, Photoshop retains it in the Type Tool dialog box. This is helpful because you can then edit your text in the dialog box. To do this, click again in the document with the Type tool to open the Type Tool dialog box. The text you last entered will be displayed in the dialog box. After you change the text, click OK and the edited text will appear in the document window.*

Examining Pixels with the Zoom Tool

In this section, you'll zoom in to text on screen so that you can see the matrix of pixels that combine to make the letters you typed. The Zoom tool allows you to point to an area in the document window and magnify it. Each time you click the Zoom tool, magnification grows by a factor of two. For instance, the first time you zoom, your image will grow to twice as large as the original. The next time you zoom, it will be four times as large; the next, eight times as large, and so on.

1. To activate the Zoom tool, click on it. The mouse pointer changes to a magnifying glass.

2. Position the Zoom tool pointer over the letter n (or the first letter of your name), and click. The screen image doubles. Notice that the magnification ratio in the title bar has changed to 2:1. Keep clicking the mouse until the magnification ratio is 8:1 (16:1 is the limit).

3. To ensure that the zoomed letter is in view, use the scroll arrows at the lower-right and lower-left of the screen to reposition the letter if necessary. Instead of scrolling, you can also use the Hand tool. Click on the tool and drag to reposition the screen. (You may need to click and drag on the Resize box in the lower-right corner to enlarge the document window. PC users can click and drag on the window border to resize.) Your screen will look similar to Figure 2-6.

Notice that the your zoomed text looks jagged; this is because the letters are made of pixels. The jaggies are the pixel edges. Notice how different combinations of pixels form the various letters. As stated earlier, all images in Photoshop are basically created the same way, from pixels. You might notice that some of the hard edges in the zoomed text are blurred or softened. Photoshop tries to eliminate the jaggies as much as possible; this blurring effect is called *anti-aliasing*.

Editing Pixels with the Eraser Tool

Since the letters in Photoshop are not individual objects but rather locked together on a grid of pixels, there's no way of slipping a cursor between them to delete or

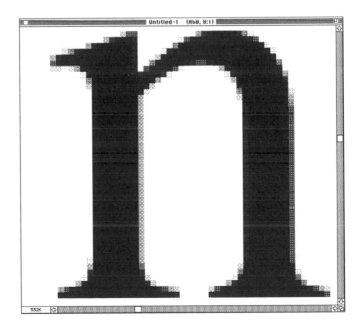

Jagged
edges
displaying
pixels in
text

FIGURE 2-6

edit them. To delete and edit in Photoshop, you'll need to white out the pixels of any letter you wish to remove, and then make your changes.

In this exercise you'll use the Eraser to white out the lowercase n from the word nancy, and then replace it with an uppercase N. (You can do the same with the first letter of whatever text you typed on the screen.)

1. Click the Eraser tool in the Toolbox. The mouse pointer changes to a small eraser.

2. Position the Eraser over any part of the n in nancy (or the first letter of your name). Click the mouse, and Photoshop replaces the black in that pixel with white.

3. Click over different parts of the letter to create a speckled effect.

   At first glance it seems the Eraser is merely removing black from each individual pixel. You are, however, actually painting with the default background color of white. This may seem like a slow way of deleting, but it's actually one of the strengths of Photoshop: You can edit any object at the smallest possible level: the pixel. In most other programs, you can edit text, but not pieces of type.

4. Continue whiting out the lowercase n until you have deleted it. To work a little faster with the Eraser tool, keep the mouse button pressed as you move the Eraser back and forth over the letter, much the same as you would use a rubber eraser on paper.

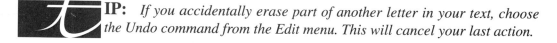

IP: *If you accidentally erase part of another letter in your text, choose the Undo command from the Edit menu. This will cancel your last action.*

Now that you've removed the lowercase n, you'll use the Type tool to enter a capital N and move it to the left of the letters currently on screen. It will be easier to perform this task if you can see all the letters of the name on the screen. Instead of zooming out and scrolling, here is a shortcut you can use to make an image fit on screen: Double-click on the Hand tool. The magnification ratio will change to 1:1.

1. To enter the capital N, activate the Type tool and then click below the letters on screen. The Type Tool dialog box will open.

2. In the Type Tool dialog box, type **N** and click OK. The letter appears in the document window in floating mode.

EMEMBER: *Because the letter is still floating you can move it with either the keyboard arrows or the mouse.*

3. While the letter is still floating, move the I-beam over the letter. When the I-beam changes to an arrow, click and drag the letter to the left of the other letters, so your screen looks like this:

Nancy

4. When you're happy with the position of your new capital letter, move the pointer away from the image and click. The letter stops floating and locks down on the screen.

This concludes your introduction to pixel editing. You have seen how to access tools in Photoshop's Toolbox, and had an introduction to "thinking like a painter" when you're using Photoshop.

STORING AND RETRIEVING FILES

Although Photoshop requires you to think like a painter, it doesn't allow you to work *exactly* like one. Unlike a painter, when your work is done you can't just turn out the lights to the studio and go home for the day. If you wish to return to your Photoshop work for another session, you need to save your file.

Saving a File

Although your file so far is merely a practice document, save it anyway so that you can practice storing and retrieving it later. The next exercises will help you become familiar with the steps involved in saving your document.

1. To save your work, select Save from the File menu. The Save As dialog box appears the first time you save your file. In the text box labeled Save this document as, you'll see the highlighted word "Untitled-1." This is the text box where you name your document.

2. Type **MyType**. (Since "Untitled-1" is highlighted, as soon as you start typing you replace it with the name of your file.)

```
┌─────────────────────────────────────────────┐
│  📁 Adobe Photoshop™... ▼                     │
│  ┌──────────────────────────┐                 │
│  │ 🔷 Adobe Photoshop™ 2.5.1 ⬆│   💾 HD #1     │
│  │ 🗀 Brushes & Patterns    ▓│                 │
│  │ 🗀 Calibration           ▓│  ┌──────────┐  │
│  │ 🗀 Color Palettes        ▓│  │  Eject   │  │
│  │ 🗀 Duotone Curves        ▓│  ┌──────────┐  │
│  │ 🗀 EfiColor for PS 2.5.1 ⬇│  │ Desktop  │  │
│  └──────────────────────────┘                 │
│  Save this document as:        ┌──────────┐   │
│  ┌──────────────────────────┐  │   Save   │   │
│  │ MyType                   │  └──────────┘   │
│  └──────────────────────────┘  ┌──────────┐   │
│                                │  Cancel  │   │
│  Format:  ┌────────────────┐                  │
│           │ Photoshop 2.5  │                  │
│           └────────────────┘                  │
└─────────────────────────────────────────────┘
```

Notice that Format displays as "Photoshop 2.5"; this is the default file format. If this field contains another format name, you or someone else changed it while working.

3. To change file formats (if necessary), click on the Format pop-up menu and choose Photoshop 2.5.

Look at the folder icons in the dialog box to see where you're saving your file. (PC users: Folders are visual representations of your directories.) Make sure you are saving it in a location that you will remember.

4. When you're ready to save, click the Save button (PC users: OK). After Photoshop saves your file, the filename, MyType in this case, appears in the title bar of your document window.

𝓃 **OTE:** *As you work on any Photoshop file, you can save as often as you like by choosing Save from the File menu or by pressing COMMAND-S. (PC users: CTRL-S) Be aware, though, that the Save command always replaces the previous version of your file. If you wish to make a copy of your file, you should use the Save As command.*

 AUTION: *System crashes, however rare, do occur. To avoid losing hours of your hard work in the electronic void, save your work frequently.*

Using Save As

The Save As command reopens the Save As dialog box so that you can save your file under a new name. This lets you create different versions of a file or save it to another hard drive or storage device as a backup.

1. To save another version of your MyType file, choose Save As from the File menu. The Save As dialog box appears, where you see MyType waiting to be renamed (PC users will see mytype.psd).

2. Position the I-beam immediately after the letter e in MyType, and click the mouse. The cursor is now blinking after the letter e. (PC users: Make sure your cursor is blinking between the e and the period in front of psd).

3. Type the number **2**. The filename changes to MyType2 (PC users will see mytype2.psd).

4. To save a copy of your document with the name MyType2, click the Save button (PC users: OK).

When the dialog box closes, you are in the document MyType2. The previous version of the file is no longer open, but remains on your hard disk still saved as MyType. You can continue to work in MyType2, knowing that MyType is still intact on your hard disk.

As you work on new versions of your practice file, you can continue to use Save As to rename your file MyType3, MyType4, and so on. This way you can always return to any previous version of your file.

Using the Revert Command

A command almost as beneficial as Save As is the File menu's Revert command. While Save As can be used to save different versions of your file, Revert always returns you to the last saved version. When you use the Revert command, you automatically load your previous version, without using the File/Open command.

To get to know the value of the Revert command, you'll need to make some changes to MyType2. Start by adding Nancy's last name, Smith. (Of course, you can do all of this next exercise using your own name if you wish.)

1. Click on the Type tool to activate it.

2. To display the Type Tool dialog box, click in the middle of your screen below the word "Nancy."

3. Type **Smith** into the text entry field and click OK. Smith appears under Nancy.

4. Position the I-beam over Smith. When it becomes an arrow, click and drag Smith away from Nancy.

5. Click away from the text to deselect it and drop it out of floating mode.

6. To save this version of your file, select Save in the File menu.

EMEMBER: *It is a good idea to save your file before you start experimenting with new ideas.*

Now that you've edited and saved your file, make a few more changes before you use Revert to get the last saved version. Try experimenting with the Eraser tool to see if you can create some interesting typographic effects.

1. Click on the Eraser tool. Move the eraser pointer over into the middle of the N in Nancy, and click and drag to the right to create a white swath through all of the letters. Create another white swath through Smith, like this:

2. You're not impressed, so you want to undo your changes. Choose Undo from the Edit menu.

Note that Undo cancels only the last change you made: Smith has returned to its original state, but not Nancy. Fortunately, you saved before beginning your Eraser experiment. You can now return to the last saved version of your file using Revert.

3. From the File menu, select Revert. The Revert alert box appears.

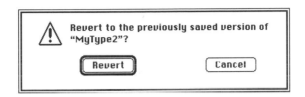

4. If you wish to revert to the last saved version, click Revert. In a few seconds, your screen returns to the way it was before you began to erase.

CAUTION: *The Revert command is irreversible. Once you revert, you can't Undo it.*

Once you decide that the image on screen is exactly the way you want it, you'll probably want to output it to your printer. The next section covers printing and Photoshop's page preview feature.

PAGE PREVIEW AND PRINTING

Before you print, it's often a good idea to preview your output, particularly because graphic images usually take a long time to be processed by most printers. Although Photoshop does not provide a print preview of your image, it does let you preview

page orientation and other specific printing options, such as crop and registration marks. For a detailed discussion of the options in the Page Setup dialog box, see Chapter 14.

To preview your file, click on the file size number in the lower-left corner of the Photoshop window. A preview of your page's orientation—landscape or portrait—pops up in the lower-left corner of the window.

The preview can also show labels, crop marks, registration marks, calibration bars, negatives, and emulsion type. These are all options that can be selected in the Page Setup dialog box accessed through the File menu.

NOTE: *If you aren't using Adobe's Print Driver 8.0, your Page Setup dialog box will not look exactly the same as the one shown here.*

If you click on the file size number with the OPTION (PC users: ALT) key pressed, Photoshop will display information about your file's size, resolution, and number of channels.

```
    Width:  504 pixels (7 inches)
   Height:  360 pixels (5 inches)
 Channels:    3 (RGB Color)
Resolution:  72 pixels/inch
```

To print your document, select Print from the File menu. The Print dialog box appears and contains standard Mac/Windows print options. In addition, Photoshop allows you to print a color image as a Grayscale, RGB, or CMYK image. The Print Selected Area option will only print an area that is selected on screen. If no area is selected, this option will be dimmed. For more information about printing, see Chapter 14.

Photoshop in Action

The highway was pasted using an 80% opacity.

The rectangle was created using the Rectangular Marquee.

The ellipse was created using the Elliptical Marquee.

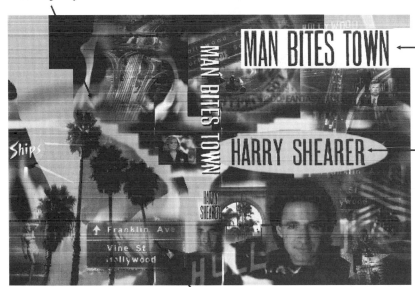

Artist: Josh Gosfield

Book cover for St. Martins Press

This image was pasted using a 70% opacity

Josh created this book cover by first filling in the background with color. He then used different selection tools to select images from other files to copy and paste in the book cover file. After an image was pasted, he lowered the Opacity setting in the Brushes palette to create a blending effect between the pasted image and the background. Once the images were in position, he added the rectangle and ellipse. After these areas were filled with color, the text was then placed over them.

Most artists add text to an image by using Photoshop's Type tool or by creating the text in a drawing or page-layout program. In this case, the publisher supplied Josh with the typeset book title and author's name on paper. This was scanned in and selected with the selection tools, then copied and pasted over the rectangle and the ellipse. Josh was also able to rotate and shrink the text to place on the spine by using the Rotate command in the Image menu and the Scale command in the Image/Effects submenu.

OTE: *If you are not using Adobe's Print Driver 8.0 your Print dialog box will not look exactly the same as the one shown here.*

You may be surprised at the low quality of the printed MyType2 file. The jagged edges are the result of the 72-ppi file resolution. Since Photoshop is a pixel-based program, the print quality of text is dependent upon the file's resolution, not the output resolution of your printer. Users who need high-quality printed text often export their files into drawing programs such as Adobe Illustrator and Aldus Freehand. In these programs, the quality of type does not depend on image resolution.

USING PREFERENCES TO CHANGE THE DEFAULTS

Before quitting Photoshop, let's take a look at how to change some of the program's default settings. Changing the defaults lets you customize your Photoshop environment to make it more comfortable for you to use, and possibly to save you some time. The defaults can be accessed from the Preferences command in the File menu.

Function Keys

Both Mac and PC users can use function keys to execute commands. But only in the Macintosh version of Photoshop can you customize your function keys. Although the function keys are not programmable in Windows, you can still take advantage of using them to execute commands.

Customizing Macintosh Function Keys

To customize function keys on the Macintosh extended keyboard, select Preferences from the File menu. Keep the mouse button pressed so that the Function Keys submenu appears. To open the Function Key Preferences dialog box, shown in Figure 2-7, select Function Keys from the Preferences submenu.

Notice that F1 through F9 are already assigned to execute the Undo, Cut, Copy, Paste, Show Brushes, Show Channels, Show Colors, Show Info, and Show Paths commands. But F10 through F15 can be customized as your own function keys. This is a very useful feature. Just type in a menu command next to the function keys; for instance, you could click in the F10 field and type **Revert**. After you click OK and exit the dialog box, you can use F10 to Revert instead of having to open the File menu.

Function
Key
Preferences
dialog box

FIGURE 2-7

If you would like to customize additional function keys, click on the Shift check box in the Function Key Preferences dialog box to open a new unassigned set of function keys.

The Save button in the Function Key Preferences dialog allows you to name and save sets of various function keys for use in documents that may require particular commands other than those you use in your day-to-day work.

NOTE: *The Save Selection and Load Selection commands found in the Select menu cannot be executed with function keys. Save Selection and Load Selection are covered in Chapter 12.*

Unit Preferences

To change the Photoshop ruler measuring units, select Units from the Preferences submenu. Then click on the Ruler Units pop-up menu; here you can change the measuring units to pixels, inches, centimeters, points, or picas.

If you are using points, you can choose either the PostScript (72 points/inch) or Traditional (72.27 points/inch) setting, by clicking on the appropriate radio button in the Unit Preferences dialog box, shown in the illustration on page 65.

Photoshop in Action

The circles in the background were created using the Paintbrush and a custom brush.

The rectangle was created using the Rectangular Marquee.

The text was created using Photoshop's Type tool. To make the text appear vertically, the RETURN key was pressed after each letter was entered into the Type Tool dialog box.

The speckled effect was created using the Airbrush tool with a small soft-edged brush.

Artist: Pamela Hobbs   Promotional poster for the Limelight

Pamela created this poster by starting with a photograph of KEDA, the musician, wearing jeans, and with a sketch of the costume he would wear the night of his performance at the Limelight in New York City.

After the photograph was scanned in, Pamela began painting over it with the painting tools, using the costume sketch as a guide. Once the image of KEDA in his costume was completed, the background was created and the text applied.

To create the fire in the background, the Paintbrush, Airbrush, and Blur/Sharpen tools were used with different foreground colors, brushes, opacities, and pressures. Next, the two rectangles on both sides of the image were created and filled with color. The text was then added, and the finishing touches were applied with the Airbrush tool.

EMEMBER: *To display the rulers in your document window, select Show Rulers from the Window menu.*

The Column Size settings allow you to specify a column width and gutter as a measuring unit. This measuring unit is named Columns. In the New, Image Size, Canvas Size, and Cropping Tool dialog boxes, Columns can be used in place of inches, points, pixels, or centimeters. This can be helpful when working with images that will be placed in columns in page-layout programs such as QuarkXPress and Aldus PageMaker.

General Preferences

The bulk of Photoshop's Preferences options are found in the General submenu. These general preferences cover a wide variety of settings, from how the screen displays imported images to whether your computer beeps when it has completed a task.

Although most preferences are simple in concept, some might be confusing until you've had a chance to work more with Photoshop. Don't worry—these options will be covered in detail as you work through the other chapters in this book.

CONCLUSION

By now you should have a sense of the fundamentals of Photoshop. In Chapter 3, you'll build on this foundation, taking a thorough look at how to use the selection tools. This chapter will set you on your way to creating shapes, separating images from their background, and cutting, pasting, moving, and filling objects.

If you wish to exit Photoshop now before going ahead with Chapter 3, select Quit (PC users: Exit) from the File menu. If you made changes to a file that you haven't saved, an alert box will appear asking if you wish to save the changes. Click the Save button if you do, or Don't Save if you don't. Click Cancel if you change your mind and want to go directly on to work in the next chapter.

3

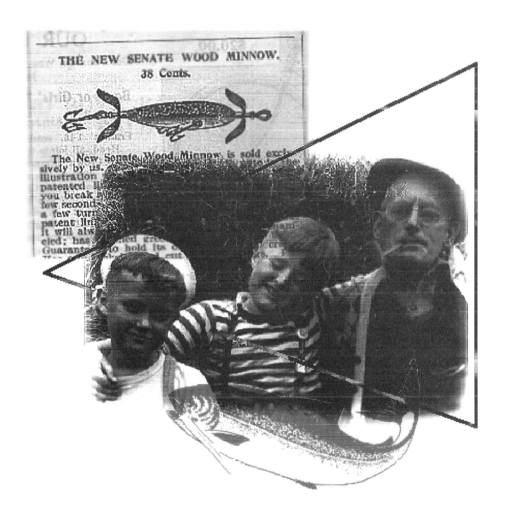

THE NEW SENATE WOOD MINNOW.
38 Cents.

The New Senate Wood Minnow is sold exclusively by us.

SELECTING AND
CREATING SHAPES

It's virtually impossible to complete any Photoshop project without using the four *selection tools:* the Rectangular Marquee, Elliptical Marquee, Lasso, and Magic Wand. These four tools, which sit at the top of Photoshop's Toolbox, are used primarily for outlining and isolating specific areas in images so they can be moved, copied, retouched, or color corrected.

The selection tools are integral to the creation of *photomontages* (multiple photographs from different images) and *collages* (various images and graphics blended together). These tools also allow you to quickly turn scanned images into line art and to create special effects such as shadows and *vignettes* (pictures that gradually fade off into the surroundings).

In this chapter you'll have a chance to try each of the selection tools. More importantly, you'll be introduced to the concept of selections and why they're so important in Photoshop. Along the way, you'll learn how to fill and *stroke* (outline or frame) a shape with the foreground and background colors. As you work through the chapter you'll use many of the commands in Photoshop's Select menu, as well as create three simple collages and a vignette.

The first image you create will be the flag collage shown in Figure 3-1. The flag image was assembled primarily by using the Rectangular Marquee selection tool. The highway in the upper-left corner of the flag was taken from a larger scanned image by selecting it with the Rectangular Marquee; once selected, it was then copied and pasted over the flag graphic.

You might be surprised to learn that the flag was *created* with a selection tool, but you'll soon see that all of Photoshop's selection tools provide a dual function: They can both be used to select and create shapes.

The exercises in this chapter use shapes as stepping stones to image creation and editing. The first exercises will help you understand what a selection is and how *floating* applies to selected objects. You'll get to practice working with simple images before you move on to more complicated ones.

Before proceeding, it's important to remember that you are using a pixel-based (sometimes called *raster*) program, not an object-oriented (sometimes called *vector*) drawing program. As discussed in the previous chapter, in object-oriented drawing programs you can select an object with the mouse and delete it. In Photoshop, however, to delete a selected object you have to paint it with the background color (often white), much like using a liquid white-out product to correct typing mistakes. Because Photoshop is pixel-based, you need to take special care when selecting,

The flag
collage

FIGURE 3-1

duplicating, and moving objects. If you don't understand the fundamentals of these actions, you may get some surprising and often unwanted results. But once you've learned the basics of how to create a selection and fill it with color, you'll be on your way to creating successful Photoshop design projects.

THE FLAG COLLAGE

Before beginning to work with the selection tools, start by creating a new document to work in. You'll use this document for the following introductory exercises and for composing the flag collage.

1. Select New from the File menu.

2. When the New dialog box appears

   a. Check to see that the Width and Height measurement units are set to inches. If they aren't, click on the pop-up menu for each field and change the units to inches.

   b. In the Width field, type **5.5**, and in the Height field, type **3.75**. These dimensions will make the flag fit snugly in the document window.

c. Resolution should be set to 72 pixels/inch. If it isn't, press TAB to move to the Resolution field and enter **72**.

d. If Mode is not set to RGB Color, click on the pop-up menu and change the setting.

e. Click OK to open the new document window.

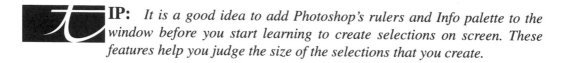 **IP:** *It is a good idea to add Photoshop's rulers and Info palette to the window before you start learning to create selections on screen. These features help you judge the size of the selections that you create.*

3. To make the rulers visible, select Show Rulers from the Window menu.

4. To open the Info palette, select Show Info from the Window menu.

Introductory Exercises: Creating, Filling, Moving, and Floating a Selection

It doesn't matter what shape a selection is; Photoshop treats them all the same. Once you select an area on the screen, Photoshop points its attention to the selection. You can execute virtually any image-editing command, and only the selected area will be affected.

Let's start with the Rectangular Marquee tool (in the top-left corner of the Toolbox), since it was used primarily to create the flag collage.

 OTE: *The selections you create with the Rectangular Marquee share the same characteristics as all selections, no matter what tool created them.*

Creating a Selection with the Rectangular Marquee Normal Option

 The Rectangular Marquee tool allows you to create and select squares and rectangles. It will also allow you to create a 1-pixel-wide vertical selection or a 1-pixel-wide horizontal selection.

1. Before you create a selection, double-click the Rectangular Marquee tool to open the Rectangular Marquee Options dialog box, as shown in Figure 3-2.

2. In the Marquee settings, check to see that the Normal radio button is selected; if it isn't, click on it. To accept the dialog box settings, click OK.

3

The
Rectangular
Marquee
Options
dialog box

FIGURE 3-2

The Rectangular Marquee Options dialog box:

Rectangular Marquee Options

Marquee
- Normal
- Constrained Aspect Ratio:
  - Width: 1
  - Height: 1
- Fixed Size:
  - Width: 64 pixels
  - Height: 64 pixels
- Single Row
- Single Column

Feather
- Radius: 0 pixels

OK Cancel

The Normal setting allows you to create rectangular selections of any size. This is the default setting, and it will be selected unless you've previously changed it. If another option is selected, such as Fixed Size, the tool will create rectangles that are always the same size. Don't worry about the other options you see; they'll be covered later in this chapter.

EMEMBER: *The dialog boxes for all of the tools in Photoshop retain the last settings used. They do not automatically return to their default settings.*

3. Move the mouse pointer to the document window. Notice that when the pointer moves over the document area, it changes to a crosshair, as shown here. Now you can start using the Rectangular Marquee tool to create a selection.

4. Position the crosshair at the 1-inch mark both vertically (x-axis) and horizontally (y-axis). To make sure you are positioned at 1 inch both vertically and horizontally, refer to the Info palette. As you move the mouse, the X and Y readings next to the crosshair icon show your horizontal (X) and vertical (Y) positions. The X and Y readings next to the anchor icon indicate your original X and Y positions.

OTE: *You change the measurement units in the Info palette by first clicking on its Options menu arrow. In the Info Options dialog box, click on the Ruler Units pop-up menu and choose Inches.*

5. When the Info palette shows both X and Y reading 1, click and drag diagonally down from left to right to make a rectangular selection about 2 inches by 2 inches, as shown in Figure 3-3. Refer again to the Info palette; notice the width (W) and height (H) readings of the selection you are creating. When your selection looks like Figure 3-3, release the mouse.

6. Your selection is represented on screen by a blinking *marquee,* which appears as a series of dotted lines. Your selection is now an isolated area that you can work with as an independent object, separate from the rest of the screen.

7. Click again anywhere in your document outside your rectangular selection. Photoshop thinks you're finished working with the selection or that you want to create another selection, so it *deselects* your original selection, and the marquee disappears.

A marquee created by a selection tool is really nothing but tiny, blinking lines on the screen, unless the selection tool has been used to isolate part of an existing onscreen image or to *create* a shape. The next sections will introduce you to techniques for creating shapes by filling selections with foreground and background colors and by moving and duplicating selections.

Filling a Selection with the Foreground or Background Color

If you wish to create an object with Photoshop's selection tools, you can't just draw it. You must first create a selection, and then make it come to life by either filling it

Clicking and dragging with the Rectangular Marquee tool to make a selection

FIGURE 3-3

with a color (either the foreground or background color) or stroking it (putting an outline around it). You'll see how to do this in the following exercise.

 To make it easier to follow the instructions in this exercise, start with the foreground and background colors at their default settings (black foreground and white background). Check the Foreground Color and Background Color icons in the Toolbox. If the foreground color is not black and the background color is not white, click the Default Colors icon to reset the colors to their defaults.

 OTE: *Until you've become familiar with Photoshop, you might find it helpful to refer back to Figure 2-2 in Chapter 2 for the locations and names of all Toolbox icons.*

To fill a selection with the foreground color, you can either choose Fill from the Edit menu or hold down the OPTION key and press DELETE (PC users: ALT-BACKSPACE). To fill a selection with the background color, press DELETE (PC users: BACKSPACE). When you fill selections using keyboard commands, you apply opaque foreground and background colors. The Edit/Fill command works with the foreground color only, allowing opacity and painting modes to be changed. Edit/Fill options will be discussed in Chapters 5 and 6.

Start by creating a rectangular selection and fill it with the foreground color, then with the background color.

1. Notice that the Rectangular Marquee tool is still selected— it's the last tool you used and Photoshop keeps it active. To create the rectangular selection, click approximately 1 inch from the upper-left corner of the screen and drag down diagonally approximately 2 or 3 inches. Release the mouse button.

2. To fill the selection with the foreground color, press the OPTION (PC users: ALT) key. Hold it down, and press DELETE (PC users: BACKSPACE).

   Your rectangular selection immediately turns black. Notice that the selection marquee still surrounds your rectangle.

3. Now fill with the background color by pressing DELETE (PC users: BACKSPACE).

The rectangle disappears but the selection remains. This often gives Photoshop beginners the mistaken impression that the DELETE (or BACKSPACE) key deletes objects. Actually, however, the DELETE or BACKSPACE key fills with the background color and could therefore be considered a painting tool. You have just painted your black rectangle white. (If you're still skeptical about this concept, be patient. When you press DELETE or BACKSPACE with a background color other than white, you'll be convinced.)

Changing the Foreground and Background Colors

Photoshop provides a variety of ways to choose and mix colors for the foreground and background. At this stage, since all you need are red and blue to create the flag collage, you can pick colors using the simplest method: from color *swatches* (small colored squares) found in the Colors palette. Once you've chosen red as your the foreground color and blue for your background color, you can proceed to fill your selections.

1. To display the Colors palette, select Show Colors from the Window menu.

2. Notice the two squares in the upper-right corner of the Colors palette. The top square is the Foreground selection box and represents the foreground color. It overlaps a second square, the Backgound selection box, which represents the background color. A white band surrounding the selection box indicates that that color is active and ready to be changed. Click on the Foreground selection box so you can change the foreground color. (At this point, don't worry about any other items in the Colors palette. Most of these will be introduced to you in Chapter 4.)

3. To change the foreground color to red, position the mouse pointer over the color swatches in the Colors palette. The mouse pointer changes to an eyedropper. Click on a red swatch. The Foreground selection box changes to red, and the Foreground Color icon in the Toolbox changes to the same red color.

4. Now change the background color to blue. Point to and click on the Background selection box, which is currently white. The white band jumps to and surrounds this box.

5. Point to the color swatches and click on a blue swatch. Again, notice the change in both the Background selection box in the Colors palette and the Background Color icon in the Toolbox.

   Now you're ready to create an object and fill it with the new backgound and foreground colors.

6. Using the Rectangular Marquee tool, create a rectangular selection. To apply the background color, press DELETE (PC users: BACKSPACE). The rectangle fills with blue.

7. To apply the foreground color, press OPTION-DELETE (PC users: ALT-BACKSPACE). The rectangle changes to red.

8. To remove the marquee from the selection, position the crosshair anywhere inside the document window (except on the rectangular selection) and click.

The marquee disappears, indicating that the rectangle is no longer selected. If you press OPTION-DELETE (PC users: ALT-BACKSPACE) or DELETE (PC users: BACKSPACE), nothing will happen. If you wish to continue experimenting with the colored rectangle on screen, you must select it again, as described in the following exercise.

Selecting a Rectangle with the Rectangular Marquee Tool

To select the rectangle on screen, position the Rectangular Marquee crosshair so that it touches the top-left corner of the object, as shown here.

Click and drag diagonally down to the bottom-right corner, and release the mouse button. Now that the rectangle is selected, you can change it—by filling it with either the foreground or background color, or by moving it to another location, as described in the next selection.

Moving a Selection

Once a selection is created, you may want to move it to the perfect location on screen. In this exercise you'll learn how to move a selection using the mouse.

1. Make sure your rectangle is selected.

2. To move the rectangle with the mouse, start by positioning the crosshair over the middle of the rectangle. The crosshair changes to an arrow pointer.

3. Once the arrow pointer appears on screen, click and drag it to move the rectangle about 1 inch to the right and about .5 inches down.

N OTE: *Clicking away from a selection will cause it to be deselected. If this occurs, you can reselect it by immediately choosing the Undo command from the Edit menu. This undoes your last action. You can also execute the Undo command by using a keyboard shortcut: press COMMAND-Z (PC users: CTRL-Z).*

As you move the object, you'll see that Photoshop leaves a duplicate of the rectangular selection in its original position, filled with the background color, as shown in Figure 3-4.

You may find it annoying that Photoshop leaves the background color on screen where an object was moved from. Most of the time when you move an object, you won't want a hole left behind filled with the current background color. Figure 3-5 shows the effects of moving a rectangular selection in a scanned image. Here, too, Photoshop has cut a hole in the image.

A simple way to avoid this is to make your selection float. In the previous chapter, you were introduced to the concept of floating when you created and moved text. When an object floats, Photoshop essentially places it in a layer above the background plane of pixels. A floating object can be deleted and moved without disturbing the underlying pixels.

Fortunately, Photoshop often automatically puts an object in Float mode after that object has been moved. You can test this by again moving the rectangle you

Moving an object leaves the current background color in the object's original position

FIGURE 3-4

Cutting and moving a portion of an onscreen image leaves the background color behind

FIGURE 3-5

created in the foregoing exercise. This time, try moving it using the keyboard: Press any directional arrow key three or four times. With each keypress, the object will move one pixel up, down, left, or right. This time, Photoshop does not rip a hole out of the background.

EMEMBER: *When you move an object that is not floating, Photoshop creates a "hole" in your image by replacing the pixels in the original position of the object with the current background color. You can use the Edit/Undo or File/Revert command to restore your original image.*

In the next exercise, you'll learn how to turn the Float mode on *before* you move and fill, so that no underlying pixels are affected. Before proceeding, let's clear the clutter from your screen so you'll have more room in which to work.

Clearing the Screen

In Photoshop, one method of clearing the screen is to execute the Select/All command, which selects the entire screen. Once the entire screen is selected, it can then be "erased" by filling it with white. The Select/All command is also helpful when you wish to apply a Photoshop command to everything on screen.

1. Change the background color back to white by clicking once on the Default Colors icon.

2. To select the entire screen, choose All from the Select menu.

3. Press DELETE (PC users: BACKSPACE). The entire screen fills with the background color, white.

4. Notice the marquee surrounding your screen, indicating that the entire screen is still selected. To deselect it, choose None from the Select menu.

Using the Float Command

In this exercise you'll create a rectangular selection and then use the Select/Float command to put it into Float mode, so it floats above the background pixels. Once the object is in Float mode, you can move it or delete it without affecting the underlying pixels.

1. Start by resetting the background color to blue (the foreground color should still be the red you selected earlier). If you don't change the background color, you won't see the effects of using the Float command.

2. Click in the upper-left corner of your window and drag diagonally about two or three inches to the right to create a rectangular selection. Do not deselect.

3. To put the object into Float mode, choose Float from the Select menu.

4. Fill the object with the foreground color by pressing OPTION-DELETE (PC users: ALT-BACKSPACE).

5. Position the pointer in the middle of the rectangle and drag about 1 inch down and to the right. Don't deselect.

   This time, when you moved the selection, the background did not change. When you switched to Float mode, Photoshop lifted the selection over the underlying pixels. You can confirm that the object is in Float mode by clicking on the Select menu. In the menu, you'll see the word Defloat, rather than Float. This means that the object is floating. (Don't select Defloat; this will drop the object out of Float mode.)

6. When an the object is floating, you can delete it by pressing DELETE (PC users: BACKSPACE). Do this now.

 EMEMBER: *In Float mode, pressing DELETE (PC users: BACKSPACE) will delete the object, **not** fill it with the background color.*

Composing the Flag

Now that you know how to create a selection, fill it, and float it, you are ready to create the flag portion of the image shown in Figure 3-1.

For the following project you will need a 5.5-by-3.75-inch file on screen. If you don't have the original practice file open, create a new one with these dimensions. Make sure all objects are cleared from your screen.

Bear in mind that the resolution of your file is set to 72 ppi. This resolution will be fine for practicing and producing *comps* (samples or simulations of the completed art design) to test designs and techniques. For professional output of the collage, you may want to use a higher resolution, such as 300 ppi. If you do this, make sure you have enough memory to handle the file. A 5.5-by-3.75-inch RGB color file at 300 ppi will consume 5.31MB, versus 314K at 72 ppi. Remember, as mentioned in Chapter 1, Photoshop generally requires memory at least three times your file size to be free on either your hard disk or in RAM.

If you do create the flag collage or any of the other projects in this chapter at a resolution higher than 72 ppi, you will need to convert the pixel measurements in order to compensate for the fact that more pixels per inch will be used. For instance, in the next exercise the height of the flag stripes is 21 pixels at 72 ppi. To convert to 300 ppi, divide the 21 pixels by 72 (72 pixels = 1 inch), to get the precise size of the object in inches. Then multiply by 300 to calculate how many pixels there will be at 300 pixels per inch, (21÷72)×300.

IP: *Use the following formula to convert a measurement from one resolution to another:* (**Measurement in ppi ÷ Original ppi**) × **New ppi.**

Creating the Red Stripes

To create rectangles with specific measurements, use the Fixed Size option in the Rectangular Marquee Options dialog box. This option allows you to type in specific measurements for rectangular objects.

IP: *The Fixed Size option is a time-saver because objects can be created at precise sizes with one mouse click. It's much easier to use Fixed Size than to create shapes with the mouse while checking against the ruler and/or the Info palette.*

1. To specify the size of the stripes, double-click on the Rectangular Marquee tool.

2. In the Rectangular Marquee Options dialog box, click on the Fixed Size radio button.

   Notice that the Fixed Size option only allows measurements to be entered in pixels. Since a pixel is the smallest element possible on screen, it is the most precise way of measuring.

3. The red stripes you are creating are approximately .3 by 5.5 inches. To set the length of the stripe to approximately 5.5 inches, type **396** ($72 \times 5.5 = 396$) in the Width field of the Fixed Size option. (Remember that there are 72 pixels per inch in a file that has a resolution of 72 ppi.)

4. To set the Height of the stripe to approximately .3 inches, type **21** ($72 \times .3 = 21.6$). Click OK.

5. To create the selection, click in the middle of the screen. A rectangular selection appears, 5.5 inches long; this is the first stripe.

6. Change the foreground color to red and the background color to white. You'll use the red foreground color to fill the stripes.

7. To color the stripe red, press OPTION-DELETE (PC users: ALT-BACKSPACE).

8. To create the top of the flag, drag the stripe to the very top of your document, as shown in Figure 3-6. Don't deselect.

   Since the background color of your file is white, you won't need to create a white stripe. What you need is the ability to create a duplicate of

Creating
the first
stripe of the
flag

FIGURE 3-6

the red stripe's selection to use as a white placeholder between the red stripes. Photoshop provides a keyboard trick that can do this for you.

9. Press OPTION-COMMAND (PC users: ALT-CTRL), and click on the selection that surrounds the red stripe. Drag down slowly. A copy of the selection marquee—but not the red stripe—moves as you drag. Notice that the copy is not a flashing marquee, because Photoshop does not consider it a selection yet.

 EMEMBER: *Pressing OPTION-COMMAND (PC users: ALT-CTRL) while clicking and dragging moves the selection marquee without moving the selected object.*

10. Move the duplicate down, so the top of the duplicate touches the bottom of the red stripe. When your screen looks like Figure 3-7, release the mouse button. The blinking marquee jumps to the copy of the selection, creating a placeholder which will act as the white stripe.

11. Now duplicate the selection you just created, but use this duplicate as a stripe, not as a placeholder. Press OPTION-COMMAND (PC users: ALT-CTRL) again, and click in the middle of the marquee on screen. Drag the selection down. Again, when the top of the duplicate touches the bottom border of the white stripe, release the mouse. A new selection marquee is created.

12. Fill the new selection with the red foreground color.

Moving the selection marquee to create a placeholder for the second stripe

FIGURE 3-7

Now that you have three stripes created, you can speed things up by selecting a white and red stripe together (since the flag ends on a red stripe) and then duplicating them using the Float command.

13. To select both the second (white) and third (red) stripes, switch from Fixed Size to Normal in the Rectangular Marquee Options dialog box. (Double-click the Rectangular Marquee tool to activate the dialog box, and then select the Normal radio button. Click OK.)

14. With the Rectangular Marquee activated, select the second and third stripes.

15. From the Select menu, choose Float. Photoshop copies your selection into a layer above the underlying pixels.

IP: *Here's a shortcut for duplicating a selected object and automatically putting it into Float mode. After selecting an object, press and hold OPTION (PC users: ALT) while you click in the middle of the object and drag. As you drag, Photoshop duplicates the object without changing the background pixels.*

16. Drag the duplicated stripes into position under the first set of stripes. Click away from the object to deselect. When you deselect the rectangle, it drops back to the background layer, creating your fourth and fifth stripes.

17. To save your work, choose Save from the File menu. Name your file **Flag**. Click Save.

18. Continue creating stripes by duplicating them with the Float command until you have created seven red stripes and six white ones. The first and last stripe should be red.

19. Save your work again.

OTE: *Throughout the next sections, you'll save your file after you've successfully finished each segment of the collage. If you keep saving, you'll always be able to use the Revert command to return to the last correct version of the file.*

Creating the Blue Rectangle of the Flag

Next you'll use the Rectangular Marquee tool's Fixed Size option to create a blue rectangle and move it to the top-left corner of the screen.

1. Double-click on the Rectangular Marquee tool and switch from Normal back to Fixed Size.

2. The blue rectangle you are creating is approximately 2.5 by 2 inches, so enter **180** (2.5×72) in the Width field, and **144** (2×72) in the Height field. Click OK.

3. Click the mouse on screen, but *do not* click and drag to move the selection. You need to use the Float command to move the selection without affecting the stripes beneath it.

4. To put the selection in Float mode, choose Float from the Select menu.

5. Now click in the middle of the rectanglular selection and move it to the upper-left corner of your screen.

6. Change the foreground color to blue, then press OPTION-DELETE (PC users: ALT-BACKSPACE) to fill the selection.

7. Click away to deselect and lock the blue rectangle into place, as shown in Figure 3-8.

You have now completed the flag. Save your work. Your next step is to place a scanned image into the flag's blue rectangle.

Placing a Photograph into the Flag File

In this section, you'll learn how to copy an image in one file and paste it into another. This example uses a scanned image of a highway that will be placed in the Flag file.

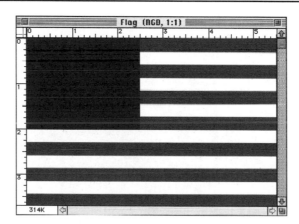

Adding the blue rectangle to the flag

FIGURE 3-8

If you do not have a similar image, you can pick any scanned image or even choose one from the Frames file (PC users: frames.jpg) located in the Tutorial folder. The Tutorial files are copied to your hard disk when you install Photoshop.

CAUTION: *No matter what digitized image you use, its resolution should match the resolution of your Photoshop collage file. The digitized image you place into the collage will enlarge if its resolution is higher or shrink if its resolution is lower. See Chapters 7 and 11 for more details.*

1. To open a digitized image in Photoshop, choose Open from the File menu. Select the filename, and then click Open (PC users: OK). The image will load on screen.

2. Double-click on the Rectangular Marquee tool. To create a selection that is the proper size for the blue rectangle of the flag, make sure that the Fixed Size option is still selected in the Rectangular Marquee Options dialog box. Enter **168** in the Width field and **134** in the Height field. Click OK, then click on screen and the selection appears.

   Don't try to move the selection by clicking and dragging with the mouse. The easiest way to move the selection on the screen is with the same technique you used to create the placeholder when working on the flag stripes earlier.

3. Press OPTION-COMMAND (PC users: ALT-CTRL). Click and drag the selection to the part of the image you wish to copy into the Flag file, as shown in Figure 3-9.

Selecting an image from a photograph to be copied and pasted in the flag's blue rectangle

FIGURE 3-9

4. To copy the area into memory so you can paste it into the Flag file, choose Copy from the Edit menu. Photoshop stores the selection in the Clipboard.

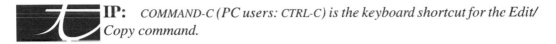

IP: *COMMAND-C (PC users: CTRL-C) is the keyboard shortcut for the Edit/ Copy command.*

5. Close the image file; the Flag file will still be open.

6. To paste the selection from the Clipboard into your Flag file, select Paste from the Edit menu.

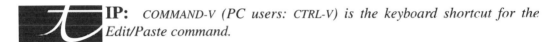

IP: *COMMAND-V (PC users: CTRL-V) is the keyboard shortcut for the Edit/Paste command.*

7. When you use the Paste command, Photoshop automatically puts the pasted image into Float mode, so you can click and drag it without worrying about altering the underlying pixels. To move the image, click and drag it into position in the top-left corner of the flag, as shown in Figure 3-10.

8. Click away from the object to deselect.

Placing Text on the Flag

In Chapter 1, the issue of type quality was discussed, and here it's worth repeating that type quality in Photoshop is dependent upon file resolution. If you work in a

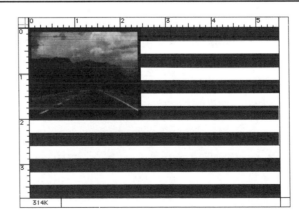

Pasting and moving the photograph into position

FIGURE 3-10

file with a resolution of 72 ppi, sending it as output to a high-resolution printer will not improve the quality. If you need to produce a Photoshop project with high-resolution text, it's often best not to create the text in Photoshop. Save the file so it can be exported to a drawing program such as Adobe Illustrator, or a page-layout program such as QuarkXPress. In these programs, text is created as a separate object that is printed at the resolution of the output device. If you wanted Photoshop's text to match the quality of text as output from these programs, you'd need to create an image at an extremely high resolution. For example, if you wanted your text output at 1,270 ppi, your file's resolution would need to be 1,270 ppi. Obviously, the file size would be gigantic. Saving files so they can be output to other programs is covered in Appendix A.

In this exercise, high-resolution text isn't necessary, so you'll just use Photoshop's Type tool to generate the words for the flag collage.

1. Select the Type tool.

2. Click in the middle of the screen.

3. If you wish to make the text appear as it does in the example in Figure 3-1, enter the following specifications:

    Click on the Font pop-up menu and change the font to Times. In the Size field, type **70** points. In the Leading field, type **125**. In the Spacing field, type **2**. In the Alignment group, click on the Right radio button. In the text box, type **USA's** and press RETURN (PC users: ENTER). Then type **HIGHWAYS** (underneath USA's). In the Style options, make sure the Anti-Aliased check box is selected. Click OK.

4. When the text appears on screen, click and drag "USA's" and "HIGHWAYS" into position, as shown in Figure 3-1. As you move the type, the underlying pixels will not be affected because the text is floating.

EMEMBER: *As discussed in the "Entering Text with the Type Tool" section in Chapter 2, Photoshop automatically puts the text you create in Float mode.*

5. When you are satisfied with the position of the text, click away from it to deselect.

That's it! You've just completed the Flag collage.

Photoshop in Action

The boxers were selected with the Lasso tool so that they could be pasted into the image.

Parts of the letter *M* were selected with the Magic Wand tool and then moved.

Artist: Marc Yankus

The Perspective command in the Image/Effects submenu was applied to the circuit board.

Client: Data Communication

Marc started this image by creating a rectangular selection with the Rectangular Marquee tool. Once the selection was on screen, he filled it with a blend using the Gradient tool. His next steps were to scan in a circuit board, select it with the Rectangular Marquee tool, and then paste it into the image. While the circuit board was still selected, he applied the Perspective command from the Image/Effects submenu. This created a sense of depth in the image.

Once the circuit board was placed, the boxers were scanned in, selected with the Lasso tool, copied, and pasted into the image. Finally, the letters IBM were scanned, copied, and pasted into the image. Then Marc used the Magic Wand tool to select parts of the letter *M* and break them away from the rest of the letter.

In the next section, you'll create another collage and will learn more about the options available in the Rectangular Marquee Options dialog box. You'll also begin to explore the other selection tools—the Elliptical Marquee, the Lasso, and the Magic Wand.

THE TRUCK COLLAGE

Your next Photoshop project, the truck collage shown in Figure 3-11, will give you additional experience with the selection tools and their dialog boxes. This collage project is divided into two parts. In the first part, you will create a truck on which you'll paste a scanned image of some fruit. In the second part, you'll outline and fill parts of a scanned image to create a landscape background. Each project section begins with a few introductory exercises designed to introduce you to the selection tools and options that you'll be using for the first time.

Introductory Exercises: Creating and Stroking Constrained Rectangular and Elliptical Selections

The first introductory exercises of the truck collage will teach you how to create perfect squares and circles. You'll be using these shapes to produce the cab and wheels of the truck. To build these objects you'll use the Constrained Aspect Ratio

The truck
collage

FIGURE 3-11

option found in both the Rectangular Marquee Options and the Elliptical Marquee Options dialog boxes. When you create a border for the fruit poster and generate the truck wheels, you'll learn how to stroke, or outline, selections. Before beginning the exercises in this section, close the Flag file or any other documents you might have open on screen. This will keep memory usage to a minimum.

1. Start by creating a file 5 inches high by 7 inches wide to use for the introductory exercises. This size will give you sufficient room to practice.

2. From the Window menu, select Show Rulers and Show Info. Use the rulers and the Info palette to help you measure when completing the exercises in this section.

3. Use black as the foreground color and white as the background color. Check to see that these are your current settings; if they aren't, click on the Default Colors icon in the Toolbox.

Using the Rectangular Marquee Constrained Aspect Ratio Option

Start by exploring the Constrained Aspect Ratio option, which creates selections according to proportions specified in the Rectangular Marquee Options and Elliptical Marquee Options dialog boxes.

1. To open the Rectangular Marquee Options dialog box, double-click on the Rectangular Marquee tool. Click on the Constrained Aspect Ratio radio button. Leave both Width and Height set at 1, the defaults. Click OK.

   These settings will constrain the mouse selection so the width and height are always drawn at a 1:1 ratio—in other words, you'll be creating a square. The width and height of the rectangular selection will always be equal to each other.

2. To create the square, move the crosshair to the upper-left corner of your document. Click and drag down diagonally from left to right. As you drag, notice that your selection is a square. Release the mouse.

   Now try creating another rectangular selection. No matter how hard you try, you won't be able to create anything other than a square selection. The selection can be any size, but it will always be a square because the width to height proportions have been *constrained* to a 1:1 ratio.

Although the Constrained Aspect Ratio option is often used to create squares, you can use it to create rectangles at other proportions. For instance, if you need to make rectangles in which the height is twice as long as the width (1:2), you can set the aspect ratio accordingly.

3. To make a rectangle with a 1:2 ratio, open the Rectangular Marquee Options dialog box. In the Constrained Aspect Ratio fields, leave Width set to 1, and change Height to **2**. Click OK.

4. Click and drag to create a selection.

No matter how large your selection, the height will always be double the width. Here are some rectangles with 1:1, 1:2, and 2:1 ratios:

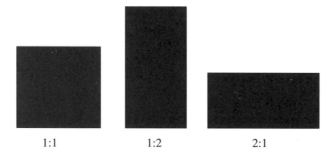

1:1   1:2   2:1

Using the Elliptical Marquee Tool

The Elliptical Marquee tool functions similarly to the Rectangular Marquee tool, except it creates round rather than rectangular shapes. In the Elliptical Marquee Options dialog box, shown in Figure 3-12, Normal is the default setting just as it for the Rectangular Marquee tool. The Normal, Constrained Aspect Ratio, and Fixed Size options work exactly as they do with the Rectangular Marquee tool.

THE ELLIPTICAL MARQUEE NORMAL OPTION   The Elliptical Marquee tool allows you to create elliptical selections. Since you haven't used the Elliptical Marquee tool before, start with it set to the Normal option, so that you can see how the tool works without any constraints.

1. Double-click on the Elliptical Marquee tool, and check to see that Normal is selected in the Elliptical Marquee Options dialog box. If it isn't, select it and click OK.

The
Elliptical
Marquee
Options
dialog box

FIGURE 3-12

Drawing an ellipse with the mouse is not too different from drawing a rectangle, primarily because you can click and drag diagonally to create the shape. The perimeter of the ellipse starts where you click, and the shape grows according to the size of the angle and distance you drag.

2. To draw an ellipse, click in the upper-left corner of your screen and slowly drag diagonally toward the lower-right corner. When you have an elliptical selection on the screen, release the mouse button.

3. To practice a bit more, try drawing another ellipse. This time, drag only about one-half inch down and then drag across to the right, almost to the edge of the screen. This produces a cigar-shaped ellipse.

THE ELLIPTICAL MARQUEE CONSTRAINED ASPECT RATIO OPTION As with the Rectangular Marquee tool, the Elliptical Marquee includes a Constrained Aspect Ratio option to allow you to create selections according to specific proportions. With this option selected and a 1:1 ratio specified, the Elliptical Marquee tool creates a perfect circle.

Try creating a circular selection with the Elliptical Marquee tool:

1. Double-click on the Elliptical Marquee tool.

2. Select the Constrained Aspect Ratio. If Width and Height aren't set to 1, type **1** in both the Width and Height fields. Click OK.

3. Click and drag diagonally down from the upper-left corner of your screen toward the bottom-right corner. Your selection will be a perfect circle.

4. Try creating another selection, but this time use different ratios. Here are some ellipses with 1:1, 1:2, and 2:1 ratios:

1:1   1:2   2:1

IP: *If the Constrained Aspect Ratio option is not activated, you can still create a perfect square or perfect circle by clicking and dragging with the SHIFT key pressed. If you click and drag with the OPTION key (PC users: CTRL) pressed, you create a square, rectangle, ellipse, or circle from the center out.*

Stroking a Selection

For the truck collage, you will create circles for the wheels of the truck by using the Elliptical Marquee tool's Constrained Aspect Ratio option. Instead of creating white circles within black circles to create the tires, you'll fill each circular selection with white and then stroke it with black.

The Stroke command in the Edit menu allows you to put a border or outline, using the current foreground color, around a selection. You can't stroke with the background color. The Stroke dialog box allows you to enter the stroke width in pixels; acceptable values are integers between 1 and 16. You can designate whether you wish the stroke to be along the outside of the selection marquee, inside it, or in the middle. You can also create a stroke with a *tint* (a percentage of the foreground color). The options in the Stroke dialog box will be discussed in Chapter 5.

1. Before you stroke an object, you need to create a selection on screen. Select the Elliptical Marquee tool, and click and drag to create a circle about 2 inches in diameter.

2. To open the Stroke dialog box, shown here, choose Stroke from the Edit menu.

```
┌─────────────────────────── Stroke ───────────────────────────┐
│  ┌─ Stroke ─────────────────────────────────┐  ┌─────────┐   │
│  │  Width: [ 1 ] pixels                       │  │   OK    │   │
│  │                                            │  └─────────┘   │
│  └────────────────────────────────────────────┘ ┌─────────┐   │
│  ┌─ Location ───────────────────────────────┐   │ Cancel  │   │
│  │  ○ Inside   ● Center   ○ Outside          │   └─────────┘   │
│  └────────────────────────────────────────────┘               │
│  ┌─ Blending ──────────────────────────────────────┐          │
│  │  Opacity: [100] %   Mode: [ Normal    ▼ ]        │          │
│  └──────────────────────────────────────────────────┘          │
└────────────────────────────────────────────────────────────────┘
```

3. To set the size of the stroke, type **5** in the Width field. Leave Location set to Center, Opacity set to 100%, and Mode set to Normal (these are the defaults). Then click OK. The circle appears, with a 5-pixel outline. In the middle of the circle's 5-pixel stroke, you'll see the selection marquee still blinking. The stroke was created in the center of the selection.

Now that we've covered all the tools and commands you'll need to create the truck, you can close this practice file.

Creating the Truck

Start by creating a new file designed to tightly fit the truck you're creating.

1. To create a new file, choose New from the File menu. Set the dimensions of the file to Width **5** and Height **3.5**. Use RGB Color and 72 ppi for the resolution. Click OK.

EMEMBER: *If you wish to create this collage at a resolution higher than 72 ppi, you'll need to convert pixel measurements to compensate for the higher resolution change. See the Tip in the section "Composing the Flag" earlier in this chapter for the conversion formula.*

2. Since the file's dimensions are small, you'll probably want to zoom in so your work area is bigger. To magnify the document window, press COMMAND-PLUS (PC users: CTRL-PLUS), the keyboard equivalent of the Zoom In command found in the Window menu. The magnification ratio in the Window title bar now reads 2:1.

3. You'll be needing both the rulers and Info palette for measuring, so open them. From the Window menu, select Show Rulers and then Show Info.

Moving the Zero Point

When you create the truck, give yourself some breathing room by creating it one-half inch from the top and one-half inch from the left side of your document. You will measure distances from the *truck's* origin, not from the *zero point*, or origin, of the rulers. To aid you in measuring in these situations, Photoshop allows you to move the zero point of both vertical and horizontal screen rulers so you can measure from anywhere on screen.

Before moving the zero point, make sure that the 0 and half-inch marks appear on both the horizontal and vertical rulers. In order to move the zero point, you'll need to be able to view this part of the ruler. If you can't see it, scroll left and/or up until you can see these marks on both rulers.

To move the zero point, select the crosshair at the intersection of the horizontal and vertical rulers in the top-left corner of your screen, as shown in the top illustration here. Click and drag diagonally down to the half-inch mark on the vertical ruler and the half-inch mark on the horizontal ruler. As you drag, horizontal and vertical guides will appear at what will be the new zero point, as shown in the bottom illustration here.

Check the Info palette to make sure that the X and Y positions of the mouse both read .5 inch. When they do, set the origin of both horizontal and vertical rulers by releasing the mouse button.

If you released the mouse at the wrong point, you can return the zero point to its original position and try again; just double-click on the crosshair in the top-left corner of the screen.

To see the effects of the relocated zero point, move the mouse across the screen and watch the X and Y coordinates in the Info palette. Notice that the values read zero when you are at one-half inch from the top and the left side of the screen. You'll start creating the trailer of the truck at this new zero point.

Creating the Truck Trailer

Both the truck trailer and the poster area within it will be created using the Rectangular Marquee tool. Later in this exercise you will paste an image into the poster area.

To make the truck's trailer, you'll need to create a rectangle that is twice as wide as it is high.

1. Double-click on the Rectangular Marquee tool to display the Options dialog box. Select the Constrained Aspect Ratio radio button. In the Width field type **2**, and in the Height field type **1**. Click OK to activate the changes.

2. Use the rulers and Info palette as guides to position the crosshair so that the X and Y coordinates both read 0. Click and drag diagonally to the right until the X coordinate is 2.75 inches. The width of the trailer will be set automatically to be a rectangle with a width of 1.375 inches because you are using a Constrained Aspect Ratio of 2:1.

3. At this point, release the mouse button.

4. Next fill the selection with the foreground color (black) by pressing OPTION-DELETE (PC users: ALT-BACKSPACE).

5. Click away from the truck to deselect, so you don't inadvertently move it.

6. Before continuing to create the poster border on the truck's trailer, save your file so you can use the Revert command if you make a mistake in the upcoming steps. Name the file **Truck**.

   Now you are going to create a smaller rectangle inside the truck's trailer. This rectangle will be used as a border for the fruit image you'll be pasting into the file.

7. Move the crosshair so that the x-axis is at approximately .250 inches, and the y-axis is at about .125 inches. Click and drag diagonally so the X coordinate in the Info palette is 2.500 inches and the Y coordinate is at 1.250 inches. This creates a rectangle with a width of approximately 2.250 inches and a height of about 1.125 inches.

8. To create a placeholder for the poster on the trailer, fill this rectangle with the background color, white. Don't deselect, because you're going to add a finishing touch by stroking the selection with a 4-pixel-wide gray border.

9. Since the Stroke command paints with the foreground color, you need to start by setting the foreground color to gray. If the Colors palette is not on screen, open it by choosing Show Colors from the Window menu. Set the foreground color to a light gray by clicking on one of the gray swatches in the palette.

10. To create the stroke, select Stroke from the Edit menu. In the Stroke dialog box, type **4** in the Width field. In the Location group, click on the Inside radio button—you want the stroke to be placed on the *inside* of the selection marquee (extending 4 pixels in from the selection), not on the outside of the selection (extending 4 pixels out from the selection) and not centered (placed directly on the selection marquee). Click OK.

11. Save your work before continuing.

Before pasting the fruit into the poster area, let's create the chassis, cab, and wheels of the truck.

Creating the Chassis and the Cab

The chassis will consist of two filled rectangles. Use the Rectangular Marquee tool to create the rectangles, and fill them with shades of gray. To make the cab, create a square selection and fill it with black. Add a white rectangle to the cab to create the window. The truck should now look like this:

 EMEMBER: *If you need to move a selection, press COMMAND-OPTION (PC users: CTRL-ALT) so that you only move the selection and don't affect any underlying pixels.*

Creating the Smoke Stack

To make the truck's smoke stack, use Figure 3-11 as a guide. Create two rectangles, a large one on the bottom (standing on its end) with a smaller one on top. Fill both with black.

Creating the Wheels

Now you are ready to create the first back wheel. After you create one wheel, you'll duplicate it to make the other three wheels.

1. Open the Elliptical Marquee Options dialog box and select the Constrained Aspect Ratio. Type in **1** for both the Width and Height fields.

2. Position the crosshair in the back of the truck chassis where you want the midpoint of the wheel to be. To draw a circle from the midpoint out, press OPTION (PC users: ALT), hold it down, and click and drag to create a smaller circle. Fill the selection with the background color, white, by pressing DELETE (PC users: BACKSPACE).

3. To create the black tire, you will stroke the circle with the foreground color. Make sure that the foreground color is black, and then choose Stroke from the Edit menu. In the Stroke dialog box, set the width to **9** pixels. The Opacity should be **100%**. Click OK. The circular selection will now look like a wheel.

    Now you'll duplicate the wheel three times and drag each duplicate into position. Before you start to drag, you'll press the SHIFT key to constrain the mouse to moving in a straight line.

4. With the wheel selected, press OPTION (PC users: ALT) then click and drag to duplicate it. Next, press SHIFT and position the mouse pointer over the wheel. With SHIFT still pressed, click and drag to the right. As you drag, a copy of the wheel appears on screen. Position the wheel using Figure 3-11 as a guide. Repeat this procedure to create and position two more wheels.

5 Before continuing, save your work.

You've just finished creating the truck. Now you're ready to paste an image of some fruit in the poster placeholder.

Creating the Poster

To create the proper selection size for the poster, use the Fixed Size option in the Rectangular Marquee Options dialog box.

1. Select the Fixed Size radio button, and type **145** in the Width field and **65** in the Height field. Click OK.

2. Click on the truck's trailer and the selection marquee appears. This is the selection size you will eventually use for the scanned image.

3. If you need to reposition the selection, just move the mouse to the upper-left corner where you want the selection to start and click again. You could also use the OPTION-COMMAND (PC users: ALT-CTRL) key combination and then click and drag the selection into the middle of the poster area of the truck, as shown here:

Keep this portion selected, because later you will copy a fruit image into this area. Notice that the selection was made slightly smaller than the poster area to provide a white border for the scanned image.

To select the fruit image to copy into the poster, you can create a selection from the fruit plate in the Frames file that is included with Photoshop (PC users: frames.jpg). The image you see on the truck in Figure 3-11 is one that was scanned from a photograph of fruit.

EMEMBER: *The resolution of your scanned image should match the resolution of your file.*

4. To open the Frames file, choose Open from the File menu. Locate the Frames file in the Tutorial folder (PC users: frames.jpg file), and double-click the filename.

5. Once the image opens on screen, you'll only need to click to create a selection because the Fixed Size option is in effect. Click in the middle of the screen to create the 145-by-65-pixel selection. Adjust the position of the selection over the fruits by pressing OPTION-COMMAND (PC users: ALT-CTRL), and clicking and dragging the mouse until you've framed a selection of fruits.

6. To copy the selection, choose Copy from the Edit menu.

7. Select Close from the File menu.

8. You are now back in the Truck file; notice the selection marquee is right where you left it, in the border area of the truck's trailer. When you paste, you will be pasting the image directly into the selection marquee. Choose Paste from the Edit menu. Your image will look like this:

9. Save your work and close the Truck file.

Next you'll perform several introductory exercises before you move on to the second part of the truck collage, where you create a background landscape from a scanned image and then paste the truck over it.

Introductory Exercises: Using the Lasso and Magic Wand Tools

To create the landscape, you will be converting a photograph of a landscape to colored line art. You'll use the Lasso and Magic Wand tools to select various parts of the landscape and fill them with a color.

In order to complete the next exercises, you'll need a new document open on screen. Create a new file, 7 by 5 inches, to give you sufficient room to practice with these tools.

Using the Lasso Tool

The Lasso tool is used for selecting irregularly shaped objects. It allows you to create a selection by drawing in a freehand mode, somewhat like drawing on screen with a pencil.

The Lasso can also be used to create *polygons*. To create these, you'll press and hold OPTION (PC users: ALT) while you click the mouse at various points on the screen. As you click, the Lasso tool connects the points where you clicked to create a selection.

No matter what shape you draw, the Lasso always closes your selection. It will not allow you to leave an open curve or angle on screen.

Before you test the Lasso, take a look at its dialog box options. As usual, you open the dialog box by double-clicking on the tool.

 The Anti-aliased check box is selected by default. Leave it selected, because this option softens the hard edges of pixels. This will cause selection edges to appear less jagged when filled with a color. (Review Chapter 2 for a discussion on pixels.)

 The Feather Radius option provides a means of softening the edges of a selection. The value that you type here determines the width in pixels of the feathered edge. You won't use feathering in this exercise, but you will later in this chapter when you create a vignette. If this value is not currently set to 0, type **0** in the field now. Click OK to close the dialog box.

CREATING FREEFORM SHAPES WITH THE LASSO   In this section, you'll try your hand at the Lasso tool by creating a freeform, kidney-shaped selection.

1. With the Lasso tool active, move the pointer into the middle of the document window. As you move the mouse, the pointer changes to a Lasso icon. Position the Lasso in the upper-left corner of the screen.

OTE: *If you press the CAPS LOCK key, the mouse pointer will turn into a crosshair. The crosshair is provided as an alternative to the Lasso pointer because it allows you to select more precisely.*

2. To create the kidney shape, click and drag as shown in Figure 3-13. As you drag the mouse, be careful not to release the mouse button. If you do, the Lasso tool will finalize the selection by connecting the starting and ending points. If this happens, click outside the selection to deselect it and start over again.

3. When you've completed the kidney shape, release the mouse button.

Next you'll try out the Lasso's Constraining mode, which you'll need later to select a mountain range for the landscape.

CONSTRAINING THE LASSO SELECTION   The Lasso's constraining option allows you to create polygons by clicking at different points on the screen. As you click, the Lasso connects the points with selection lines. To make the Lasso work in this mode, press OPTION (PC users: ALT) while you use the tool.

Creating a
freeform
selection
with the
Lasso tool

FIGURE 3-13

OTE: *While selecting with the Lasso constraining option, it's often a good idea to use the crosshair to make more accurate selections. As stated earlier, you activate the crosshair by pressing the CAPS LOCK key.*

Start learning the Lasso's constraining option by creating a simple triangle.

1. With the Lasso tool activated, press CAPS LOCK to activate the crosshair. Press OPTION (PC users: ALT) to constrain your selection. Keep OPTION (PC users: ALT) pressed as you create the triangle.

2. Move the crosshair about 1 inch down from the left side of your file and 4 inches directly across to the right. Click the mouse button. Next, move the pointer diagonally, about 2 inches to the right and about 3 inches down. Click again.

   You now have a straight line connecting your first and second mouse clicks.

3. Move the mouse horizontally to the left about 4 inches and click. Now return to your original starting point and click again. Release OPTION (PC users: ALT). Your screen will look like Figure 3-14.

Constraining
a selection
with the
Lasso tool

FIGURE 3-14

Don't deselect yet, because you'll need to use this triangular selection in the next exercise, where you'll be introduced to the Magic Wand. In order to see the Wand's color-selecting capabilities in action, you'll need to fill the triangle you just created with a color.

4. If the Colors palette is not on screen, open it by choosing Show Colors from the Window menu. Change the foreground color to orange by clicking on an orange swatch. Fill the selection by pressing OPTION-DELETE (PC users: ALT-BACKSPACE). Click away from the object to deselect, and release CAPS LOCK.

5. Use the Elliptical Marquee tool to create a circle in the middle of the triangle. Change the foreground color to yellow, and fill the circle with yellow.

You now have two shapes and two colors on which to test the Magic Wand tool's powers.

Using the Magic Wand

Of all Photoshop's selecting tools, the Magic Wand is usually considered the most powerful because it can create selections that would be nearly impossible to reproduce by hand. This tool works by selecting a color range with one click of the mouse. It is normally used to select areas according to similarity of color.

Before you begin to use the Wand with a scanned image in the landscape exercise, let's examine the Magic Wand Options dialog box. Open it in the usual way, by double-clicking on the Magic Wand in the Toolbox.

Notice that Anti-aliased is also an option in the Wand's dialog box. It functions exactly as it does in the Type and Lasso Options dialog boxes.

The value you see in the Tolerance field controls the color range that the Wand will select. The greater the Tolerance setting, the broader the color range. The smallest value you can enter is 0; the largest is 255. The default value is 32. If the Wand's Tolerance is set to 0, it will select an area of contiguous pixels that are only the same color as the pixel that you click on. If you increase the Tolerance setting, the Wand will expand the selection to include a greater range of color, using the color you clicked on as its starting point. A very high Tolerance setting will create a selection over a color range that can vary greatly from the color originally clicked on.

Before closing the Magic Wand Options dialog box, change the Tolerance setting so you can begin testing the Wand.

1. In the Tolerance field, type **0**. To accept the new settings and close the dialog box, click OK.

2. Point to the yellow circle you just created. Notice that the mouse pointer changes to a wand icon when you move it over the document area. (If the mouse pointer is a crosshair and not a wand icon, CAPS LOCK is on.)

3. Click on the circle. The Wand selects only the circle. Click on the triangle and the Wand selects only the orange area of the triangle. Since the Tolerance value is set to 0, in both cases the Wand only selects one color.

4. Now change the Tolerance setting in the Magic Wand Options dialog box to see how it affects the selection. Double-click on the Magic Wand tool, and type **255** in the Tolerance field. Click OK.

5. Click again on the yellow circle. This time the Wand selects both the circle and triangle because the high Tolerance setting allowed more colors to slip into the selection.

Even with this less-than-intricate selection, the Wand still proves to be a time-saver: If you had to reselect the triangular selection on screen, you'd have to use the Lasso tool to click precisely over your original mouse clicks.

If you'd like to experiment more with the Magic Wand, try filling various selections with different colors and then testing the Wand's selections. When you're finished, proceed to the next section, where you'll learn several very helpful selection tips for all of the program's selection tools.

Adding to and Subtracting from Selections

Even though you've learned to use all of Photoshop's selection tools, your selection knowledge won't be complete until you know how to change your selections by adding to them, subtracting from them, and intersecting them.

If you've used other Mac or Windows programs, you can probably guess that you add to a selection by *shift-clicking.* Just hold down the SHIFT key when you make a new selection, and Photoshop adds to a previous selection. However, unlike many Mac and Windows programs, you cannot subtract from a selection by pressing SHIFT and clicking on a selection.

Suppose you want to remove a selection from the screen but leave other areas selected. To subtract from a selection, press and hold COMMAND (PC users: CTRL) while you click and drag over or within a selection.

Try removing a corner from a rectangular selection, using the Lasso tool. Activate the tool, and while holding down COMMAND (PC users: CTRL), click and drag to create a curved selection over any corner of the rectangle on screen. When you release the mouse, the corner is subtracted from the selection.

You can also create a selection that is the intersection of two selections. To try this, press both COMMAND and SHIFT (PC users: CTRL and SHIFT); then click and drag to make a selection that overlaps the rectangular selection on screen. Fill with the foreground color, and you'll see that Photoshop paints the intersection—that is, only the common areas of the two selections.

The Select menu includes two commands that can help when you are selecting with the Magic Wand. Execute the Select/Grow command, and the selection on screen will expand as if you had doubled the Tolerance range in the Wand's dialog box. Execute the Select/Similar command, and the selection will jump over areas beyond the Wand's tolerance to select areas that fit within its tolerance. For instance, if an image contained a black bridge over a river, which prevented the Wand from selecting the entire river, the Select/Similar command would cause the selection to jump over the bridge and select the rest of the water.

In the next section, you may need to add to or subtract from a selection when you use the Magic Wand to create the background landscape in the truck collage.

EMINDER: *The Select menu includes two commands, Grow and Similar, that can assist you when you are selecting with the Magic Wand.*

Creating the Landscape for the Truck

Now that you've been introduced to the Lasso and the Magic Wand, and you know how to add and subtract from selections, you're ready to create the landscape for the background of the truck collage. You'll use both these tools to select areas in a scanned image and fill them with colors.

In order to create the landscape, open any suitable image that provides shapes and colors that you can select. For this example, a scanned image of the Rocky Mountains was used. Once the image is on screen, you'll want to enlarge your working area. This will make it easier to select intricate areas when you use the Lasso tool. Press COMMAND-PLUS (PC users: CTRL-PLUS) to magnify your work area.

Once you've selected an area, fill it with a color. Try experimenting with different selection tools and fill the areas with different colors. Our completed landscape is shown in Figure 3-15.

Creating the Highway

Before you paste the truck into its setting, create a highway for it. The easiest way to create the highway is to use the Single Row option in the Rectangular Marquee Options dialog box, which will create a 1-pixel-wide selection the entire width of the document window. (The Single Column option creates a 1-pixel-wide selection the entire height of the document window.) You'll stroke the selection with gray to pave this roadway with color.

1. Access the Rectangular Marquee Options dialog box and select the Single Row radio button. Click OK.

2. Create a selection by positioning the crosshair just above the bottom of document window and clicking the mouse. A 1-pixel-wide horizontal selection appears.

3. Next, select a gray foreground color.

4. Stroke the selection by choosing Stroke from the Edit menu. In the Width field box, type **4**; choose the Center option in the Location group; keep Opacity at 100%; and leave Mode set to Normal. Click OK, and then save your work.

Once you've created the highway, you're finished with the landscape portion of the collage. Now it's time to tie it all together by placing the truck into the landscape.

Pasting the Truck into the Landscape

Before you can add the truck into the landscape, you need to reopen the Truck file and select the entire image.

Once the file is opened (by choosing Open in the File menu), you're faced with a problem. How do you select the truck so it can be copied into the file containing

The
completed
landscape

FIGURE 3-15

the landscape? There doesn't seem to be a tool in the Toolbox that will easily allow you to select this object. However, though it's true the Magic Wand won't select the entire truck, it can help you out—by selecting everything *but* the truck. Use the Magic Wand to select the white background, and then use the Inverse command in the Select menu to select everything on screen except the current selection. In this case, Select/Inverse will deselect the white background and select everything but the white background (the truck).

1. Double-click on the Magic Wand. Set the Wand's Tolerance value to **0**.

2. Position the Magic Wand in the white background area of the Truck file, and click the mouse. This selects the entire white area.

3. To select everything on the screen *except* the white area, choose Inverse from the Select menu. This selects the truck.

n **OTE:** *If you see that any white area surrounding the truck is selected, subtract it from the selection using the Lasso tool and the COMMAND key (PC users: CTRL). To do this, activate the Lasso tool; then, while holding down COMMAND (PC users: CTRL), click and drag over the white area that you wish to remove.*

4. Choose Copy from the Edit menu to copy the truck to the Clipboard.

5. Open the Landscape file.

6. Choose Paste from the Edit menu to paste the truck into the landscape.

7. Photoshop automatically places the truck in Float mode when it is pasted, so you can click and drag without worrying about changing the underlying pixels. Move the truck into position as shown in Figure 3-11 and then deselect.

8. Since you will later use the Landscape file again without the truck, use the Save As command to save your new collage under a new name: **Truck Collage** (PC users: **Trklage**). By using Save As, you'll retain both files on your hard disk: Landscape without the Truck, and Truck Collage with the truck.

That's it. You have successfully created a truck and a landscape and placed the two together into a collage.

FEATHERING THE EDGES OF A SELECTION

The last selection tools exercise is creating a vignette using the Feather option available for the Rectangular Marquee, Elliptical Marquee, and Lasso tools.

To take a look at how the Feather option works, start by creating a new file, 5 by 5 inches, to use as a practice document. Click on the Default Colors icon to reset the foreground and background colors.

Let's start with the Feather option in the Rectangular Marquee; it allows you to soften the edges of a rectangle. The value that you type in the Feather's Radius field determines the width of the feather edge. This value defaults to 0 pixels; the maximum value allowed is 64. Since the feather edge extends both inside and outside the selection, the actual feather will be twice the radius value.

Double-click on the Rectangular Marquee tool, and in the Radius field type **15**. This Radius value will give you a Feather edge of 30 pixels. Click on the Normal radio button, and then on OK. Now click and drag to make a rectangle. Press OPTION-DELETE (PC users: ALT-BACKSPACE) to fill the rectangle with the foreground color. The feathered rectangle will look like this:

Notice what has happened: The edges in the object have been feathered 30 pixels; the feathering begins 15 pixels within the selection and extends 15 pixels beyond the selection. The outer edges of the black rectangle have a *gradient* effect; they start out black and then turn gray, until they blend into the white background. This effect, called a vignette, is also sometimes called a *halo* or *glow*.

Creating a Vignette

The Feather option for the Elliptical Marquee tool has been used to create the vignette shown in Figure 3-16. If you wish to try creating this type of special effect, start by opening an image file on your screen. If you don't have an image file, you can use the Portrait file (PC users: portrait.jpg) in Photoshop's Tutorial folder.

1. Double-click on the Elliptical Marquee tool. Leave the Marquee set to Normal in the Elliptical Marquee Options dialog box, and set the Feather Radius to **10**. Click OK.

2. Click and drag to create an ellipse surrounding the area where you want to add the vignette effect. (The vignette will not appear until after you copy and paste the selection.)

3. From the Edit menu, choose Copy.

Creating a
vignette

FIGURE 3-16

4. Create a new file where you will paste your selection. From the File
menu, choose New, and change the Width and Height settings to make
them larger, if desired. Click OK.

5. From the Edit menu, choose Paste. The image is pasted with the
feathering effect that creates the vignette.

𝓃 OTE: *Depending upon the resolution and dimensions of your image, you
may wish to experiment with different Radius values.*

The vignette exercise is the last of the selection tools design projects in this
chapter. If you've read through and completed all the exercises in this chapter, you
are now prepared to move on to more advanced topics, particularly those involving
the use of color in your Photoshop work. The next chapter lays the groundwork for
painting and image editing by covering the fundamentals of color theory. It will also
provide a thorough discussion of how to use the colors in the Colors palette, as well
as help you understand the differences between RGB and CMYK colors.

Photoshop in Action

Elements for the image were selected with the Lasso tool using different Feather Radius settings to create soft-edged effect when pasted.

Areas of the background were selected with the Magic Wand and colored with the Edit/Fill command.

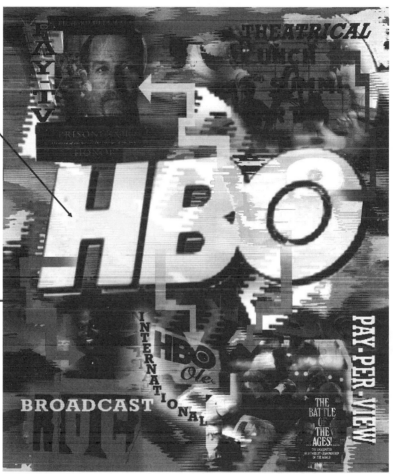

Artist: Josh Gosfield   A Time Warner Annual Report

Josh first created the background of the image by scanning a photo he took of a television screen with interference. Once the photo was scanned, different areas were selected with the Magic Wand tool and then painted with the Edit/Fill command.

After the background was completed, Josh scanned various images and selected them using the Lasso tool with different Feather Radius settings. This created a soft-edged effect when he pasted them into the final image.

color evokes a mood
creates contrast
enhances the feeling
can make a tired image
suddenly sparkle with life.

UNDERSTANDING
COLOR THEORY

Color evokes a mood; it creates contrast and enhances the beauty in an image. It can make a dull scene vibrant and a tired image suddenly sparkle with life.

To the graphic designer, painter, artist, or video producer, creating the perfect color is essential. When the colors aren't correct, the concept isn't complete; the image may fail to convey its information and the artistic experience may be lost. If the rich green that should radiate from a forest setting is too yellow and sickly, the magnificence of nature is not portrayed, and the "healthy" feeling of the great outdoors is lost. If the forest's reds that should glow with fire and vibrance turn dull, a sense of decay and rust is conveyed, rather than excitement.

Producing the perfect color is no easy task. A painter must mix and remix paint, blending to get the perfect shades to match images seen or imagined. Photographers and filmmakers must spend hours testing, refocusing, and adding lights until the proper scene is created. In many respects, working with color on the computer is no different. The computer creates its own set of special complications and technical difficulties. How can you ensure that the colors you see on your screen match the colors of nature or your artistic vision? And then how do you get the same colors you see on screen to appear in your printed image?

Producing the right colors in Photoshop requires a knowledge of color theory. Once you understand the basics of color theory, you'll begin to recognize the color terminology used throughout Photoshop's dialog boxes, menus, and palettes. You'll also understand the process of adding and subtracting colors when you're doing color correcting. With a knowledge of color theory, you'll know how to paint the sky a richer, fuller blue. You'll be able to pick colors so that the same luscious emerald green you create in Photoshop appears in the forest on your printed page.

To be successful in choosing the right colors in Photoshop, you must first understand color models. *Color models* were created to provide a way of translating colors into numerical data so that they can be described consistently in various media. For instance, referring to a color as "greenish-blue" leaves it open to interpretation based largely on personal human perception. On the other hand, assigning that color specific values in a color model—in the CMYK model it would be 100% cyan, 3% magenta, 30% yellow, and 15% black—makes it possible to reproduce that color the same way, again and again.

As you use Photoshop's color features, you'll work with several different color models: RGB, CMYK, HSB, and Lab. The RGB and CMYK color models are a constant reminder that the colors of nature, the colors on your monitor, and colors on the printed page are created in completely different ways. Your monitor creates colors by emitting red, green, and blue beams of light; it uses the RGB (red/green/blue) color model. To reproduce the continuous-tone effect of color photographs, printing technology uses a combination of cyan, magenta, yellow, and black inks that reflect and absorb various wavelengths of light. Colors created by overprinting these four colors are part of the CMYK (cyan/magenta/yellow/black) color model. The HSB (hue/saturation/brightness) color model provides an intuitive way to translate the colors of nature to the colors your computer creates because it is based on the way humans perceive colors. The Lab color model provides a means for creating "device-independent" color, meaning that Lab colors shouldn't vary, regardless of the monitor or printer used.

WHAT IS COLOR?

Color exists because of three entities: light, the object being viewed, and the viewer. Physicists have proven that white light is composed of wavelengths of red, green, and blue. The human eye perceives color as various wavelengths of red, green, and blue that are absorbed or reflected by objects. For example, assume you are at a picnic on a sunny day, ready to reach for a red apple. Sunlight shines on the apple and the red wavelength of light is reflected off the apple back to your eyes. The wavelengths of blue and green are absorbed into the apple, as shown in Figure 4-1. Sensors in your eye react to the reflected light, sending a message that is interpreted by your brain as the color red.

Your perception of the red color depends upon the apple, the light, and you. One apple will absorb more green and blue than another, and thus its color will appear redder. If clouds cover the sun, the apple's red will appear darker. Your interpretation of the apple will also be affected by your own physiology, by your experience as an apple eater, or by the fact that you haven't eaten all day.

The apple absorbs the green and blue wavelengths; the red wavelength is reflected back to the eye

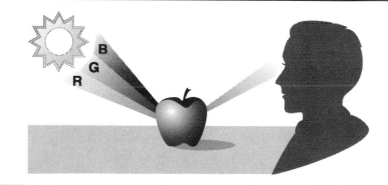

FIGURE 4-1

The red, green, and blue wavelengths that allow you to see the apple are the basis for all colors in nature. That is why red, green, and blue are often called the *primary colors* of light. All colors of the spectrum are created by different intensities of these wavelengths of light. Figure 4-2 (reproduced on the "Color Theory" page of the color insert in this book) is a simple example of how different colors can be created with the primary red, green, and blue wavelengths. When the three primary colors overlap, they create the secondary colors: cyan, magenta, and yellow. The primary and secondary colors are complements of one another. *Complementary colors* are colors that are most unlike each other. In Figure 4-2 you can see that yellow is made up of red and green. Blue is the missing primary color; therefore, blue and yellow are complements. The complement of green is magenta, and the complement of red is cyan. This explains why you see other colors besides red, green, and blue. In a sunflower, you see yellow because red and green wavelengths of light are reflected back to you, while the blue is absorbed by the plant.

Figure 4-2 also shows that all primary colors combine to create white. You might think that adding these colors together would produce a darker color, but remember that you are adding *light*. When light wavelengths are added together, you get lighter colors. This is why the primary colors are often called *additive* colors. By adding all of the colors of light together, you obtain the lightest light: white light. Thus, when you see a white piece of paper, all of the red, green, and blue wavelengths of light are being reflected back to you. When you see black, all of the red, green, and

The primary (additive) colors and their complements. When all three primary colors are mixed together, they create white

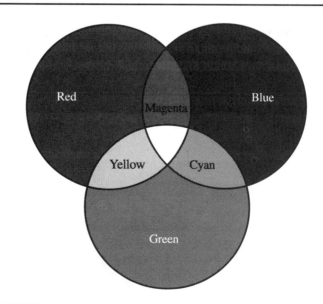

FIGURE 4-2

blue wavelengths of light are being completely absorbed by the object; thus no light is reflected back to you.

THE RGB COLOR MODEL

The system of creating colors on your monitor is based on the same fundamental properties of light that occur in nature: that colors can be created from red, green, and blue. This is the basis of the RGB color model.

Your color monitor creates colors by emitting three light beams at different intensities, lighting up red, green, and blue phosphorescent material overlaying the inside of your monitor's screen. When you see red in Photoshop, your monitor has turned on its red beam, which excites red phosphors, lighting up a red pixel on your screen. Thus, seeing a scanned image of an apple on screen is different from seeing the apple that sits on top of your computer, waiting to be eaten. If you turn off the lights in your room, you won't see your red snack; but you'll still see the scanned apple, because light is being emitted from your monitor.

In Photoshop's RGB color model, pixel colors can be changed by combining various values of red, green, and blue. Each of these three primary colors has a range of values from 0 to 255. When you combine the 256 possible values of red, 256 values of green, and 256 values of blue, the total number of possible colors is approximately 16.7 million (256×256×256). This may seem like a lot of colors, but remember that these are only a portion of the visible colors in nature. Nevertheless, 16.7 million colors is sufficient to reproduce crystal-clear digitized images on a monitor equipped with 24-bit color.

Using RGB Colors in the Colors Palette

In this section, you'll experiment with RGB Color in the Colors palette. You'll see how colors are created from RGB color values, and learn how to set RGB color values to mix colors. If the Colors palette isn't open, open it now by choosing Show Colors from the Window menu.

By default, the Colors palette will display the RGB color model palette, unless it was changed in a previous session. You should see three bars, called *color sliders*, labeled R, G, and B. If you do not see the letters R, G, and B, you are in another color model's palette. To change to the RGB palette, click on the Colors palette Options menu arrow (PC users: Control menu button). A list of Photoshop's color models will appear. Select RGB Color from the list, and the palette with the three RGB sliders will load. Beneath each slider is a triangular-shaped slider *control*. Using the mouse, you can click and drag on the slider controls to change the values of red, green, and blue in the foreground or background color. The foreground and background colors are indicated in the selection boxes (the overlapping squares in the upper-right corner of the Colors palette).

Using Swatches to Pick Colors

Start by clicking on the red, green, and blue color squares, or swatches, in the bottom half of the Colors palette, and examine the color values of the primary colors. This will demonstrate the full range of each color component in the RGB color model. When you click on a swatch, Photoshop displays the swatch color in either the Foreground or Background selection box, as well as displaying its R, G, and B values to the right of the sliders.

OTE: *In order to see the foreground or background colors in each slider, Photoshop's Dynamic Sliders option must be activated. When the Dynamic Sliders option is activated, each slider displays the current foreground or background color above the slider control. Also, each slider shows the range of colors available when you click and drag the slider control left or right. If the Dynamic Sliders option is not enabled, each slider will only show color values for red, green, or blue color components. For instructions on installing the Dynamic Sliders option, see Chapter 1.*

In this exercise, you will only work with Photoshop's foreground color. Before you begin, make sure that the Foreground selection box (the top overlapping square to the right of the sliders) is activated. If the white band is not surrounding the Foreground selection box, click on that box to activate the foreground color.

To see the RGB values of the primary color red, position the mouse pointer over the red color swatch in the upper-left corner of the color swatches, in the first row. When the pointer turns into an eyedropper, click on the red swatch.

Notice that the R slider control jumps to the far right. The number to the right of the slider indicates the red value of the color swatch you just clicked. (If you clicked the correct shade of red, the value will be 255.) The active color in Photoshop (the foreground color) has now changed to this value of red. Take a look at the sliders for green and blue; they are both at 0, because the shade of red you clicked contains no green or blue.

To see the RGB values of the primary color green, click on the green swatch (the third from the left in the first row). The G value jumps to 255, and the values of blue and red drop to 0. To see the values of the primary color blue, click on the fifth swatch from the left in the first row. Pure blue's value is 255, with no red and no green.

You can see from the foregoing color swatch tests that each primary color has a range of values from 0 to 255, to produce 256 separate color values.

Using Sliders to Create RGB Colors

Now that you've seen the color values of pure red, green, and blue, take a look at some colors created from the primaries. Click on any swatch, and you'll see its combination of RGB color values. Try the yellowish color, the one directly below the pure blue swatch. Notice the combination of values: R 255, G 236, and B 103. Click on a few of the other color swatches, and notice the combinations of the three primary colors.

The palette swatches obviously can't contain all 16.7 million colors, but by adjusting the slider controls with the mouse, you can create every one of the 16.7 million colors Photoshop can display.

All three sliders work in the same manner. When you click and drag a slider control to the right, you are adding more color. When you drag left, you are subtracting color. With any color swatch selected, try dragging the G slider control from left to right. Notice that as you drag to the right, the green values increase, and the foreground color you are creating in the Colors palette grows brighter. Now drag left; as you do, the color values decrease and the green gets darker.

To create black, drag all of the slider controls to the left, setting them to 0. Watch as the foreground color in the Colors palette grows darker. When all of the values reach 0, the foreground color displays black. If red, green, and blue are equal in value but are not 0 or 255, a shade of gray is created. To create white, move the slider controls in the opposite direction. By doing this you are adding light. Set each slider to its full value of 255, and you'll create white.

Using the Sliders to Display RGB Complements

If you are using the Dynamic Sliders option, you'll see a range of colors displayed in each slider when all of the RGB sliders are set to 255. The R slider displays white turning to cyan; the G slider displays white changing to magenta; and the B slider displays white changing to yellow.

Why do the sliders change colors? The designers of Photoshop are shrewdly reminding you about color theory. In each slider, you see the opposite of each primary color (its *complement*). The color towards the left end of each slider is showing you what happens if you subtract a primary color from white (by dragging the slider control all the way to the left). Remember the discussion earlier in the chapter of why you see yellow when you look at a sunflower? The sunflower absorbs (subtracts) the blue wavelength of light. When red and green are reflected back to you, you see yellow.

You can easily demonstrate this with the sliders. To create yellow, which is the complement of blue, drag the B slider control back to 0, and leave the R and G sliders set to 255. Thus yellow is created by subtracting blue from white.

To create cyan, which is red's complement, first set all the sliders back to 255, and then drag the R slider control to 0. By subtracting the red value from the primary colors, you have created cyan.

To create magenta, the complement of green, drag the R slider control back to 255 and the G slider control to 0. Magenta is created by subtracting green from the primary colors.

This concept of subtracting colors is the foundation of the CMYK color model, described in the following section.

THE CMYK COLOR MODEL

The CMYK color model is based not on adding light, but on subtracting it. In the RGB model, colors were created by adding light; the monitor (or a television) is a light source that can create colors. But a printed page doesn't emit light; it absorbs and reflects light. So when you want to translate the monitor's colors to paper, another color model, CMYK, must be used. The CMYK color model is the basis for *four-color process* printing, which is used primarily to print continuous tone images (such as digitized photographs) on a printing press. In four-color process printing, colors are reproduced on a printing press by using four different printing plates; C (cyan), M (magenta), Y (yellow), and K (black—black is represented by the letter K because B might also stand for blue).

Because the printed page cannot emit light, a press cannot use RGB colors to print; instead, it uses inks that can absorb specific wavelengths of light and reflect other wavelengths. By combining inks of cyan, magenta, and yellow, a commercial printer can reproduce a significant portion of the visible spectrum of colors. In theory, these three colors should combine to produce all colors necessary for printing, including black. However, because of the impurity of inks, the cyan, magenta, and yellow colors produce a muddy brown rather than black. Therefore, printers often add black to cyan, magenta, and yellow to produce the darker and gray portions of images. Figure 4-3 (reproduced on the "Color Theory" page of the color insert in this book) shows the subtractive colors overlapping to create a muddy brown. Notice that each two subtractive colors creates a primary color.

Using CMYK Colors in the Colors Palette

To introduce yourself to the CMYK color model, start by taking a look at how to change colors using the CMYK sliders in the Colors palette. First, you'll need to switch to the CMYK color model by clicking on the Options menu arrow (PC users: Control menu button) in the Colors palette. Mac users drag to the CMYK Color choice (PC users: click on CMYK Color).

You'll immediately notice some differences between the RGB and CMYK palettes. First, CMYK utilizes four sliders, not three. There is a slider for each *subtractive* color: C for cyan, M for magenta, Y for yellow, and K for black. Also, the colors are measured in percentages. The percentages provide a standard way of conveying various ink values from the design studio to the printing press.

Using CMYK percentages can be confusing, but it helps to understand that you can produce the primary colors using CMYK percentages. When you know how to produce red, green, and blue from CMYK values, you'll be better able to orient yourself when mixing colors or correcting color in this color model. To aid you in

The secondary (subtractive) colors and their complements. When all three secondary colors are mixed together, they create a muddy brown

FIGURE 4-3

creating these colors, it's helpful to have a color wheel at hand. The color wheel shown in Figure 4-4 (reproduced on the "Color Theory" page of the color insert in this book) is a simplified version of the color wheels professional color correctors use to help them add and subtract colors.

In a color wheel, colors are arranged in a circle to show the relationship between each color. The primary colors are positioned around the circle equidistant from one another. Each secondary color is situated between two primary colors. In this arrangement, each color is directly opposite its complement, and each color on the wheel is situated between the two colors that are used to create it.

By studying the wheel, you can see that adding yellow and magenta creates red. If you subtract both yellow and magenta, you remove red. Thus, if you want to subtract red from an image, you decrease the percentages of yellow and magenta. Another point to realize about the color wheel is that when you are adding color to an image, you are subtracting its complement. For instance, when you are making an image redder, you are decreasing the percentage of cyan (which is red's complement, directly opposite it in the color wheel).

Using Sliders to Create CMYK Colors

Now you'll practice using both the color wheel and the CMYK sliders to create red, green, and blue. This simple exercise will demonstrate how CMYK inks absorb different light waves and reflect others to produce colors, as shown in Figure 4-5.

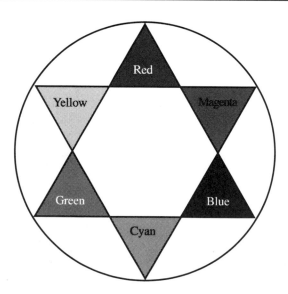

The color
wheel

FIGURE 4-4

Red   Green   Blue

Wavelengths of light, absorbed and reflected

White   Black

FIGURE 4-5

To create red, drag magenta and yellow to 100%, and leave cyan and black at 0%. Notice that red is between yellow and magenta on the color wheel. When you see red in an image printed using four-color process printing, yellow and magenta inks have combined to absorb the blue and green wavelengths of light. The result is the color red.

To create green, drag yellow and cyan to 100%, and put magenta and black at 0%. Green is between yellow and cyan on the color wheel. When you see green in an image printed using four-color process printing, yellow and cyan inks have combined to absorb the blue and red wavelengths of light.

To create blue, drag cyan and magenta to 100%, and yellow and black to 0%. Blue is between cyan and magenta on the color wheel. When you see blue in an image printed using four-color process printing, cyan and magenta inks have combined to absorb red and green wavelengths of light.

Now try experimenting with the sliders to create additional CMYK colors. If you have a swatch book displaying CMYK percentages and the colors they produce, use the sliders to re-create a few of these colors, and see how close the screen color comes to the real thing.

OTE: *If you're interested in creating and printing four-color separations, your file mode must be CMYK color. See Chapters 9 and 14 for more information.*

The Out-of-Gamut Alert

Before you leave the CMYK color model and move on to the next section, it's important to realize that the color ranges of the RGB and CMYK color models are different. The professional term for the visible color range of a color model is *gamut*. The gamut of RGB is larger than that of CMYK, as shown in Figure 4-6. Therefore, if you only work with RGB color on your computer, be aware that you may be designing and editing with onscreen colors that cannot be printed.

 Fortunately, Photoshop provides a warning when you overstep the bounds of printable colors. You may even have already noticed this warning: it's a small Alert symbol—a triangle with an exclamation mark inside—that appears in the Colors palette. Even when you are working in the CMYK palette, you can still activate the Alert feature by clicking on any of the first six color swatches from the left in the top row.

For example, click on the red swatch in the top row of the Colors palette. The Alert will immediately appear, indicating that this color is beyond the CMYK gamut. If you click on the Alert, Photoshop will select the nearest printable color. Try clicking the Alert now; the closest printable red will be displayed as the foreground color. But even though Photoshop is showing you that the red is printable, it is only displaying an RGB monitor's simulation of red. Never assume that the color you see on screen is an exact representation of the printed color.

OTE: *If you are in a CMYK color file and try to paint with an out-of-gamut color, Photoshop will convert it to the nearest printable color.*

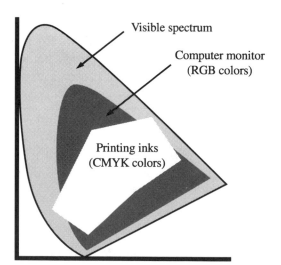

Visible
color
ranges
(gamuts)
for the
RGB and
CMYK
color
models

 FIGURE 4-6

OTE: *If you are outputting your work to slides or video, you needn't worry about the out-of-gamut Alert, because slides and video use RGB colors. The Alert indicates that the color cannot be created by commercial printers' inks.*

THE HSB COLOR MODEL

Although both RGB and CMYK are essential color models for computer graphics and printing, many designers and graphic artists find it unnecessarily complicated to try to mix colors using values or percentages of other colors. Using a color wheel helps, but neither RGB nor CMYK are very intuitive. The human mind doesn't divide up colors into models of red/green/blue or cyan/magenta/yellow/black. To make such choices easier, a third color model—HSB (hue/saturation/brightness) —was created.

HSB is based on human perception of colors, rather than the computer values of RGB or printers' percentages of CMYK. The human eye sees colors as components of hue, saturation, and brightness.

Think of hues as the colors you can see on a color wheel. In technical terms, *hue* is based upon the wavelength of light reflected from an object, or transmitted through it. *Saturation*, often called chroma, is the amount of gray in a color. The higher the saturation, the lower the gray content and the more intense the color. *Brightness* is a measure of the intensity of light in a color.

Using HSB Sliders in the Colors Palette

Let's take a look at how to choose colors using the HSB color model. In the Colors palette, click on the Options menu arrow (PC users: Control menu button) and choose HSB Color. You'll see three sliders: H for changing hue values, measured in degrees; S for saturation, and B for brightness, both measured in percentages. As with the sliders in the other two color models, you move through the different hue, saturation, and brightness values by clicking and dragging the slider controls.

Try this now by clicking and dragging the H slider control to the right. As you move through different degrees of hue, the Foreground or Background selection boxes in the Colors palette will display the same colors that you would see if you were traveling the perimeter of a color wheel. When you reach 360 degrees, you'll see the same red that is displayed when you are at 0 degrees because you are traveling around the circumference of a circle.

The major color values of hue, with saturation and brightness set to 100%, are as follows:

Color	Hue Setting
Red	0 or 360°
Yellow	60°
Green	120°
Cyan	180°
Blue	240°
Magenta	300°

Now we'll experiment with changing saturation and brightness to other percentages and see how they affect the color red.

Changing Saturation and Brightness

To follow along with the next steps in this exercise using the HSB color model, start by selecting the red color swatch in the first row of the color swatches.

Let's begin by observing the effects of changing the saturation percentage for the red color. Move the S slider control. The intensity of the red will diminish as you decrease saturation by dragging the slider control to the left. Try it, and you'll move from red to light red to pink. When you reach 0%, the red will have changed to white.

NOTE: *You cannot create white and black with the hue slider. To create white, the saturation slider control must be set to 0% and the brightness slider control to 100%. To create black, the saturation slider control must be set to 0% and the brightness slider control to 0%.*

Before you test the brightness slider, click and drag saturation back to 100%, to give you a reference point for observing the effects of changing brightness. Dragging the brightness control to the left will decrease the percentage of color brightness, dragging to the right will increase the brightness.

Try it now: Drag the B slider control to the left, and you'll see that red gradually darkens. When you reach 0%, the red will have turned to black. To bring brightness back to the red, drag the control back toward 100%.

If you wish, continue to experiment with the HSB color sliders by picking a hue and then adjusting its saturation and brightness. It probably won't take long before you agree that HSB is the easiest of the color models to use, because it's the most intuitive. There's less guesswork involved in color creation when you don't have to worry about mixing other colors together. You may even decide to do all of your work in the HSB model—particularly if you're going to use Photoshop as a painting program and will not be creating output for four-color printing.

THE LAB COLOR MODEL

One more color model remains to be explored. Though it's not used as frequently in Photoshop as the RGB, CMYK, and HSB color models, the Lab color model is worth investigating, particularly because it may prove helpful in certain color editing situations. When you learn about changing modes in Chapter 9, you'll see that Lab color can be used when editing Photo CD images and when outputting to PostScript Level-2 printers.

Although you may never need to use Lab color, this color model is vital to Photoshop. Lab is the internal color model that Photoshop uses to convert from one color mode to another. In Chapter 9, you'll learn how to change modes from RGB to CMYK so that you can produce a four-color separation. When Photoshop converts from RGB to CMYK, it first converts to Lab color, then from Lab to CMYK. One reason why it uses Lab is because the Lab color gamut encompasses both the color gamuts of RGB and CMYK.

The Lab color model is based upon the work of the Commission Internationale de l'Eclairage that was formed in the early 1900s to try to standardize color measurement. The commission designed a color model based upon how color is perceived by the eye. In 1976, the original color model was refined and called CIE Lab. It was created to provide consistent colors, no matter what monitor or printer is being used; this is called *device-independent color*. Device-independent color isn't affected by the characteristics or idiosyncrasies of any piece of hardware.

Using Lab Sliders in the Colors Palette

You might wonder why you should know anything about the Lab color model, if Photoshop uses it internally. The reason is that Lab divides colors using an approach different from that of RGB, CMYK, and HSB, and gives you another perspective to editing colors: the Lab model comprises a lightness, or luminance, factor and two color axes.

Take a look at Lab color in the Colors palette. Click on the Options menu arrow (PC users: Control menu button) and switch to Lab Color. You'll see three sliders, labeled L, a, and b. The L slider allows you to change a color's lightness, in values from 0 to 100. The a slider represents an axis of colors ranging from green to magenta; and the b slider is an axis of colors ranging from blue to yellow. The values accessible from both axes are –120 to 120. 100 at L, a at 0, and b at 0 create white.

Lab is useful if all you wish to do is change the lightness of a color. Also, if you need to change only the red and green components of a color, or the blue and yellow components, you can click and drag on the Lab slider controls to do this.

To see how the Lab sliders affect color, start with the L slider control set all the way to the right at 100. This provides the brightest levels for the colors you will be creating.

To see how the a slider changes colors from green to magenta, set the b slider to 0. Then, click and drag on the a slider control, moving first to the right, then to the left. As you drag the a slider control to the left, the color will turn to green. Now drag the a slider control to the right to see the color change to magenta. When you are done, leave the control in the middle of the a slider (set to 0). This will best enable you to see the effects of changing the b slider.

Now observe how the b slider changes colors from blue to yellow by clicking and dragging the slider control. First drag it to the right, and the color will turn to yellow. Drag to the left to see the color change to blue.

If you wish to keep experimenting, try clicking and dragging on the L slider control to see how lowering the L value darkens colors.

THE COLOR PICKER

Now that you've examined each of the color models in the Colors palette, take a look at Photoshop's Color Picker. The Color Picker provides another tool for picking foreground and background colors. The chief differences between the Color Picker and the Colors palette are that the Color Picker allows you to see the values of all four color models (RGB, CMYK, HSB and Lab) at the same time, and you can enter specific values for most color settings. The Color Picker also lets you access color-matching systems such as PANTONE and TRUMATCH.

To access the Color Picker, click on the Foreground Color or Background Color icon in the Toolbox. You may also open the Color Picker from the Colors palette, by clicking on either the Foreground or Background selection box. If the Foreground selection box is activated, your settings in the Color Picker will affect the foreground color. If the Background selection box is selected, your settings change the background color.

Take a look at the Color Picker in action. Start by accessing the Color Picker dialog box from the Colors palette to change the foreground color. Here's how: Make sure the Colors palette is set to change the foreground color; a white band should surround the Foreground selection box in the upper-right of the palette. If the white band surrounds the Background selection box instead, click the Foreground selection box to activate it. Then click it again to display the Color Picker dialog box, as shown in Figure 4-7.

n **OTE:** *The Color Picker will not appear if you have switched to either the Apple or Windows color picker in the General Preferences dialog box. If you use either the Apple or the Windows color picker, be aware that neither alerts you when you are picking unprintable colors. To switch back to Photoshop's Color Picker, select Preferences in the File menu and then click General from the submenu. In the Color Picker pop-up menu, click and choose Photoshop.*

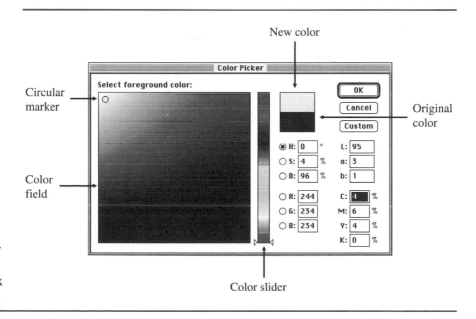

The Color
Picker
dialog box

FIGURE 4-7

Exploring the Color Picker

You'll notice that all of the color models—RGB, CMYK, HSB, and Lab—are included in the Color Picker dialog box, with entry fields where you can type values for the various color components. Thus, if you know the precise CMYK values you want for an image, you can just type them in, rather than having to nudge the CMYK slider controls into position in the Colors palette.

IP: *Before you start experimenting with the settings in the Color Picker dialog box, notice the color in the bottom half of the small box next to the top of the color slider. This box displays your original color. As you work, the top part of the box will change to show you the new color currently being edited (see Figure 4-7). The bottom portion of the square always remains the same. If you wish to return to the original color, you can click on the bottom of the square. This is a very handy "undo" feature.*

As you choose or edit colors, you can choose the color model that best suits your needs. For instance, suppose you need to add more green to an image that must be output in CMYK for process printing. If you were working in the CMYK model in the Colors palette, you might have to refer to a color wheel or try to figure out which sliders would add green. With the Color Picker, however, you can add green by simply entering a higher value into the G field of the RGB values.

Though the Color Picker doesn't provide sliders for all color models, it does offer one vertical slider that can be used for any of the RGB or HSB color components. You convert the slider's role by clicking in one of the radio buttons that appear to the left of the HSB and RGB value fields. For instance, if you click on the R radio button, the vertical slider lets you move through red values in the RGB color model. Click on the H radio button, and you can move through hue values.

The large colored square that occupies the entire left half of the Color Picker dialog box is called the *color field*. A small circular marker in the color field allows you to change color components by clicking on it and dragging the mouse. For instance, if you click on the H radio button, the vertical slider changes hue values; now clicking and dragging on the marker in the color field changes saturation and brightness. (Dragging the circle horizontally changes saturation; dragging vertically changes brightness.)

If you don't click and drag the circle, but instead click anywhere in the color field, the circular marker will jump to the new position. The values in the dialog box and the foreground or background color displayed will change accordingly.

If the Color Picker is confusing to you at first, imagine yourself in a three-dimensional version of the color model you are using. This is often called a color model's *color space*. Figure 4-8 (reproduced on the "Color Theory" page of the color insert in this book) illustrates a three-dimensional view of the HSB color model. As you are swimming in this three-dimensional pool of HSB colors, the hue levels change around the perimeter of the pool. The saturation levels change as you swim out to the middle of the pool. The brightness levels change as you dive deeper into the pool.

As you move along the edges of the pool, you pass through various hues. This is the equivalent of clicking and dragging on the vertical slider control with the Hue

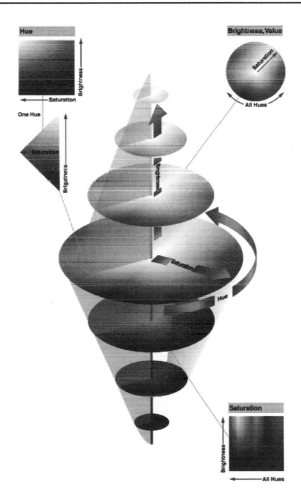

The HSB color model, in 3-D (courtesy of Agfa Corporation)

FIGURE 4-8

radio button selected, while viewing saturation and brightness in the color field. As you look across the water of the pool, you see the saturation and brightness values of each hue you pass through.

If you dive straight down along the edge of the pool, you pass through various levels of brightness. From your vantage point, you see the saturation and hue values of the colors according to your brightness depth. This is equivalent to clicking on the Brightness radio button while viewing saturation and hue in the color field.

Now imagine that you're swimming out to the middle of the pool, moving through the saturation levels of colors. Dive deeper and view the colors around you. The colors you see are similar to those in the color field when you clicked on the Saturation radio button.

Changing Colors Using the Color Picker

Now try the Color Picker and see how you can use the combination of radio buttons, vertical slider, and value fields to change colors. Assume that you wish to edit a color by adding more green to it. First set the vertical slider to change green RGB values, by clicking on the G radio button.

When you drag the control for the vertical slider, you'll see that it functions much the same way as the horizontal sliders do in the RGB model. Dragging the slider control upward raises the green value, and dragging downward lowers it. Try this now: Click on the control and drag toward the top of the slider. As you drag higher, the green color value grows. Drag up to 255, and then back down. The highest value that appears in the G entry field is 255, and the lowest is 0.

When you clicked on the G radio button, the circular marker in the color field is set to change the R and B values of the RGB model. (If you had clicked on the R radio button, instead, the color field marker would change the G and B values of RGB; clicking on the B button makes the marker control the G and R values.) When the G radio button is selected, dragging the marker upward adds red to the color you are creating, and dragging to the right adds blue.

Experiment with the marker to see how the color field controls the R and B values. Click and drag the circular marker up. As you drag, notice that the value in the R field increases. As you drag down, it decreases. Now drag to the right; this causes blue levels to increase. Drag left, and the levels decrease. You can probably guess what happens if you drag diagonally—you can change both R and B values at the same time.

Now that you have oriented yourself in the Color Picker, can you guess how to create pure green? Drag the slider control all the way up to 255, and then drag the color field marker to the bottom-left corner of the color field. When your color changes to green, you'll see the same Alert sign that you saw in the Colors palette, again warning you that you are viewing an unprintable color. If you click on the Alert, Photoshop will choose the closest printable color for you.

If you'd like, you can continue to experiment with the Color Picker. As you grow accustomed to it, you may find yourself beginning to prefer it to the Colors palette. But don't give up on the Colors palette; you'll find more uses for it later in this chapter.

ACCESSING CUSTOM COLORS FROM THE COLOR PICKER

An important feature in the Color Picker is the Custom button. This button allows you to choose colors using color-matching systems to make printed colors more predictable.

As you've worked through this chapter, you've become aware that it is often difficult to precisely translate colors displayed on your computer screen to the printed page. The problem is compounded by the fact that not all monitors are the same, not all inks are the same, and a printed page cannot completely reproduce the color sensation of the video monitor. Video colors often look brighter than their counterparts on the printed page.

One way to obtain a better idea of how the colors on your screen will print, or at least to better predict color output, is to pick colors not by how they look on the computer screen but by their appearance in a color swatch book—a book of many color samples printed on paper, used to label or classify colors.

Suppose you wish to print a blue border around an image. You could pick a blue from a swatch book and then choose that same blue color from Photoshop's Custom Colors dialog box. During the printing process, your commercial printer will be able to match the swatch's custom color when producing your image.

 OTE: *To accurately match colors, make sure that the colors in your swatch book have not faded.*

In deciding which swatch book to use, consider the following:

 Are you printing on newsprint, coated paper, or uncoated paper? Inks spread differently depending upon the type of paper being used. For more information on how paper stock affects printing, see Chapter 14.

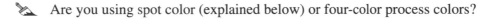 Are you using spot color (explained below) or four-color process colors?

The most commonly used color-matching system was created by PANTONE. It's important to understand that PANTONE has traditionally been used for *spot*-color printing, not in four-color separation work. Spot color is similar to printing an overlay, separate from any other color; this is quite different from four-color separation, where cyan, magenta, yellow, and black combine to create a color. In spot color, the printer mixes inks to create a matching color and prints that one color on an individual plate. This is fine for one or two colors but would be very expensive for multiple colors.

Spot colors can be used as "fifth" colors; this is a term used when a job is printed with the standard four-color process and needs a fifth color picked for a specific match of a certain color. Fifth colors are used to create silvers, coppers, golds, deep blues, and certain greens, because they can't be created with four-color inks. Although Photoshop does not directly support spot color, a technique for creating and printing spot colors is discussed in Chapter 12.

 OTE: *Second Glance of Laguna Hills, California, produces spot-color separation software for Photoshop called PhotoSpot.*

Using Color-Matching Systems

In this section you'll learn how to use color-matching systems. Then you'll add a custom color to the Colors palette and save the new palette.

If the Color Picker isn't open, click on the Foreground Color icon in the Toolbox. The Color Picker dialog box will open. Click on the Custom button to open the Custom Colors dialog box.

IP: *Photoshop can search for a custom color that matches a color you have created with sliders or the Color Picker. First, the color you wish to match must be active in either the Foreground or the Background selection box. Then, access the Book pop-up menu from within the Custom Colors dialog box and select which swatch book (e.g., PANTONE, TRUMATCH) you want the match to come from. The Custom Colors dialog box then displays the custom color that most closely matches the color you created.*

Selecting a Color-Matching System and a Color

To access a custom color, you first have to access the Book pop-up menu and choose one of the following ink-matching systems, as shown in Figure 4-9.

  ANPA Color   These colors are used for printing to newsprint.

  FOCOLTONE   This system, popular in England, includes 763 CMYK colors.

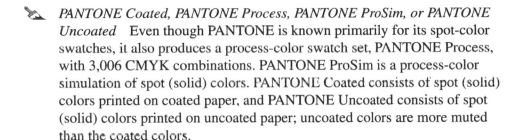

PANTONE Coated, PANTONE Process, PANTONE ProSim, or PANTONE Uncoated   Even though PANTONE is known primarily for its spot-color swatches, it also produces a process-color swatch set, PANTONE Process, with 3,006 CMYK combinations. PANTONE ProSim is a process-color simulation of spot (solid) colors. PANTONE Coated consists of spot (solid) colors printed on coated paper, and PANTONE Uncoated consists of spot (solid) colors printed on uncoated paper; uncoated colors are more muted than the coated colors.

TOYO 88 CF 1050   This system from Japan provides 1,050 colors.

TRUMATCH   The TRUMATCH system uses strictly CMYK process colors. It has approximately 2,000 process colors, arranged according to hue, saturation, and brightness.

Once you've selected the color-matching system you want to use (for this exercise, choose PANTONE Process), you can select a color. To find a color you can either click the up or down arrow in the vertical slider of colors, or click anywhere within the slider, or type in a swatch number in the Find # field. In Figure 4-9 we have chosen a reddish PANTONE color, number 73-1, and typed it in the Find # field. Do this on your own computer, and the PANTONE Process color 73-1 will be selected on screen in the list of custom colors and in the swatch box. The vertical slider on screen will also be set to the custom color. (You can, however, select any color you want).

Custom
Colors
dialog box,
with list of
Book
options
open

FIGURE 4-9

Click OK to close the Custom Colors dialog box. Notice that your foreground color has been changed to the PANTONE color (or the custom color) you selected. If you position the mouse pointer over the Foreground selection box in the Colors palette (without clicking), the title bar of the Colors palette will display the name of the PANTONE (or custom) color you picked.

OTE: *If you intend to export your Photoshop file to any program that uses short PANTONE names, choose Short PANTONE names in the General Preferences dialog box before you select any PANTONE colors.*

Saving Custom Colors in the Colors Palette

If you want to keep this custom color handy, you can add it to the swatches that appear in the Colors palette.

To add a custom color, or any color, to the Colors palette, position the mouse pointer in the white area to the right of the last color swatch in the Colors palette. When the pointer turns into a paint bucket, click to create a swatch of your active color. To insert the custom color between two existing swatches, press and hold down SHIFT-OPTION (PC users: SHIFT-ALT) while you click on a swatch or between two swatches to insert the active custom color. To replace an existing swatch with the current foreground color, press OPTION (PC users: ALT), then click on the swatch. Note that if the Background selection box (in the Colors palette) is active, you will add a swatch of your background color to the Colors palette.

Paint bucket

To delete a swatch, position the mouse pointer over a swatch and press COMMAND (PC users: CTRL). When the pointer turns into a scissors, click and the swatch will be deleted.

Saving Cutomized Palettes

You can continue to add your own custom colors to the Colors palette and then save it so that you can access it at a later time. Just click on the Options menu arrow in the Colors palette (PC users: Control menu button) and choose Save Colors to open the Save dialog box.

It might be a good idea to save your custom palette in Photoshop's Color Palettes folder (PC users: palettes), so that all of your palettes are in the same place. For the filename, type **Mycolors**, and then click Save (PC users: OK). You are now working in the Colors palette called Mycolors.

IP: *If you'd like, you can create your own color swatch book. Open a new file, and using the Rectangular Marquee tool, create a small rectangular selection. Fill the rectangle with a swatch color by using the Fill command in the Edit menu. With the Type tool, label the selection by typing in the name of the swatch color. Continue to create and label rectangles until you have applied all the color swatches from your palette to the new file. Save the file and print it to whatever output device you will be using with this collection of swatches. Then use the printout of the color swatches as a guide for what the swatch color will look like when printed from your output device.*

Loading and Appending Palettes

If at any time you want to reopen Photoshop's default Colors palette, or any other palette created by Adobe, you can do so by clicking the Options menu arrow (PC users: Control menu button) in the Colors palette and choosing Load Colors.

To reload Photoshop's default palette, select Default Colors (PC users: default.aco) from within the Color Palettes folder (PC users: palette), then click

Open (PC users: OK). After you load the Default Colors palette or any other color palette, it will replace the current palette on screen.

As you continue to experiment with the various palettes, you may wish to append a saved palette to the Colors palette on screen. To do this, choose Append Colors from the Options menu. A dialog box will appear, allowing you to load a palette from your hard disk.

CONCLUSION

In this chapter we've laid the foundation for further exploration into Photoshop's color spectrum. As you progress to more advanced topics, you'll see that it's vital to have an understanding of the differences between the color models. In future chapters you'll be introduced to such topics as converting from RGB Color to CMYK Color mode, calibrating your system for RGB to CMYK conversions, color-correcting in CMYK Color mode, and printing spot colors and four-color separations.

Next, in Chapter 5, you'll go one step further into the world of color as you begin to explore the painting tools and the painting modes in the Brushes palette.

5

INTRODUCTION TO
PAINTING TECHNIQUES

Even if you're not an artist, the scope, power, and rich diversity of Photoshop's painting capabilities are certain to inspire the creativity within you. You'll marvel at the realistic and electronic effects within your grasp. At times, you might even expect to see the paint dripping down your screen, or sparks flying from your electronic brushes. In this chapter, you'll try your hand at being a painter, using electronic versions of a paintbrush, pencil, eraser, paint bucket, and airbrush. These tools, along with the Line, Gradient, and Eyedropper tools, and Photoshop's Brushes and Colors palettes, will open a world of infinite artistic possibilities for you.

If you're not interested in Photoshop's painting features and are using the program more for its image-editing and photo-retouching capabilities, don't skip this chapter. You'll need to know the tools and techniques covered here because they are a fundamental part of electronic composition. As you continue to read this book, you'll see the need for these tools and techniques arise again and again.

The chapter is primarily divided into short introductory exercises and projects. Although the focal point is primarily the Toolbox's painting tools, you'll also use the Brushes palette and learn how to change brushes, to create, save, and load custom brushes, and to change the opacity of colors. At the conclusion of the chapter you'll explore Photoshop's painting modes, also accessed through the Brushes palette, which can change the results of painting based on the color being applied, the color over which it is painted, and the painting mode that is chosen.

INTRODUCTION TO THE LINE, ERASER, AND PAINT BUCKET TOOLS

The best way to learn the painting tools is to start with the easiest ones—the Line, Eraser, and Paint Bucket. Creating artistic effects with these tools requires only a click or a click-and-drag of the mouse, and knowledge of how to use the Brushes palette.

Preparation for the Exercises

When working with the Line tool (and all other painting tools), you'll make extensive use of the Colors palette to change colors. In the exercises in this chapter, you'll be using the HSB color model because it's the most intuitive one. Switch to the HSB color model by accessing the Options menu in the Colors palette and choosing HSB Color.

In preparation for the introductory exercises in this section, make sure that the Brushes palette is visible on your screen. If necessary, open it now by choosing Show Brushes from the Window menu.

Mode pop-up menu

Although you do not paint with a brush while using the Line tool, the Brushes palette does control the opacity and painting mode of the lines you create. The Brushes palette also controls the opacity and painting mode of the Pencil, Paint Bucket, Paintbrush, Gradient, Rubber Stamp, and Type tools. After you set the opacity and mode of a tool, they stay set for that tool until you change them. You can thus maintain different Brushes palette settings for each tool.

> **NOTE:** *The element controlled by the slider in the Brushes palette depends on which tool you are using. When you use the Line, Pencil, Paint Bucket, Paintbrush, Gradient, Rubber Stamp, and Type tools, the slider sets opacity. For the Airbrush, Smudge, and Blur/Sharpen tools, the slider sets pressure. For the Dodge/Burn tool, the slider sets exposure. (You will be introduced to the Rubber Stamp, Smudge, Blur/Sharpen, and Dodge/Burn tools in Chapter 6.)*

To activate the Mode pop-up menu and the Opacity slider in the Brushes palette, click on the Line tool. When the Line tool (or any other tool) is selected, the Brushes palette will display either the default settings or the last settings used for that tool.

If Opacity is set at less than 100%, you will not be painting with an opaque color, but rather a *tint*—a transparent version of a color. Painting with a tint can create a transparent effect and different shades of colors. When you lower the opacity percentage, you make a color more transparent; when you raise it, you make the color more opaque.

Later in this section, you'll lower the opacity to create tinted lines. For now, though, start with opaque lines. If the opacity setting is not 100%, reset it by clicking and dragging the Opacity slider control all the way to the right.

Before continuing, look at the Mode pop-up menu in the Brushes palette to see which painting mode is in effect. You will see one of the following words: Normal, Darken, Lighten, Hue, Saturation, Color, Luminosity, Multiply, Screen, or Dissolve. These are the painting modes, and they control how Photoshop applies one color over another.

For now, you will work in Normal mode (the default). When you paint in Normal mode, you paint all of the underlying pixels with the foreground or background color that is set in the Colors palette or Color Picker dialog box. If the painting mode is not Normal, change it now by clicking on the pop-up menu and selecting Normal from the list that appears.

Now that the Brushes palette options are set, you can create a new file to begin working with the Line tool. Choose New from the File menu. Set both Width and Height to 5 inches. Set Resolution to 72 pixels/inch, and use RGB Color for Mode. These settings will create a practice file that does not consume too much memory. Click OK, and once the new file appears, display the rulers and open the Info palette by selecting Show Rulers and Show Info from the Window menu. You'll be using the rulers and the Info palette as measuring guides in the Line tool exercise.

Using the Line Tool to Create Lines and Arrows

 As you can probably guess, the Line tool is used to create lines. You can create vertical or horizontal lines, or lines drawn at a diagonal in increments of 45 degrees. The Line Tool Options dialog box allows you to control the thickness of a line, as well as create arrowheads at the beginning and end of a line. In this section, you'll be using the Line tool to create lines at various thicknesses, angles, and shades, with and without arrowheads, as shown in Figure 5-1.

As with most other tools, the dialog box for the Line tool provides its various options. To view the Line Tool Options dialog box, double-click on the Line tool. In the dialog box, the Width field allows you to change the pixel width of the lines you create; the default width is 1. In the Arrowheads section you can specify the size of arrowheads to appear at either or both ends of a line.

Use the Line tool now to create a wide, red line. In the dialog box, type **16** in the Width field and click OK. Before creating the line, use the Colors palette to change the color in the Foreground selection box. Move the H (hue) slider control so that it is set to red (either 0 or 360 degrees). The S (saturation) and B (brightness) sliders should be set to 100%.

 OTE: *Don't worry about setting the background color, because the Line tool only paints with the foreground color.*

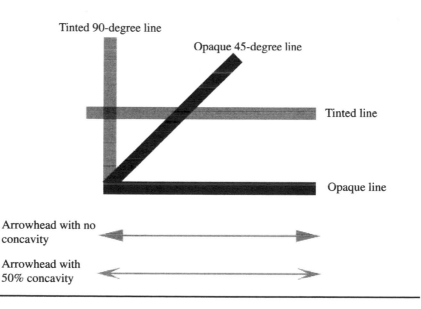

Tinted 90-degree line

Opaque 45-degree line

Tinted line

Opaque line

Examples
using the
Line tool

Arrowhead with no concavity

Arrowhead with 50% concavity

FIGURE 5-1

Creating a Line

Drawing a line is simple. Once you've set your Line Tool options, move the mouse pointer toward the middle of your document. As you move the mouse, the mouse pointer will change to a small crosshair. To create the line, all you need to do is click and drag.

1. Position the crosshair about 1 inch from the left side of the screen and 2.5 inches from the top of the screen; then click and drag to the right. As you drag, Photoshop creates an outline of the line that will appear on screen.

   Notice that as you drag the mouse, the values in the Info palette change. In addition to the X and Y coordinates that appear next to the crosshair icon, look at those adjacent to the icon of the square with arrows. These X and Y coordinates, which have a triangle in front of them, indicate the distance moved horizontally or vertically from one position to another. Next to the angle icon are A and D coordinates—the A coordinate shows the angle that you are dragging the mouse, and the D coordinate indicates the distance.

2. When you get near the right edge of the document window, release the mouse button. Not until you release the mouse will Photoshop use the foreground color to fill the linear outline it has drawn on screen.

 OTE: *Look carefully at the line you just created, and notice that it has a soft edge. This is because lines created by the Line tool are anti-aliased, so they do not appear jagged.*

 OTE: *If a selection exists on screen, you will only be able to use a painting tool in the selected area. To remove a selection from the screen, click away from it, or press COMMAND-D (PC users: CTRL-D)—the keyboard equivalent to choosing None from the Select menu.*

Drawing Lines to Create Angles

The Line tool allows you to draw lines in increments of 45 degrees; to do this, press SHIFT as you're drawing a line. Since you'll be using this *constraining* technique in the File Manager with File Cabinet project later in the chapter, practice it now by drawing a line at a 45-degree angle from the left endpoint of the one already on your screen.

1. Move the crosshair to the left edge of the existing line. Press and hold SHIFT, and click and drag diagonally up and to the right.

    You'll see that your movement is constrained to a 45-degree angle. When you've dragged about 3 inches, release the mouse, and Photoshop will draw a diagonal line at 45 degrees to the original one.

    Next, you'll press the SHIFT key while clicking and dragging to draw a 90-degree angle, but this time you'll change the opacity setting in the Brushes palette to create a tinted line.

2. In the Brushes palette, click and drag the slider control to the left, decreasing the Opacity percentage. (You can also use the keyboard to change the Opacity value in increments of 10 percent. For instance, type **3** and Opacity will jump to 30%.) Before you draw the next line, use the keyboard now to set Opacity to 50% by typing **5**.

    The next line you paint, at a 90-degree angle, will illustrate the effect of placing a translucent color over an opaque color. Once again, you'll start painting the line at the left endpoint of the first line you drew.

3. Position the crosshair on the left endpoint of the horizontal red line, press and hold SHIFT, and click and drag up to constrain the line to a 90-degree angle.

When you release the mouse, you'll see that the new line is 50% red. Notice that even though you drew the 50% red line on top of the opaque line, the opaque line's color has not changed to the tinted shade. It's as if the intensity of the 100% red burns through the translucent version of the same color.

For an example of painting a translucent color over another translucent color, click and drag to create a horizontal line that intersects both the 90-degree red-tinted line and the 45-degree opaque red line, as shown in Figure 5-1. Where the two translucent colors intersect, a square appears with a more intense red. But once again, when the red with the 50% opacity is painted over the opaque red, only the opaque version of the color shows.

IP: *If you set the width for the Line tool to zero pixels, you can use the tool as a screen-measuring device. When you click and drag, Photoshop creates an electronic tape measure, a thin line on screen that you can use to drag over items that you wish to measure. The linear dimensions of the object will appear in the Info palette. When you release the mouse, the measuring line will disappear.*

Creating Lines with Arrowheads

Next, try the Arrowheads options. This time, you'll create a thinner line so the effects of the arrowhead settings will be clearly visible.

1. Reopen the Line Tool Options dialog box by double-clicking on the Line tool. In the Width field, type **2**.

2. In the Arrowheads section, click on the At Start and At End check boxes. When these options are selected, the Line tool will create arrowheads at both ends of the next line you create.

   You can also control the width and the length of the arrowhead, using the Width and Length fields in the Arrowheads settings. Both the Width and Length fields will accept values between 1 and 1,500 pixels.

   a. To create an arrowhead that is twice as long as it is wide, type **15** in the Width field and **30** in the Length field.

   If you wish, you can also change the shape of the arrowhead by setting its *concavity*. Concavity determines the curve on the back of the arrowhead, as shown in some examples in Figure 5-1.

   b. Set Concavity to 0, so you can see how an arrowhead looks without concavity.

3. Click OK to accept the Line tool settings.

4. To see the arrowheads, draw a line from left to right below the other lines on your screen. This time, the line features arrowheads at both ends.

Take a look at how concavity changes the arrowhead. First, you'll need to reopen the Line tool dialog box and change the concavity of the arrow to 50% (values can be between -50% and 50%) and click OK. Then click and drag to create another line below the last one you created. Your screen will now look like Figure 5-1. Notice that the back of the 50%-concavity arrowhead has a very distinctive curve.

If you wish to continue experimenting with the Line tool, try creating one more line below the others with Concavity set to a negative number. This will create a line with an arrowhead that looks like a diamond.

After you've finished testing the Line tool, you can proceed to the next section, where you'll learn how to paint and fill using the Paint Bucket.

Using the Paint Bucket Tool to Paint and Fill

The Paint Bucket tool lets you quickly fill areas of an image with the foreground color. The area painted by the tool is determined by how similar in color the adjacent pixels are to the pixel that you click on.

The Paint Bucket and Magic Wand tools work in a similar way, by first analyzing the color of the pixel that is clicked and then using the Tolerance settings in the tools' dialog boxes to determine the range of pixels affected. As with the Magic Wand, the greater the Tolerance, the larger the pixel range affected; the lower the Tolerance, the smaller the pixel range.

There is a clear difference between the two tools, however, that you need to understand: The Magic Wand *selects* according to the Tolerance setting, but the Paint Bucket *paints over image areas* according to the Tolerance setting. The Magic Wand selects; the Paint Bucket paints. (To review the properties of the Magic Wand tool, see "Using the Magic Wand" in Chapter 3.)

In this section, you'll observe how various Tolerance settings determine how the Paint Bucket fills the four adjoining red lines created in the previous section. Double-click on the Paint Bucket tool to open the Paint Bucket Options dialog box. Start by examining the Tolerance setting; by default, it is set to 32. Like the Magic Wand, the Paint Bucket's Tolerance range is 0 to 255. If you type a low number in the Tolerance field, Photoshop will apply the foreground color to contiguous areas that are very similar in color to the pixel you click on. If you enter a large number in the Tolerance field, Photoshop applies the foreground color over contiguous areas that vary greatly from the pixel you click on.

In the Contents section of the dialog box, you'll see that the Paint Bucket tool paints with either the foreground color or a pattern. (You'll be creating and using patterns in Chapter 6.) The Anti-aliased option assures that the paint applied with the Paint Bucket tool will appear smooth, without jagged edges.

Start by testing the effects of a low Tolerance setting.

1. Change the value in the Tolerance field to 0, then click OK.

2. In order to see the Paint Bucket tool in action, you'll need to change the foreground color. In the Colors palette, click on a bright blue color, like the first blue square in the first row of swatches. To fill with an opaque blue, make sure that the Opacity slider in the Brushes palette is set to 100% and that Mode is set to Normal.

3. Now move the mouse pointer to the first red horizontal line that you drew in the previous section. As you move into the document window, the mouse pointer changes to a paint bucket. Position the paint bucket directly over any part of the thick, horizontal red line and click.

 OTE: *If you want to use a crosshair instead of the paint bucket, turn on CAPS LOCK before you use the Paint Bucket tool.*

With a zero Tolerance setting, the Paint Bucket tool fills only the two opaque red lines with blue. When you clicked the paint bucket (or crosshair) on the horizontal opaque red line, Photoshop hunted down only the adjacent opaque red pixels and filled them with the blue color, but not the pixels painted at a lower opacity (the 50% tinted lines).

To force the Paint Bucket tool to spread its paint over all the red lines, opaque and tinted, you'll need to increase the Tolerance setting.

4. Before testing this, choose Undo from the Edit menu to reset the line's color back to red. Then double-click on the Paint Bucket tool, and in the dialog box change Tolerance to 200 and click OK to accept the new setting.

5. Once again, move the paint bucket (or crosshair) over the horizontal opaque line and click. This time the Paint Bucket tool paints all of the adjoining lines, including the tinted ones. The higher Tolerance level causes the Paint Bucket tool to paint over pixels that have a color range that is broader than just opaque red.

CAUTION: *If you click on one of the tinted lines instead of the opaque red lines, the Paint Bucket tool will paint the entire screen blue because the white background is within the 200 Tolerance range when applied to the 50% red tint. If this occurs, choose Undo from the Edit menu.*

6. Before continuing, save your work and name it **Bucket.**

You'll be using the Paint Bucket tool throughout this chapter, primarily to paint over areas that have been outlined with either the Paintbrush or Pencil tools, or that have been previously painted. The Paint Bucket tool can also be used to fill a selection. When a selected area exists on screen, the Paint Bucket, like all painting tools, will only paint within the selection.

Next you'll work with the Eraser tool you learned about in Chapter 2 and try out the Magic Eraser.

Using the Eraser Tool to Erase and the Magic Eraser to Revert

Now that you have several lines on your screen, you might want to erase everything so you have more room to work. The fastest way to clear the screen is to use the Eraser tool. Recall that the Eraser tool always erases (paints) with the background color. Make sure your background color is white, then double-click on the Eraser tool. An alert box will appear, asking you to confirm that you wish to erase the entire image. Click OK to confirm.

Now that you've cleared the entire screen, let's assume you acted too rashly and shouldn't have erased the lines that have arrowheads. A handy feature of the Eraser tool, called the Magic Eraser (▣), will put a smile on your face in this situation. The Magic Eraser works like the File menu's Revert command, except that the Magic Eraser only reverts the part of your document that you click and drag over. As you can imagine, the Magic Eraser is an extremely handy feature for any Photoshop project.

To try out the Magic Eraser, press OPTION (PC users: ALT) while clicking and dragging with the Eraser tool over the bottom portion of your screen. At first, nothing will happen, but be patient—Photoshop is loading the previously saved version of the file (the one you named Bucket). In a few moments, you'll see parts of two lines reappearing. Keep clicking and dragging until you at least see the arrowheads. Notice that the Magic Eraser tool is not really erasing, but rather is reverting part of the image back to your last saved version.

When you are ready to proceed to the next section, close the file on screen. You don't need to save the changes because you won't use this file anymore.

INTRODUCTION TO THE PENCIL, PAINTBRUSH, AND EYEDROPPER TOOLS

In this section you will be introduced to the painting tools, the Pencil, Paintbrush, and Eyedropper. If you wish to create the File Manager with File Cabinet project in this chapter, these are the tools you'll use. The Pencil and Paintbrush tools let you paint with brushes from the Brushes palette. The Eyedropper tool aids you in changing foreground and background colors.

Start by creating a new file large enough for the next few practice exercises. Set both Width and Height to 5 inches, the resolution to 72 pixels/inch, and Mode to RGB Color. When you are ready to begin, click OK to display a new, untitled document.

Using the Pencil Tool to Draw and Erase

Photoshop's electronic Pencil tool is unlike any pencil you've ever used before. It not only emulates a real pencil but can also draw lines between mouse clicks and erase by painting with the background color. It also allows you to pick different "lead" sizes from the Brushes palette.

You may be surprised to learn that the Pencil tool's "lead," or stroke, is controlled by a brush chosen in the Brushes palette. This gives the Pencil tool tremendous versatility. When you use the Pencil tool, the stroke can be thick, thin, round, or square. The tool's smallest stroke is one pixel wide, which is handy for retouching images one pixel at a time.

Apart from retouching individual pixels, the Pencil tool can be used for freehand sketching. When you click and drag on the screen with the Pencil tool, it paints with the foreground color, using a stroke, opacity, and mode determined by the Brushes palette. No matter what the brush size or shape, the Pencil tool will always paint with a hard-edge brush—unlike the Paintbrush and Airbrush tools, which can paint with soft edges. To see this in action, activate the Pencil tool and draw a line by clicking and dragging on screen. The line is created with the foreground color and is the width of the currently active brush.

Now take a look at the features in the Pencil Options dialog box. As usual, to access the dialog box, double-click on the Pencil tool. Notice the Fade-out, Stylus Pressure, and Auto Erase options. (Fade-out and Stylus Pressure also appear in the dialog boxes for the Paintbrush and Airbrush tools.) The Fade-out options work similarly for the Pencil, Paintbrush, and Airbrush tools, and are covered later in this chapter when you learn how to use the Paintbrush and Airbrush tools.

```
========= Pencil Options =========

┌─ Fade-out ──────────────┐      ┌──────────┐
│ Distance: ┌──────┐      │      │    UK    │
│           └──────┘      │      └──────────┘
│   ○ To Transparent      │      ┌──────────┐
│   ○ To Background       │      │  Cancel  │
│                         │      └──────────┘
│                         │      ☐ Auto Erase
│                         │
├─ Stylus Pressure ───────┤
│ Uary: ☐ Size            │
│       ☐ Color           │
│       ☐ Opacity         │
└─────────────────────────┘
```

The Stylus Pressure Options

The Stylus Pressure options can only be activated if you have a stylus and graphics tablet connected to your computer. If you do have a stylus, these options are invaluable: You can control the size, color, and opacity of your painting by applying different amounts of pressure to the stylus.

Here are brief explanations of the Stylus Pressure options available for the Pencil, Paintbrush, and Airbrush tools:

Size   Select this check box, and you can control the size of your brush strokes by applying different pressure with the stylus. Light pressure creates a small brush stroke; heavy pressure creates a large brush stroke. (The Stylus Pressure options for the Airbrush tool do not include size.)

Color   Select this check box, and you can apply either the foreground color, the background color, or an *intermediate color*—a blend of the foreground and background colors. Applying heavy pressure administers the foreground color, applying light pressure administers the background color, and applying a medium amount of pressure administers an intermediate color.

Opacity   Select this check box, and you can use stylus pressure to control how opaque or transparent your brush strokes will be. The heavier the pressure, the more opaque the color; the lighter the pressure, the more translucent the color.

The various Stylus Pressure options shown in the following illustration were created with a Wacom stylus with the Pencil tool activated.

Size   Color   Opacity

The Auto Erase Option

The Auto Erase option in the Pencil Options dialog box allows the Pencil tool to work as an eraser. Remember, "erasing" in Photoshop means painting with the background color. Turning on the Auto Erase option triggers the Pencil tool to automatically switch to the background color when you paint over the foreground color.

Take a look at the Auto Erase feature in action.

1. If the Auto Erase option isn't selected, click the check box and then click OK to close the Pencil Options dialog box.

   Next, select a vivid color for the foreground color and its complement for the background color from the Colors palette. For instance, try blue as the foreground color and yellow as the background color.

2. If the Foreground selection box is not active in the Colors palette, click on it. To choose a blue foreground color, you can either click on the first blue swatch in the first row of the Colors palette, or move the hue (H) slider control to 240 degrees, with saturation (S) and brightness (B) set to 100%.

3. Click on the Background selection box in the Colors palette. To choose a yellow color, click on the yellow swatch in the first row of swatches, or move the H slider control to 60 degrees, with the S and B sliders set to 100%.

   After you've chosen your colors, the next step is to select a brush from the Brushes palette to set the brush stroke the Pencil tool will use.

4. Start with a large brush size, so the Pencil tool's stroke will be dramatic. Click on the largest brush in the first row of the Brushes palette. After you click, the brush will be outlined, indicating it is the active brush for the Pencil tool.

OTE: *Brushes that are too large to be depicted by icons in the Brushes palette are represented by a circle with a number inside, representing the pixel width of the brush's diameter.*

Now, with the Pencil tool's Auto Erase option enabled, create the word *ART*, using capital letters.

5. Begin by clicking and dragging to start creating the left, slanted side of the capital letter *A*. As you drag, the Pencil tool paints with the foreground color. Continue drawing the letter, creating the right, slanted side of the *A* and connecting the two slanted sides with the small crossbar. Now, as soon as the Pencil tool touches an area of the foreground color, the Auto Erase option causes the Pencil tool to paint with the background color.

When you've completed the letter *A*, start drawing the letter *R*. Immediately, the Pencil tool returns to the foreground color. As you draw the *R*, the Auto Erase feature causes the Pencil tool to switch to the background color whenever it touches the foreground color.

To create the letter *T*, try a different painting technique as a special effect: Instead of dragging with the mouse, create the *T* with mouse clicks. Begin by clicking once to create a foreground-colored spot, then move the mouse halfway into the colored spot and click again. This creates a background-colored spot. Keep using overlapping mouse clicks to gradually create the letter. When you've finished, the letter will be entirely created from Pencil marks alternating between the foreground and background colors.

SHIFT-Clicking with the Pencil Tool

After you've completed your penmanship exercise, turn off the Pencil tool's Auto Erase option and experiment with the SHIFT constraining option, which constrains all lines to 45-degree increments. Click on screen with the Pencil tool; then move the mouse to another area, press and hold SHIFT, and click again. The Pencil tool connects your mouse clicks.

When you're ready to move on to the next section and explore the Paintbrush tool, you'll need to clear your screen. But don't double-click on the Eraser tool yet, or you'll paint the entire screen with the current background color (yellow). First, reset the background color to white, and then double-click on the Eraser tool to clear the screen. Click OK to confirm.

 EMEMBER: *Double-clicking on the Eraser tool paints the document window with the background color.*

Painting with the Paintbrush Tool

 The Paintbrush tool is Photoshop's electronic version of an artist's paintbrush. The Paintbrush tool paints with the foreground color, using your choice of brush strokes. Using the tool's Fade-out options, you can also create colors that *fade out,* or dissolve, as you paint.

Like the Pencil tool, the Paintbrush tool allows you to connect painted brush strokes by pressing SHIFT while clicking the mouse. Unlike the Pencil tool, though, the Paintbrush tool offers soft brush strokes that simulate paint applied with a paintbrush. When you activate the Paintbrush, take a moment to examine the Brushes palette; it includes a row of soft-edged brushes that weren't available when you were using the Pencil tool.

Double-click on the Paintbrush tool to open the Paintbrush Options dialog box. You'll notice that the Paintbrush's options are almost identical to those of the Pencil tool, except that the Paintbrush does not have an Auto Erase feature. Both tools have the same Stylus Pressure controls, and both feature the Fade-out option. The choices in the Fade-out option allow you to create effects where the stroke you are painting gradually disappears (Fade-out To Transparent) or gradually turns into the background color (Fade-out To Background). In the Distance field you specify how many pixels the Paintbrush tool will paint before the fade-out begins.

```
═══════════ Paintbrush Options ═══════════
┌─ Fade-out ──────────────────┐   ┌────────┐
│ Distance: [        ]        │   │   OK   │
│      ○ To Transparent       │   └────────┘
│      ○ To Background        │   ┌────────┐
└─────────────────────────────┘   │ Cancel │
                                  └────────┘
┌─ Stylus Pressure ───────────┐
│ Vary:  ☐ Size               │
│        ☐ Color              │
│        ☐ Opacity            │
└─────────────────────────────┘
```

Beginning the Painter's Palette Exercise

As you work through the next few sections, you'll be performing the steps of an exercise to create a painter's palette like the one shown in Figure 5-2. Your experimentation with the Paintbrush tool's Fade-out options will be the start of the exercise. Since you'll begin by painting without a Fade-out option chosen, check to see that there is a value currently in the Fade-out Distance field. If there is, delete it

The
Painter's
Palette
exercise

FIGURE 5-2

now. When you are ready to continue, close the Paintbrush Options dialog box by clicking OK.

Before you start painting

1. Set the foreground color to a dark gray. In the Brushes palette, choose a medium, hard-edged brush from the second row of brushes. Click and drag the Opacity slider control to 100%, or press **0** on your keyboard.

2. Position the Paintbrush tool about .5 inches from the top of your screen, and click and drag to create a kidney shape, representing the palette. Refer to Figure 5-2 as a guide. To paint the handle hole in the middle of the palette, click and drag again with the Paintbrush in a circular motion.

   To create the paint dabs in the palette, use the Paintbrush's Fade-out To Transparent feature.

3. Double-click on the Paintbrush tool; in the dialog box, type **75** in the Distance field. If the To Transparent radio button is not selected, select it now. These settings will cause the painting color to fade out after 75 pixels. To accept the dialog box settings, click OK.

4. Create a couple of paint dabs in the painter's palette. Pick a foreground color, and choose a medium, soft-edged brush in the Brushes palette. Again using Figure 5-2 as your guide, click and drag with the Paintbrush tool in a circular motion in the palette. As you click and drag, the paint will gradually fade out. Do this one more time with another color to create another paint dab.

   To paint the small, waved lines in the upper-left part of the palette, you'll need to reset the Fade-out Distance option so the paint fades before you finish creating the lines.

5. Double-click on the Paintbrush tool to bring up the Paintbrush Options dialog box again, and type **35** in the Distance field and click OK. Set the foreground color, and then click and drag to create the two waved lines at the top-left side of the palette. You'll notice that the fade-out occurs as you're drawing these lines.

6. Click three times to apply three soft-edged dots adjacent to the handle hole. To finish up, draw two more short, straight lines at the top-right side of the palette. Your painter's palette should look similar to Figure 5-2.

Now assume that you want to add a few more artistic touches to the palette, with the same colors that you used to paint the lines and circles. For this, you need to use the Eyedropper tool.

Sampling Colors with the Eyedropper Tool

The Eyedropper tool doesn't paint, but is an invaluable tool in the painting process; it is used to *sample*, or read, an image's color so it can be used as the foreground or background color. With one quick click of the Eyedropper tool, the foreground or background color can be changed to the color of the pixel you clicked on with the tool. For example, it would be a lot of work to mix colors in the Colors palette to obtain a particular flesh tone that appears in a scanned image. With the Eyedropper tool, on the other hand, you need only click on that colored portion of the image, and Photoshop's foreground color instantly changes to the flesh tone you need. This technique is a tremendous time-saver when you are color correcting and retouching scanned color images.

Before trying out the Eyedropper tool, take a look at its options. Double-click on the Eyedropper tool to open the Eyedropper Options dialog box, and then click on the Sample Size pop-up menu.

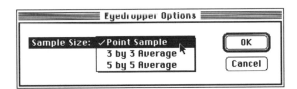

All of the Eyedropper options reside in the Sample Size pop-up. The default Sample Size setting is Point Sample, which narrows the Eyedropper's sample to the color value of the pixel on which you click. The 3 by 3 Average option reads the average color value of a 3-pixel-by-3-pixel area, and the 5 by 5 Average option operates similarly. To test the Eyedropper tool at its default setting, make sure the Sample Size option is set to Point Sample; then click OK to close the dialog box.

Changing the Foreground and Background Colors with the Eyedropper

Move the mouse pointer toward the first paint dab you created in the painter's palette. As you move the mouse into the document window, notice that the pointer changes to an eyedropper. (If CAPS LOCK is on, the pointer will be a crosshair, but it will still function as the Eyedropper tool.) Position the pointer over the first paint dab you created, but don't click the mouse yet. First, examine the color value readings in the Info palette.

The Info palette displays the color values of the pixels underlying the Eyedropper tool, using various color models. You can display one or two color model values at a time. If you will be sending your file to a printing press, it can be helpful to view CMYK colors at the same time as RGB or HSB colors are displayed. When CMYK colors are displayed in the Info palette, an exclamation point appears next to CMYK percentages that are out of gamut. As you paint and color correct, it's very helpful to have both RGB and CMYK colors on screen because you will have a readout of the primary colors and their complements.

Although it is helpful to view both RGB and CMYK color values in the Info palette, you can also change to HSB, Lab, or Grayscale by clicking on either of the eyedropper icons in the Info palette. When you click, the pop-up menu shown here will appear, allowing you to choose the Color model of your choice.

NOTE: *If you set both eyedropper icons in the Info palette to the same color model, the bottom eyedropper and color model readout will disappear. To return both eyedroppers to the Info palette, click on the top eyedropper icon, and choose another color model. You can also click on the Options menu arrow (PC users: Control menu button) and choose a second color model in the Info Options dialog box. Once two different color models are chosen, both color model readouts will appear in the Info palette.*

With the Eyedropper tool pointer positioned over the first paint dab that you created, click the mouse. Notice that the foreground color immediately changes to match the color you clicked on. To further test the Eyedropper's sampling power, move it to the outer edge of the paint dab circle, and click the mouse. The foreground color changes to a lighter shade, reflecting the color created by the Fade-out To Transparent option you used with the Paintbrush tool to make the paint dab.

OPTION-CLICKING (PC USERS: ALT-CLICKING) WITH THE EYEDROPPER   From time to time, you may wish to use the Eyedropper tool to change the background color when the Foreground selection box is activated in the Colors palette, or to change the foreground color when the Background selection box is activated. If the Foreground selection box is activated, you can change the background color by pressing OPTION (PC users: ALT) while clicking on a color in the image with the Eyedropper tool. If the Background selection box is activated, you can change the foreground color by pressing OPTION (PC users: ALT) while clicking on a color in the image with the Eyedropper tool.

Try this. Change the background color by pressing OPTION (PC users: ALT) and clicking with the Eyedropper tool on any colored element in the painter's palette you created.

IP: *The designers of Photoshop recognized the tremendous value of the Eyedropper tool and made it readily available for changing the foreground color. Press OPTION (PC users: ALT) while using the Pencil, Line, Paintbrush, Paint Bucket, Airbrush, or Gradient tools, and that tool will change to the Eyedropper tool. Many experienced Photoshop users take full advantage of this feature by using it with the Colors palette's scratch pad area, as explained in the following section.*

Using the Eyedropper Tool and the Scratch Pad Together

The scratch pad in the Colors palette is the large square to the left of the color sliders. Here you can test colors, brush strokes, blends, and special effects without altering your document. You can also use the scratch pad in conjunction with the Eyedropper tool as a holding area for colors you wish to keep readily accessible.

Scratch pad

Suppose you wish to use a few of the fade-out colors from the painter's palette over and over again. One way to facilitate this is by first transferring a color into the Foreground selection box using the Eyedropper tool, and then dropping the color into the scratch pad with the Paintbrush tool. Here's how to do this without having to go to the Toolbox more than once. Click on the Paintbrush tool to activate it. Then press and hold OPTION (PC users: ALT), which switches you to the Eyedropper tool, and move the eyedropper to the edge of one of the paint dabs on the palette. To change the foreground color to the color of the paint dab, continue to hold OPTION (PC users: ALT) and click. Next, to place that color in the scratch pad, first release OPTION (PC users: ALT) so that the Paintbrush pointer returns. Position the

Paintbrush pointer over the scratch pad in the Colors palette and click. You have now copied a color from your image into the scratch pad. To practice, try the same technique with another color.

While you work on a project, you can add more colors into the scratch pad. You can even drop colors of varying opacities into the scratch pad to mix and test them. You can then easily access any of them when you need them by changing the foreground color to one of the "custom" colors, as described next.

To change the foreground color to a color from the scratch pad, first press OPTION (PC users: ALT) to turn the Paintbrush tool into the Eyedropper tool. Position the eyedropper over the desired color in the scratch pad and click. The foreground color changes to the color you clicked in the scratch pad.

Close the painter's palette image now, and save it with an appropriate file name if you wish to use it again.

THE FILE MANAGER WITH FILE CABINET PROJECT

Before proceeding to learn about more painting tools, you may wish to practice using the painting tools that have been covered so far. Using the Line, Paintbrush, Pencil, and Paint Bucket tools, you can create the image shown in Figure 5-3. You'll start by creating the file cabinet first, then create the file manager character in another file, which will then be pasted into the file cabinet file. Although the steps are detailed as follows, feel free to improvise and experiment as you work.

The File Manager with File Cabinet project

FIGURE 5-3

1. Create a new file, 7 inches wide and 5 inches high. (This size will accommodate both the file cabinet and the file manager character.) Set the resolution to 72 ppi and Mode to RGB Color.

OTE: *If you wish to use this or any of the other images in this chapter as the basis for a project that you will output professionally, you'll probably want to use a resolution higher than 72 ppi. Make sure that you have enough memory to handle the file size—a 5 by 7 inch RGB file at 300 ppi consumes 9MB as compared to 532K at 72 ppi.*

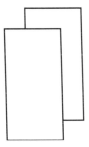

2. Your first step is to use the Rectangular Marquee tool and the Edit/Stroke command to create a rectangle. In the Stroke dialog box, set Width to 2 pixels and Location to Inside. After the first rectangle is stroked, don't deselect. Duplicate the rectangle by pressing OPTION (PC users: ALT) while you click and drag on a selection edge. Drag downwards and to the left so that your image looks like the illustration shown here.

3. Use the Line tool with a 2-pixel width to connect the two offset rectangles to create a three-dimensional effect. Next, use the Paint Bucket tool to fill the side of the file cabinet. Make sure that no gaps appear in the outline of the area you are filling; otherwise the Paint Bucket tool will spread paint over the entire image. Clean up the image by removing any unwanted lines with the Eraser tool.

4. Once you have the basic structure of the cabinet created, use the Rectangular Marquee tool and the Edit/Stroke command to create two rectangles for the file cabinet drawers. Duplicate the top drawer rectangle and offset (as you did with the rectangles to create the file cabinet).

5. Use the Line tool to create a three-dimensional effect for the top drawer, and fill with the Paint Bucket tool to create a shadow along the side.

Again, use the Eraser tool to remove any unwanted lines. Then use the Line tool with a 75% opacity to create the drawer handles. To create the file folders in the cabinet, draw lines with a 50% opacity setting. Your image should look similar to this:

6. When you've completed the filing cabinet, save the file and name it **Cabinet**.

Creating the File Manager Character

Follow these steps to create the file manager character shown in Figure 5-3.

1. Create a new file, with the width and height both set to 5 inches. This should provide enough room to work with the file manager character, which will be about 4 inches by 4 inches.

2. Use the Elliptical Marquee and Rectangular Marquee tools and the Edit/Stroke command to create simple shapes, as shown here, to use as a rough guide for the file manager.

3. After creating the foundation for the character, use the Paintbrush tool to paint in details. Use the Eraser tool to erase any of the unwanted foundation lines that remain. Choose the color you want for the mouth, nose, eyes, ears, and hair.

4. Use the Pencil tool to create details in the shirt—the buttons, cuffs, and cuff links. Then, use the Pencil tool with your choice of colors to add the pocket, pencil, and bow tie.

5. Use the Paintbrush tool to paint in the hands. Create the disk with the Pencil tool, then continue using the Pencil tool to outline the character's pants.

6. Fill in the pants using the Paint Bucket tool. Again, when you fill them in, make sure that no gaps appear in the outline of the area you are filling; otherwise the Paint Bucket will spread paint over the entire image.

When you are satisfied with the file manager's appearance, save your work. Now you're ready to copy the file manager character into the file cabinet document.

Pasting the File Manager into the File Cabinet File

In this section, you'll use the Magic Wand tool to select the white background of the file manager character and then invert the selection so that you can copy the image.

1. With the file manager character on screen, double-click on the Magic Wand tool. To ensure that you will only select the white background, type **0** in the Tolerance field. Click OK. Next, click on the white background; only the background should be selected. Choose Inverse from the Select menu; now only the file manager character should be selected.

2. From the Edit menu, select Copy. Close the Manager file and open the Cabinet file.

3. Select Paste from the Edit menu, and the file manager character will appear in the Cabinet document.

4. While the character is still floating, click and drag it to a suitable position, as shown in Figure 5-3. Lock the character into position by choosing None from the Select menu.

5. To save your work, use the Save As command and name your file **FileMan** so you can keep the original Cabinet file intact.

You now have three files on your disk: the original file, Cabinet; the original file, Manager; and the final project file, FileMan. By keeping the original Cabinet and Manager files, you can always edit them and then re-create the final project.

Now that you've mastered Photoshop's basic painting tools, you are ready to progress to more advanced painting tools and techniques.

INTRODUCTION TO THE AIRBRUSH TOOL

The Airbrush tool is an electronic version of the mechanical airbrush that artists use to create three-dimensional shading effects. The tool is also used to soften images with a hint of color. In retouching and painting work, the Airbrush tool is often the best tool for adding highlights and shadows.

The Airbrush tool paints in much the same manner as the Paintbrush tool, except the Airbrush colors with a softer edge. Like the Pencil and Paintbrush, the Airbrush allows you to pick from a variety of brushes from the Brushes palette. Unlike the other tools, however, the Opacity slider in the Brushes palette is not available with Airbrush; instead, you have a Pressure slider. The greater the pressure setting, the more paint that gets sprayed when you click and hold down the mouse button.

Brushes	▶
Normal ▼	Pressure: 100% △

In this section you will experiment with the Airbrush tool and its Fade-out options. In order to perform the exercises, create a new file 6 inches wide by 4 inches high. This is the size you will need to accommodate the Summer Sale Postcard project (shown in Figure 5-4) after the introductory exercises.

Click now on the Airbrush tool to activate it. For the foreground color, choose any color swatch in the Colors palette. From the Brushes palette, pick a large, soft-edged brush. Examine the Pressure slider; if it is not set to 100%, click on the slider control and drag all the way to the right.

Now move the mouse pointer toward the document area. As you move, the pointer changes to an airbrush. (If CAPS LOCK is on, your pointer will be a crosshair, but the tool will still work as the Airbrush.)

Move the Airbrush pointer anywhere in the document. Click the mouse and keep it pressed for a second or two. Notice that paint keeps spilling out. Now click and drag slowly for a few inches to see the soft, diffused spray created by the tool.

To observe the effects of painting with a lower pressure, click and drag the Pressure slider control in the Brushes palette to 50%. Move the Airbrush pointer back into the document, and click and hold the mouse button. This time, less paint is sprayed by the brush onto the screen.

Continue experimenting with the Airbrush tool, choosing various brush sizes and pressure settings. When you're ready, continue to the next section and explore the Airbrush's Fade-out options.

The Airbrush Fade-out Options

To open the Airbrush Options dialog box, double-click on the Airbrush tool. Notice that the options here are very similar to those for the Paintbrush and Pencil tools. The Fade-out options for the Airbrush work exactly as they do with the Paintbrush and Pencil. You'll remember them—they are Fade-out To Transparent and Fade-out

To Background. When one of these options is selected, painting starts with the foreground color and fades out to either a completely transparent color or to the background color. The Fade-out Distance field controls how much paint appears before the fade-out occurs. For both Fade-out options, the brush size you choose in the Brushes palette controls the width of the fade-out.

```
╔══════════════ Airbrush Options ══════════════╗
║  ┌─ Fade-out ─────────────┐                   ║
║  │ Distance: [        ]    │   ┌──────────┐   ║
║  │                         │   │    OK    │   ║
║  │   ○ To Transparent      │   └──────────┘   ║
║  │   ○ To Background       │   ┌──────────┐   ║
║  │                         │   │  Cancel  │   ║
║  └─────────────────────────┘   └──────────┘   ║
║  ┌─ Stylus Pressure ──────┐                   ║
║  │ Vary:  ☐ Color          │                  ║
║  │        ☐ Pressure       │                  ║
║  └─────────────────────────┘                  ║
╚═══════════════════════════════════════════════╝
```

To try out the Fade-out options, type **100** in the Distance field of the Airbrush Options dialog box. Click on the To Transparent radio button and then click OK. In the Brushes palette, choose a medium, soft-edged brush with Pressure set to 100%. Change the foreground color, if you wish. To see the fade-out, click and drag in a spiral motion. As you drag you'll see a soft edged brush stroke that gradually fades out after 100 pixels of paint have been applied.

Next, try the Fade-out To Background option. Return to the dialog box by double-clicking on the Airbrush tool. This time, click on the To Background radio button. Leave the Distance set to 100. This will make it easier to compare the difference between the To Transparent and To Background fade-outs.

Before you begin to paint, set the foreground color to green and the background color to yellow. These two colors are near each other on the color wheel, and so there won't be a great contrast as one switches to the other. The fade-out effect will appear smoother and more realistic. Keep Brightness and Saturation set high to ensure that the colors will be bright. Now click and drag to create another spiral on screen. This time, the green, soft-edged brush stroke will gradually dissolve into the yellow you picked as the background color.

If you wish to keep experimenting, use a few other color pairs. Try working with colors that are near each other on the Hue slider, and then compare the effects to what you get when you pick a color and its complement, such as blue and yellow.

Before you continue to the next section, set the background color back to white and clear the screen by double-clicking on the Eraser. Click OK to confirm.

Photoshop in Action

The flaring light effect was created by applying the Lens Flare filter in the Filter/Stylize submenu.

The Airbrush tool was used to create the glow effects in the planet and in the arm.

©ER/VEGA

Artist: Enrique Rivera-Vega   Promotional Material

Enrique began this image by creating two rectangular selections. He filled the bottom selection with color, then applied the Add Noise filter to create a gravelly texture in the foreground. He filled the top selection with black, then used the Airbrush tool to create the lighter areas in the dark background. Next, Enrique created a circular selection for the planet, then used the Airbrush again to create the different lighting effects within it.

The robot was first sketched with the Pencil tool, then filled using the Paintbrush and Airbrush tools. All of the glow effects were created with the Airbrush tool.

THE SUMMER SALE POSTCARD PROJECT

If you'd like to practice using the Airbrush tool, try your hand at creating the Summer Sale postcard, shown in Figure 5-4. This project was designed to convey a feeling of lightness and delicacy to match the type of clothes people buy in the summer. In order to create this mood, a very soft brush stroke was needed, one that would taper off. The Airbrush tool is perfect for the job.

Creating the Sun

The first step in this project is creating the sun. You'll use the Airbrush tool with both the Fade-out To Background and Fade-out To Transparent options. Using both Fade-out options adds variety and realism, as they are perfect for giving a soft edge to the sun and for blending its colors from yellow to orange.

1. Double-click on the Airbrush tool. In the Fade-out Distance field, type **200**. Select the To Background radio button. Click OK.

2. In the Brushes palette, pick any small, soft-edged brush.

3. In the Colors palette, choose an orange foreground color and a yellow background color.

4. Now create the spiral that is the center of the sun by clicking and dragging in a spiral motion.

The
Summer
Sale
Postcard
project

FIGURE 5-4

5. Return to the Airbrush Options dialog box and switch to the Fade-out To Transparent option to create the rays of the sun. Type **10** in the Distance field. Click OK.

6. In the Brushes palette, pick a medium, soft-edged brush.

7. Position the mouse at the edge of the sun's spiral, and click and drag outward to create several rays, as shown in Figure 5-4.

8. Save your work and name the file **Summer.**

Creating the Butterfly

In this section, you'll continue using the Airbrush to create the butterfly on the Summer Sale postcard.

1. Double-click on the Airbrush tool and delete whatever value is in the Fade-out Distance field. Click OK.

2. Click on the Default Colors icon to reset the foreground to black and the background to white. In the Brushes palette, set the Pressure to 25% and choose a small brush.

3. Use the Airbrush to sketch an outline of a short ellipse and a long ellipse for the butterfly's body. Then create the outline of the wings.

4. Once you've sketched the outline of the butterfly, paint the wings using various shades of blue. Use different Pressure settings in the Brushes palette and different Fade-out options in the Airbrush Options dialog box.

5. When you have finished coloring the wings, you are ready to fill in the body of the butterfly. Use the Fade-out To Transparent option with Pressure set to 30%, but change the foreground color to black and choose a medium, soft-edged brush.

6. Now apply the finishing touches. Create the black strokes for texture in the butterfly's body, wings, eyes, and antennae by airbrushing with a small, hard-edged brush and Pressure set to 90%.

Feel free to continue to experiment with different colors and effects in the butterfly. If you try something and don't like the results, use the Undo command.

Also, don't forget that you can activate the Magic Eraser to revert a portion of your document to the last saved version.

Creating the Text and Clothing Items

The next step in the postcard project is using the Type tool to add the words, SUMMER SALE. Remember, when you use the Type tool, Photoshop paints using the current foreground color and current opacity setting in the Brushes palette.

1. Activate the Type tool and click in the upper-left side of your document window.

2. In the Type dialog box, choose Times (or another typeface) in the Font pop-up menu. Type **40** in the Size field. Make sure the Anti-Aliased check box is selected. In the text field, type **SUMMER SALE.** To have Photoshop drop the type into your painting, click OK.

3. While the text is floating, move it into position by clicking and dragging in the middle of the text. Do not deselect.

4. Try creating a special effect in the text by changing the foreground color and using the Airbrush tool to apply another color. When you paint over selected text, Photoshop applies the color to the text only, not to the underlying pixels. With the Airbrush tool, dab a bright color over the SUMMER SALE letters to create highlights.

5. To finish off the project, create the clothes and the hangers. Draw the hangers with the Pencil tool, and then paint the clothes over them; use the Airbrush and Paintbrush tools with whatever colors you like. If you wish, add more items.

When you're satisfied with your work on the Summer Sale postcard project, save and close the file.

INTRODUCTION TO THE GRADIENT TOOL AND CUSTOM BRUSHES

In this section, you'll learn how to create blends and custom brushes. A *blend* is a gradual transition from the foreground to background color. A *custom brush* is a brush you create by specifying its size, shape, and other characteristics. After you create a custom brush, Photoshop automatically adds it to the Brushes palette.

To get started, create a new file 6 inches wide by 4 inches high. You'll use this file for both the introductory exercises and for the final project. The file resolution should be set to 72 and the mode to RGB Color.

Using the Gradient Tool to Create Blends

The Gradient tool allows you to fill the screen or a selection with a blend that gradually changes from the foreground color to the background color. Blends are frequently used to produce shading and lighting effects, as well as to quickly create visually pleasing backgrounds. By changing opacity and/or painting mode settings in the Brushes palette, you can create interesting effects by applying blends over images and over other blends.

To access the Gradient Tool Options dialog box, double-click on the Gradient tool icon in the Toolbox.

```
╔══════════ Gradient Tool Options ══════════╗
║  ┌─ Style ─────────────────────┐           ║
║  │ ⦿ Normal                    │  ┌──────┐ ║
║  │ ○ Clockwise Spectrum        │  │  OK  │ ║
║  │ ○ Counterclockwise Spectrum │  └──────┘ ║
║  └─────────────────────────────┘  ┌──────┐ ║
║                                   │Cancel│ ║
║  ┌─ Type ──────────────────────┐  └──────┘ ║
║  │ ⦿ Linear                    │           ║
║  │ ○ Radial                    │           ║
║  └─────────────────────────────┘           ║
║                                            ║
║  Midpoint Skew: [ 50 ] %                   ║
║  Radial Offset: [    ] %                   ║
╚════════════════════════════════════════════╝
```

The Gradient Tool Style Options

The Style options in the Gradient Tool Options dialog box determine how colors are used in the blend. If Normal is selected, Photoshop will blend the colors, creating a smooth transition between the foreground and background colors. The next two options, Clockwise Spectrum and Counterclockwise Spectrum, alter the blend so the colors change from foreground to background, using the colors in the color wheel in either a clockwise or counterclockwise direction.

CAUTION: *Be aware that various factors may affect the way a blend prints. The blend's printed output will depend on the colors you use, the length of the blend, the file mode you are in, and the resolution at which you are printing. For more information about printing blends, see Chapter 14.*

The Linear Gradient Option

The Linear option for the Gradient tool creates a blend along a straight line. The blend is created from the point where you start clicking and dragging the mouse and ends where you release the mouse.

The Midpoint Skew field at the bottom of the dialog box determines where the blend begins to change from the foreground to background color. The default Midpoint Skew value is 50%; if you type in a larger number, the blend will be produced with more foreground color than background color. Enter a smaller number, and the blend will be created with less foreground color and more background color.

You can specify where you want the blend to occur by selecting an area on screen with one of the selection tools before you create the blend. You can even create a blend inside text by clicking and dragging with the Gradient tool over floating text. If you don't designate a selection or create the blend over floating type, the entire screen will be filled with the blend.

Try creating a blend that will simulate a change in lighting. To produce a blend for a lighting effect, you don't want to pick colors that contrast too much. Choose a yellow foreground color (the first yellow color swatch in the Colors palette). For the background color, lower the Hue slider about 20 degrees. This will produce an orange color.

1. You'll create the blend in a rectangular selection, so activate the Rectangular Marquee tool. Click and drag to create a rectangle about 2.5 inches wide by 2 inches high.

2. Double-click on the Gradient tool, and make sure that Style is set to Normal, Type is set to Linear, and Midpoint Skew is set to 50%. Click OK.

3. Now create a gradient that starts on the left with the foreground color and blends to the right into the background color. Position the crosshair about .5 inches inside the selection. Click and drag from left to right—the direction in which you want the blend to go. As you drag, Photoshop will create a line on screen indicating where the blend will be created. To

produce the blend, release the mouse about .5 inches away from the right side of the selection.

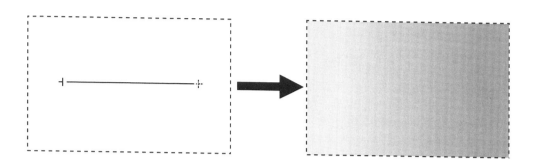

Notice that the blend appears between the two endpoints of your mouse selection. Photoshop fills the area directly before the blend with the solid foreground color and the area after the blend with solid background color. To get a sense of how Photoshop fills in the intermediate colors, open the Info palette (if it isn't already open), slowly move the mouse pointer over the blend from left to right, without clicking, and watch the color values gradually change.

If you'd like to experiment with a few more linear blends, clear your screen first; then try adjusting the Midpoint Skew setting in the Gradient Tool Options dialog box, and create another blend. You also might want to try some *angled blends*. This is easily done by clicking and dragging at an angle with the Gradient tool. You can even hold down the constraining SHIFT key to create blends at a 45-degree diagonal. After you've created a few more blends, continue on to the next section to create a radial gradient.

TIP: *If you wish to test a blend without altering your document, create it in the scratch pad of the Colors palette. After setting the foreground and background color and the Gradient tool options, click and drag with the Gradient tool in the scratch pad. To erase the scratch pad, first change the background color to white, and then create a rectangular selection over the scratch pad. Click and drag to move the selection out of the scratch pad, and the scratch pad will be painted white. A slower method is to click and drag over the scratch pad with the Eraser tool.*

The Radial Gradient Option

The Radial option for the Gradient tool is similar to a linear blend, except the radial blend radiates outward from a central starting point.

Try creating a radial blend in a circular selection.

1. Activate the Elliptical Marquee tool, and then click and drag to create a circular selection.

2. Double-click on the Gradient tool to open the Gradient Tool Options dialog box, and click on the Radial radio button in the Type section. Click OK.

To create the blend, position the mouse in the center of your elliptical selection. Click and drag in any direction toward the edge of the elliptical selection. This time Photoshop creates the blend radiating out from the center, instead of in a straight line.

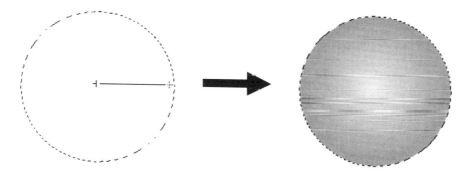

At this point you'll probably want to do some experimenting with radial blends. If you wish, you can also try out various settings for the Radial Offset option (at the bottom of the Gradient Tool Options dialog box). The Radial Offset percentage controls the distance from the start of the blend, where the foreground color is displayed as a solid color. For example, a radial offset of 25% makes the solid foreground color appear for 25% of the distance from the starting point to the end of the blend.

IP: *If you create a blend with an opacity less than 100% over an image, the underlying object will appear through the translucent blend.*

CREATING A GLOWING PLANET EFFECT   Here's how you can use the Gradient tool's Radial Offset option with the Elliptical Marquee's Feather Radius option to create a glowing planet effect.

1. Start by choosing a reddish foreground color and a reddish-yellow background color.

2. Double-click on the Gradient tool and choose the Radial option. Leave Midpoint Skew set at 50%. Change Radial Offset to 60%. Click OK.

3. Double-click on the Elliptical Marquee tool. Click on the Constrained Aspect Ratio radio button, and set Width to 1 and Height to 1. Set the Feather Radius to 15. Click OK.

4. Now click and drag on screen with the Elliptical Marquee tool to create the circular selection.

5. Activate the Gradient tool and position the crosshair in the center of the selection. Click and drag toward the edge of the circular selection. When you release the mouse, the blend will be created with a large central red area. The Radial Offset setting of 60% is responsible for creating this red mass in the circle. The Feather Radius setting creates the soft edge of the blend.

Before continuing, reset the Elliptical Marquee tool to Normal and change the Feather Radius to 0.

Creating and Using Custom Brushes

Thus far in this chapter, you've been using the default brushes that appear automatically in Photoshop's Brushes palette. But it's likely you will want to create your own custom brushes to add more variety and style to your work, and this section tells you how. You'll also learn how to save a palette of custom brushes and load it from your hard disk.

Examining the New Brush Dialog Box

You'll start by creating a new brush based on one of the brushes already in the Brushes palette. You'll use a large brush as the model because its diameter, hardness, and roundness attributes will be more noticeable than those of a smaller one. Click once on the largest, hard-edged brush in the first row of the Brushes palette.

Photoshop in Action

The light beams were created with linear blends

The lighting effects under the plane were created with blends

The Airbrush tool was used to create the the movie marquee lights

Artist: Leslie Carbaga   Art Director: Ron Kellum   Client: Vision Cable of South Carolina

Leslie created this image for a pay-per-view advertisement. The outline for the image was sketched in Adobe Illustrator, then placed in Photoshop.

Using the Pen tool, Leslie created paths to outline each part of the image, then converted each path into a selection. Most of the lighting effects were created using the Gradient tool to produce blends in the different selections.

Leslie then touched up the image by using the Airbrush tool to paint the lights in the movie marquee and to fill the area under the marquee.

Your next step in creating a new brush is to choose the New Brush command in the Options menu (PC users: Control menu) of the Brushes palette. The New Brush dialog box will appear, with the settings for the brush that was selected in the Brushes palette. In the dialog box you'll see there are sliders for controlling Diameter, Hardness, and Spacing, and boxes for entering Angle degrees and Roundness percentages.

Angle/Roundness
preview box

Diameter/Hardness
preview box

DIAMETER   Start by exploring the Diameter setting, which determines the size of the brush. To change this, click and drag the slider control, or type a value (in pixels) into the Diameter field. Try clicking and dragging the slider control to the right. As you drag, watch the preview box in the lower-right corner of the dialog box. It may take a moment or two, but eventually a preview of the new brush size will appear. As you drag the slider to the right, the brush's diameter grows. Change the diameter to 29. If you make it any larger, the brush's representation in the Brushes palette will be replaced by a number.

HARDNESS   Now test the Hardness slider, which controls whether the brush paints with a soft or hard edge. This value is a percentage of the center of the brush. The best way to visualize this is to gradually drag the Hardness slider to the left and stop at every 25% interval to watch the changes in the preview box. As you drag, you'll see a light shade surrounding the brush gradually grow. This shading indicates the soft area of the brush. Drag all the way to 0% to see the preview of the softest setting. In the Hardness field, 0% produces the softest brush, 100% the hardest.

SPACING   Next, test the Spacing option, which controls the distance the brush paints as make you make a stroke. The Spacing option is turned off or on with a check box.

 When the Spacing option is on, the distance you set with the slider (or typed in the Spacing field) is a percentage of the brush's diameter. Thus, when Spacing is set at 100%, the brush will leave dabs of paint spaced the same distance apart as the brush's diameter. The largest value you can enter is 999%.

When the Spacing option is off, the brush's stroke is controlled by your mouse or stylus dragging speed. Drag slowly, and more pixels on screen are absorbed with paint; drag quickly, and the brush jumps over pixels.

Turn the New Brush Spacing option on and set the value to 300%, a change that will be easily seen when you start painting with your custom brush.

5

ANGLE AND ROUNDNESS   The next two options in the Brushes palette, Angle and Roundness, work together. The Angle setting changes the brush shape only if Roundness is *not* set to 100%. (A roundness setting of 100% produces a circular brush.) Therefore, start by changing the brush shape from a circle to an ellipse.

You can change the roundness by either typing a value in the Roundness field or by clicking and dragging either of the two dots in the preview box in the lower-left corner of the dialog box. So, to create an elliptical brush, you would click and drag one of the two dots toward the other one. As you drag, you will decrease the percentage of roundness. The lower the percentage of roundness, the more elliptical your brush will be.

Once you've created the elliptical brush, you can change the Angle setting; you either type in a value between -180 and 180 degrees, or click and drag on the arrowed axis line in the preview box.

Now try this out: Change the Angle value to create a brush that will be dramatically different from the original one. Set the Angle to 45 degrees and the Roundness to 40%. Notice that both preview boxes reflect the changes. Before closing the New Brush dialog box, examine all the settings of your custom brush. Diameter should be 29 pixels, Hardness 0%, Spacing 300%, Angle 45%, and Roundness 40%. Click OK to accept the settings. Your new brush appears in the bottom row of the Brushes palette.

Angle: 45 °
Roundness: 40 %

Experiment with your custom brush using the Paintbrush tool. Click on the tool, and then activate the custom brush in the Brushes palette. Click and drag on screen to test it. You'll see that the brush paints a stroke at an angle of 45 degrees and creates a dotted effect, as shown here, because of the Spacing setting in the New Brush dialog box. This brush stroke was created with the following settings: Hardness 0%, Spacing 300%, Angle 45 degrees, and Roundness 40%.

Now return to your new brush's settings and change the Spacing and Hardness options. To do this, double-click in the Brushes palette on the brush you just created. Change Spacing to 25% and set Hardness to 100%. To accept the new settings, click OK. To see the change, try painting once again with your custom brush. As you paint, you'll see the brush now has a hard-edged stroke, and the white spaces between the brush strokes have disappeared. This brush stroke was created from these settings: Hardness 100%, Spacing 25%, Angle 45 degrees, and Roundness 40%.

If you wish to continue experimenting, try turning off the Spacing option by deselecting the Spacing check box in the New Brush dialog box. Try a few quick brush strokes and then a very slow brush stroke. You'll see that when you paint slowly, more paint is absorbed by the pixels on screen. When you paint faster, fewer pixels are filled in.

Defining a Custom Brush

With Photoshop you can design unusual custom brushes, something only an electronic painting program could produce. In this next example, you'll create a brush using the Type tool. Instead of using the New Brush command in the Brushes palette Options menu, you'll use the Define Brush command, which turns a selection or floating text into a brush. To demonstrate this, try creating a custom brush out of the dollar sign character on the keyboard. This will allow you to paint dollar signs on the screen with the painting tools.

1. To begin, activate the Type tool and click anywhere in your document. In the Type Tool dialog box, choose any font from the pop-up menu; then type **24** in the Size field and type $ in the text box. Click OK to make the text appear on screen.

2. While the dollar sign is floating, choose Define Brush from the Options pop-up menu (PC users: Control menu) in the Brushes palette. A $ (dollar sign) should appear in the Brushes palette.

3. Double-click on this brush in the Brushes palette. Notice that your options for altering the brush have been changed: Spacing and Anti-aliased are the only choices available. (The Anti-aliased option is only available for small brush sizes.) Before you close the Brush Options dialog box, feel free to change the settings if you wish.

4. To use your new brush, activate a painting tool and then select the $ (dollar sign) brush. All you need to do now is just click on the screen, and the dollar sign will appear in the current foreground color.

You can purchase different typefaces that are symbols and/or ornaments and use them to create different custom brushes. (These typefaces include Dingbats, Carta, Sonata, Wood, and Wingdings.) For example, if you are using the Dingbat font, you can create star (★ ☆), snowflake (❄), sun (☉), flower (❁), and heart (♥) brushes. To create stars, press SHIFT-H or SHIFT-P. Press the letter f to create a snowflake Dingbat. Press the letter b to create a sun. To create a flower, press SHIFT-MINUS. To create a heart, press OPTION-2 (PC users: ALT and type **0164** on the numeric keypad).

IP: *In addition to using the Type tool to create custom brushes, you can create custom brushes from any selected object on screen. It doesn't matter what tool you use to create the object, or whether the image was created from scratch or digitized.*

You can also create, select, and define brushes in the Colors palette's scratch pad. Just type a letter, or paint an object, or copy an item into the scratch pad. If the item isn't selected, use a selection tool to select it. While the item is selected in the scratch pad, choose Define Brush from the Brushes palette Options menu (PC users: Control menu).

Continue experimenting, creating various custom brushes using the techniques described in this section. When you are done, proceed to the next section to learn how to save your custom brushes.

Saving and Loading Custom Brushes

If you like the custom brushes you create and wish to use them again, you can save the entire Brushes palette to disk. When you need it again, you can load the palette from the disk.

To save your Brushes palette, including all the custom brushes you have designed, select Save Brushes from the Brushes palette Options menu (PC users: Control menu). To keep all of your custom brushes together, it might be a good idea to save them in the Brushes & Patterns folder (PC users: brushes) within the Adobe Photoshop folder (PC users: Photoshop). When you install Photoshop, the Brushes & Patterns folder (PC users: brushes) is automatically installed. Once you've located the folder, name your brush palette **MyBrush** and click Save.

n OTE: *If you wish to add custom brushes that already exist in a saved brushes file to the current Brushes palette on screen, use the Append Brushes command in the Brushes palette's Options menu (PC users: Control menu) of the Brushes palette.*

Incidentally, since you've opened Photoshop's Brushes & Patterns folder, take a look at the custom brushes Adobe includes with Photoshop. Within this folder are three different brush files: Assorted Brushes, Drop Shadow Brushes, and Default Brushes (PC users: custom.abr, shadows.abr, and default.abr files).

Once you've saved a custom brush file, when you want to load it just select Load Brushes from the Brushes palette Options menu (PC users: Control menu). For example, in the Load Brushes dialog box, locate the Adobe Photoshop 2.5 folder (PC users: Photoshop), and open it if it isn't already opened. Then open the folder called Brushes & Patterns (PC users: brushes) if it isn't already opened. Inside this folder you will see the brush files. Click on the Assorted Brushes file (PC users:

custom.abr) and open it. The brushes in the Brushes palette have now changed. Your Brushes palette should now look like this:

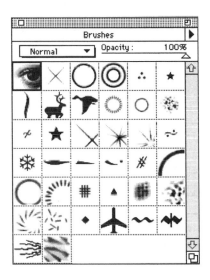

Take a few moments to experiment with the various brushes.

 OTE: *Whenever you wish to return the default Brushes palette to the screen, load the Default Brushes file (PC users: default.abr) from the Brushes & Patterns folder (PC users: brushes).*

This concludes the exercises and projects for the painting tools and techniques. In the next section, you'll learn about changing painting modes.

PAINTING MODES

In the Brushes palette, you can choose from a wide range of color-painting modes. These modes are generally used to change colors and create special effects when painting, or when pasting or painting over previously colored areas. How those areas are affected depends upon the painting mode, the color being applied, and the range of pixels that are painted or pasted over. For instance, if you apply a red color to an image in Darken mode, only the underlying pixels that are lighter than red will be darkened with the red color. If you paint in Lighten mode, only pixels darker than your red will be lightened by the red color.

In addition to the Brushes palette, painting modes appear in the dialog boxes for the Edit/Fill, Edit/Stroke, and Edit/Composite Controls commands, and for the Fill Path option in the Paths palette. (You'll learn about Paths in Chapter 10, and how to use the Composite Control dialog box in Chapter 11.)

This section describes the fundamental purpose of each painting mode. As you work through this book, you'll gain experience with all the painting modes and see how they can produce effects from simple to startling. At the conclusion of this section, you'll have a chance to create some special effects using the Lighten and Darken painting modes.

Here are basic descriptions of the painting modes:

Normal   This painting mode modifies every underlying pixel with the color being applied. In Normal mode, with Opacity set to 100%, underlying pixels will be completely replaced with the color being applied. If Opacity is less than 100%, the color of underlying pixels will show through the color being applied.

Darken   Only colors lighter than the color you are applying are affected, causing them to be darkened by the painting color.

Lighten   This mode is the opposite of Darken mode. Only colors darker than the color you are applying are modified. The darker colors are lightened by the painting color.

Hue   When you apply color in Hue mode, only the Hue values of underlying pixels will change. Thus, only the hue of the affected pixels are modified by the painting color, but not their Saturation and Luminosity values. Applying colors to black or white pixels in Hue mode will have no effect.

Saturation   When you apply color in Saturation mode, only the Saturation values of underlying pixels will change. Applying colors to black or white pixels in Saturation mode will have no effect.

Color   In this mode, the Hue and Saturation values of pixels will change, but not Luminosity. The Color mode is frequently used to colorize gray or monochrome images because underlying shadows and contours will show through the color that is being applied. The effect is similar to colorizing old black-and-white movies. This technique is demonstrated in Chapter 9.

 OTE: *If you wish to colorize a grayscale file, you must convert the file to Color mode using the Mode menu. For more information about changing modes, see Chapter 9.*

Luminosity   Luminosity measures a color's brightness. In Luminosity mode, the lightness and darkness values of a color's pixels will change, but the color values won't. The Luminosity mode is the opposite of the Color mode.

Photoshop's internal formula for computing a pixel's luminosity is

30% of Red value + 59% of Green value + 11% of Blue value

This formula always produces a number between 0 and 255. The closer a number is to 255, the closer the luminosity is to white; the lower the number, the closer the luminosity is to black. By analyzing the formula, you can see that colors with a high green content will produce a brighter effect. When you apply color in Luminosity mode, all RGB color values will switch to the luminosity value produced by the formula, which will apply a gray shade to your image.

OTE: *The Hue, Saturation, Color, and Luminosity modes are based on a Hue/Saturation/Luminosity (HSL) color model. This color model is slightly different from the Hue/Saturation/Brightness (HSB) color model. Thus, if you try to evaluate the effects of painting in these modes using the HSB readouts in the Info palette, it may seem that the modes do not work exactly as specified. For instance, when you paint over a color using Hue mode, the HSB readout in the Info palette may show that the color's saturation as well as hue have changed.*

Multiply   This mode multiplies color values, causing underlying pixels to darken. Each time when a color is applied, pixels will receive more of the painting color's values.

Screen   This mode whitens underlying pixels, leaving them in a tint of the color being applied. If you repeatedly apply color in Screen mode, pixels grow lighter and lighter. The Screen mode is the opposite of the Multiply mode.

Dissolve   When colors are applied in Dissolve mode, the painting color randomly replaces underlying pixels. This can produce anything from a speckled paint to a sandpaper effect. For more dramatic results, use Dissolve mode with a large brush and experiment with different opacities.

Color Mode Exercise

In this section, you'll try using the Darken and Lighten modes with the Type and Gradient tools to see how these modes completely change how a blend is applied. First you'll create a radial blend behind some text; then you'll create a linear blend within the letters of the text.

1. Begin by opening a new file, 5 inches by 5 inches. Set the mode to RGB and the resolution to 72 ppi.

2. Click on the Default Colors icon to reset the foreground and background colors. This will ensure that the text you create is black.

3. Select the Type tool and click on the screen. When the Type Tool dialog box appears, click on the Font pop-up menu and choose Times (or the font of your choice). In the Size field box, type **100**. Leave the Leading and Spacing fields empty. In the Style group, check to see that Anti-Aliased is selected. In the Text field, type **BLEND**. When you are finished, click OK.

4. While the text is still floating, move it to the center of your document, using the mouse or the keyboard arrow keys. Once the text is in position, deselect it by choosing None from the Select menu.

5. Next, create the blend. Double-click on the Gradient tool to open the Gradient Tool Options dialog box. Select the Clockwise Spectrum radio button, leave Midpoint Skew set to 50%, and select the Radial blend type. Click OK.

6. In the Brushes palette, click on the Mode pop-up menu and choose the Darken mode. Set Opacity to 100%.

7. Pick a yellow foreground color and a blue background color.

8. Now create the radial blend. With the Gradient tool activated, click and drag diagonally from the top-left corner of your document to the bottom-right corner. The blend appears with the text over it. Because you used the Darken mode, only the areas lighter than the painting color were affected, not the darker areas. Thus, even though you created the blend over the entire screen, only the white pixels were affected, not the black text.

   Now, you'll work with the Lighten mode, the opposite of Darken.

9. In the Edit menu, select Undo to remove the effects of the blend that was created in Darken mode.

10. In the Brushes palette, click on the Mode pop-up menu and change the mode to Lighten.

11. Before creating another blend, open the Gradient Tool Options dialog box and change Type to Linear. Click OK.

12. To create the blend, position the mouse to the left of the word *BLEND*, and click and drag to the far-right side of the screen. When you release the mouse, you'll see that the blend is created inside the text, without affecting the white background. The Lighten mode only lightens areas darker than the painting color. Thus, the black text was lightened by the blend, and the background white area was not affected. By switching to Lighten mode, you were able to change the text without first selecting it.

You've just seen a very clear example of how powerful the painting modes can be in your Photoshop work. You now have new options at your disposal that edit pixels not according to whether they are selected but according to their color values.

All the exercises in this chapter have offered but a taste of the features and special effects that await you in Photoshop. In Chapter 6, the electronic magic will continue as you learn the basics of image editing.

INTRODUCTION TO
IMAGE EDITING

Image editing is where the magic of Photoshop truly comes alive. With Photoshop's image-editing tools at your command, objects once hidden in darkness will suddenly emerge from the shadows. Images almost lost in the distance will gradually sharpen into focus. Images that are bland, barren, or unbalanced can be populated with just the right objects in exactly the right place. In short, Photoshop's image-editing tools allow you to produce or improve an image to look the way you want it to look.

The goal of this chapter, though, is not to concentrate on the fantastic and amazing, but rather to provide you with an introduction to the basics of image editing. We'll begin here by performing a little image-editing magic with the Blur/Sharpen, Dodge/Burn, Rubber Stamp, and Smudge tools. As you did in Chapter 5, you'll use these tools from the Toolbox in conjunction with the Brushes palette's Mode pop-up and its Options menus.

You'll begin the exercises in this chapter by opening a digitized image. With this image on screen, you will use the Dodge and Burn tools to lighten overexposed and darken underexposed areas. Once you've improved the image's exposure levels, you'll use the Blur and Sharpen tools to soften and clarify certain areas. With the Smudge tool, you'll blend small parts of the image to create watercolor and finger-painting effects. Finally, you'll use the powerful Rubber Stamp tool to clone areas of the image, create impressionistic effects, and apply a pattern to the digitized image.

When you are ready to begin, open any digitized image as your practice document. If you don't have a digitized image available, open the Frames (PC users: frames.jpg) file in the Adobe Photoshop Tutorial folder.

The examples in this chapter use a scanned image of an oriental fan. Figure 6-1 shows the original scanned image of the oriental fan with its imperfections. You can see that light areas needed to be darkened, and shadowed areas needed to be lightened. The flowers needed to be sharpened so that they would stand out. The edges of the fan also needed to be softened, so that the fan would blend into a background photograph. Figure 6-2 shows the corrected fan as part of a completed project. Notice that the fan now has more flowers than in the original image—these flowers were *cloned*, or copied, to make the fan look more interesting. The translucent effect of the type was created by setting Opacity to 50% in the Brushes palette and using the Type tool to add the text.

Sharpen flowers

Lighten shadows

Clone flowers

Soften edges

Darken highlights

Midtones okay

Corrections
needed for
the oriental
fan image

FIGURE 6-1

6

Oriental
fan and text
added to
the image.
(Background
setting
photograph
courtesy of
Stacy
Kollar
Photography)

FIGURE 6-2

USING THE DODGE AND BURN TOOLS

The Dodge and Burn tools are two tools that have begun enticing photographers out of the darkroom and into the Photoshop studio. These tools are simulations of traditional darkroom techniques. Photographers can often improve even their best work by using Dodge and Burn to block out or add light from a negative in order to enhance image definition. In photography, dodging is usually employed to lighten *shadow areas* (the darkest portions of an image), and burning is employed to darken *highlights* (the brightest parts of an image)—both techniques increase the detail in a photograph. Photoshop's Dodge and Burn tools produce the same effects in a digitized image.

As discussed in "The Editing Tools" section in Chapter 2, the Dodge and Burn tools share one location in the Toolbox, with only one icon visible at a time (Dodge is the default tool). You can switch tools using a pop-up menu in a dialog box that appears whenever the tool in the Toolbox is double-clicked.

When either Dodge or Burn is activated, the slider in the Brushes palette measures exposure. In photography, an *overexposed* image is one that is too light; an *underexposed* image is too dark. By clicking and dragging on the slider control, you can set the exposure level from 1% to 100%. By typing a number on your keyboard, you can step through exposure settings in intervals of 10%. Increasing the exposure while using the Dodge tool intensifies the Dodge tool's lightening effect. Increasing the exposure while using the Burn tool intensifies the Burn tool's darkening effect.

When you use Dodge or Burn, the Mode pop-up menu in the Brushes palette displays the following options: Shadows, Midtones, and Highlights (shown in the following illustration). Highlights are the brightest components of an image; midtones are halfway between the highlights and shadows; and shadows are the darkest components of an image. By selecting one of these options, you can apply the Dodge or Burn tools to correct either shadows, midtones, or highlights. For instance, if you select Highlights, only highlight areas will be affected.

The width of the area you edit is determined by the size of the brush you pick in the Brushes palette and whether it is hard-edged or soft-edged. By allowing you to choose a brush size, an exposure level, and an image's highlights, midtones, and shadows, Photoshop provides tremendous control over brightness and darkness levels. Using a soft-edged brush with a low exposure creates a subtle effect; a hard-edged brush with a high exposure rate produces a more dramatic effect.

As you see in Figure 6-1, the light areas on the left side of the fan are too light, almost white. The dark areas on the top of the fan are almost the same color as the flowers, causing the flowers to fade into the background and appear less visible.

In the image that you have on your screen, look for areas that are too bright and too dark. These are the areas to focus on when you put the Dodge and Burn tools to work. Before you begin, however, use the Save As command so that you don't alter the original image. Name your practice file **Editing.** If you are using the Frames file, an Image Quality dialog box will appear after you click Save (PC users: OK). This is because the file was saved using a compression format called JPEG. Click Save to save the file in a compressed format. (For more information about JPEG and other file formats, see Appendix A.)

Using the Dodge Tool to Lighten Image Areas

Start by using the Dodge tool to lighten shadow areas, so that more detail is visible in the dark areas of your image. If the Dodge tool is not shown as the active tool in the Toolbox, double-click on the Burn tool icon. When the dialog box opens, click on the Tool pop-up menu and select Dodge. Click OK.

IP: *A quick way to switch between the Dodge and Burn tools in the Toolbox is to press the OPTION key (PC users: ALT) while clicking on either tool. This same technique also works with the Blur and Sharpen tools.*

Now use the Dodge tool to lighten shadow areas that are too dark.

1. First, in the Brushes palette, set Exposure to 20% and use a soft-edged brush to make subtle changes. Click on the Mode pop-up menu and select Shadows.

2. Move the mouse pointer over a dark area of your image. (The mouse pointer changes to the Dodge tool when it enters the document window,

unless CAPS LOCK is depressed.) Click and drag with a few short mouse movements. As you do, you'll see that the darkest areas that you are clicking and dragging over become lighter. In Figure 6-3, you can see that the Dodge tool has lightened shadowed areas to add tonal balance to the fan.

3. Continue using the Dodge tool to lighten all of the unwanted dark areas in your image. You might need to change the brush size, exposure, and mode to produce the desired effect.

 OTE: *Using a stylus and digitizing tablet provides even more control when editing images with Dodge and Burn. If you turn on the Size and/or Exposure check boxes in the Stylus Pressure section of the Dodge/Burn Options dialog box, you can change the exposure and size of the area you are editing by applying more or less pressure to the stylus pen.*

Using the Burn Tool to Darken Image Areas

To switch to the Burn tool, double-click on the Dodge tool. In the Dodge/Burn Options dialog box, click the Tool pop-up menu, select Burn, and then click OK.

1. With the Burn tool active, change the settings in the Brushes palette. To create a subtle effect, use a soft-edged brush with Exposure set to 20%. Since you only want to darken the brightest areas of the image, choose Highlights in the Mode pop-up menu.

Dodge tool

Lightening shadows with the Dodge tool

FIGURE 6-3

2. In your image, look for a bright portion to start working on, and then position the Burn tool pointer over this area. (As you move the mouse pointer over the document area of the screen, the pointer changes to the Burn tool.)

IP: *If you wish to zoom in, use the keyboard shortcut: Hold down COMMAND-SPACEBAR (PC users: CTRL-SPACEBAR) and click over the area that you wish to zoom. To zoom out, click the mouse while pressing OPTION-SPACEBAR (PC users: ALT-SPACEBAR).*

3. When you are ready to begin, click and drag several times over the area using short strokes. As you drag, the lightest part of the image turns slightly darker. Now you can see how the rate of the darkening reflects the brush size and exposure setting you are using. Because the exposure setting is low and you are using a soft-edged brush, the darkening progresses slowly.

Figure 6-4 shows an example where the Burn tool is adding tone to an overexposed area of the fan.

Darkening highlights with the Burn tool

Burn tool

FIGURE 6-4

IP: *If an image area requires you to lighten or darken in a straight line or at 45-degree increments—for example, if you're lightening or darkening the edges or corners of a book—press SHIFT while clicking and dragging with either the Dodge or Burn tool activated.*

4. If you wish to darken shadow or midtone areas that are too light, you will need to change mode settings in the Brushes palette first. Continue editing by changing to Shadows or Midtones and using various brush sizes and exposure percentages.

When you've finished darkening the light areas of your image, move on to the next section, where you will use the Blur and Sharpen image-editing tools.

USING THE BLUR AND SHARPEN TOOLS

The Blur tool softens parts of an image by, as you probably guessed, blurring it. Its counterpart, the Sharpen tool, makes image areas sharper and more distinct. Photoshop's Blur tool works by decreasing the contrast among the pixels you drag over; the Sharpen tool works by heightening contrast in neighboring pixels.

Like the Dodge and Burn tool combination, Blur and Sharpen are often used to enhance the quality of digitized images. You may wonder, though, why anyone would want to make an image more blurry. It's because scanners sometimes accentuate edges too much, causing images to look too harsh. These edges can be softened with the Blur tool. The Blur tool can also be used to help soften the jagged edges of an image that is pasted into a document, so that it blends more smoothly into its surroundings.

The Blur and Sharpen tools share one location in the Toolbox, as do Dodge and Burn. By default, when Photoshop is first loaded, only the Blur tool appears in the Toolbox. Again, as with Dodge/Burn, you can switch between the Blur and Sharpen tools by using the Tool pop-up menu in the Blur/Sharpen Options dialog box or by pressing the OPTION key (PC users: ALT) and clicking on the active tool in the Toolbox. Try using the OPTION key (PC users: ALT) and clicking to switch between the Blur/Sharpen tools.

```
╔══════════ Blur/Sharpen Options ══════════╗
║                                           ║
║  Tool: ✓△ Blur                            ║
║         △ Sharpen        ┌──────────┐     ║
║  ─ Stylus Pressure ─     │    OK    │     ║
║  Vary: ☐ Size            └──────────┘     ║
║         ☐ Pressure       ┌──────────┐     ║
║                          │  Cancel  │     ║
║                          └──────────┘     ║
╚═══════════════════════════════════════════╝
```

Now take a look at the Brushes palette. Click on the Mode pop-up menu to view the different modes. When the Blur or Sharpen tool is activated, the modes available to you in the Brushes palette are Normal, Lighten, Darken, Hue, Saturation, Color, and Luminosity. Also, notice that the slider in the palette now controls Pressure. (See Chapter 5 for a discussion of the modes in the Brushes palette.)

The Pressure slider controls the amount of sharpening and blurring that these tools produce. The greater the Pressure percentage, the greater the effect of the sharpening or blurring. As usual, the size of the area that changes is determined by the brush size you are using—smaller brushes affect smaller areas, larger brushes affect larger areas.

 OTE: *If you have a stylus and digitizing tablet, you can also take advantage of the two Stylus Pressure options for the Blur and Sharpen tools: Size and Pressure.*

Using the Sharpen Tool to Increase Contrast

 Because it's easier to recognize the need for sharpening image areas rather than for blurring them, start by experimenting with the Sharpen tool first. If the Sharpen tool is not active, switch to it.

Before you begin sharpening your own image, pick a brush size, Pressure value, and Mode in the Brushes palette. Leave Mode set to Normal. By switching modes, you can control which image areas will be affected; for instance, if you choose Darken, only lighter pixels will be changed. If you use a medium-sized, soft-edged brush and a low Pressure setting, the sharpening effect will be barely noticeable. A large, hard-edged brush with a high Pressure value will produce a more intense effect.

Be aware of sharpening too much. If you overdo it, the colors will break up and become pixelated, as shown in Figure 6-5. Here the Sharpen tool is being used to heighten the contrast in the fan's flowers. To avoid oversharpening, use the Zoom tool to zoom in and keep a close eye on the pixels being affected.

Now decide which area you want to work on, move the Sharpen tool over that area, and click and drag the mouse to begin increasing contrast. Try moving to other areas in the image to see the results of sharpening with different Pressure settings.

 EMEMBER: *Oversharpening will cause pixelation.*

Sharpen tool

Pixelation
occurs if
you
oversharpen

FIGURE 6-5

Using the Blur Tool to Soften Hard Edges

You can use the Blur tool to soften hard edges in an image and to correct any pixelation caused by oversharpening.

Press and hold OPTION (PC users: ALT) to switch to the Blur tool from the Sharpen tool. Look for areas in your image that are too sharp or that have hard edges that need to be softened. Work these edges first with a low-pressure setting in the Brushes palette, so you don't blur your image too much.

Figure 6-6 shows the Blur tool being used to correct the pixelation that occurred when the fan's flowers were being sharpened (in Figure 6-5). The Blur tool was also used to soften all of the hard edges of the fan, including the ridged perimeter after it was pasted into the final photograph.

n **OTE:**   *In addition to using the Blur and Sharpen tools, you can apply filters to make entire images more or less distinct. Filters will be discussed in Chapter 8.*

If you wish, continue to experiment with the Blur and Sharpen tools. When you're done, save your work and close the practice file. Then proceed to the next section to try your hand at more image-editing techniques with the Smudge tool, which can make your image look as though it is hand painted.

Using the
Blur tool to
soften
pixelated
area of
image

FIGURE 6-6

Blur tool

6

USING THE SMUDGE TOOL TO MIX COLORS AND CREATE WATERCOLOR EFFECTS

The Smudge tool lets you blend colors as if you had smudged them together with your finger. When you use the Smudge tool, Photoshop starts with the color you clicked on and mixes it with the colors you drag over. Besides blending colors and mixing paint, the Smudge tool can be used to produce a watercolor effect in your image.

In this section, you'll have a chance to experiment with the Smudge tool by transforming a digitized image into a watercolor painting. You'll also learn how to add colors to an image by activating the Smudge tool's Finger Painting option.

1. Before proceeding, open any scanned image file, or reopen the Frames (PC users: frames.jpg) file you started with at the beginning of this chapter. Use Save As to create another copy of your file. Name your file WaterPainting (PC users: WaterPtg). By using Save As, your original file will not be affected by the changes you are going to make in the following exercises.

EMEMBER: *Saving different versions of your file enables you to experiment with various designs and keep them as you are working on a project.*

2. Double-click the Smudge tool to examine the Smudge Tool Options dialog box; you'll begin by using the Smudge tool without the Finger Painting option. If necessary, deselect this option by clicking in the check box, then click OK.

```
╔══════ Smudge Tool Options ══════╗
║                                  ║
║  ☐ Finger Painting               ║
║  ┌─ Stylus Pressure ─┐  ┌──OK──┐ ║
║  Vary:  ☐ Size       │  └──────┘ ║
║         ☐ Pressure   │ ┌─Cancel─┐║
║                      │ └────────┘║
╚══════════════════════════════════╝
```

To control how the colors are smudged together, you can pick a brush size, a mode, and a Pressure value in the Brushes palette. If you use a large brush with a high pressure value, you will create a large smudge that will completely distort your image. A lower pressure value with a small- or medium-sized brush will decrease the size of the smudge and create a less dramatic effect.

 OTE: *The Smudge tool can be used to soften unwanted wrinkles and blemishes in fleshtones. This technique is discussed in Chapter 13.*

The modes that are available in the Brushes palette are the standard choices (as discussed in Chapter 5). These can provide further control of your smudge. For example, if you use Hue mode, only the hue values will be smudged (not the saturation or the luminosity values). Similarly, use Saturation mode to change only the saturation values, and Luminosity mode to smudge only the luminosity values.

3. Pick a medium-sized, soft-edged brush from the Brushes palette. Set the Pressure to 50% and Mode to Normal. Move the smudge pointer anywhere in your document, and click the mouse. You'll see that a small smudge of colors appears on screen. Zoom in to see a close-up view of the smudge. If you create a few more smudges, your image will start looking more like a watercolor painting, as in Figure 6-7.

Experiment with various brush sizes. Also, try switching modes a few times before smudging different parts of your image.

Smudge tool

Creating a
watercolor
effect using
the Smudge
tool

FIGURE 6-7

6

The Smudge Tool's Finger Painting Option

To this point, you have created a watercolor effect by smudging the colors of your
image together. What if you want to create a watercolor effect and add new color to
your image at the same time? You can do this by activating the Smudge tool's Finger
Painting option, which smudges using the foreground color.

1. Double-click on the Smudge tool, select the Finger Painting check box in
   the Smudge Tool Options dialog box, and click OK.

2. For this exercise, set the foreground color to a bright color so you can
   easily view the Finger Painting effects.

3. In the Brushes palette, continue to use a medium-sized, soft-edged brush
   with Pressure set to 50%.

4. Click and drag over an area on your document, and notice how the
   Smudge tool smudges with the selected foreground color. Continue to
   experiment using other foreground colors. When you're finished, close
   the file and save it, if you wish.

In the next section, you'll learn about one of Photoshop's most versatile tools,
the Rubber Stamp.

USING THE RUBBER STAMP TOOL

The Rubber Stamp is a multipurpose tool. Although it can be used for reverting, applying a pattern, or creating an impressionistic effect, its most valuable feature is undoubtedly its cloning capability. *Cloning* means choosing parts of an image and duplicating them to areas in the same file or in another file. This is quite different than copying and pasting. During the cloning procedure, Photoshop *samples,* or reads, a source area and clones it to a target area. As you click and drag in the target area in the file, a clone of the sampled area gradually appears. This process can produce an undetectable blend of old pixels and new. When executed properly, the cloning effect is often seamless and—even to the experienced Photoshop user—frequently amazing.

To see the Rubber Stamp tool's options, double-click on the tool in the Toolbox. In the Rubber Stamp Options dialog box, the Option pop-up menu displays the currently selected option. Click on the Option pop-up menu to see what else is available. The choices are numerous: Clone (aligned or non-aligned), Pattern (aligned or non-aligned), From Snapshot, From Saved, and Impressionist.

OTE: *The Rubber Stamp tool also has two Stylus Pressure options, Size and Opacity.*

In the next sections, the oriental fan image will be used to demonstrate the basics of the Rubber Stamp tool. To follow along, open the file you named Editing (earlier in this chapter), or load any digitized image.

Photoshop in Action

New sky was created with the
painting and editing tools.

The Rubber Stamp tool's cloning option
was used to help blend the characters
into the mountain.

Artwork by: R/GA Print

Client: Acclaim Entertainment

The characters were combined with
a scan of Mount Rushmore.

6

R/GA Print gave artist David Mattingly photographs of the characters that would appear in this final image. David then created a painting of the characters to make it look as if they were created from stone.

Karen Sideman at R/GA Print scanned an image of Mount Rushmore, then scanned Dave's painting and combined the two together. To blend the images together, she used the Edit menu's Composite Controls command and the Rubber Stamp tool's cloning option. To create a brilliant blue sky in the background, Karen used Photoshop's painting and editing tools.

Mount Rushmore will never be the same.

Using the Clone Options to Duplicate Image Areas

Cloning can be tremendously helpful when you edit an image or retouch a photo. For example, one of the authors of this book retouched a cover for a proposed Reader's Digest travel guide. The picture that the book's art director wished to use was a photograph of a small New England town. Everything in the photo was beautiful—except for the telephone wires criss-crossing through the scene. Using the Rubber Stamp tool's Clone option, parts of the trees that surrounded the wires were easily cloned over the wires to make them disappear. You'll see this example in Chapter 13, where advanced retouching techniques are introduced.

The Clone (aligned) option allows you to clone different parts of an image to different areas of the same file or another file. When you clone using the aligned option, Photoshop retains the same distance and angle relationship between the source area that you are sampling and the target area where the clone appears. Say, for instance, you wish to clone an image two inches directly above the original sample. After you finish cloning, if you move the mouse to another area of the file and then click and drag, Photoshop will clone whatever is two inches directly above the mouse pointer.

The Clone (non-aligned) option automatically samples the original source area, so you can clone the same sample in many places after you release the mouse. For the completed fan image in Figure 6-2, the Clone (aligned) option was used to duplicate different flowers in various areas of the fan. Had the designer wanted to clone the same flower in many parts of the fan, the Clone (non-aligned) option would have been used instead.

1. To start the exercise, choose Clone (aligned) from the Option pop-up menu in the Rubber Stamp Options dialog box.

2. Pick a large brush in the Brushes palette. With a large brush and a high opacity setting, the cloning will happen faster and its effect will be more obvious.

3. To clone part of your image, move the rubber stamp pointer so that it's over the area you wish to duplicate. Press and hold the OPTION key (PC users: ALT) and then click the mouse to sample the area. Notice that the small black triangle at the base of the rubber stamp (⬚) turns white (⬚). This indicates that an area has been sampled. Once you've sampled an area, release the OPTION key (PC users: ALT) and move the rubber stamp pointer to the area where you wish the clone to appear.

To begin cloning, click and drag the mouse, moving the rubber stamp pointer over the target area. As you move the mouse, the clone will begin to appear in that area. Notice that a crosshair in the source area follows the movements of your rubber stamp pointer in the target area. The crosshair always remains the same distance and the same angle from the rubber stamp pointer, as shown in Figure 6-8. Continue clicking and dragging the mouse. The greater the area that you click and drag over, the greater the area that is cloned.

When you use the Clone (aligned) option, it's important to remember that the distance and the angle between the sampled area and the area where the clone is placed are always the same. To verify this, release the mouse button and then move the rubber stamp pointer to another area on the screen. Click and drag—Photoshop resamples and starts cloning again. Notice that when you clone the new area, the distance and angle between the crosshair and the rubber stamp pointer is the same as the previous sample/clone pair. If you want to reset the distance between the source area and the target area, move the rubber stamp pointer to another area that you wish to sample, then press OPTION (PC users: ALT) and click the mouse. Now you can move the Rubber Stamp tool to the other area where you wish to clone the new sample. Subsequent sample/clone pairs will then be separated by this new distance and angle. The cloning will begin as soon as you click and drag

Using the
Rubber
Stamp
tool's
Clone
(aligned)
option to
clone a
flower

FIGURE 6-8

Crosshair pointer   Rubber stamp pointer
(sampled area)   (cloned area)

If you wish to clone the same sample to different areas in your image, use the Clone (non-aligned) option. Try this now. Double-click on the Rubber Stamp tool and choose Clone (non-aligned) from the Option pop-up menu in the dialog box. Click OK. When you are ready to begin, pick an area that you wish to clone. Once again, press OPTION (PC users: ALT) and click the mouse to sample. Move the Rubber Stamp tool to the area where you want to apply the clone, then click and drag. After you've created the clone of the image, release the mouse button. Move to another area of the screen where you wish to duplicate the sample, and click and drag again to get another clone of the first sampled area.

IP: *You can press the CAPS LOCK key to turn the rubber stamp pointer into a crosshair. It's easier to use the middle of the crosshair than the rubber stamp icon as a guide to judge the specific area that you are cloning. When you use this technique, you'll have two crosshairs on screen—one indicating the sample area and the other indicating the target area where the clone appears.*

As you work, you'll want to make the cloned image look as natural as possible. You don't want the clone to stand out from its surroundings. To make your clone blend in, experiment using the Rubber Stamp tool with different brushes, opacities, and modes. In the fan example, a soft-edged brush was used. This helped blend the new flower at the top of the fan to look as though it has always been there.

When you've finished cloning, save your file and proceed to the next section, where you'll experiment with more Rubber Stamp options.

IP: *You can also clone an image from one file to another. To do this, open the two files side-by-side on screen. Press OPTION (PC users: ALT) and click over the area you wish to sample; then activate the target file. Position the rubber stamp pointer over the area where you wish to place the clone, then click and drag.*

Reverting Using the From Saved and From Snapshot Options

The Rubber Stamp tool's From Saved and From Snapshot options work much like the Magic Eraser feature of the Eraser tool. Recall from Chapter 5 that the Magic Eraser allows you to click and drag to revert, or unerase—that is, to resurrect parts of images that have been changed. You can also revert with the From Saved and

From Snapshot options; and with these options you also are able to choose *how* you want to revert, by choosing a mode, opacity, and brush in the Brushes palette. The From Saved option allows you to revert to the last saved version of your file. The From Snapshot option allows you to revert to a *snapshot,* a version of the file captured using the Edit menu's Take Snapshop option, which is temporarily stored to an area of memory called the *image buffer.*

Reverting using the Rubber Stamp tool allows you to resurrect just a part of the previous version of an image by painting it on the screen. You can use the Brushes palette to choose a brush type, as well as the opacity percentage and the mode. These options—for example, using a soft-edged brush or lowering the opacity—can prove valuable for blending the reverted part of a file into the image on screen.

Using the From Saved Option

In this exercise, you're going to alter a file by coloring the entire screen with the background color. After you have changed the screen, you'll use the From Saved option to return part of the file to its original form.

6

1. Open the Frames (PC users: frames.jpg) file or any other digitized image.

2. Double-click on the Eraser tool and erase the entire screen by filling it with the background color.

3. Open the Rubber Stamp Options dialog box and choose From Saved in the Option pop-up menu.

4. Before you start reverting, pick a large brush from the Brushes palette and set Opacity to 100%. The Mode should be Normal. When you start using the Rubber Stamp tool, these settings will return your file to its original form using a large brush stroke and its original opacity.

5. Now move the rubber stamp pointer to an area that you want to revert, and click and drag over the area. Photoshop takes a few minutes to read the file information of the saved version. As you move with the brush, you'll see parts of your image being restored; they will match the size and shape of your brush.

6. Before you finish, change Opacity to 50%, and then click and drag in the document window. Now the image is being restored with a 50% opacity.

Keep this technique in mind. It might come in handy when you wish to create special effects.

IP: *Using the Rubber Stamp tool's From Saved option with an Opacity setting lower than 100% can produce a ghostlike effect.*

Continue experimenting with the From Saved option. Keep Opacity set to 50% and the large, soft-edged brush selected, but switch modes from Normal to Dissolve. Dissolve, as mentioned in the "Painting Modes" section of Chapter 5, randomly changes the colors of pixels. The results of this effect will vary according to the image and its color. When you're done, keep your file on screen and proceed to the next section.

Using the From Snapshot Option

Before you begin exploring the From Snapshot option, you must take a "snapshot" of your work. A snapshot saves your file's image in an area of memory called the image buffer, rather than to your hard disk. If you change an image that has already been saved and then take a snapshot, you have a choice between reverting to the disk version or the snapshot version of the image.

To see how this works, take a snapshot of your image now. (If you don't have an image on screen, load one, then make a few changes to it.) To take a snapshot of your work on screen, select the Take Snapshot command from the Edit menu.

OTE: *Photoshop can hold only one snapshot in memory at a time. When Take Snapshot is executed, any previous snapshot is replaced by the current snapshot.*

In order to see the From Snapshot option in action, you'll want to either make changes to your image on screen or revert the image to an earlier version. For simplicity's sake in this exercise, choose Revert from the File menu to revert to the previous version of the entire image.

Next, double-click on the Rubber Stamp tool and select From Snapshot in the Option pop-up menu in the dialog box. Click OK to accept the setting change. In the Brushes palette, set the painting mode from Dissolve back to Normal; otherwise, when you revert, you'll be painting a dissolved version of the snapshot on the screen.

Now you're ready to revert to your snapshot. Position the Rubber Stamp pointer over the area that you previously changed with the Rubber Stamp's From Saved option, and click and drag. As you move the mouse, you'll see the Rubber Stamp tool return the image to the snapshot version of the file.

You have now seen how Photoshop gives you the ability to re-create a file based on either a saved or snapshot version.

n OTE: *Starting in version 2.5.1, Photoshop added revert capabilities to the Edit/Fill command. Using Edit/Fill, you can revert a selection to either the last saved version or to the snapshot version. To revert using Edit/Fill, first select an area. From the Edit menu, choose Fill. From the Use pop-up menu, choose either Saved or Snapshot.*

Your next stop is the Rubber Stamp tool's Impressionist feature. Once again, you'll probably want to start with a fresh version of your file. To do this, use the Revert command in the File menu to revert the entire image to the last saved version.

Using the Impressionist Option

Another of the Rubber Stamp tool's many specialties is its ability to take a scanned photograph and transform it by applying the characteristics of an impressionist painting. The Impressionist option takes the pixels from the last saved version of the file and blends them into the pixels of the current version of the file.

The Impressionist effect will vary depending upon the brush, opacity, and painting mode used. If you use either a large, hard-edged brush or a small, soft-edged brush with a low Spacing value, you will produce a very spotted effect, making it difficult to decipher what the image is supposed to be. If you wish to produce a more realistic, less impressionistic effect, use a small brush with a high Spacing value. (See "Creating and Using Custom Brushes" in Chapter 5 for a discussion on brush attributes.)

1. For this first experiment, keep the Brushes palette at the default setting—Opacity at 100% and Mode at Normal.

2. To set the Spacing value of a brush, click on any brush in the Brushes palette. Then click on the Options menu arrow in the Brushes palette and choose New Brush from the list that appears. In the New Brush dialog box, set the Spacing to 300%, Hardness to 50%, and Diameter to 19 pixels. If you want your strokes to be round, keep Roundness at 100%.

For strokes that look more elliptical than round, set Angle to 50 degrees and Roundness to 40%. Click OK to accept the changes.

3. To use the Impressionist option, double-click on the Rubber Stamp tool. Click on the Option pop-up menu, choose Impressionist, and click OK.

4. Click and drag over any area of your file. As you drag, you'll see the pixels appear to smear together, as shown in Figure 6-9, almost as if Renoir had taken control of the painting.

Additional effects can be created by using painting modes (Normal, Lighten, Darken, Hue, Saturation, Color, Luminosity, Multiply, Screen, and Dissolve) to change different areas. Continue experimenting with various modes and opacities. When you are done, make sure to use either the Save or the Save As command if you wish to save your file. Before proceeding to the next section, close the file.

Using the Pattern Option

The other options for the Rubber Stamp tool are Pattern (aligned) and Pattern (non-aligned). To experiment with these options, you need to create and define a pattern. Patterns can be used to create special effects, background textures, and fabric

An effect created with the Rubber Stamp tool's Impressionist option

FIGURE 6-9

or wallpaper designs. In this section you'll learn how to create a pattern and then use the Rubber Stamp tool to apply it.

Using Adobe Photoshop's Patterns

When you install Photoshop, a Brushes & Patterns folder (PC users: patterns) is created. This folder contains PostScript patterns that were created in Adobe Illustrator for you to use in Photoshop.

To access one of Adobe's patterns, choose Open from the File menu. In the Open dialog box, locate the PostScript Patterns folder (PC users: patterns) and open it. In this folder you will see a long list of files. Select the Mali Primitive file (PC users: mali.ai) and open it. In a few moments, Photoshop's EPS Rasterizer dialog box will appear. Since the pattern was created in Illustrator, which is a vector program, Photoshop needs to convert it to Photoshop's native format, bitmap. You do not need to change any of the dialog box settings, just click OK. (The rasterizer options are discussed in Appendix A.)

EPS Rasterizer	
┌─ Image Size: 4K ─	
Width: `90` `pixels ▼`	`OK`
Height: `45` `pixels ▼`	`Cancel`
Resolution: `72` `pixels/inch ▼`	
Mode: `Grayscale ▼`	
☒ Anti-aliased ☒ Constrain Proportions	

When the file appears, you are ready to define it as a pattern. In order to define any image or part of an image as a pattern, it must first be selected. In this example, you'll select the entire image.

1. Choose All from the Select menu. To define the pattern, choose Define Pattern from the Edit menu. The pattern has now been defined, and you can proceed to use the Rubber Stamp or Paint Bucket tool, or the Fill or Stroke command to apply it to your file.

2. With the pattern defined and in memory, you no longer need the pattern file (Mali Primitive) open, so close it.

3. Create a new 5-inch-by-5-inch RGB file, which you'll use to see the effects of painting with a pattern using the Rubber Stamp tool.

4. When you have a new file on screen, double-click on the Rubber Stamp tool. From the Option pop-up menu, select Pattern (aligned) and click OK.

   The Pattern (aligned) option allows you to apply a continuous pattern, no matter how many times you stop and start. If you pick the Pattern (non-aligned) option instead, the pattern will restart every time you release the mouse button and click and drag again in your image.

5. In the Brushes palette, choose a large brush size, set Opacity to 100%, and change the mode to Normal.

6. Click and drag with the Rubber Stamp tool to start painting. As you paint the Rubber Stamp tool applies the selected pattern. If you wish, test out other brush sizes and opacity settings.

   As you work, you might decide that the pattern would look better with a little color, perhaps some green. One easy way of doing this is to paint the entire screen green and then use the painting modes and the Rubber Stamp tool to help paint the pattern back into the picture.

7. Change the background color to green, or to any color that you want to add to your pattern (other than black or white). Then double-click on the Eraser tool to fill your document with this color.

8. Once the document has become the background color, activate the Rubber Stamp tool. Pick a large brush and set Opacity to 100%.

   Establish a reference point on screen by painting a few brush strokes with the mode set to Normal, and then switch to the Lighten mode. This will only lighten areas that are darker than the pattern you are painting with. Thus, when you paint the pattern with the Rubber Stamp tool in Lighten mode, the white part of the pattern will paint over the green colors on the screen. The black part of the pattern is not painted because it is darker than the green color on screen. Try painting several brush strokes on the screen to see the effect.

If you wish to reverse the colors in the previous example, choose the Darken mode. Now, only the black part of the pattern is applied because black is darker than the underlying green color. Figure 6-10 shows the Mali Primitive pattern applied with the Normal, Lighten, and Darken modes.

OTE: *You can add colors to one of Photoshop's pattern files by opening the file and choosing RGB Color or CMYK Color from the Mode menu.*

Normal mode

Lighten mode

Darken mode

Applying a pattern with the Rubber Stamp tool using Normal, Lighten, and Darken modes

FIGURE 6-10

Creating, Defining, and Applying Custom Patterns

Now that you know how to apply one of Adobe Photoshop's patterns, you're ready to learn how to create one of your own. Although you can create a pattern in any file, it's probably best to make one in a new file. If you create each pattern in a separate file that you name and save, you'll have an easier time accessing your patterns when you wish to use them again. Since these files will be used solely to hold the design of your pattern, they don't need to be very large.

To create a pattern, follow these steps:

1. Open a new file, 2 inches by 2 inches.

2. Use any of Photoshop's tools to create a pattern.

 IP: *You can also select a portion of a digitized image to use as a pattern.*

3. Select with the Rectangular Marquee tool the area you wish to include in your pattern file, as shown in the following illustration. If you select any

white background area with your pattern, that white area will be included when you paint with the pattern.

4. While the pattern is selected, choose Define Pattern from the Edit menu.

5. Save your file and close it.

nOTE: *Photoshop, unfortunately, can only remember one pattern at a time. The defined pattern is stored in memory until you either define another pattern or quit the program. Thus, if you want to use a pattern again, you must save the file that the pattern was created in.*

6. To apply your pattern, create a new file, 5 inches by 5 inches.

7. When the new file appears, you can use either the Rubber Stamp or Paint Bucket tool, or the Fill or Stroke command to apply the pattern. For this exercise, use the Rubber Stamp tool. Double-click on the Rubber Stamp tool, and from the Option pop-up menu, choose Pattern (aligned). Click OK.

8. Click and drag in the document to paint with the pattern using the Rubber Stamp tool.

Try experimenting by applying your pattern with the Pattern (non-aligned) option, with the Paint Bucket tool, or with the Edit/Fill command. To make your pattern more interesting, you may wish to create a custom brush and apply it to different areas in the image. The music notes shown in this illustration were created with a custom brush from the Sonata typeface.

RENOVATING A KITCHEN

Here's a tip for architects, interior designers, or anyone who might be involved in a renovation project. This project demonstrates how to take a scanned image of an old, dusty kitchen and transform it into a clean, modern one.

Certainly, one of the major advantages of a computer is that you can experiment with various interior and scenic designs without paying anyone to lift a hammer or a paint brush. If you wish to use Photoshop for this type of project, you will need to scan (or have a service bureau scan) photographs of the rooms that you wish to renovate. (You'll learn more about digitizing your images in Chapter 7). If you are thinking of using different wallpaper or colors, take photographs that include the wallpaper samples. This way, you can easily create a pattern in Photoshop from the wallpaper, and it will be at the proper proportions. Of course, you can also create your own patterns for wallpaper and floor tile designs.

Once you have digitized an image of a room, with its wallpaper and floor patterns, load your file. Figure 6-11 is a digitized image of a photograph of a kitchen before image editing in Photoshop. Notice the wallpaper samples hanging on the wall. Figure 6-12 displays the same digitized image after the electronic renovation. In this example, the Rubber Stamp tool's cloning powers were used to remove unwanted items such as the dishes, bottles, old-fashioned light fixture, paper towel holder, and pots and pans. The Edit/Fill command was used to fill a pattern created from a

The kitchen before image editing

FIGURE 6-11

The kitchen
after image
editing

FIGURE 6-12

wallpaper sample taped to the wall. The Burn tool dissipated the highlights, and the Sharpen tool made certain areas of the image more distinct.

This example should give you an idea of how money can be saved and mistakes can be avoided by first visualizing (via computer) various wallpaper designs, floor coverings, and cabinet treatments.

From the examples and exercises in this chapter, you can see that Photoshop provides numerous possibilities when editing an image. Now that you've seen the potential of image editing, you'll probably want to learn more about digitizing images so they can be edited with Photoshop. That's the subject of the next chapter.

DIGITIZING IMAGES

Digitized images are at the core of most Photoshop design projects. When you digitize a visual image, you are translating it into digital signals so it can be broken down into pixels and loaded into the computer. Assuring that images are digitized correctly is crucial to the success of your work. If the digitization process is not conducted properly, image quality will likely be unacceptable and colors may be flawed. Images that are digitized at too low a resolution may look jagged or blurred, and too high a resolution may cause the file size to increase to the point where the file can't even be edited on your computer.

Since scanning is the most widely used digitizing process, this chapter focuses on using a scanner to digitize an image directly through Photoshop. In addition, you'll experiment with some simple commands that are generally used right after scanning, including those that allow you to manipulate, correct, resize, and create special effects. You'll put your skills to work on a design project, as well as learn about other digitizing alternatives rapidly gaining popularity, such as Photo CD.

Before you can begin digitizing any image, you must first decide what equipment is necessary to properly digitize an image. For digitizing flat art, slides, or photographic prints, you will undoubtedly use a scanner. If your images are on film, you can have them digitized through Kodak's Photo CD process and then view the results in Photoshop with the aid of a CD-ROM XA (extended architecture) player. If you don't already have photographs or slides to work with, you may want to use a digital or video camera to digitize your images at the time you are shooting them. You can also digitize a still frame from videotape by using a video capture card connected to a video recorder.

SCANNING

The most important point to remember about scanners is that different scanners provide different quality output, just as different types of cameras produce photographs of various quality. An expensive camera with a sophisticated optical system will produce sharp, crisp images with a full range of accurate colors. Images produced from a cheaper camera will, of course, be of lower quality.

Using a low-end scanner is much like shooting a picture with an inexpensive camera. A low-end desktop scanner may well suit your needs for newspaper work and other low-resolution printing. Low-end desktop scans can also be placed in documents to test layout and design concepts; this is often called *FPO* ("for position only"). After the design has been finalized, the FPO image is replaced with a high-end scan before the project starts its journey to the printing press.

High-end digitizing is the domain of the service bureau. A service bureau will scan your image on expensive prepress equipment, such as Scitex's flatbed scanner, or a rotary drum scanner manufactured by DuPont Crosfield, Linotype-Hell, or Optronics. All of these scanners employ sophisticated optical and color-correcting systems to make your images crisp and sharp. Most will also convert an image from RGB Color to CMYK Color.

C AUTION: *Be aware that any image editing you do in Photoshop to FPO images cannot automatically be converted to the high-resolution scan. The work will need to be re-created on the higher-quality image. Most service bureaus and prepress houses will do this work for you if your own computer system cannot handle the file size of the high-resolution scans.*

You may be able to avoid the expense of high-end equipment by using a midrange scanner. These produce highly acceptable images because they can process more color information than low-end scanners, and they are more sensitive to the color range of an image. See Chapter 1 for more information on scanning hardware.

Before you begin scanning, you should know the dimensions of your final image and calculate the correct scanning resolution. Like monitor resolution, scanning resolution is measured in pixels per inch. More pixels in an image means it contains more information. Thus, in general, the more pixels you can pack into an image, the sharper it will be. If you scan at too low a resolution, your image may be blurry, or you may see the individual pixel elements in the image.

Notwithstanding the value of high-resolution images, it's generally unnecessary to scan at the highest possible resolution, because eventually a point of diminishing returns is reached. Printing presses can only produce images at a limited number of lines per inch, so the extra resolution will be wasted and may even result in images that look flat. The same holds true if your scans will be output for television, which has a top resolution of 640 by 480 pixels (72 ppi)—the NTSC (National Television System Committee) standard. Since television cannot produce images at a quality higher than that standard, it is generally unnecessary to scan at a higher resolution.

Why not just scan everything at a high resolution, just to be safe? Consider that file size is directly related to an image's resolution. Images that are scanned at higher resolutions produce larger file sizes than images scanned at low resolution. For instance, if you take a 72-ppi image and rescan it at twice the resolution (144 ppi), the new file will be approximately four times as large as the original 72-ppi image. Thus, if you scan at too high a resolution, an image's file size may become so large that it overwhelms your computer's memory capacity.

EMEMBER: *File size is directly related to an image's resolution. It's advisable to have at least three to five times your image's file size available in RAM or on your hard disk.*

Calculating Resolution and Image Size

If you are producing output for a printing press, calculate the image's resolution based upon the printing resolution.

The resolution of a printing press is measured in lines per inch (lpi), often called *line screen* or *screen frequency*. Your scanning resolution (measured in ppi) is directly related to the screen frequency. In the electronic printing process, screen frequency is produced by rows and columns of different-sized dots called *halftones*. These halftones are built from cells of the tiniest dots that can be produced by printers—from lasers to imagesetters. (Imagesetter dots are sometimes called *rels*, or raster elements; laser printer dots are frequently called pixels.) The following illustration shows how a halftone is built from a cell of pixels. Halftones and gray levels combine to produce the illusion of continuous tones of grays and colors in photographs. Halftones will be discussed in greater detail in Chapter 14.

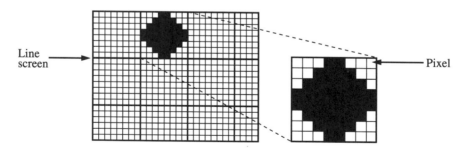

Halftone dot

When scanning, use this as a general rule: Two image pixels are needed for every halftone dot to produce high-quality output for images that will be printed on a printing press. Thus, the process of calculating the correct scanning resolution can often be reduced to the simple formula of doubling the screen frequency:

scanning resolution = 2 × screen frequency (lpi)

OTE: *When an image is printed, a file scanned at two times the line frequency actually has four times as much information, compared with the same file scanned at one times the line frequency. The number of pixels is quadrupled because pixels are added for each horizontal and vertical line screen.*

If you don't know what screen frequency will be used to print your work, ask your printer. When discussing printing resolution with your printer, you should also know what type of paper will be used. Generally, newspapers are printed at 85 lpi. Most magazines are printed on an offset press using 133 or 150 lpi. Some art books printed on coated paper use 200 lpi. Once you know what lpi you'll be using, you can calculate the resolution, or how many pixels per inch (ppi), you will need when you scan.

If you'd like, you can have Photoshop calculate the scanning resolution for you, as explained next. When Photoshop calculates the resolution, it will also reveal the file size of the image that you will be scanning.

Letting Photoshop Calculate Image Size and Resolution

In this section, you'll have Photoshop calculate both the file size and resolution for a grayscale or color image. Later in the chapter you'll read about calculating resolution for black and white line art and for images that will be enlarged.

Start by creating a new file. Select File/New, and in the dialog box enter the dimensions of the image you will be scanning. For the example here, use 3.5 inches for the Width and 5 inches for the Height. For now, leave the resolution set to 72 ppi. (Eventually Photoshop will change this value.) If you are scanning a color image, leave the mode set to RGB Color, because both your monitor and scanner produce colors from red, green, and blue values. If you are scanning a grayscale image, switch to Grayscale mode.

OTE: *If you are scanning in Grayscale mode, your file size will be smaller than in RGB Color mode because Photoshop will not need to store as much information. Rather than 24 bits per pixel of information to create colors, Photoshop uses only 8 bits per pixel for grayscale.*

At this point, notice that Photoshop has already calculated a file size. At 3.5 by 5 inches and Mode set to RGB Color, the dialog box displays 266K as the file size. When you are ready to continue, click OK.

After the new file appears, select Image Size from the Image menu. Notice that the Image Size dialog box, shown in Figure 7-1, contains all of the information you entered in the New dialog box: Width and Height are set to the size of your image, Resolution is set to 72 ppi, and the file size is the same as it was in the New dialog box. You'll also see the Constrain option check boxes called Proportions and File Size; these options will be discussed later.

Now you're ready to have Photoshop calculate your scanning resolution. In the Image Size dialog box, click the Auto button to display the Auto Resolution dialog box.

```
┌─────────────────── Auto Resolution ───────────────────┐
│                                                        │
│   Screen: [150]    [ lines/inch ▼ ]    ┌─────────┐    │
│                                         │   OK    │    │
│   ┌─ Quality ──────────────────────┐    └─────────┘    │
│   │  ○ Draft                       │    [ Cancel  ]    │
│   │  ○ Good                        │                   │
│   │  ◉ Best                        │                   │
│   └────────────────────────────────┘                   │
│                                                        │
└────────────────────────────────────────────────────────┘
```

In the Screen field, type in the screen frequency that you'll be using (if you don't know this, type **150**). Then click on one of the three Quality radio buttons to designate how you want Photoshop to calculate image resolution. If you click Best, Photoshop will multiply the screen frequency by 2 to compute the resolution; for Good, Photoshop will multiply the screen frequency by 1.5. If you pick Draft and your screen frequency is not less than 72, Photoshop will enter 72. If you enter a screen frequency less than 72 in the Screen field, Photoshop will use that number as your scanning resolution. Click OK, and Photoshop will calculate your resolution and return you to the Image Size dialog box.

The Image Size dialog box lets you tell Photoshop how to calculate file size and scanning resolution

FIGURE 7-1

When the Image Size dialog box reappears, notice that the New Size and Resolution values have changed. Resolution now displays the desired resolution, according to your screen frequency (if you used a screen frequency of 150, your new resolution will be 300 ppi). New Size displays the size of the file you will be working with. Now you can compare the anticipated file size to your computer's memory capacity.

Changing Image Dimensions and Resampling

If the new file size is too large for your system to handle, you can reduce the file size by decreasing the dimensions of the image in the Image Size dialog box.

Before you start making changes in the Image Size dialog box, note whether the Constrain Proportions check box is selected. If it is, the width-to-height ratio will remain constant no matter what values you enter (that is, altering the Width field will cause a proportional change in the Height field). The chain-link icon next to these two fields indicates that the two values are linked.

```
percent
pixels
✓inches
cm
points
picas
columns
```

If you know the percentage of enlargement or reduction for the file to be digitized, you can change the measurement units in the New Size fields from inches to percent. To do this, click on the pop-up menu to the right of either Width or Height and choose percent. (You'll also see a columns measurement unit in this menu, which can be used if you will be exporting your file into a desktop publishing program that has multicolumn page-layout capability. The columns measurement uses the units specified in the Unit Preferences dialog box, discussed in the "Unit Preferences" section of Chapter 2. In this dialog box you can set the column width and the gutter size as well.)

If you don't want a proportional change, deselect the Constrain Proportions check box. Be aware, however, that if you turn off the Proportions option and then change the dimensions of an image, you will distort it.

The other Constrain option in the Image Size dialog box is for File Size. When this option is *not* selected, Photoshop reduces the file size when the New Size Height and Width values are decreased. It will also decrease the file size if you lower the Resolution value. If you increase Resolution or Width and Height, the file size will grow. If the File Size checkbox is selected now, deselect it so you can experiment; then type a smaller number into the Width or Height field. Notice that the New Size value decreases.

When Photoshop increases or decreases the file size, it adds or subtracts pixels in your image. Adding or subtracting pixels is called *resampling*. It's important to realize that when you resample, Photoshop must make some sacrifices in image quality. If you decrease the dimensions of your image size, Photoshop must subtract pixels; if you increase your image size, Photoshop must add pixels. When Photoshop adds pixels, it *interpolates*. During interpolation, Photoshop attempts to smooth the difference between the original pixels and the ones it adds. This can result in a somewhat blurred image.

If you resample down (that is, decrease file size) and then later resample back up, the final image will not be as sharp as the original. This is because Photoshop must remove pixels, and when you resample back up Photoshop interpolates and cannot add the original pixels that were subtracted earlier.

Changing Image Dimensions Without Resampling

At this point, you may be wondering whether it's possible to change an image's size or resolution without resampling (adding or subtracting pixels). You can—using the Constrain File Size option. When the File Size check box is selected, the size of your image will not change when you modify its dimensions or resolution. In order to keep the file size constant, though, Photoshop must compensate by changing the resolution when you change dimensions, or changing dimensions when you change the resolution. To avoid adding or subtracting pixels, Photoshop decreases the resolution if you increase the dimensions of your image. If you decrease the dimensions of your image, Photoshop increases the resolution.

OTE: *If you resize without resampling, the display of your image on screen will not change because you have not added or subtracted pixels. If Photoshop's rulers are displayed, they will indicate any change in image dimensions.*

Take a moment and try this out—it's important to understand how file size, image dimension, and resolution are related because they all affect your work. Select the Constrain File Size checkbox. Notice that the chain-link icon now shows that the image dimensions and resolution are linked. Enter a higher value for either Width or Height, and you'll see that Resolution drops. This makes sense: If you want to make an image larger, but you don't add any information to it, the resolution will be lower.

The inverse is true when you change the Resolution setting. Increase it, and Photoshop decreases the image dimensions; decrease Resolution, and Photoshop increases the image dimensions. Try entering a higher value into the Resolution field, and watch the file's dimensions drop. If you want more pixels per inch and you don't want the file size to change, the image dimensions will have to decrease.

If this concept seems confusing, here's an analogy: Assume that you have a balloon with a painted image on it, consisting of many tiny dots of paint. If you stretch the balloon out to make the image size greater, the space between each dot grows, and you have fewer dots per square inch. This is the same as decreasing resolution when file dimensions are increased. Squeeze the balloon to make the image smaller, and the dots get closer together. Similarly, the image resolution increases when the file dimensions are decreased. In both cases, whether you stretched or compressed the balloon, the actual mass of rubber or the number of dots did not change. Likewise, the file size and number of pixels in your image always remain the same even if you change its dimensions or resolution with the Constrain File Size check box selected.

The following chart summarizes how the Constrain File Size option affects your image, when working in inches:

	Increase Dimensions	Decrease Dimensions	Increase Resolution	Decrease Resolution
File Size check box OFF (resampling)	Increases file size	Decreases file size	Increases file size	Decreases file size
File Size check box ON (no resampling)	Decreases resolution; file size is unchanged	Increases resolution; file size is unchanged	Decreases dimensions; file size is unchanged	Increases dimensions; file size is unchanged

At this point, you should have a good idea about how you can control Photoshop image dimensions, file sizes, and resolutions. You can even test how fast Photoshop will operate on your computer at different image sizes and resolutions. If you'd like to "test-drive" your computer at your digitized image's size and resolution, return the settings in the Image Size dialog box to those needed by your image. (In our example, width is 3.5 inches, height is 5 inches, and resolution is 300 ppi.) Click OK to continue.

After you click OK in the Image Size dialog box, you'll probably see your document window enlarge—because you have increased the file's resolution over its previous setting of 72 ppi. The new window size reflects the fact that more pixels are consuming each inch of the image. Remember, if you are working on any file that has a resolution higher than your monitor's 72 ppi, your image will be displayed larger than actual size. (For more information, see "Creating a New File" in Chapter 2.)

Now you can test to see how fast your computer will work with the anticipated file size of your soon-to-be-scanned image. Try painting with a couple of different tools to see how Photoshop responds. You don't need an image in the file to do this. Remember, even though the file has no image, pixels are pixels; it doesn't matter whether they're white, black, or colored.

Calculating Resolution for an Enlarged Image

Now that you have calculated your scanning resolution and image size, you are just about ready to scan your image. But there are two more issues you might need to consider—whether the image will be enlarged during scanning or in Photoshop, and whether black-and-white line art will be scanned.

If you are going to enlarge the scanned image dimensions (likely if you are scanning slides, for instance), you'll need to increase the scanning resolution before you scan. Increasing the number of pixels in the image will ensure that the quality is maintained when the image is enlarged. If you don't boost the resolution, image clarity will suffer, and the image may become pixelated (the individual pixels in the image become evident when the image dimensions are enlarged).

To calculate the correct scanning resolution for an image that will be enlarged, use the following formula:

$$\begin{matrix} \text{longest} \\ \text{dimension} \\ \text{in final} \\ \text{image} \end{matrix} \times \begin{matrix} \text{screen} \\ \text{frequency} \\ \text{(lpi)} \end{matrix} \times \begin{matrix} \text{pixel-} \\ \text{to-line screen} \\ \text{ratio} \end{matrix} \div \begin{matrix} \text{longest dimension} \\ \text{of original image} \end{matrix}$$

As an example, assume you scan an image of 2 inches by 3 inches and want to enlarge it to 4 inches by 6 inches. (Also assume your screen frequency is 150 lpi.) Here's a step-by-step explanation of how to apply the formula:

1. Multiply the longest dimension (height or width) of the final image by the screen frequency (lpi). This produces the minimum number of pixels necessary to produce the longest dimension of the image. In our example, 6×150 equals a total of 900 pixels.

2. As discussed earlier in the chapter, to produce a high-quality image 2 pixels are needed for every line-screen inch (or per halftone dot); thus, 2 is the pixel-to-line screen ratio. In our example, 2 times 900 equals 1,800, the optimum number of pixels necessary to produce the longest dimension of the image.

3. To obtain the scanning resolution, divide the optimum number of pixels needed to produce the longest dimension by the longest dimension of the original image. In our example, 1,800 divided by 3 equals 600 ppi, the final scanning resolution.

After you've calculated the correct resolution and scanned your image at that resolution, you would then use the Image Size dialog box with the Constrain File Size check box selected to enlarge your image.

OTE: *If you are uncertain about what screen frequency or pixel-to-line screen ratio you should use, check with your service bureau and/or commercial printer.*

As previously mentioned, the foregoing calculation is extremely important when scanning slides. For example, let's say you are enlarging the longest dimension of a slide to 5 inches. Since the longest dimension of a 35mm slide is 1.375 inches, you would use the following calculation (if your screen frequency is 150): $5 \times 150 \times 2 \div 1.375$, and your scanning resolution would be a little less than 1,100 ppi.

Choosing a Resolution for Black-and-White Line Art

Black-and-white images such as line art, logos, and text are frequently referred to as *bitmap* images. This term is used because only 1 bit is necessary to make each pixel of the image black or white. As discussed in "Video Display Cards" in Chapter 1, a bit can be either off or on. If the bit is on, the pixel is black; if it is off, the pixel is white.

If you are scanning bitmap images, you may be surprised to learn that resolution must sometimes be set higher than when working with color. In color and grayscale images, gradations of colors and grays can hide edges and make an image blend into its background. In black-and-white images, on the other hand, the stark contrast between black and white draws the eye's attention to outlines.

Many printing professionals suggest scanning at a resolution as high as your output device. As mentioned in "Output Devices" in Chapter 1, resolution for both printers and imagesetters is measured in dots per inch (dpi). If you are producing output for an imagesetter with a resolution of 1,200 dpi, you should scan at 1,200 ppi. If you are printing to a laser printer that outputs 300 dpi, you may as well scan at 300 ppi. Even if you scan at a 1,000 ppi, your 300-dpi printer cannot add any more resolution to the image.

Using File/Acquire to Scan an Image

After you've decided which scanner to use and have calculated your scanning resolution, you are ready to start scanning. This section takes you step by step from previewing your image to scanning it from within Photoshop.

TWAIN

In order to scan, you will need to install the plug-in (driver) that is provided by your scanner's manufacturer, which allows you to operate the scanner from within Photoshop. To install the plug-in, copy it into the Plug-ins folder (PC users: plugins). If you are using a scanner that supports the TWAIN standard—such as the Hewlett-Packard Scanjet—you will need to install the TWAIN software that comes with your scanner. PC users might need to update scanning software that was released earlier than the Windows version of Photoshop.

 OTE: *If your scanner did not come with a Photoshop plug-in, you may need to scan using the software that came with your scanner.*

If you install the plug-in while you have Photoshop open, you'll need to Quit and restart Photoshop before you continue.

Once your scanner plug-in is installed, and before you begin digitizing an image, read the instructions that come with your scanner. In particular, find out whether your scanner allows you to set the *white point* (sometimes called *highlight point*) and the *black point* (sometimes called the *shadow point*). From these two endpoints, your software may be able to create a tone curve to ensure that the scanner captures the widest density or dynamic range.

 OTE: *Scanning software, such as PixelCraft Color Access and Light Source Ofoto, may provide features not found in your scanning software.*

Agfa PhotoScan 2.13

The explanations in this section are based on the Agfa Arcus scanner, a midrange scanner available for both Mac and PC users, using the Agfa PhotoScan plug-in. The steps described here are similar to those you'll perform for most desktop scanners.

When you're ready, turn on the scanner (if it isn't already on). Place the image facedown on the scanner's glass plate. Try to get the image placed as straight as possible; otherwise, the scanned image will appear crooked. If you are using a slide scanner, place the slide in the slide holder. The Arcus scanner scans reflective objects, such as photographs and line art, as well as transparencies, such as slides. In this procedure, we will use the reflective option.

To begin the scanning process within Photoshop, select Acquire from the File menu. If your scanner has a plug-in, you will see it in the Acquire submenu. Select your scanner driver from the Acquire submenu.

If you have a TWAIN-compatible scanner, the first time you use your scanner you must select it as the scanning source. In the Acquire submenu, choose TWAIN Select Source, and then select your scanner in the dialog box that appears. To start the scanning process, choose File/Acquire again, and choose TWAIN Acquire.

Your next step is to preview the scanned image and choose a specific area of the image to scan. If you don't do this, the final image will be as large as the scanner's entire scanning area and you'd wind up with a very large file size. Another reason for previewing is to make sure you haven't put the image in the scanner upside down. To begin the preview, click on the Preview button. In a minute or so the preview will appear on screen.

After the miniature image appears, select the specific area to scan, as shown in Figure 7-2. Most scanner selection controls work similarly; typically you only need to click and drag over the specific part of the previewed image that you wish to scan. Don't worry about selecting too precisely. Once the image has been scanned, you can crop out extraneous portions in Photoshop. Notice, as shown in Figure 7-2, that the Arcus scanner dialog box produces a handy readout of the image dimensions, image size (5505K), and output resolution (screen frequency 150 lpi) for printing.

Next, after selecting the area to be scanned, you're ready to choose a mode and scanning resolution for the digitized image. Click on the Mode pop-up menu and choose either Color, Grayscale, or Lineart (sometimes called Bitmap), then choose a resolution. In this example, the Input pop-up menu will be used to change the resolution to 300 ppi.

The Arcus scanner plug-in previews an image and its file size, and allows the dynamic range to be set automatically

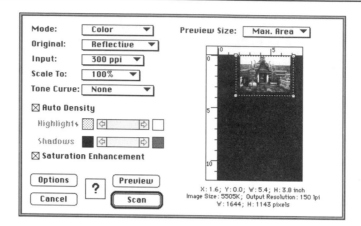

FIGURE 7-2

Before scanning, examine the controls in your own scanning window. If you don't know the purpose of each option, consult your scanner's manual. Notice that the Arcus scanning window includes an Auto Density setting. When Auto Density is enabled, the scanner will automatically set its *density range,* or *dynamic range.* A scanner's dynamic range is the range of colors it can identify, from the brightest to the darkest. With Auto Density on, the scanner prescans the image to measure the brightest highlight and the darkest shadow. This helps the scanner capture the broadest dynamic range possible.

The Arcus plug-in also features commands to eliminate *color casts,* shifts in color toward red, green, or blue. If an image displays too much of any of these colors, the cast can be eliminated by clicking the Options button to open the Color Options dialog box and adjusting the sliders for the red, green, and blue values.

Many scanners allow you to change exposure settings before you scan. If you wish, you can experiment with these settings, or make adjustments to your image later in Photoshop.

When you're ready to scan the image, click the Scan button. In a few minutes, the scan will be completed and the image will appear in a Photoshop window.

ROTATING AND FLIPPING A SCANNED IMAGE

When the scanned image appears in Photoshop, you may see that, despite your best efforts, the image is tilted. The Rotate commands in Photoshop's Image menu help you fix this. These commands can also be used to rotate an image that had to be scanned sideways so that it would fit on the scanner flatbed, or to turn over an image that was inadvertently scanned upside down.

If you wish to rotate your entire image, you need not select it (except when using the Image/Rotate/Free command). If you rotate a selected portion of the image or select the entire image, Photoshop may crop part of it when you execute one of the Rotate commands. This can occur because Photoshop allows you to rotate an image so that parts of it extend beyond the document window. If you rotate the entire image without first selecting it, Photoshop will change the size of the window, so no part of the image will be cropped.

OTE: *If you want to follow along with these steps, but you don't want to rotate or change your scanned image on screen, you can load one of the images from the Frames file (PC users: frames.jpg) in the Tutorial folder.*

To rotate the image, choose Rotate from the Image menu. The Rotate submenu provides you with several choices, as shown here. Each option will rotate your image according to the angle indicated (CW means clockwise and CCW means counterclockwise). The Arbitrary option allows you to specify a particular degree of rotation. Since this command is more flexible than the others, it's a good place to start, so select Arbitrary.

In the dialog box that appears, you will enter the rotation degree that you wish to use and specify clockwise or counterclockwise rotation. In the Angle field you can enter values from –359.99 to 359.99 degrees. So you can easily see the results of this test, enter **45**. Click the CCW radio button to rotate counterclockwise. Click OK.

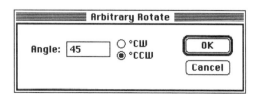

You'll see that the entire screen image rotates 45 degrees counterclockwise. To return the screen to its original position, rotate the image again, this time 45 degrees clockwise.

Before moving on, try one more test, using the Rotate submenu's Free option. This option allows you to click and drag with the mouse to control the rotation. When you rotate with the Free option, it's often helpful to have the Info palette on screen; this palette will display your rotating angle as you are working.

Now try this out. Select part of your image with the Rectangular Marquee. Select Image/Rotate and choose Free. Handles will appear at the corners of the selection marquee. To rotate, position the mouse pointer over any handle, and click and drag it in any direction. The selection marquee will provide you with a preview of your selection. When you are happy with the rotation, position the mouse over the selection, and the pointer will change to a gavel (⌐⊣). This indicates that Photoshop will hammer down the selection when you click the mouse.

Flipping an Image

The Flip commands in the Image menu let you flip an image to face it in a different direction. The Flip, as well as the Rotate, commands can be applied to a selected area in an image to create special effects.

If you wish to flip the entire image, you do not have to select it. (However, if the image you are working with now is large and you wish to test this command, it's wise to use the Rectangular Marquee to create a small selection to flip. Otherwise, you may be waiting some time for Photoshop to finish its task.) If you wish, you can continue to use the Frames file or any digitized image to experiment with.

To flip your image horizontally, choose Flip from the Image menu, and choose Horizontal. Your image will flip along a vertical plane and face in a new direction.

Return to the Flip submenu and choose Vertical to see the image flip along a horizontal plane, turning it upside down. Flip your image again to make it right-side up.

Now that you've rotated your image so it's straight and flipped it to face in the direction you want, you might wish to crop it, as explained next.

USING THE CROPPING TOOL

Cropping is very similar to taking a pair of scissors and cutting an image so that only a portion of the original is visible. You can also crop to remove unwanted border areas left over from a scan. Removing unwanted border areas is also a good way to keep the size of your file under control.

Before you begin to crop, double-click on the Cropping tool and examine its dialog box to make sure that no previous settings for the tool will interfere with your work.

```
╔══════════════ Cropping Tool Options ══════════════╗
║                                                    ║
║     Width: [          ]  [ inches    ▼ ]  ┌──────┐ ║
║                                           │  OK  │ ║
║    Height: [          ]  [ inches    ▼ ]  └──────┘ ║
║                                           ┌──────┐ ║
║ Resolution: [          ] [ pixels/inch ▼ ]│Cancel│ ║
║                                           └──────┘ ║
╚════════════════════════════════════════════════════╝
```

The Cropping Tool Options dialog box contains dimension settings that are by now familiar to you. You can specify Width and Height measurement units in inches, centimeters, points, pixels, or columns. Notice that you can also change the resolution of the cropped area. If you change the width and height measurements and you want to maintain your image's current resolution, it's important to type that resolution into the Resolution field. If you don't, Photoshop will change the resolution to compensate for the change in width or height when you eventually execute the crop.

The Cropping tool also works somewhat like the Image Size dialog box. If you don't enter a resolution, it's the same as telling Photoshop to readjust the file dimensions without changing the number of pixels in the image. So if you reduce the width or height, Photoshop will increase the resolution proportionally.

Conversely, if you enter a resolution without changing the height or width, Photoshop will change the image dimensions proportionally. If you increase the resolution, Photoshop will decrease the image size; decrease the resolution, and Photoshop will increase the image size.

If you exit the Cropping Tool Options dialog box without setting any values, you can crop freely with the mouse, and the resolution of the image will remain unchanged. If any values are now in the dialog box, delete them for this experiment. When you are ready to continue, click OK.

To begin cropping, click on the Cropping tool in the Toolbox. The mouse pointer turns into the cropping tool icon.

IP: *If CAPS LOCK is on, the pointer will be a crosshair instead of the cropping tool icon. The crosshair pointer is more precise, because you can set the starting point of the cropping area to be exactly at the intersection of the crosshair.*

With the Cropping tool selected, click and drag over the image area that you want to retain. The area *outside* the selection is the portion that will be cropped.

When you are satisfied with the selection, release the mouse button. Notice that the selected area on screen now includes one handle at each corner. If you need to make any adjustments to the crop, click and drag any of the handles to resize the selected area. To move the entire selection marquee, press COMMAND (PC users: CTRL), click on one of the four handles, and drag with the mouse.

If you crop your image incorrectly or accidentally, it's easy to undo the crop by immediately choosing Edit/Undo.

IP: *You can also use the Cropping tool to rotate a selection. Press OPTION (PC users: ALT) and click and drag on any of the selection handles.*

You'll probably notice that if you move the mouse outside the selected cropping area, the pointer will change to a circle with a bar through it (⊘). This indicates you can cancel the selected cropping area by clicking the mouse. If you move the mouse inside the selected area, the pointer will change to a scissors icon (✄). The scissors icon indicates that you can crop the image by clicking the mouse.

When you have selected the area you wish to crop, move the Cropping tool into the middle of the selection. The scissors icon will appear, as shown in Figure 7-3. At this point, click the mouse to crop the area.

IP: *To crop an image, you can also use the Rectangular Marquee tool to select an area and then choose the Crop command from the Edit menu.*

Now that you have the image cropped exactly the way you want it, you may want to make some simple adjustments to your image's brightness and contrast.

ADJUSTING BRIGHTNESS AND CONTRAST

Contrast is the difference between the lightest and darkest parts of an image. *Brightness* is the degree of light that is reflected from an image or transmitted through it.

Some scanners have a tendency to darken images, causing them to lose contrast. Images frame-grabbed from videotape also may have a tendency to darken when loaded into Photoshop. When you need to make simple adjustments to the brightness and contrast levels of your image, you'll find that the Brightness/Contrast command

Crop line →

The scissors icon shows that the area selected with the Cropping tool can be cropped by clicking the mouse

FIGURE 7-3

Crop handle   Scissors icon

7

in the Image/Adjust submenu may solve the problem. (If your image needs more extensive color correction and retouching, refer to Chapter 13.)

To use the Brightness/Contrast controls, first select an area to be adjusted, or don't select in order to adjust the entire image. Choose Adjust from the Image menu, and then Brightness/Contrast. The Brightness/Contrast dialog box is a simple one: It contains a Preview check box and sliders for adjusting Brightness and Contrast.

First, make sure the Preview check box is selected so you can watch the results of your adjustments, and then begin by testing the Brightness slider. Drag the slider control to the right to brighten your image, or to the left to darken your image. Take a few moments now to adjust Brightness to the best level for your image. Be careful not to overexpose or underexpose the image.

When you are satisfied with the brightness level, try adjusting the contrast. Moving the slider control to the right adds more detail; this increases the difference between the lightest and darkest portion of the image. If you drag the slider control to the left, the lightness and darkness levels will begin to merge.

Once you are satisfied with the new brightness and contrast levels, click OK. If the image doesn't look as good as it did when you started, you can either drag both sliders back to their zero points or click Cancel.

RESIZING AN IMAGE

You may need to increase or decrease the size of a digitized image so that it will fit in a specific area when you print it. To resize an image, you'll use the Image Size command in the Image menu, which is fully explained earlier in this chapter.

Remember, if you increase image dimensions (with the Constrain File Size check box deselected), Photoshop must interpolate. By default, Photoshop uses its best possible interpolation method. As you can probably guess, the best method is also the slowest.

Changing Interpolation Methods

To view the interpolation choices, select Preferences in the File menu, and choose General. Click on the Interpolation pop-up menu to see the choices. Nearest Neighbor is the fastest but least exact interpolation method. If you use this method, your image will probably look jagged after rotating or using other manipulation commands. With Bicubic, the best interpolation method, Photoshop attempts to improve contrast while interpolating. Bilinear is the middle ground between Nearest Neighbor and Bicubic.

Interpolation: | Nearest Neighbor / Bilinear / ✓ Bicubic

If you wish to change interpolation methods now, select one from the list, click OK in the General Preferences dialog box, and continue.

Changing the Image Dimensions

To change the dimensions of the image, enter a new value in either the Width or Height field (under New Size) in the Image Size dialog box. If the Constrain

Proportions check box is selected, Photoshop will automatically change the other value. If the Constrain File Size option is off, your resolution will remain the same, but the new file size in bytes will change.

Later in this chapter, in the "Working with Image Effects" section, you will work through a design project in which the example image will be reduced by one half-inch. Go ahead and do this to your own image now, if you wish. But before you click OK, remember that when you decrease the size of your image (with the Constrain File Size check box deselected), Photoshop removes pixels from it. Thus, if you later try to resample up, the image will not look as sharp as the original. Once Photoshop removes the pixels, they're gone for good; Photoshop cannot re-create them. When Photoshop resamples up, it resamples based upon the contents of the current file. When you are ready to have Photoshop resample your image, click OK.

INCREASING THE CANVAS SIZE

Now that you have the image the size you want, you may wish to increase your work area on screen. You can do this by changing the *canvas size* of your image. When you increase the canvas size, you extend the perimeter of your document. This puts a border of the background color around the image. Later in this chapter, you'll see how you can utilize this border as an area for adding text and extra images to a document.

When a border is added, Photoshop uses the current background color as the canvas color. Before you change the canvas size, pick a background color that you like. If you want the canvas color to match one of the colors in your image, you can use the Eyedropper tool and OPTION key (PC users: ALT) to switch background colors (as long as the Foreground selection box is activated in the Colors palette). Activate the Eyedropper by clicking on it, press OPTION (PC users: ALT), move the eyedropper pointer over the color you wish to use as your background color, and click.

To change the canvas size, choose Canvas Size from the Image menu. In the Canvas Size dialog box, notice that your image's current dimensions appear in the Width and Height fields. At this point, they are the same as the canvas. If you increase these values in the Width and Height fields for New Size, the perimeter or surrounding canvas will grow. This will produce a border around the image in the current background color.

The Canvas Size dialog box also allows you to indicate the placement of your image in the canvas. At the bottom of the dialog box is the Placement area, a grid of nine boxes. The selected box represents the position of your image in relation to the canvas. If you select the center box, Photoshop will center your image in the Canvas. If you click on the lower-middle box, Photoshop will drop your image to the bottom-middle part of the canvas. This is the placement chosen for the design project, shown in Figure 7-6, presented later in this chapter. Also, 1 inch was added to both the Width and Height, as shown in Figure 7-4. The result is a half-inch border on the left and right sides of the image, and a one-inch canvas area on top.

To create a canvas background for your image now, increase the Width and Height settings in the New Size area of the Canvas Size dialog box. Try adding 1 inch to both. If you wish your image to appear as shown in the design project, choose the bottom-middle Placement box. Click OK to see the results.

At this point you have learned how to rotate, flip, crop, change brightness and contrast, resize, and border your digitized image. We'll look now at some special effects that will add variety to your image. You will use these techniques to create a sample design project.

WORKING WITH THE IMAGE/EFFECTS COMMANDS

The commands available in Photoshop's Image/Effects submenu allow you to scale, skew, change perspective, and distort floating text or any selected part of an image. Use the Scale command to resize part of an image, Skew to slant an image, Perspective to create the appearance of depth in an image, and Distort to stretch an image in different directions.

To try any of these commands, you must first create a selection, and then choose either Scale, Skew, Perspective, or Distort from the Image/Effects submenu. These

One inch was added to the Width and Height to increase the canvas (work area)

FIGURE 7-4

commands work similarly to the Rotate/Free command. After you choose an Image/Effects command, Photoshop adds handles to the selection. With the mouse,

you click and drag on the handles to preview the effect. Once you position the mouse over the selection, the gavel icon appears, and when you click inside the selection, Photoshop executes the command.

CAUTION: *Be aware that when you execute any of the Image/Effects menu commands, Photoshop interpolates. Thus, image quality depends upon the interpolation method set in the General Preferences dialog box.*

Take a few moments to try out each Image/Effects command. If you don't wish to apply the commands to your current image, open a new file and create some text that you can experiment with. Remember, these commands can only be applied to selections or to floating text. Here are some guidelines for using Image/Effects commands:

- To scale an object in proportion, press the SHIFT key while you use the Scale command.

- When you use the Perspective command, try dragging one handle up and the opposite one down or diagonally in and out. As you drag one handle, another one will move in the opposite direction, to create depth or dimensionality. Figure 7-5 illustrates the effect of the Perspective command applied to a text selection. Here, clicking and dragging downward on the lower-right handle caused the top-right handle to move upward.

- When you skew a selection, click and drag on any handle. All handles will always move along a horizontal plane as the object is slanted.

- You can distort a selection by clicking and dragging on any handle in any direction. With Distort you can create effects that look like Perspective and Skew, except you have more control over the selected area.

After you've finished experimenting, you may want to use the Revert command to retrieve the last saved version of your file before you continue to the next section, where you'll see the image effects demonstrated in a design project.

Photoshop in Action

The sphinx was scanned and then selected with the Lasso tool. It was pasted into the monitor, then shrunk with the Image/Effects/Scale command.

The monitor was selected and then stretched using the Image/Effects/Scale command.

Artist: Marc Yankus   **Client: Computer World**

Marc started by scanning black-and-white images of various pyramids. These were selected with the selection tools and filled with color using the Edit/Fill command. In the Fill dialog box, Marc set the mode to Darken, so that only the light areas would be painted and not the dark areas. Then he scanned a picture of a computer. Once the computer was scanned, he selected it with the Lasso tool and pasted it into the final image.

With the
Perspective
command,
dragging a
handle
distorts the
image and
creates
depth

FIGURE 7-5

Image Effects Design Project

If you wish to complete a project like the one shown in Figure 7-6, load any digitized
image, or the image you used in the "Increasing the Canvas Size" section earlier in
the chapter (and skip step 1).

1. Choose a background color and then use the Image/Canvas Size
   command to add 1 inch to both the Width and Height of your image. Set
   Placement in the Canvas Size dialog box so that the bottom-middle box is
   selected. This will create a .5-inch canvas border area on the left and right
   or your image, and a 1-inch canvas border area above your image.

2. Next, to fill the half-inch border on the right and left sides with a
   duplicated portion of your image (see Figure 7-6 as an example), use the
   Rectangular Marquee tool to create a selection. It doesn't matter whether
   the selection is bigger than the half-inch canvas border because you can
   scale it to fit.

3. With the image area selected, duplicate it by pressing OPTION (PC users:
   ALT) while you click and drag the selection toward the upper-left canvas
   border area. *Don't deselect.* (You can also create a duplicate by choosing
   Select/Float and then clicking and dragging the selection.)

A design
project
created
using the
Image/Effects
commands

FIGURE 7-6

4. Choose Scale from the Image/Effects submenu. Scale the image by clicking on one of the four corners. If you wish, press SHIFT to constrain proportionally.

5. When you are satisfied with the scaling, move the mouse pointer into the center of the scaled image. When the gavel icon appears, as shown in Figure 7-7, click the mouse. After the scaled image has been hammered down on your screen, *do not deselect it.*

6. Keep the scaled image selected so that you can reproduce it several times in order to cover the entire left and right borders. While pressing OPTION (PC users: ALT), click and drag to duplicate the image as many times as needed to cover the borders.

Once you've assembled the border, you are ready to start creating the distorted text. Before you begin, make sure that the foreground color is set to the color you wish to use for the text (we used white).

7. Select the Type tool and click on the top canvas area. When the Type Tool dialog box appears, pick an appropriate font and size. So that the text does not appear jagged, select the Anti-Aliased option.

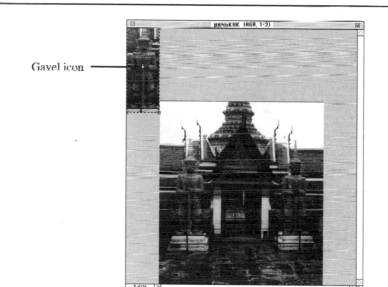

Gavel icon

The Scale command is used to shrink a selection that was created by duplicating part of the image

FIGURE 7-7

7

8. Type the heading you want to appear in your image. In our example, we used BANGKOK. Click OK. Don't deselect.

10. Your next step is to distort the type. While the text is still selected, choose Distort from the Image/Effects submenu. (If you prefer, you can create a different effect by choosing Perspective or Skew.) When the handles appear, click and drag on them to create the look you want. In this example, all four handles were dragged to create the distortion.

11. When you are ready to apply the effects of your adjustments, move the mouse into the center of the selection. When the gavel appears, as shown in Figure 7-8, click to seal in your changes.

12. Move the distorted text into position. If you'd like, duplicate the text, fill it with another color (we used black), and offset it; this effect can be seen in Figure 7-6.

If you wish to execute any more image effects, feel free to experiment.

The remaining sections of this chapter discuss some alternative digitizing methods for use with Photoshop; these options require hardware other than scanners.

With the Distort command, selection handles can be adjusted to create the distortion

FIGURE 7-8

PHOTO CD

If you need to have your images photographed first before digitizing them, you might be able to avoid scanning altogether. Eastman Kodak's Photo CD process transforms a roll of film into a CD-ROM disc filled with digitized images. Each disc stored in Kodak's standard Master format can hold 25 to 100 35mm images. The images are stored at five different resolutions, from 128 by 192 pixels to 2,048 by 3,072 pixels. Expect the low-resolution color images to be about 72K in size; high-resolution images will be around 18MB.

Kodak's newest format, Pro Photo CD, allows film sizes of up to 4 inches by 5 inches and a top resolution of 4,000 by 6,000 pixels. For a 4-by-5-inch image, this would provide you with a resolution of approximately 1,200 ppi. Thus, you easily could enlarge to an 8-by-10-inch image without sacrificing quality.

In order to use the Photo CD images, you need a CD-ROM player that incorporates XA (extended architecture), which most new CD-ROM players have. You'll also want to get a multisession drive, because it will let you add photos to CD-ROMs that are not filled to the 100-picture capacity. Once you've connected your CD-ROM to your computer, you can load the images into Photoshop using the File/Open command. When you load the file, you will be able to choose a file format and a resolution.

Kodak sells a plug-in (driver) for Photoshop. After choosing the Photo CD plug-in from the File/Acquire submenu, you see the dialog box shown in Figure 7-9, in which you choose an image and a resolution. You can see that there is a preview of the image, and a Sharpening option. There are also a variety of Metric options, which give you a choice of importing the file into Photoshop as a Video RGB, Grayscale, or Photo YCC image (Kodak's own color space model). The Metric option also allows you to change gamma levels for the midtones of the image. A gamma setting higher than 1 brightens; a gamma setting lower than 1 darkens.

If you select Video RGB or a gamma level, and then click on the Edit Image button, you can change the color balance of the image by clicking and dragging on slider controls for Saturation, Cyan/Red, Magenta/Green, Yellow/Blue, and Dark/Light.

DIGITAL AND VIDEO CAMERAS

Digital and still-video cameras provide even more versatile alternatives to scanning. With these cameras, you don't have to wait for film to be developed and then scan or convert to Photo CD. By digitizing with a still-video or digital camera, you can quickly see the results by shooting in a studio with the camera connected to a computer. If the image doesn't please you, you can usually change your lighting setup and reshoot.

Photo CD
images can
be loaded
and their
resolution
chosen
using the
Kodak
Photo CD
Acquire
Module

FIGURE 7-9

Still-video and digital photography is growing in popularity—particularly in catalog work, where many products need to be digitized quickly. Many digital cameras provide Photoshop plug-ins, so you can use the File/Acquire command to load the image directly into Photoshop. Many digital cameras feature on-board disks, memory cards, or hard disks. To download files to a computer, some cameras require an interface card to be installed in the computer; others, such as Kodak's DCS 200, can be plugged into a computer via a SCSI port.

Using Kodak's DCS 200 Digital Camera

The Kodak DCS 200 comes with a plug-in that is accessed using the File/Acquire command. The Acquire dialog box provides a preview of the image. Using the mouse, you can click on a white area of the preview to set the image's *white point*—the lightest part of the image. Once the white point is captured, the image can be opened into Photoshop at the proper dynamic range.

The example you see in Figure 7-10 was digitized by Image Technologies, Inc., a New York City prepress house, using the Kodak DCS 200 camera. In the image, notice there is a Kodak Gray Scale alongside the art being digitized. After the image was digitized, Photoshop's Eyedropper tool was used to click on the various gray

A Photoshop screen shot of an image digitized by Kodak's DCS 200 camera

FIGURE 7-10

levels to analyze whether pure gray was being produced. This test ensured that no color cast (excess of any color) was being produced during the digital photography session.

Sony SEPS-1000 Digital Camera

Figure 7-11 is another example of an image created for a catalog with a digital camera. The camera that digitized the image is the camera you see in the image, the Sony SEPS-1000 Digital Studio Camera. The image appeared in Tegra-Varityper's PrePRESS DIRECT catalog. Like the Kodak camera, the Sony camera can be used to digitize directly into Photoshop through a plug-in module.

FotoMan Plus

If you don't need high-resolution color images but you still want to save time and avoid the cost of film and processing, Logitech's FotoMan Plus might be the option for you. This small digital camera sells for less than $800 and saves up to 32 grayscale photos in its internal memory. Image resolution is 496 by 360 pixels. Pictures can be downloaded to both Macs or PCs.

7

A Sony SEPS-1000 digital camera digitized this image of another Sony SEPS-1000 camera (image courtesy of Tegra-Varityper)

FIGURE 7-11

FotoMan has been used successfully by real-estate companies to take pictures of houses and catalog them, or mail printouts to customers.

VIDEO CAPTURE

Photoshop's plug-in capabilities allow still-frames to be captured from videotape. To capture video, a card must be installed in your computer to convert the television signals (NTSC) to RGB so the images can be input to Photoshop. The plug-in and video card combination also allows the RGB signals to be converted to an NTSC television signal for output back to videotape. One of the best-known manufacturers of video cards for both PCs and Macs is TrueVision. TrueVision makes the Targa board for the PC and the NuVista board for the Mac. If you are using a Mac, you should investigate Apple's new AV computer models, which have video input and output capabilities built in.

To obtain frame-accurate control over the input and recording of the video signal, most multimedia systems require a video card that controls a videotape recorder.

Figure 7-12 shows two dialog boxes that appear in Photoshop when used with DiaQuest's video controller card and plug-in. The dialog box options allow you to control a videotape player and pick a frame from the tape.

DiaQuest video controller dialog boxes allow videotape control directly from Photoshop (images courtesy of Microcomputer Publishing Center)

FIGURE 7-12

Digitized
video
frames
from a
commercial
advertising
Andersen
Consulting

FIGURE 7-13

Microcomputer Publishing Center (a video and prepress service bureau) in New York digitized a variety of Effie-award-winning TV commercials for *BRANDWEEK* magazine. The images appeared as part of a special color insert featuring freeze frames from the commercials. All images were digitized and enhanced in Photoshop. A few of the images are reprinted in the following figures (with permission of *BRANDWEEK* and Microcomputer Publishing Center)—Figure 7-13 shows an image from a commercial for Andersen Consulting (with permission also from the company), Figure 7-14 is from a commercial for Rhone-Poulenc's Buctril Corn Herbicide (with permission also from the company and Rhea & Kaiser Advertising), Figure 7-15 is from a commercial for Little Caesars Pizza (with permission also from the company and Cliff Freeman & Partners), and Figure 7-16 is from a

Digitized
image
from a
commercial
for Buctril
Corn
Herbicide

FIGURE 7-14

Digitized
video
frame from
a
commercial
advertising
Little
Caesars
pizza

FIGURE 7·15

commercial for MobileComm (with permission also from the company and G. Williams & Assoc).

DIGITIZED STOCK PHOTOS

If your image needs are not specific, and you don't need to scan or photograph images, numerous sources of stock digital images are available. Several stock photo collections are now sold on CD-ROM discs for both the PC and the Mac. Many collections allow unlimited usage, and some contain images that are scanned on high-end drum scanners in 24-bit color. Before purchasing stock photos, check to see that the resolution and size of the images meet your needs. Also, find out whether the images are compressed, and if they are, whether a lossy or lossless compression method was used. Lossless compression means that no loss of picture quality occurs during compression.

Digitized
video
frames
from a
commercial
advertising
MobileComm

FIGURE 7·16

Photoshop in Action

The different musicians were scanned separately and then pasted into the final image.

After all the musicians and hands were in place, the file was converted from Grayscale to Duotone mode. It was then saved in EPS format so that it could be placed into Adobe Illustrator where the line art was created.

All of the hands were scanned, scaled, and then placed into the final image.

Artist: Lynda Kusnetz   Client: Columbia House

Lynda created this spirited image for a Columbia House mail-order catalog of inspirational music. She started by scanning a photograph of a sky with clouds to use for the background. Then she scanned her hands in different positions by placing them under the scanner lid with the help of a co-worker who controlled the scanner. Once the hands were scanned, they were scaled using the Image/Effects/Scale command. Then the Add Noise filter was applied to create the textured background effect.

After the background was created, the photographs of the different musicians were scanned and pasted into the image (clockwise from top are Tramaine Hawkins and Alvin Chea, Quincy Jones, Mervyn Warren, Al Jarreau, and Mervyn Warren). Next, the Mode menu was used to change the image into a Duotone. The file was saved as an EPS file so it could be placed into Adobe Illustrator, where the frames around the images were created.

IMAGE DATABASE SOFTWARE

If you start building a library of digitized images, you'll soon long for an efficient means to keep track of them. If you are storing many files on disk, consider purchasing image-management software that will help you catalog, archive, and find images. Examples of these programs include Fetch from Aldus, Kudo from Imspace Systems, Kodak's Shoebox, and Nikon's Image Access. Both Shoebox and Image Access are available for both Macs and PCs.

Perhaps the chief advantage of most of these programs is that the actual images in the database do not need to be on the same hard disk as the image cataloging software. The programs maintain low-resolution images for quick access, and the high-resolution files can be stored on removable media. Virtually all cataloging software lets you sort your images and search by title or keyword.

Now that you've learned the basics of digitizing images, you're ready to explore further into the world of image enhancement and editing. In the following chapter, you will learn how Photoshop's electronic filters can sharpen your images, blur them, and apply special effects that make them ripple, twirl, and even melt before your very eyes.

FILTERS

Photoshop's magical filters are designed to do what your scanner can't do: enhance an image and disguise its defects. A filter can turn soft, blurred contours into sharp, crisp edges, or it can soften an image with jagged or harsh edges. Filters can also help eliminate *color banding,* abrupt changes in color values, and *noise*, randomly colored pixels that can appear in a scanned image.

Although many filters are designed to subtly improve scanned images, others will create dramatic alterations, for example, twisting, bending, or spinning an image into motion. Some filters can grab a continuous-tone or painted image and make it appear to be made of three-dimensional blocks or pyramid shapes. Many filters create unusual, eerie, or humorous effects. Digitized images, as well as original images created in Photoshop, can be spherized, zigzagged, or twirled into a digital "soup."

The complex digital effects produced by Photoshop's filters have their roots in photography. Photographic filters are used to filter out light, to enhance images, and to create special effects. But the photographic filter can't match Photoshop's digital filters in effects or versatility. In Photoshop, filters can be applied again and again, one after another, until just the right effect is achieved for the entire image or within selections in the image. For instance, one filter might be applied to enhance the edges of an image and another to give it an embossed effect. The possibilities are endless.

HOW A FILTER WORKS

Each of Photoshop's filters produces a different effect. Some filters work by analyzing every pixel in an image or selection and transforming it by applying mathematical algorithms to create randon or predefined shapes, such as tiles, three-dimensional blocks or pyramids. Many filters, though, achieve their effects by first sampling individual pixels or groups of pixels to define areas that display the greatest difference in color or brightness. Once it zeroes in on one of these transitional areas, the filter starts changing color values—sometimes replacing one pixel's color with that of an adjacent pixel, sometimes substituting pixel colors with the average color value of neighboring pixels. The result, depending upon the filter, can be a sharpening of the image, a softening of harsh edges, or a complete transformation.

Many filters invite you to be an active participant in determining the outcome of the filter's effects. Before these filters begin their work, a dialog box is presented to you, where you can control the magnitude of the filter's effects and often specify the *radius* (range) in which changes will occur.

HOW TO APPLY A FILTER

Despite the differences among Photoshop's numerous filters, the process of applying each one is virtually the same. Start by opening, or activating, the image you will be changing. If you wish to apply the filter to only a portion of the image, select that area with one of the selection tools; otherwise, Photoshop will apply the filter to the entire image.

From the Filter menu, choose one of the filter groups: Blur, Distort, Noise, Sharpen, Stylize, Video, or Other. From the submenu that appears, select the filter that you wish to apply. Several of the filters are applied immediately when you select them. For others, you'll need to set dialog box options to control the filter's results, and then click OK.

NOTE: *Filters cannot be applied to Bitmap or Indexed Color images. If you are working on a Bitmap or Indexed Color image and wish to apply a filter, change modes first by choosing either Grayscale or RGB Color in the Mode menu. Indexed Color and Bitmap images and changing modes are discussed in Chapter 9.*

Sometimes the effect of a filter on an image will be so subtle that you won't notice it, and you may wish to apply the filter again to enhance the results. To facilitate the process of reapplying filters, Photoshop copies the name of the last filter used from a submenu and installs it at the top of the Filter menu. To reapply the filter, just click on the first menu item in the Filter menu or press COMMAND-F (PC users: CTRL-F). If the filter requires dialog box settings, you can press OPTION-COMMAND-F (PC users: ALT-CTRL-F) to open the dialog box before reapplying the filter.

Because many Photoshop filters are somewhat sophisticated and require extensive computer processing, they may take some time to execute, particularly in a large image or selection. If you apply a filter and wish to halt it before it is finished processing, you can usually press COMMAND-PERIOD (PC users: CTRL-PERIOD) to cancel.

If you'd like to try out the filters as you work through the discussions in this chapter, open the scanned image you used in Chapter 7, or choose one of the files available in the Tutorial folder.

NOTE: *Some filters do not use your scratch disk while executing, so you must have sufficient RAM to complete the entire filter operation. If you do not, you may still be able to apply the filter to the image one channel at a time. See Chapters 9 and 12 for more information.*

THE BLUR FILTERS

The five Blur filters are often used to smooth areas where edges are too sharp and contrast is too high. They soften image edges by removing contrast. Blur filters can also be used to blur the background of an image so the foreground stands out, or to create a soft shadow effect.

BLUR The Blur filter creates a light blurring effect that can be used to decrease contrast and eliminate noise in color transitions.

BLUR MORE The Blur More filter blurs about three to four times more than the Blur filter.

GAUSSIAN BLUR The Gaussian Blur allows you to control the blurring effect, creating anything from a slight softening of image edges to a thick haze that blurs the image beyond recognition. This filter is named because it maps pixel color values according to a Gaussian bell-shaped curve.

In the Gaussian Blur dialog box, you specify a value from .1 to 250 in the Radius field to control the range of the blur from transitional areas. The higher the number, the greater the blur.

```
╔══════════ Gaussian Blur ══════════╗
║                                    ║
║   Radius: [1.0]  pixels   ( OK )   ║
║                         ( Cancel ) ║
║                                    ║
╚════════════════════════════════════╝
```

By experimenting with different Radius values, you can often eliminate moiré patterns in scanned images. A *moiré* pattern is an unwanted mottled effect that sometimes occurs during the scanning of printed photographs or when an image is printed at an incorrect screen angle. Figure 8-1a shows a photograph, scanned from a Pratt Manhattan Art School's course catalog, of Puck standing on top of New York City's Puck building; notice the moiré pattern over the entire image. Figure 8-1b shows the same image after the Gaussian Blur filter was applied. As you can see, after applying the filter, the pattern is hardly noticeable.

MOTION BLUR The Motion Blur filter creates the illusion of motion. It imitates the effect of photographing a moving object using a timed exposure.

(a) Image
showing a
moiré
pattern, and
(b) after
applying
Gaussian
Blur
(courtesy
of Pratt
Manhattan
and
photographer
Federico
Savini)

(a)

(b)

FIGURE 8-1

The Motion Blur dialog box allows you to control the direction and strength of the blur. To set direction, type a degree value from –360 to 360 in the Angle box, or use the mouse to click and drag on the radius line in the circle. To control intensity, enter a pixel value from 1 to 999 in the Distance field.

If you experiment with Motion Blur, zoom in on the pixels after blurring, and you will easily see how the filter works. It copies the image using the number in the Distance field as a guide, then offsets (shifts) the duplicate according to the Angle value, and overlays the copy of the image over the original as it lowers the opacity of the duplicate.

This illustration shows the results of Motion Blur. In order to prevent the deer image itself from appearing blurred, the original image was selected with the Magic Wand and copied into the Clipboard before the blur was applied. In the Motion Blur dialog box, Distance was set to 60 pixels; Angle was set to 45 degrees to match the deer's jumping angle. Then the copy of the deer from the Clipboard was pasted over the blurred image. While the pasted image was floating, it was offset about a quarter of an inch away from the blur.

RADIAL BLUR The Radial Blur creates numerous interesting effects. It can spin an image into a circular shape or make it radiate out from its center.

When you activate Radial Blur, a wireframe preview appears in the filter's dialog box, providing a skeletal view of the blur's effect. This is extremely helpful because the Radial Blur often takes a long time to execute.

In the Radial Blur dialog box, you can select either Spin or Zoom as the blur method. If you select Spin, the blur is created in concentric circles, often making your image look as if it were spun on a potter's wheel. With Zoom, blurred image lines zoom out from the image's center point.

To control the intensity of the blur, enter a value between 1 and 100 in the Amount field, or drag the Amount slider control until the blur in the preview box shows the effect you desire. The higher the value, the more intense the blur. To change the center of the blur, click and drag on the dot in the center of the Blur center box.

The Radial Blur dialog box also allows you to specify the quality of the blur. The Best option produces the smoothest blur, but it takes the longest to execute. With the Draft option, Photoshop completes the blur faster, but the results will be grainy.

Photoshop in Action

The kids were photographed
with the table and balloons.

Shaquille O'Neal from the
Orlando Magic was photographed
with a tray in his hand.

Artist: Nik Kleinberg

With the cake selected, the
Motion Blur filter was applied.

Client: Sports Illustrated for Kids

It's a bird, it's a plane, it's a birthday cake! Covers for *Sports Illustrated for Kids* are always creative, unusual, and playful. This cover began when George B. Fry III photographed the children and balloons around the table. Later he photographed basketball star Shaquille O'Neal holding a tray beside the table, while an assistant held the cake over the middle of the table at the angle seen above. For an added effect, a photograph was taken of smoke created by candles that were blown out.

After the photographs were scanned, Nik selected then copied and pasted Shaquille into the image with the kids. Next, he selected the cake with the Rectangular Marquee tool's Feather Radius option, and then copied and pasted it into the image with the kids. After the cake was pasted and moved into position, the Motion Blur filter was applied to it. To create the streams of smoke trailing the cake, Nik pasted the digitized photograph of the smoke. Then he pasted a portion from the original children's image over the smoke. Next, he used the Rubber Stamp tool's From Save option with a low opacity and a soft-edged brush to bring the smoke back into the image. Nik also used the Airbrush tool's Fade-out option and a low opacity with a soft-edged brush to create more streams of smoke trailing from the cake.

The Good option will produce a level of quality between Best and Draft, although for large files, there may be little noticeable difference between Best and Good.

In the following illustration, the Radial Blur filter was applied to the wheel graphic at the left to produce the spinning wheel at the right. The filter was applied with an Amount setting of 30; Spin was selected as the blur method; and Quality was set to Best.

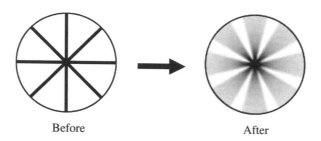

Before   After

THE NOISE FILTERS

Noise, randomly colored pixels, is occasionally introduced during the scanning process. The Noise filters will blend noise to make it less apparent. Or you can use Add Noise to drown an image with so much noise that it is completely transformed into colored pixel patterns; this effect can be used to quickly create interesting and unusual textured backgrounds.

ADD NOISE   The Add Noise filter adds noise to an image, blends noise into an image, and helps diffuse color banding that can occur in blends. This filter is sometimes used to help blend images created with painting tools into their surroundings, or to create interesting patterned backgrounds. When you use it to create background patterns, experiment with different file resolutions because the pattern will change depending upon the resolution.

Use the Add Noise dialog box to indicate the amount of noise you wish to add to an image. Enter a value from 1 to 999 in the Amount field; the greater the amount, the greater the noise effect.

```
╔═════════════ Add Noise ═════════════╗
║                                     ║
║  Amount: [32]          ┌────────┐   ║
║                        │   OK   │   ║
║  ┌─ Distribution ─┐    └────────┘   ║
║  │ ◉ Uniform      │    ┌────────┐   ║
║  │ ○ Gaussian     │    │ Cancel │   ║
║  └────────────────┘    └────────┘   ║
║                                     ║
╚═════════════════════════════════════╝
```

There are two Distribution options in the Add Noise dialog box. When you select Uniform, Photoshop generates the noise randomly, using the Amount field value to calculate the random values. For instance, if you enter 5 in the Amount field, Photoshop will calculate random color values between –5 and 5 for each pixel's color. With the Gaussian distribution option, the noise is mapped along a bell-shaped curve. This often produces a noisier effect than that of the Uniform setting. The Gaussian option also tends to produce a greater number of light pixels than the Uniform setting.

The following illustration shows a pattern created with the Add Noise filter. This effect was generated by first creating a dark-to-light linear blend horizontally (left to right) on the screen. Then the Add Noise filter was applied once with the Gaussian option selected and an Amount value of 100.

DESPECKLE   The Despeckle filter seeks out areas of greatest color change in an image and blurs everything except transitional edges; thus detail is not lost. Use this filter when you need to reduce noise or to blur areas that have been pixelated due to oversharpening. The Despeckle filter can sometimes help reduce moiré patterns that can occur after scanning images that have been printed.

MEDIAN   The Median filter also reduces noise by blending the brightness of pixels within a selection. It's called the Median filter because it replaces the center pixel in a radius area with the median brightness value of the pixels in the area. In the Median dialog box, you may enter a Radius value between 1 and 16 pixels. The Radius value is the distance the filter searches from each pixel to analyze brightness.

THE SHARPEN FILTERS

The four Sharpen filters clarify images by creating more contrast and are often used to enhance the contours of scanned images. It is often helpful to apply these filters after reducing or distorting images that have been edited with Image/Effects submenu commands; the Sharpen filters will reduce the blurring that can occur after interpolation.

AUTION: *Be careful not to sharpen too much or distinct pixels will begin to show through, causing the image to look pixelated.*

IP: *If you need to sharpen small, intricate areas, it's better to work with the Sharpen tool in the Toolbox because it is more precise. See Chapter 6.*

SHARPEN   The Sharpen filter sharpens by increasing the contrast between neighboring pixels.

SHARPEN EDGES   The Sharpen Edges filter works like the Sharpen filter, except it sharpens only the edges of an image (smooth areas are unaffected).

SHARPEN MORE   The Sharpen More filter provides a stronger sharpening effect than the Sharpen filter.

UNSHARP MASK   The Unsharp Mask filter exaggerates the sharpness of an image's edges. It is often helpful to apply this filter after converting an image from RGB to CMYK, or after any other Photoshop operation that involves interpolation. Unlike the other Sharpen filters, Unsharp Mask lets you control the amount of sharpening when you apply it.

The name of the Unsharp Mask filter is based on a traditional photographic masking technique in which a negative and blurred positive of an image are combined to make the image stand out.

You can control the intensity of this filter's effect by entering a percentage from 1 to 500 in the Amount field of the Unsharp Mask dialog box. The greater the percentage, the greater the sharpening. A percentage of 150 usually provides good results with 300-ppi color images. Higher resolution images will often require a higher percentage. In the Radius field, you can specify the distance (in pixels) out from transitional edges that you want sharpened. If you enter a low Radius number, the sharpening occurs closer to image edges. The higher the Radius number, the greater the distance sharpening will occur beyond image contours.

```
┌══════════════ Unsharp Mask ══════════════┐
│                                          │
│    Amount: [50   ] %        ┌────────┐   │
│                             │   OK   │   │
│    Radius: [1.0 ] pixels    └────────┘   │
│                             ┌────────┐   │
│  Threshold: [0   ] levels   │ Cancel │   │
│                             └────────┘   │
└──────────────────────────────────────────┘
```

FIG 4-2

The primary (additive) colors and their components. When all three primary colors are mixed together, they create white.

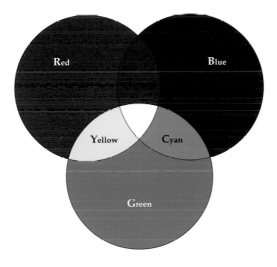

FIG 4-3

The secondary (subtractive) colors and their complements. When all three secondary colors are mixed together, they create a muddy brown.

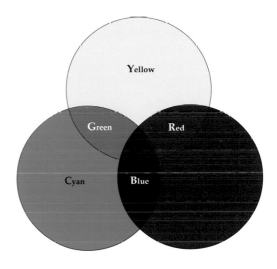

FIG 4-4

Each color in the color wheel is opposite its complement and between the two colors that create it.

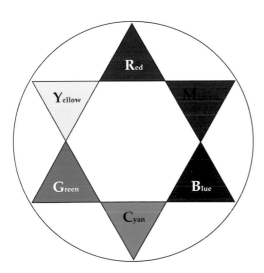

FIG 4-8

The Hue, Saturation, and Brightness color model. (Courtesy of Agfa Corporation)

The Photoshop Portfolio

1 This photograph (also shown in Chapter 13) of a beautiful New England town was taken by Gene Ahrens for the cover of a proposed Reader's Digest book titled *Back Roads of America.* The image was almost perfect, however, the power lines and telephone wires running through the town marred the landscape. The art director of Reader's Digest General Books, David Trooper, felt that areas of the sky were too dark and would conflict with the color of the book's title. He also wanted the road signs in the foreground removed. To make the changes, the image was scanned and saved as a CMYK file, then retouched and color-corrected by Adele Droblas Greenberg.

2 This image (also shown in Chapter 13) shows the final cover for the proposed book after retouching and color-correcting. To remove the road signs, telephone wires, and power lines, Adele used the Rubber Stamp tool's Cloning option. Before color-correcting, several masks were created using the selection tools and the Quick Mask mode. To make the water bluer, she added Cyan using the Levels command in the Image/Adjust submenu. The clouds behind the title were lightened using the Curves command in the Image/Adjust submenu. The colors on the hills across the water were made to look more autumn-like and the foliage in the town was made more vibrant. For a full discussion of the steps involved, see Chapter 13.

3 This photograph (also shown in Chapter 13) was taken in the late 1800s of a 24-year-old French nobleman who came to the United States in hopes of fulfilling his dream of raising cattle. The photograph was selected for the Reader's Digest book, *Discover America's Past,* where it appears as a sepia. Notice that the lower part of his left leg and his left foot are badly faded and barely noticeable. In addition to restoring the leg and foot, the book's art editor, Ken Chaya, asked Adele Droblas Greenberg to paint in the left elbow, add tone to the pistol, and enhance the detail in the rifle and hat.

4 Here is the image (also shown in Chapter 13) after retouching. Adele began restoring the lower left leg and left foot by copying, pasting, and flipping part of the right leg and foot into a new file. She then used the Rubber Stamp tool's Cloning option to clone the foot back into the image, and the Airbrush tool to provide a seamless transition between the restored and original areas. Before painting the left elbow, Adele used the Eyedropper tool to set the foreground color so it matched the tone of the original. Next, she used the Airbrush and Paintbrush tools to paint in the left elbow. For complete details on how this image was retouched, see Chapter 13.

1

2

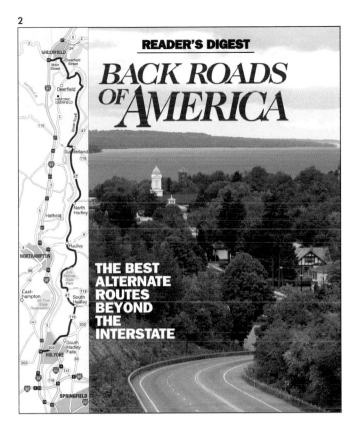

READER'S DIGEST

BACK ROADS OF AMERICA

**THE BEST
ALTERNATE
ROUTES
BEYOND
THE
INTERSTATE**

3

4

1
Image before retouching
and color-correcting
Photograph courtesy of Gene Ahrens

2
Image after retouching
and color-correcting
Artist: Adele Droblas Greenberg
Client: Reader's Digest General Books

3
Image before retouching
Photograph courtesy of Library of
Congress

4
Image after retouching
Artist: Adele Droblas Greenberg
Client: Reader's Digest General Books

The Photoshop Portfolio

5 This fantastic image won the 1991 APA Gold Award for Special Effects and Kodak's VIP Image Search '91 awards for Best in Show and Best in Digital Photography. The image was created as a self-promotion piece for R/GA Print, a division of R/Greenberg Associates, which is well known for its creation of a Diet Coke television commercial featuring Paula Abdul dancing with Gene Kelly.

The dove, the parrot, and the sky in this image were photographed by Ryszard Horowitz. The cone was created using R/GA Print's own proprietary 3-D computer software and was rendered twice, once with the sky and once with "wild" colors. In order to create the opaque blue sky and the clear sky, a linear blend was applied using the Gradient tool in an alpha channel. All of the images were then composited together using the Image/Calculate and Edit/Paste commands. The mirrored image of the cone was created by copying, pasting, and then using the Edit/Composite Controls command.

Alpha channels and the Calculate commands are covered in Chapter 12.

6 Josh began creating this inspirational campaign image by selecting parts of a scanned photograph of a crowd at a Clinton/Gore rally and pasting them into a new file. He also scanned an American flag, then selected, copied, and pasted it several times into the new file using the Edit/Composite Controls command with different opacity settings. He flipped and rotated the flag using the commands in the Image menu. Chapter 11 covers the Composite Controls command.

After a few flags were pasted, he scanned pictures of Clinton and Gore. He selected each image using the Lasso tool with a Feather Radius set so that both would blend into the background when pasted. Next, using a very low opacity setting, he again pasted the flag image--this time on top of Clinton, so that his face would appear through the flag's stripes. As a finishing touch, he selected, rotated, and pasted a Clinton banner over several parts of the background with a low opacity setting.

7 This collage, created for a Time Warner annual report, was begun by scanning an old wedding album, movie images, the Warner Brothers logo, and the number one. Josh then selected different areas of the digitized album and, using the Edit/Fill command, filled them with color. Next he selected, copied, and pasted the movie images provided by Time Warner into the final file. To make the images and the background blend together, he used both the Select/Feather and the Edit/Composite Controls commands. After all the elements were placed, he created the lines using Photoshop's Line tool.

5

5
Artist: R/GA Print
Client: R/GA Print
(promotional materials)

6
Artist: Josh Gosfield
Client: Newsweek Magazine

7
Artist: Josh Gosfield
Client: Time Warner Inc.

6

7

The Photoshop Portfolio

8 This image was created from a set designed by Santa Barbara Studios for the movie, "500 nations" (from Pathways Productions; Jack Leustig, owner and producer; Kevin Costner and Jim Wilson, executive producers), which will air on CBS as a miniseries. Christopher started creating this image by scanning a slide of the sky. After retouching the image, he added rays of light using the Airbrush and Gradient tools and the Rubber Stamp tool's Cloning option. He also used the Airbrush tool to create the sky's haze. To paint the trees, he used the Paintbrush tool with a one-pixel-wide brush. Based upon the staff archaeologist's design, he created an oil painting of the pyramids on canvas. He photographed it and then scanned and synthesized it into the final image. The images of the Indians, who were actors in costumes, were digitized using a video camera, then frame-grabbed. Christopher then scaled down the actors in Photoshop using the Image/Effects/Scale command, and color-corrected the images using various commands in the Image/Adjust submenu. Image/Effects commands are covered in Chapter 7.

9 The concept of Ted Turner's global village is perfectly conveyed in photographer Greg Heisler's cover for *Time* magazine's 1992 Man of the Year issue. To begin the project, Greg had approximately 100 video images frame-grabbed and converted to slides. He digitized them and chose 42 for the final image. Using Photoshop's Image/Adjust submenu commands, he color-corrected the images and assembled them in a grid of seven rows by six columns. To create the globe effect, he applied Photoshop's Spherize filter. The highlight on the right side of the globe was created by first photographing a plastic sphere with a spotlight pointed towards it. Then the Edit/Composite Controls command with the Lighten mode selected was used to blend the sphere with the globe image.

To produce the gap in the middle of the globe, Greg created a selection with the Elliptical Marquee tool and filled it with black. Next, he used the Elliptical Marquee tool to create a selection in the middle of the gap and, with the Paste Into command, pasted a digitized image of his photograph of Ted Turner.

10 This imaginative magazine cover is comprised of a variety of photographs which were scanned and placed into one file. The first image to be digitized was the wide-eyed child at the table. After the three images of the standing players were scanned, they were outlined using the Pen tool, converted to selections, then scaled using the Image/Effects/Scale command. The player images were also rotated using the Image/Rotate command. Then they were copied and pasted into the file with the child, and their shadows were created using the Pen tool and the Image/Adjust/Levels command.

The players on the cards were also outlined with the Pen tool, converted to selections, then filled with white. For the finishing touch, a football was scanned in, selected, scaled, copied, and then pasted into the final image. Finally, the Motion Blur filter was applied to the football to make it look like it was flying through the air. Using the Pen tool is covered in Chapter 10.

8

8
Artist: Christopher Evans
Client: Pathways Productions

9
Artist: Greg Heisler
Client: Time Magazine

10
Artist: Nik Kleinberg
Client: Sports Illustrated for Kids

9

10

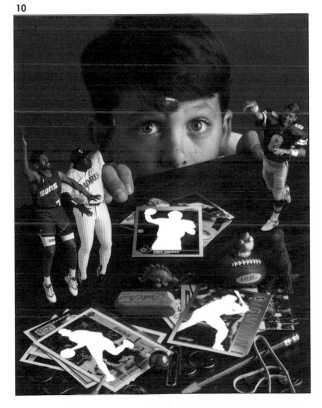

The Photoshop Portfolio

11 Anne created this montage for the front and back covers of a J.P. Morgan financial brochure by scanning different images, selecting them, and placing them into one file. She first worked on the background; the pavement, blue sky, and water. Then she began the process of selecting and pasting the images using primarily the Lasso tool, and the Pen tool to create paths and change them into selections. Anne created the montage as a low-resolution file and then had it printed on a color printer for the client's approval. Once it was approved, the image was re-created as a high-resolution file at a prepress house. When the image was finally printed, a screen frequency of 200 lpi was used.

To learn more about the selection tools see Chapter 3.

12 This image was used as the cover illustration for an issue of the *Washington Post* magazine which featured an article titled "What's Wrong with Newspapers." To digitize the image, Rico and Mauricio used a camcorder. After the pens were digitized, they were individually scaled and distorted using commands in the Image/Effects submenu. The artists then created the target by scanning different newspapers and applying tinted rings using circular selections filled at a low opacity setting. The borders of each separate ring were enhanced with the Select/Border, Select/Feather, and Edit/Fill commands. The shadows were created with the Lasso tool's Feather option and the Edit/Fill command. Finishing touches were applied with the Airbrush and other painting tools. Finally, the Dodge and Burn tools were used to balance specific areas of shadow, textures, and light sources.

The Dodge and Burn tools are discussed in Chapter 6.

13 Rico created this intriguing image as a cover for the *Boston Globe* magazine to illustrate the article, "New World Borders, Madness for Mapmakers." Using a flat-bed scanner, Rico digitized different maps and objects such as a Band-Aid, tacks, tape measure, thread, and yarn. Before assembling the elements together on screen, he used the Gradient tool to achieve a linear blend from dark to light for the background. The globe was created with a circular selection that was then saved to an alpha channel. Next, he applied the Spherize filter to the different scanned elements and pasted them into the circular selection. Using the Elliptical Marquee tool with the Feather Radius set to 25 pixels, Rico created the elliptical shadow below the globe and filled it with black. The smooth shadow on the underside of the globe was created with Adobe Illustrator.

To learn how to use the Spherize filter and other powerful Photoshop filters, see Chapter 8.

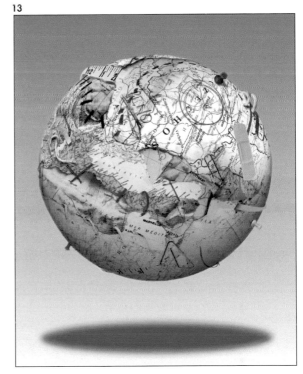

11
Artist: Anne Wren
Client: J.P. Morgan & Co. Incorporated

12
Artists: Rico Lins and Mauricio Nacif
Client: Washington Post Magazine

13
Artist: Rico Lins
Client: Boston Globe Magazine

The Photoshop Portfolio

14 Both Adobe Photoshop and StrataVision, a photo-realistic 3-D program, were used to produce this sci-fi image. George created the earth, moon, and stars in Photoshop. To produce the glow around the earth, he created a Pen path that was stroked with the Airbrush tool.

Once the earth, moon, and stars were created, George used Photoshop's Airbrush tool with a Wacom stylus and tablet to paint the woman. The 3-D spaceship cabin and futuristic laptop computers were created in StrataVision.

15 From photographs taken by Mark Sokol of the water, fire, sky, circuit board, and the rock on a sandy beach, Daniel created this surrealistic image for a California service bureau. In order to work efficiently, he first produced the entire image as a low-resolution comp. As he worked, he created masks for the various elements in the image which allowed him to isolate and edit each area without affecting surrounding regions.

To create the CMYK page edges, he used Aldus Freehand and then imported the image into Photoshop to add color and shadows. Once he perfected the various design elements, he reloaded the high-resolution versions of the images and masks, and used Photoshop's painting tools to blend them together.

16 Marc created this intriguing cover for *Art Direction* magazine by first scanning a circuit board. With green selected as the foreground color and lavendar as the background color, he used the Gradient tool to fill the circuit board with a linear blend. To produce the bottom part of the background, he made a rectangular selection using the Rectangular Marquee tool, then filled the area using the Gradient tool to create a black-to-purple linear blend.

Marc then scanned a black-and-white picture of a jar from an old medical catalog and an engraving of a man's face. Once the face was scanned, Marc colorized it using the Edit/Fill command's Darken mode. The Darken mode painted only the white areas and left the black areas untouched. He then selected the face and saved it to an alpha channel.

Using the Magic Wand tool, Marc selected two different portions in the jar and filled one with blue. He pasted the face inside the other selection by using the Edit/Paste Into command. When the jar was completed, he selected and pasted it into the final image. To create the reflection of the face, Marc returned to the original scanned image and loaded the selection from the alpha channel. He then copied and pasted it into the final image using the Composite Controls command with Opacity set to 50%. While the face was still selected, he applied the Ripple filter. This same technique was used on the reflection of the pen. To achieve the blend from yellow to pink in the pen, the Gradient tool was used with the Darken mode selected so that the black areas were not affected.

14

14
Artist: George H. Krauter
Client: ANALOG Science Fiction
and Fact Magazine

15
Artist: Daniel Clark
Client: Raging Fingers

16
Artist: Marc Yankus
Client: Art Direction Magazine

15

16

The Photoshop Portfolio

17   Paul created this intricate three-dimensional image of a space station for the museum in Ontario, Canada, using both StrataVision and Photoshop. Since the size of the final file was fairly large, Paul selected and copied individual areas and pasted them into new files where he could work more efficiently. After he completed work on one area, he reselected it, and then copied and pasted it back into position in the original file.

    He created the 3-D renderings in StrataVision. The StrataVision file was saved in a TIFF format and then imported into Photoshop. In Photoshop, he touched-up the 3-D renderings, adjusted colors, and added details. He also used Photoshop to create the texture maps that were applied to the 3-D shapes in StrataVision.

18   This humorous animal balancing act was created from several photographs taken by Howard Berman. With the assistance of a professional animal handler, Howard took at least two photographs each of the dog and the cat in different positions. Separate photos were taken of the fish and the fish bowl. The fish were shot in a calm, stable fish tank and the fish bowl was shot while water was being splashed in it. The two birds that look like parrots are actually one bird, a canary, that was enlarged in the computer to look like a parrot. The bird and the wheel, which was made by model maker, were photographed separately. The ball under the dog was shot and then enlarged in Photoshop. After the photographs were taken, they were scanned, then copied and pasted by Bob Bowen and Frank Lance at R/GA Print using the selection tools and alpha channels. The shadow was created using the selection tools and the Image/Adjust submenu's Levels and Curves commands.

19   Ruth Kedar, former art director of Adobe Systems, created this surreal image as a promotional piece to demonstrate filter affects for Andromeda Software. Ruth started by creating a new CMYK Color file. To create the background, she used the Gradient tool to produce several vertical color blends. She then created an alpha channel in which she applied an Andromeda Designs filter. Next, Ruth scanned a grayscale photograph of a child. She used various selection tools and the Quick Mask mode to separate the child from its background, then copied and pasted the image into the CMYK Color file. To colorize the child's hair, Ruth selected it, feathered it with the Select/Feather command, and then filled it with a reddish-brown color. The bubbles were created using the Andromeda cMulti filter. They were selected using the Elliptical Marquee tool, then duplicated and scaled using the Image/Effects/Scale command. Each bubble was colorized using the Image/Adjust/Color Balance command. Next, the Andromeda Prism filter was applied to create the look of multiple floating bubbles. Ruth's final touch was to paste one of the bubbles on top of the child's hand. She used a 60% Opacity setting in the Composite Controls dialog box to create the illusion that the child is indeed blowing bubbles.

17

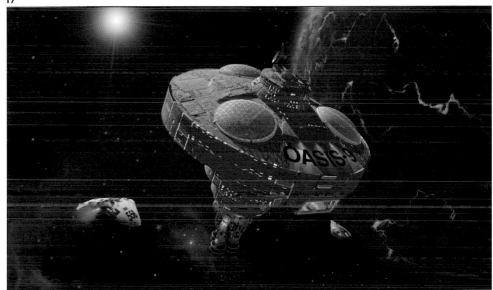

17
Artist: Paul Cosby
Client: National Museum of
Science and Technology

18
Artist: R/GA Print
Client: Computor Associates

19
Artist: Ruth Kedar
Client: Andromeda Software

18

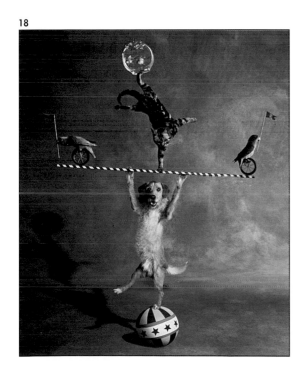

19

20 José created this image by first using a scratchboard and a blade to create black-and-white line art. He scanned it into Photoshop and then used the Pencil tool to touch up the black lines. In order to paint the image, he converted the black-and-white file into a CMYK Color file. Next, he selected the image with the Rectangular Marquee tool and used the Lighten mode in the Edit/Fill dialog box to fill only the black lines with red. To complete the colorization, he used the Paint Bucket tool to fill the various white areas.

The Pencil and Paint Bucket tools are covered in Chapter 5.

21 Pamela created this appealing image using both Adobe Photoshop and Aldus Freehand. She first scanned a photograph of an Absolut vodka bottle and then selected one side of it with the Rectangular Marquee tool. Using the Image/Map/Invert command, she inverted the selection which turned the light portions of the bottle dark and the dark portions light. After the bottle image was completed, the file was saved in an EPS format and then imported into Aldus Freehand. Using Freehand, she began painting all of the images around the bottle.

Saving in different file formats so you can export Photoshop files to other programs is covered in Appendix A.

22 Adele began this image by creating a black-and-white still life with pencils and markers. She scanned the image in as a color file and then applied color to the plants using the Paintbrush tool and a Wacom stylus and tablet. Then she selected the window area with the selection tools and created a mask using the Quick Mask mode. Once the area was masked, Adele saved the selection to an alpha channel. She then loaded the selection and pasted a digitized photograph of a sky and mountains into the masked area using the Edit/Paste Into command. The Image/Effects/Scale command was then used to slightly distort the perspective.

To add depth to the image, Adele used StrataVision to create the cubes and textures, which were saved as TIFF files. The two cubes were positioned into the final image using the Rubber Stamp tool's Cloning option. Selections of the wall and vase were created, saved to alpha channels, and then loaded before the textures were pasted into them. The shadow of the vase was produced by converting a Pen path into a selection, then filling it with 20% black.

20

22

21

20
Artist: José Ortega
Client: Money Magazine

21
Artist: Pamela Hobbs
Client: Carallion Importers

22
Artist: Adele Droblas Greenberg
Client: AD. Design and Consulting

The Photoshop Portfolio

How the Color Insert Was Created

The color separations for this insert were produced by the New York City office of Applied Graphics Technologies, Inc. (AGT), a prepress house with offices throughout the United States. The authors asked them to create the separations because of AGT's reputation for high-quality output and extensive experience with Photoshop.

The layout with the high-resolution images was created in QuarkXPress and proofed by the authors on a Tektronix Phaser IISDX dye-sublimation printer. Once the layout was approved, it was supplied to AGT. Since many of the color images were RGB Color files, AGT needed to convert them to CMYK Color. When converting, AGT used its own customized separation table. Images that were supplied as chromes were digitized on a Dupont Crosfield drum scanner.

Once all of the images were digitized and the RGB Color files converted to CMYK color, AGT created proofs using its Kodak Approval Digital Color proofing system. After the proofs were analyzed, several were color-corrected. The final separations were output on a Scitex Dolev 400 imagesetter at a resolution of 2,540 dpi, and then proofed with 3M matchprints.

If you would like to contact Applied Graphics Technologies, the company has offices in Foster City, Glendale, and Los Angeles, CA; Boulder, CO; Washington, DC; Detroit, MI; Carlstadt and Moonacie, NJ; and New York City, Oceanside, and Rochester, NY.

The Threshold field allows you to specify a comparison between neighboring pixels for sharpening. It allows you to prevent sharpening unless contrast between pixels is above the Threshold value. For instance, if the brightness values of neighboring pixels differ by 5, typing in a Threshold of 4 will cause sharpening to occur. Enter 5 or larger in Threshold, and Photoshop will ignore the pixels. Thus, the Threshold value can be used to prevent oversharpening in the entire image or selected area. If you keep Threshold set at the default level, 0, the filter will change the most pixels possible. The higher you set Threshold, the fewer number of pixels are affected.

Figure 8-2 shows a Santa Fe landscape with part of the image sharpened. The Unsharp Mask filter was applied three times, with Amount set to 50%, Radius set to 1, and Threshold set to 0.

THE DISTORT FILTERS

The Distort filters are used to create distortions that vary from rippling an image to twirling and twisting it. How you use them is up to you. If you are creating original

Area sharpened

Unsharp
Mask
applied to
a portion
of a
Santa Fe
landscape
(photograph
courtesy of
Stacy
Kollar
Photography)

FIGURE 8-2

art with Photoshop's tools, you'll find that many of the Distort filters can help save you time when you are creating unusual effects.

In Photoshop 2.5.1, most Distort filters feature miniature dialog box previews that help take the guesswork out of applying filters. The previews are a great help in giving you a sense of how each filter option will affect your image *before* the filter is applied. When you're working with large files, that means you're saving time by avoiding trial runs.

On the Mac, the previews can be turned off or on. In Photoshop 2.5.1, all previews are turned on by default. To access the off/on switch for the previews, click on the Apple menu and choose About Plug-ins. Included in the list that appears will be all of Photoshop's filters. Press and hold the OPTION key while you click on any Distort filter to access the dialog box to set the preview on or off. When the Distortions Plug-in dialog box appears, click on the Show Previews & Sliders check box to turn the previews off or on.

DISPLACE   Of all the filters in Photoshop's varied collection, the Displace filter is probably the most difficult to understand and the hardest to predict. The results seem unpredictable because the filtered image's pixels can be shifted in different directions, and the shift is based not only on dialog box settings but also on a *displacement map,* which can be any Photoshop file saved in a 2.0 or 2.5 format that is not a Bitmap file.

The Displace filter also works differently from any other Photoshop filter. After the Displace dialog box settings are accepted, the filter doesn't immediately begin processing. Instead, an Open dialog box appears, allowing you to select a file to use as the displacement map. After the displacement map file is chosen, the Displace filter shifts image pixels according to color values in the displacement map.

Color values in the displacement map are measured on a scale from 0 to 255. Low values (darker colors) produce a displacement down and to the right in the filtered image. Midrange values (near 128) produce little displacement. High values (lighter colors) produce a displacement up and to the left.

If you wish to experiment with the Displace filter, you can use a variety of displacement maps included with the Photoshop package, in the Displacement Maps folder in the Plug-ins folder (PC users: dispmaps in the plugins folder).

PRACTICE WITH THE DISPLACE FILTER   The best way to get a feel for the Displace filter is to first use one of Photoshop's displacement maps, and then analyze the effects.

1. Before you begin, load the displacement map, Crumbles, to take a look at how the light and dark areas are dispersed in the image. After examining the Crumbles file, it's a good idea to close it (so you don't inadvertently apply the Displace filter to it, rather than to your image).

2. Open an image on screen that you wish to apply the filter to. If you like, you can choose any file from the Tutorial folder.

3. From the Filter menu, choose Distort. From the Distort submenu, choose Displace.

   In the Displace dialog box, you can enter values that control the degree of horizontal and vertical displacement. By entering a value in the Horizontal Scale field, you specify how much the filter will shift your image left or right according to the color values in the displacement map. The value in the Vertical Scale field specifies the amount the filter will shift your image up or down according to the color values in the displacement map. The highest allowed percentage, 100, displaces your image 128 pixels in areas corresponding to black or white in the displacement map.

   ```
   ┌──────────────── Displace ────────────────┐
   │                                          │
   │  Horizontal Scale: [10  ]    ┌────────┐  │
   │    Vertical Scale: [10  ]    │   OK   │  │
   │                              └────────┘  │
   │                              ┌────────┐  │
   │                              │ Cancel │  │
   │                              └────────┘  │
   │  Displacement map:    Undefined Areas:   │
   │    ◉ Stretch to fit     ○ Wrap Around    │
   │    ○ Tile               ◉ Repeat edge pixels │
   └──────────────────────────────────────────┘
   ```

4. For this exercise, you'll use low displacement values. (Higher values would displace your image so much that you wouldn't be able to decipher the results.) Enter **20** for the Horizontal Scale and **20** for Vertical Scale.

   There are two choices for handling displacement maps that are not the same size as the area you are applying the filter to. The Stretch to Fit option transforms the size of the displacement map to match the image. The Tile option uses the displacement map as a repeating pattern.

You can also control the destiny of pixels that would normally be outcast from the screen by the displacement effect. Under Undefined Areas, the Wrap Around option will wrap the image so that it appears on the opposite side of the screen. The Repeat Edge Pixels option disperses the extra pixels over the edges of the image; this can sometimes create distinct color bands if the color of the extra pixels is different from the rest of the edge.

5. To keep your image from becoming too distorted, select the Tile and Repeat Edge Pixels options, and click OK.

6. An Open dialog box appears, where you will choose a file to use as a displacement map. Open the Crumbles file from the Displacement Maps folder (PC users: dispmaps in the plugins folder).

The progress indicator on the screen now indicates that the filter is being applied. In a few moments, your image will be displaced according to the Crumbles displacement map.

Now that you know how to run the filter, you can begin to analyze how the Displace filter works. Perhaps the most complicated factor about this filter is that its behavior depends on the number of channels in the displacement map. As mentioned in Chapter 2, a channel is somewhat similar to a color plate in printing. RGB and Lab images consist of three channels, a CMYK file has four channels, and a Grayscale image has one channel.

In one-channel displacement maps, the Displace filter displaces along x- and y-axes. Darker values in the displacement map displace pixels downward according to the Vertical Scale value in the dialog box, and to the right according the Horizontal Scale value. White values are displaced upward according to the Vertical Scale value and to the left according to the Horizontal Scale value.

When the displacement map has more than one channel, the filter displaces according to the first two channels only: horizontally according to the first channel and vertically according to the second channel. In the first channel, darker areas will cause displacement to the right, and lighter areas will cause displacement to the left, according to the dialog box values. In the second channel, dark areas displace the image downward and white areas displace upward, according to the dialog box values. Thus, to predict the outcome of the filter, you not only need to think in different dimensions but you must also try to figure out how the color range in the displacement maps will affect the image.

If the Displace filter seems confusing to you, try creating your own simple one-channel displacement map and analyze the results. Follow these steps:

1. Create a new Grayscale file, and set the width and height to be about the same size as the image that you will be applying the filter to.

2. Create a radial blend from black to white in the middle of the screen. Save the circle file in Photoshop's native 2.5 format. This will be your displacement map.

3. Open the image or one of the Tutorial files that you wish to apply the filter to. From the Filter menu choose Distort, and select the Displace filter.

4. In the Displace dialog box, type **50** in the Vertical Scale field, and type **0** in the Horizontal Scale field. Choose both the Stretch to Fit and Repeat Edge Pixels options. Click OK.

5. When the Open dialog box appears, select the file that contains your radial blend.

    After the filter is finished processing, you will see that the image pixels corresponding to the darkest areas of the displacement map area have moved down. Pixels corresponding to the white displacement areas have moved up.

6. Now undo the changes so that you can analyze the horizontal displacement. Select Edit/Undo.

7. Select the Displace filter again. This time, type **50** in the Horizontal Scale field, and **0** in the Vertical Scale field. Click OK. Use the same displacement map that you used before.

This time, when the filter is applied, the darker areas displace your image to the right; white areas are displaced to the left.

The Displace filter was applied to the car image shown in Figure 8-3a using the white-to-black radial blend shown in Figure 8-3b as the displacement map. A 25% radial offset was used to enlarge the white area (foreground color) of the blend. When the filter was applied, 70 was the value for both Horizontal Scale and Vertical Scale in the Displace dialog box. The result is shown in Figure 8-3c. The car was bent up and slightly left in the areas corresponding to the light areas in the displacement map, and bent down and to the right in areas corresponding to the dark portions of the displacement map.

PINCH   The Pinch filter is used to squeeze an image inwards or outwards. Figure 8-4a shows a clock graphic before the Pinch filter was applied; Figure 8-4b shows it after applying an outward pinch at −100% (100% results in an inward pinch).

(a)

(b)

(a) The
original car
image;
(b) the
displacement
map;
(c) the
image after
applying
the
Displace
filter

(c)

FIGURE 8-3

(a) The
clock
graphic
before and;
(b) after
applying
the
(outward)
Pinch filter

(a)

(b)

FIGURE 8-4

Before the Pinch filter was applied, it was selected with the Rectangular Marquee. By leaving more space in the marquee selection on the right side of the clock, a slight leftward tilt in the pinch effect was produced.

POLAR COORDINATES The Polar Coordinates filter converts an image's coordinates from Rectangular to Polar or from Polar to Rectangular.

This filter can take a rectangular object and bend it into a circular shape. Figure 8 5a shows a pencil graphic before using the Polar Coordinates filter with Rectangular to Polar selected; in Figure 8-5b the pencil has been bent by the filter. When the filter was applied, no selection was made on screen. If the pencil had been selected, the filter would have made it look somewhat like a round pie with a wedge cut out of the top.

The pencil graphic before and after applying the Polar Coordinates filter using the Rectangular to Polar option

(a)　　　　　　　　　　　　　　(b)

FIGURE 8-5

When you select the Polar to Rectangular option in the dialog box, the Polar Coordinates filter will take a circular object and stretch it. The following illustration shows the effects of applying this filter to the clock graphic from Figure 8-4a using the Polar to Rectangular option. The snaking line at the bottom was created because a rectangular selection was made around the clock before the filler was applied.

RIPPLE The Ripple filter transforms an image by displacing its pixels to create a ripple effect. The following illustration shows what happened to the Polar Pencil from Figure 8-5a after the Ripple filter was applied. To create this effect, the Ripple Amount was set to 100 and the Ripple Frequency to Large.

SHEAR The Shear filter bends an image according to a curve established in the Shear filter's dialog box. The effect can be used to bend and elongate an object.

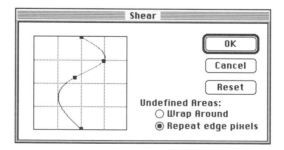

To establish the curve in the Shear dialog box, you click and drag on the vertical band in the dialog box grid. Each click will produce another control point that can be dragged to create the curve. If you need to reset the curve back to its starting position, click the Reset button. When the filter is applied to an object, it will bend along the curve you have established in the dialog box.

Here is the clock graphic that was shown in Figure 8-4a, this time with the Shear filter applied:

SPHERIZE   The Spherize filter transforms a selection into a spherical shape. Use it to give text or an object a three-dimensional or bloated effect. In Figure 8-6, the Spherize filter has been applied to the truck (from Chapter 3) with a grid background. To create this effect, the Amount field in the Spherize dialog box was set to 100%, and the Mode was set to Normal. To view more examples of the Spherize filter in action, see the *Time* magazine (image 9) and *Boston Globe* magazine (image 13) covers in the color insert in this book.

The truck
image from
Chapter 3
after
applying
the
Spherize
filter

FIGURE 8-6

TWIRL   The Twirl filter creates swirling pinwheel effects, with the rotation focused toward the center of the object. When you apply it at maximum strength, the Twirl filter will make your image look as if it were whipped by a blender. Here once again is the clock graphic, showing the Twirl filter's effect when set to 150 degrees:

WAVE   The Wave filter helps you create many different undulating effects by providing, in the filter's dialog box, various wavelength options to distort an image. Values can be entered by clicking and dragging on slider controls or by typing numbers into fields.

In the Number of Generators field you can control the number of waves generated, from 1 to 999. The more waves you generate, the more distorted the effect because the peaks and dips of the wavelengths begin to intersect, causing more and more havoc in your image. Creating multiple waves is somewhat analogous to one ocean wave crashing into others: The more waves that crash together, the greater the turbulence.

You can specify the distance between wave crests by entering a minimum and maximum Wavelength value. The height of each wave is controlled by the value specified for the minimum and maximum Amplitude values. Wavelength and Amplitude values can be from 1 to 999.9.

You can select a wave Type of Sine (curved), Triangle, or Square. The Scale percentages determine the degree of the distortions horizontally and vertically; values can be from 0% to 100%.

AUTION: *If you wish to replicate your wave results on other images, do not click the Randomize button because it creates a random starting point for the wave effect.*

When using the Wave filter, the image can sometimes blend and twist off the screen. The Undefined Areas options allow you to control the destiny of these outcast pixels. If you select Wrap Around, images will wrap to the opposite side of the screen. The Repeat Edge Pixels option disperses the extra pixels over the edge of the image; this can sometimes create distinct color bands if the color of the extra pixels is different from the rest of the edge.

Figure 8-7 shows the Wave filter applied to create an earthquake effect on the highway image used in Chapter 3.

The highway image from Chapter 3 after applying the Wave filter

FIGURE 8-7

ZIGZAG   This filter can be used to create ripples-in-a-pond and twirling effects. This effect is controlled by the value entered in the Amount and Ridges field and whether you choose the Pond Ripples, Out from Center, or Around Center options in the Zigzag dialog box. Figure 8-8 demonstrates how the Zigzag filter's Pond Ripples option can be used to create pond ripples out of almost anything. In this case, the ripples were created in the Santa Fe landscape image shown earlier in Figure 8-2.

THE STYLIZE FILTERS

The Stylize filters are used to create the look of impressionist paintings and other painterly effects. Many of these effects are so dramatic you may hardly recognize your original.

CAUTION: *Don't be too heavy-handed with the Distort and Stylize filters or you run the risk of turning something interesting and possibly humorous into something bizarre or grotesque.*

COLOR HALFTONE   The Color Halftone filter makes an image appear to be created from large halftone dots. Photoshop creates this effect by dividing the image into

The Santa Fe landscape after applying the Zigzag filter using the Pond Ripples option rectangular grids and then filling each rectangular grid with pixels to simulate the halftone dots. The Width and Height of the grid is controlled by the Max. radius field.

CRYSTALLIZE   The Crystallize filter sharpens images by moving similarly colored pixels together into a polygonal grid of pixels. The size of the polygon is controlled by the value entered in the Cell Size field. Figure 8-9 shows the effect of the Crystallize filter applied to the Santa Fe landscape photo with a cell size of 10 pixels.

DIFFUSE   The Diffuse filter creates an unfocused effect that breaks up an image as though seen through frosted glass. The effect is created by shifting pixels at random (Normal option), by replacing light pixels with darker ones (Darken Only option), or by replacing dark pixels with lighter ones (Lighten Only option).

EMBOSS   The Emboss filter creates a raised effect by outlining the edges in a selection and lowering surrounding color values. This filter is often used for designing raised type or creating a relief effect.
    In the Emboss dialog box, the direction of the embossing is controlled by the Angle field. Values can range from –360 to 360 degrees. You can type in the value

The
Santa Fe
landscape
after
applying
the
Crystallize
filter

FIGURE 8-9

or click and drag the angle indicator in the circle; dragging clockwise increases the angle, and dragging counterclockwise decreases the angle.

```
┌─────────────────── Emboss ───────────────────┐
│                                                │
│   Angle:  [135]  °                    ┌──────┐ │
│                              ╱         │  OK  │ │
│  Height:  [3]    pixels     ╱          └──────┘ │
│                          (    )        ┌──────┐ │
│  Amount:  [100]  %          ╲          │Cancel│ │
│                              ╲         └──────┘ │
│                                                │
└────────────────────────────────────────────────┘
```

The height of the embossing is controlled by the value in the Height field, which can range from 1 to 10 pixels. To raise or lower the color values in the embossed image, enter a value from 1% to 500% into the Amount field. The lower the percentage, the lower the amount of color; the higher the percentage, the more color is applied to edges.

Figure 8-10 shows the effects of the Emboss filter applied to the car image from Figure 8-3a. In the Emboss dialog box, the Angle was set to 135, the Height was set to 10 pixels, and the Amount was set to 200%. Before the filter was applied, the contrast of the image was increased with the Brightness/Contrast command in the

The car image after applying the Emboss filter

FIGURE 8-10

Photoshop in Action

The Centurion character was lightened so that the message would be readable.

The text was embossed using various filters and alpha channels.

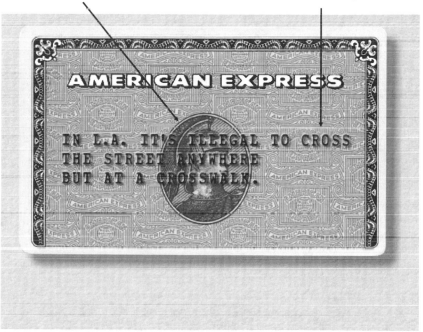

Artist: Russell Cook, Ogilvy and Mather Advertising   **Client: American Express**

Russell Cook, an artist at Ogilvy and Mather Advertising, created the above image as a public service sign for American Express. Variations of the sign have appeared in many airports around the world. After an American Express card was digitized, Russell used the Rubber Stamp tool to clean up the scan.

The type was imported from Adobe llustrator. Once the type was in Photoshop, an alpha channel was created for it. The alpha channel was duplicated and the Emboss filter was applied. The embossed alpha channel was duplicated and inverted so that one alpha channel could be used for the highlights and the other for the shadows. Russell then used the Image/Map/Threshold command to isolate highlight and shadow areas. The Gaussian Blur and Motion Blur filters were applied to the shadowed text alpha channel.

Once the card was perfected it was laid over a textured background where a shadow was added. When the card was complete it was imported into QuarkXPress, where the following text was added: "Welcome to Los Angeles. We're here to help."

Image/Adjust submenu. This emphasized the edges in the image, thereby enhancing the effect of the Emboss filter.

EXTRUDE   The Extrude filter transforms an image into a series of three-dimensional blocks or pyramids depending upon the option set in the dialog box. Use it to distort images or create unusual 3-D backgrounds. Figure 8-11 shows the Extrude filter Pyramids option applied to a radial blend grading from a dark color to a lighter one.

In the Extrude filter dialog box, you can set the size of the base of the blocks or pyramids by typing a value from 2 to 255 in the Size field. Enter a value from 0 to 255 into the Depth field to control how far the objects extrude from the screen. Choose the Random radio button if you wish the depth of each extruding object to be set to a random value.

If you want brighter parts of the image to protrude more than darker parts, select the Level-Based radio button. This option links the pyramid or block depth to color values. If you choose the Solid Front Faces check box, the face of the block is filled with the average color of the object, rather than the image. To ensure that no extruding object extends past the filtered selection, choose the Mask Incomplete Blocks check box.

FACET   The Facet filter gives a hand-painted look to an image, by grouping and changing sampled pixels into blocks of similarly colored pixels. When this filter is applied, solid and similar colors are emphasized.

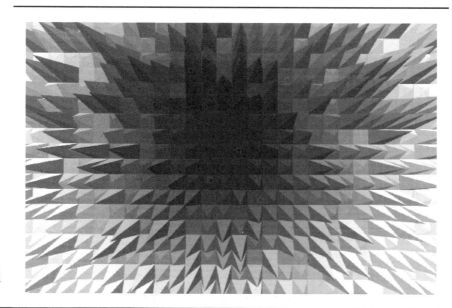

The effects of the Extrude filter applied to a radial blend

FIGURE 8-11

The car image after applying the Find Edges filter

FIGURE 8-12

FIND EDGES   The Find Edges filter searches for image areas that exhibit major color changes and then enhances transitional pixels. It can make an image look as though it were outlined with a pencil. In Figure 8-12, the Find Edges filter has been applied to the car image. First, though, the contrast of the image was increased, using the Brightness/Contrast command in the Image/Adjust submenu. This enhanced the effect of the filter by adding more edges for the filter to outline.

TRACE CONTOUR   The effect of the Trace Contour filter is similar to that of the Find Edges filter, except Trace Contour draws thinner lines around edges and allows you to specify a tonal level for transition areas. In the Trace Contour dialog box, you can enter a value between 0 and 255 in the Level field. Darker pixels correspond to lower numbers; lighter pixels to higher numbers. The Upper and Lower options allow you to choose whether you want contours traced above or below the Level value.

FRAGMENT   The Fragment filter creates an unfocused effect by copying an image's pixels four times, averaging them, and then offsetting them. This filter will quickly create an unfocused background over which you can paste objects to make them stand out.

LENS FLARE   The Lens Flare filter creates an effect similar to a bright light shining into the lens of a camera, as demonstrated in Figure 8-13.

The highway image after applying the Lens Flare filter

FIGURE 8-13

The Lens Flare dialog box allows you to set the brightness of the light, the center of the light source, and the lens type. In the Brightness field, type in or use the slider control to enter a value between 10% and 300%. Click anywhere on the image icon to choose a center point for the light source. After you click, a crosshair indicates the center point. Before executing the filter, choose one of the Lens type radio buttons.

Crosshair —

OTE: *The Lens Flare filter only works on RGB files. Also, the filter does not work in computers without a math coprocessor (FPU chip).*

MOSAIC   The Mosaic filter gives your image a mosaic effect. If you are using Photoshop to create video animation, you can use the Mosaic filter to replicate a technique commonly used in television, where an image gradually breaks up into pieces and then disappears. Enter a number between 2 and 64 pixels in the Cell Size field. The filter creates the mosaic effect by making all pixels in a cell the same color.

POINTILLIZE   The Pointillize filter breaks up an image into random dots, producing an effect much like a pointillist painting. To control the size of dots in the filtered image, you can enter a cell value between 3 and 999.

SOLARIZE   The Solarize filter creates the effect of a positive and negative of an image blended together. In photography, you accomplish similar results by adding light during the developing process. See Chapter 13 to learn how to create a solarized effect using the Image/Adjust/Curves command.

TILES   The Tiles filter divides an image into tiles according to values specified in the filter's dialog box. Figure 8-14 shows the effect of the Tiles filter when it is applied to the Santa Fe landscape using the default settings. In the Number of Tiles

The
Santa Fe
landscape
after
applying
the Tiles
filter

FIGURE 8-14

field, enter the minimum number of tiles you wish to appear in each row and column of tiles. In the Maximum Offset field, enter the maximum distance (as a percentage) that you want the tiles offset from their original positions. If you want the area between the tiles filled with color, choose the Background Color or Foreground Color radio buttons in the Fill Empty Area With section. Choosing the Inverse Image radio button causes a reverse color image of your original image to appear through the tile cracks. Choosing the Unaltered Image radio button makes the tiles appear over the original image.

WIND   The Wind filter creates a windblown effect by adding small horizontal lines. The Wind filter dialog box allows you to choose how strong the wind is and what direction you wish the wind to blow. In Figure 8-15, the Wind filter was applied to the car image first with the filter's Blast option selected, and then with the Wind option selected. The Direction was set to Right, rathar than Left (the default).

VIDEO FILTERS

Photoshop's Video filters were designed for images that will be input from video or output to videotape.

NTSC COLORS   These filters reduce the color gamut of the image to acceptable levels for television.

The car image after applying the Wind filter

FIGURE 8-15

DEINTERLACE   This filter smooths video images by removing odd or even interlaced lines. This filter is needed when a video frame is captured between an odd and even field, and a blurred scan line becomes visible. The filter's dialog box gives you a choice of substituting the line by duplication or interpolation.

THE OTHER FILTERS

The filters in this menu are a diverse group that don't fit into any other major category. Perhaps the most interesting is the Custom filter choice, which allows you to create your own filter.

Custom

If you would like to try your hand at creating your own filters, select Custom from the Other submenu. You won't be able to create filters as sophisticated as Photoshop's filters, but you can design your own sharpening, blurring, and embossing effects.

In the Custom dialog box, you can control the brightness values for all pixels that will be filtered. Each pixel evaluated is represented by the text field that is in the center of the matrix of text fields in the dialog box (in the following illustration, it's the one with the 5). The value entered in this box is the number by which Photoshop multiplies the current pixel's brightness. You can enter between –999 and 999.

```
┌──────────────────────── Custom ────────────────────────┐
│                                                         │
│  ┌────┐ ┌────┐ ┌────┐ ┌────┐ ┌────┐    ┌──────────┐     │
│  │    │ │    │ │    │ │    │ │    │    │    OK    │     │
│  └────┘ └────┘ └────┘ └────┘ └────┘    └──────────┘     │
│  ┌────┐ ┌────┐ ┌────┐ ┌────┐ ┌────┐    ┌──────────┐     │
│  │    │ │    │ │ -1 │ │    │ │    │    │  Cancel  │     │
│  └────┘ └────┘ └────┘ └────┘ └────┘    └──────────┘     │
│  ┌────┐ ┌────┐ ┌────┐ ┌────┐ ┌────┐                     │
│  │    │ │ -1 │ │ 5  │ │ -1 │ │    │    ┌──────────┐     │
│  └────┘ └────┘ └────┘ └────┘ └────┘    │  Load... │     │
│  ┌────┐ ┌────┐ ┌────┐ ┌────┐ ┌────┐    └──────────┘     │
│  │    │ │    │ │ -1 │ │    │ │    │    ┌──────────┐     │
│  └────┘ └────┘ └────┘ └────┘ └────┘    │  Save... │     │
│  ┌────┐ ┌────┐ ┌────┐ ┌────┐ ┌────┐    └──────────┘     │
│  │    │ │    │ │    │ │    │ │    │                     │
│  └────┘ └────┘ └────┘ └────┘ └────┘                     │
│                                                         │
│         Scale: ┌────────┐                               │
│                │ 1      │                               │
│                └────────┘                               │
│        Offset: ┌────────┐                               │
│                │        │                               │
│                └────────┘                               │
└─────────────────────────────────────────────────────────┘
```

By typing numbers in the surrounding text fields, you control the brightness of adjacent pixels in relation to the pixel represented in the center box. Photoshop multiplies the brightness value of adjacent pixels by this number. In other words, with the Custom dialog box's default settings, the brightness value of the pixel to the left of the central pixel will be multiplied by –1.

In the Scale field, you can enter a value that will be used to divide the sum of the brightness values. In the Offset field, you can enter a value that you wish to have added to the Scale's calculation results.

When the filter is applied, Photoshop recalculates the brightness of each pixel in the image or selected area, summing up the multiplied values used in the dialog box matrix. It then divides this result by the Scale value and adds the Offset value, if there is one.

> To create a sharpening filter, you'll need to increase the contrast between neighboring pixels. If you balance a set of negative numbers around the central matrix pixel, you will sharpen your image.

> To create a blur filter, surround the central matrix pixel with positive numbers. The positive numbers reduce the contrast between pixels as the matrix formula passes over the images.

> To create an embossing filter, balance positive and negative values around the central matrix area, as shown here:

Figure 8-16 shows an image before and after increasing contrast and applying a custom emboss filter.

Try your hand at creating a filter or two, using the foregoing suggestions and examples as a guide. You can save and reload your custom filters by using the Save and Load buttons in the Custom dialog box.

Before and after applying a custom emboss filter (photograph courtesy of Stacy Kollar Photography)

(a)

(b)

■ FIGURE 8-16

HIGH PASS   The High Pass filter suppresses areas that contain gradual increases in brightness and preserves portions of the image that exhibit the sharpest transitions in color. When you apply this filter, it removes shading and accentuates highlights.

HSL&HSB   The HSL&HSB filter was added to version 2.5.1 of Photoshop to allow users of previous versions to work in the HSL (Hue/Saturation/Lightness) and HSB (Hue/Saturation/Brightness) modes. (In Photoshop 2.5, HSL and HSB were removed from the Modes menu, and Lab Color was added.)

When the HSL&HSB filter is applied, a dialog box appears allowing conversion from RGB to HSL or to HSB. You can also return from HSL or HSB to RGB. When this filter is applied, the RGB components of an image are converted to HSL and HSB components, and vice versa.

When you convert an RGB file to either HSB or HSL, RGB's red channel becomes the hue channel, the green channel becomes the saturation channel, and the blue channel becomes the brightness or lightness channel. Once the filter is applied, you can make changes to each separate channel and then use the filter to convert the image back to RGB as well.

OTE: *See Chapter 9 for information about viewing images in separate channels; see Chapter 12 for information about editing images in channels.*

MAXIMUM The Maximum filter expands light areas and diminishes dark areas. The filter can be used in an alpha channel to increase the light area in the channel. (*Alpha channels* can be used for masking out parts of an image so they can be edited in an isolated area, as discussed in Chapter 12.)

MINIMUM This filter is similar to the Maximum filter except that it expands *dark* areas and diminishes *light* areas. The Minimum filter can be used in an alpha channel to increase the dark areas.

OFFSET The Offset filter moves the filtered image according to values entered in the Offset dialog box. You can use this filter to create a shadowed effect.

```
┌══════════════════════ Offset ══════════════════════┐
│                                                     │
│  Horizontal: [0        ] pixels right   ( OK )      │
│                                                     │
│  Vertical: [0      ]    pixels down    [ Cancel ]   │
│                                                     │
│  ┌─ Undefined Areas ──────┐                         │
│  │ ⦿ Set to Background    │                         │
│  │ ○ Repeat Edge Pixels   │                         │
│  │ ○ Wrap Around          │                         │
│  └────────────────────────┘                         │
│                                                     │
└─────────────────────────────────────────────────────┘
```

In the Offset filter dialog box, specify whether you wish the image to move horizontally and/or vertically. In the Vertical and Horizontal fields, you can enter values between –30,000 and 30,000. Positive values offset right and up, negative values offset left and down. If you wish to have the background of the image filled with the current background color, select the Set to Background radio button.

The Offset filter also includes options for handling pixels that would be offset out of the screen area. The Wrap Around option wraps these pixels so they appear on the opposite side of the screen. The Repeat Edge Pixels option disperses the extra pixels along the edges of the image.

FILTERS FROM THIRD-PARTY MANUFACTURERS

Now that you've seen the tremendous capabilities of Photoshop filters, you may feel that you have more than enough filters to meet your image-editing needs. However, if you ever grow tired of Photoshop's filters, you'll be happy to know that there's a small industry of third-party manufacturers of plug-in filters. For example, Alchemy by Xaos Tools, Inc., and Gallery Affects by Aldus offer filters that add more painting effects to a scanned image. And if you want more in the way of startling and unusual effects, investigate Andromeda Software Inc. and Kai's Power Tools. An example of the effects of an Andromeda filter is shown in image 19 in the color insert in this book.

9

CONVERTING FROM
ONE MODE TO ANOTHER

Throughout this book you've been working primarily in RGB Color mode, Photoshop's default file mode. Although RGB Color allows you to access the full range of Photoshop image-editing menus and commands, many Photoshop projects will require that you convert images from RGB Color to another mode. For instance:

- To output a file for four-color process printing, you will need to convert to CMYK Color mode.

- When you need to work with a display of 256 (or fewer) colors, you can switch to Indexed Color mode.

- To add color to a grayscale image, you'll need to convert from Grayscale mode to one of Photoshop's color modes (RGB Color, Indexed Color, CMYK Color, or Lab Color).

- For other projects, you may need to remove all color from an image. In this case, you can convert from any color mode to Grayscale mode, and from Grayscale you can convert to Bitmap (black and white) mode.

Switching modes also allows you to create special printing effects such as duotones and mezzotints. A *duotone* is a grayscale image in which two inks, usually black and another color, are printed over each other. The resulting extra color can add interest and depth to a grayscale image. A *mezzotint* is a bitmap image created from randomly shaped dots.

In this chapter, you'll have a chance to explore Photoshop's eight modes: Bitmap, Grayscale, Duotone, Indexed Color, RGB Color, CMYK Color, Lab Color, and Multichannel. You'll learn how to switch between one mode and another and, most importantly, from RGB Color to CMYK Color.

RGB COLOR MODE

RGB Color is Photoshop's native color mode. As discussed in Chapter 4, in RGB Color mode, all colors are created by combining different values of red, green, and blue. In Photoshop's RGB Color mode, over 16.7 million colors are available to you. You can view and edit each of the red, green, and blue color components, called *channels,* individually. Viewing an image's channels can help you better understand the difference between one mode and another.

In order to see the RGB channels that make up an RGB Color image, open any RGB Color file on your screen. (If you don't have an RGB image, load the Portrait file (PC users: portrait.jpg) from the Tutorial folder. With your file displayed, open the Channels palette by choosing Show Channels from the Window menu.

Using the Channels Palette

When the Channels palette opens, you'll see the three RGB channels listed. There's also a composite channel, where all channels combine to produce one color image.

The pencil icon (✒) to the left of each channel name indicates that the contents of the channel will be affected when the image is edited. The eye icon (👁) indicates that the components of a particular channel are being viewed.

You'll have a better sense of how RGB colors combine to create an image if you take a look at each channel. To do this, click on the name of the channel in the Channels palette. For instance, to view only the Red channel, click on Red, or use the keyboard shortcut COMMAND-1 (PC users: CTRL 1). In the image on your screen, you will only see the Red channel.

𝓃 **OTE:** *You'll probably see the channel as a grayscale image; Photoshop does not display the individual channels in color unless you change one of the default General Preferences settings. To see the channels in color, open the File menu and select Preferences and then General from the submenu. In the General Preferences dialog box, select the Color Channels in Color option. Click OK.*

Take a look at each one individually. Press COMMAND-2 (PC users: CTRL-2) to view the Green channel, and then COMMAND-3 (PC users: CTRL-3) to view the Blue channel. Notice that the eye and pencil icons are only next to the Blue channel in the Channels palette. This means that the Blue channel is the only channel in view and the only channel that can be edited. If you'd like, you can view and edit two channels together, independently of the third. While viewing the Blue channel, press and hold SHIFT while you click on Green in the Channels palette. You will see both Blue and Green channels together. Now you can begin to see how the colors combine to create the image. If you wish to deactivate or hide a channel, you can SHIFT-click on the channel name in the palette. To return to the composite view, click on the RGB composite channel, or press COMMAND-0 (PC users: CTRL-0).

Besides viewing the RGB channels, you can also edit within them to create special effects. For example, you could click on a channel name so it will be the only channel that can be viewed and edited, then apply a filter to it. In addition, you can apply paint to each channel separately. If you paint with white in a channel, you will be painting with that channel's color (red, green, or blue); if you paint with black, you add that channel's complementary color to the image.

Switching from RGB to Other Modes

The three RGB channels and the million of colors that can be produced in RGB images will provide you with the proper colors for output to slides and video or for printing to an RGB color printer. But as you work with Photoshop, your design goals or the output requirements of a project may necessitate switching modes. The following chart lists the modes to which you can convert from RGB Color, with a brief explanation of each one.

OTE: *From RGB Color, you cannot convert directly to Bitmap (black and white) or Duotone; you must convert from RGB Color to Grayscale mode first.*

Mode	Description
Grayscale	256 shades of gray. (From Grayscale you can switch to Bitmap to work in black and white, or to Duotone.)
Indexed Color	Restricts number of colors to 256 or fewer.
CMYK Color	Allows you to print color separations.
Lab Color	Encompasses both RGB and CMYK color gamuts. Used by Photo CDs and PostScript Level 2 printers.
Multichannel	No composite channel is created. Channels are viewed separately. When you delete a channel from RGB, Lab, or CMYK modes, Photoshop automatically switches to Multichannel.

When you convert from RGB Color to another mode (except Multichannel), Photoshop changes the color data in the image's file. If you save the file after converting, you will not be able to return to the original color data, unless you are converting between RGB and Lab Color. Thus, before converting from RGB Color to another mode, it's wise to use the Save As command to create a second copy of your file. That way you can always return to your original RGB file, if necessary.

In the next section, you will convert your RGB Color image to a CMYK Color image. Before proceeding, use the Save As command to save a copy of your image, and rename the new file **ModeTest**.

CMYK COLOR MODE

The CMYK Color mode is used for viewing and editing images for output by a commercial printer. If you are working with an RGB Color file and need to produce four-color separations, you must convert the image from RGB Color to CMYK Color. CMYK Color images are divided into four channels, one for each of the process colors used to create four-color separations: Cyan, Magenta, Yellow, and Black. From the four channels, a prepress house produces the four pieces of film needed by a print shop to create the cyan, magenta, yellow, and black printing plates. When the image is printed, the tiny colored ink dots from each plate combine to create countless varieties of color.

If your images are digitized on a high-end scanner, they will probably be saved as CMYK files. These scanners can convert from RGB to CMYK "on the fly"—during the process of digitizing the image. When the scanned image is loaded into Photoshop, it will open as a CMYK image in CMYK Color mode. Photo CD "profiles," available from Kodak, can convert Photo CD files directly to CMYK Color when the images are opened.

OTE: If you are working with a CMYK Color file, it is not advisable to convert it to RGB Color and then back to CMYK Color. When you convert to RGB Color, you lose color data that will not be restored when you convert it back to CMYK Color.

When you work in CMYK Color mode, you have a choice as to how the CMYK colors are displayed. In the General Preferences dialog box (File/Preferences/General), you can change the CMYK Composites option from Faster (the default) to Smoother. Photoshop will then display the colors as accurately as possible. The disadvantage of the Smoother option is that it slows down the screen display.

Converting from RGB Color to CMYK Color

Before you convert a file from RGB Color to CMYK Color, bear in mind that CMYK Color files are larger than RGB Color files, due to the addition of the fourth channel. Thus, working in RGB Color mode is generally faster, and it's often advisable not to convert a file to CMYK Color until all image editing is complete. On the other hand, if you have a fast computer, a lot of RAM, and available space on your hard disk, you may want to convert to CMYK Color before you complete a project, so you can edit using the same colors that will be used when the image is printed. When you edit in CMYK Color, you'll be able to color correct and edit in the four individual channels.

Although converting an RGB Color file to CMYK Color is a simple process, it's vital to understand the steps Photoshop goes through to complete the conversion. If you don't, you may not be happy with the color quality of the printed image. To begin the conversion process, you simply select CMYK Color from the Mode menu. The conversion process can take several minutes. When it's done, the RGB colors will be converted to CMYK equivalents, and you will have a larger file because of the fourth channel.

IP: *After a conversion to CMYK, it is often advisable to run the Unsharp Mask filter to sharpen image details. See Chapter 8 for more information.*

When the conversion begins, Photoshop first uses the information in the Monitor Setup dialog box (accessed from the File/Preferences submenu) to *internally* convert from RGB Color to Lab Color. Thus, if your monitor is not properly calibrated, you could be on your way to a separation that will produce unsatisfactory colors in the printed image. If you need to, review the section on monitor calibration in Chapter 1.

Next, Photoshop analyzes the settings in two dialog boxes that will be discussed in later sections of this chapter: Printing Inks Setup and Separation Setup, both of which are accessed via the File/Preferences command. Using the information in these two dialog boxes and the Monitor Setup dialog box, Photoshop creates the CMYK Color file.

OTE: *Once a file is converted to CMYK Color, changing the settings in the Monitor Setup and Printing Inks Setup dialog boxes will only affect the CMYK Color image's on-screen display. It will not affect the color data in the file. Thus, if you convert a file with incorrect settings, you will then need to change the settings, return to the original RGB Color file, and again convert to CMYK Color.*

Printing Inks Setup Dialog Box

The primary purpose of the Printing Inks Setup dialog box is to provide Photoshop with information about the ink and paper your commercial printer will be using. Photoshop uses this information to fine-tune the conversion so that the CMYK colors are the most appropriate for your particular print job. When you change the settings in the dialog box, only the display of a CMYK Color image will be affected—not the display of an RGB Color image.

To access the Printing Inks Setup dialog box, choose Preferences from the File menu, and select Printing Inks Setup from the submenu. The Printing Inks Setup options allow you to choose from various printers and printing inks.

When the dialog box appears, open the Ink Colors pop-up menu to view the choices available. The default setting is SWOP (Coated). The SWOP (Specifications Web Offset Proofing) organization has published specifications for web offset printing. Choosing one of the SWOP settings means you are choosing inks and papers according to these specifications. Notice the other choices: SWOP (Newsprint), QMS, NEC, and Tektronix printers, as well as Canon laser copiers.

When you make a choice in the Ink Colors pop-up menu, the value in the Dot Gain field, explained next, is updated automatically.

Understanding Dot Gain and Gray Balance

The Dot Gain percentage indicates the percentage of dot gain expected on a printing press. *Dot gain* is the bleed or spreading of the ink that occurs on paper when an image is printed on a printing press. Dot gain is caused by halftone dots that print larger or smaller than their actual size on film or on the printing plate. This unavoidable phenomenon is most noticeable in midtones and shadow areas of printed images, where the halftone dots are the largest. The degree of dot gain is primarily determined by the printing paper. When Photoshop converts to CMYK Color, it adjusts CMYK percentages in the converted image to compensate for dot gain.

At first glance, the number in the Dot Gain field may seem frighteningly large—but it's really not as bad as it seems. The percentage is measured in terms of the ink increase beyond the size of midtone halftone dots in the film output from the imagesetter. Photoshop then takes the dot gain value and creates a curve which it uses to calculate dot gain in other areas beside midtones.

Since the dot gain value is entered automatically when you change the Ink Colors selection, there's generally no need to enter a number in the Dot Gain field. As long as you know the printing process you will be using, you won't need to change the value in the Dot Gain field. You may, however, wish to change the Dot Gain setting when you calibrate your system to a proof (or sample printout). This subject is covered in Chapter 14.

n **OTE:** *By default, the Use Dot Gain for Grayscale Images check box is turned on. When the check box is on, display of grayscale images is changed in order to compensate for dot gain. For more information, see the section "Converting from Any Color Mode to Grayscale" later in this chapter.*

The Printing Inks Setup dialog box also allows adjustment of gray balance settings. The four fields here allow you to control the levels of CMYK colors to compensate for color casts. For instance, a color cast may appear if one of the process inks has a higher dot gain than the others.

Usually, the Gray Balance fields are only changed when you're recalibrating your system to a proof (or sample printout) while you are in a CMYK Color file. In an RGB Color file, changing these values affects the separation settings but not how colors are displayed. In a CMYK Color image, *increasing* the value of any of the Gray Balance fields will lighten that color's display on screen, and vice versa. Chapter 14 tells you how to use a proof as a guide for adjusting for the Gray Balance fields.

The Printing Inks Setup dialog box also includes Save and Load buttons, which allow you to save your settings and reload them to use again in another file.

If you are working with an image in the Photoshop screen, and you are certain of the correct Printing Inks Setup settings for your project, go ahead and select the appropriate choice in the Ink Colors pop-up menu and click OK. Otherwise, if you made changes to the Printing Inks Setup dialog box while working through this section, click Cancel now so that the default settings remain intact. Next, take a look at the Separation Setup dialog box, which is also used during CMYK conversion.

Choosing a Separation Setup

To open the Separation Setup dialog box, choose Preferences from the File menu and then select Separation Setup. The Separation Setup dialog box controls how the black plate is created during the separation process. In most cases, the default dialog box settings should provide good results. The Save and Load buttons allow you to save and reload the settings you make here; this is helpful when you need to return to a particular set of print settings or wish to reload the Black Generation custom curve (explained below).

AUTION: *If you experiment with the Separation Setup dialog box settings as you work through this section, be sure to change them back to the defaults. These settings should only be changed on the advice of your commercial printer or prepress house.*

As discussed in Chapter 4, cyan, magenta, and yellow can theoretically produce all of the colors needed for commercial printing. Unfortunately, however, when the three colors overprint, ink impurities produce a muddy brown color instead of pure black. To remedy this, a black plate is added to increase contrast and produce blacker blacks. When black is added, levels of cyan, magenta, and yellow can be reduced to enhance printing quality. The two primary techniques used to substitute black for CMY colors are UCR (Under Color Removal) and GCR (Gray Component Replacement).

The decision to use either GCR or UCR in Photoshop is often determined by paper stock and printing requirements. GCR is generally used for coated stock and UCR for uncoated stock.

For the UCR separation type, levels of cyan, magenta, and yellow are subtracted from gray and shadow areas and replaced with an appropriate amount of black. For the GCR separation type (Photoshop's default), levels of cyan, magenta, and yellow are subtracted from both gray and colored areas. To compensate for the removal of one or all three of the these colors, when GCR is chosen, an appropriate amount of black is added. The degree of black replacement can be specified in the Black Generation pop-up menu of the Separation Setup dialog box.

Most of you won't need to delve deeply into the inner workings of GCR; the basic theory is that one of the three process inks (CMY) often is the gray component of a color. The gray component is the ink that lightens or darkens; the other two inks provide most of the color. When GCR is applied, the gray component ink is reduced and black is added. For instance, consider a digitized image of green grass that is primarily composed of cyan and yellow, with a small percentage of magenta darkening the image. During the separation process with the GCR option selected, a portion of the magenta can be reduced and replaced with black. Theoretically, GCR can result in better gray balance and better reproduction of saturated colors.

OTE: *Despite what you read or are told about the advantages of GCR over UCR (or vice versa), don't make any choices without contacting your print shop.*

In the Separation Setup dialog box you'll also see a grid where a slope portraying the *gray ramp* is displayed. The Gray Ramp grid provides a visual representation of how the process inks produce neutral or gray colors based upon the settings in the dialog box. The x-axis charts the color value from 0% to 100%. The gray bar depicts the actual shade of gray from white to black. The y-axis charts the ink that will be used to produce the gray value.

GCR AND THE GRAY RAMP   The best way to understand how the Gray Ramp works is to see what happens when you turn off the black plate with the GCR option enabled. To turn off the black plate, select None in the Black Generation pop-up menu. This menu controls the amount of black substituted in the image when the GCR option is used.

As soon as you click None, the Gray Ramp changes, showing you that the grays will be produced with approximately equal amounts of cyan, magenta, and yellow, but not black. Now click on Medium in the Black Generation pop-up menu. The Gray Ramp now shows that CMY levels are reduced, with black used to help produce grays starting in areas just lighter than the image's midtones. Switch among the choices in the Black Generation menu, and you'll see that as more black is added, the CMY inks are reduced; when black is reduced, the CMY levels are increased.

The Custom selection in the Black Generation pop-up lets you manually control the generation of the black plate. When you choose Custom, a Black Generation dialog box appears, where you can customize black generation by clicking and dragging on a curve. After you adjust the curve and click OK, the cyan, magenta, and yellow levels are changed according to the black curve.

When you choose the GCR separation type, the UCA (Undercolor Addition) Amount field at the bottom of the Separation Setup dialog box allows you to add cyan, magenta, and yellow back into the areas that contain the highest percentage of black in an image. When you add cyan, magenta, and yellow, black is not subtracted. This results in more intense blacks, which can help prevent shadow areas from appearing too flat. Acceptable values in the UCA Amount field are between 0 and 100%. Once again, if you change settings, you will see the results in the Gray Ramp. And remember: *Any value entered in this field should also be approved by your commercial printer or prepress house.*

Before continuing, if you have changed the Black Generation menu selection, return it now to the default setting, Medium. In most situations, Medium will provide good results when you convert from RGB to CMYK.

UCR AND THE GRAY RAMP   To see how the UCR option affects the Gray Ramp, click on the UCR radio button in the Separation Setup dialog box. Notice that the black ink increases in the dark shadow areas while the appropriate CMY colors are decreased in this area.

SETTING INK LIMITS   The Black Ink Limit field in the dialog box allows you to tell Photoshop the maximum ink density that your commercial printer's press can support; the default value is 100%. This means that the darkest black (K) value in your converted CMYK Color image can be 100%. The default setting for the Total Ink Limit is 300%. This means that the total percentage of your CMY inks together will not be over 200% (300%-100%=200%, the 100% being the Black Ink Limit). If you lower the values in these fields, you'll see that the maximum values for the CMYK inks will drop in the Gray Ramp. The same warning applies here: *Do not change any values without consulting your print shop.*

To close the Separation Setup dialog box and exit without changing the default settings, click Cancel.

Separation Tables

If you are going to be printing Photoshop projects with various inks or printing systems, the settings you choose in the Printing Ink Setup and Separation Setup dialog boxes can be saved together, as a *separation table*. If you save a separation table, you do not need to save the individual settings in these dialog boxes. Saving the table essentially saves the settings in both the Printing Inks Setup and Separation Setup dialog boxes on disk.

When you want to convert an image that needs a particular group of settings, you just load the settings from the Separation Tables dialog box, instead of having to reenter the settings in the Printing Inks Setup and Separation Setup dialog boxes. Using a separation table also results in a speedier completion of the RGB-to-CMYK conversion because the separation table Photoshop will use in that conversion will have already been created.

Once you have established the settings in the Printing Inks Setup and Separation Setup dialog boxes, you can have Photoshop build a separation table. To do this, choose Preferences from the File menu and then select Separation Tables to display the Separation Tables dialog box. Click the Save button, and wait for Photoshop to build a separation table. Next, when a dialog box appears, name your table and save it on your disk. After you name your separation table, load it by clicking on the Load button and choosing the table file from the list of files in the dialog box.

When a separation table is loaded, the Separation Tables dialog box displays the name of the table alongside the Use Table radio button. When the Use Table radio button is selected, it means that the table will be used when you convert to CMYK and that the table will be used to display the CMYK color values on your RGB monitor. If you wish to use the settings in the Printing Inks Setup dialog box instead of the separation table, select the Use Printing Inks Setup radio button.

```
╔═══════════════════════ Separation Tables ═══════════════════════╗
║  ┌─ To CMYK ──────────────────────────────┐      ┌──────────┐   ║
║  │  ○ Use Separation Setup                │      │    OK    │   ║
║  │                                        │      └──────────┘   ║
║  │  ● Use Table:   Fundamental Photoshop   │      ┌──────────┐   ║
║  └────────────────────────────────────────┘      │  Cancel  │   ║
║                                                   └──────────┘   ║
║  ┌─ From CMYK ────────────────────────────┐      ┌──────────┐   ║
║  │  ○ Use Printing Inks Setup             │      │  Load... │   ║
║  │                                        │      └──────────┘   ║
║  │  ● Use Table:   Fundamental Photoshop   │      ┌──────────┐   ║
║  └────────────────────────────────────────┘      │  Save... │   ║
║                                                   └──────────┘   ║
╚═════════════════════════════════════════════════════════════════╝
```

The Separation Tables dialog box is also used if you are loading separation tables created by third-party software vendors such as EFI (Electronics for Imaging). EFI has created a variety of separation tables designed to work with specific printers and printing systems. For more details about using EfiColor for Photoshop, see Chapter 14.

OTE: *When you load a separation table, the Separation Setup dialog box will be disabled. Also, if you try to open the Printing Inks Setup dialog box, an alert message will appear, warning you that the Printing Inks Setup dialog box will not affect the CMYK conversion because a separation table has been selected.*

Completing the CMYK Conversion

Now that you have an understanding of what goes on behind the scenes, you can proceed to convert your image from RGB Color to CMYK Color. First, if you haven't already backed up your file, use the Save As command to create another version of your image. Then, to begin the conversion, choose CMYK Color from the Mode menu. When the conversion is completed, the mode in the title bar will change from RGB to CMYK. After converting, it is often advisable to run the Unsharp Mask filter, as explained in Chapter 8, to sharpen the image.

After the file has been converted, open the Channels palette and notice that it now is comprised of four channels. If you look at the File Size indicator (towards the bottom left-hand corner of your screen), you'll see that the extra channel has increased the size of the image file. Take a moment to click on each of the channels to see how the image is created from the four process colors: cyan, magenta, yellow, and black.

One of the advantages of working in a CMYK Color file is that Photoshop will not allow you to paint with out-of-gamut colors. Also, you can edit in the four individual channels or in any combination of the four channels. This is helpful when you want to color correct in the individual channels or when you are creating interesting special effects.

Here's a design tip for adding color to a black-and-white (bitmap) image, without affecting the underlying black color. This technique is possible because you can click on the pencil in the Channels palette to turn off editing in the black channel while you paint in the CMY channels. First, convert the black-and-white line art to CMYK Color. If you have a bitmap image, you will need to use the Mode menu to convert from Bitmap to Grayscale, then from Grayscale to CMYK Color. Once the image is in CMYK Color mode, deactivate the Black channel so that the black plate will not be affected. To do this, click the pencil icon adjacent to the Black channel in the Channels palette. (*Don't* deactivate the eye icon for the Black channel or you won't be able to see the black image when editing the CMY channels.) Then use Photoshop's painting tools to add color to your image.

After converting to CMYK, you'll probably want to save the file so it can be output for proofing purposes. Often this means saving the file in EPS, TIFF or Scitex CT format before sending it to a service bureau or prepress house. Before you send the file to the service bureau, you may need to export your EPS or TIFF file to a page-layout program such as QuarkXPress. For more information about saving Photoshop files in EPS, TIFF, and Scitex CT formats, see Appendix A.

INDEXED COLOR MODE

The Indexed Color mode is used to create and edit files that only require a maximum of 256 colors. Converting to Indexed Color is often necessary when editing files that will be exported to programs that only support 256 colors. The Indexed Color mode can also be used if you are creating applications or silkscreens that only require a few colors.

When you convert a file to Indexed Color, Photoshop reduces the channels in the image to one and creates a color table that is essentially a palette of colors that is tied to the document. This table is called a *color lookup table* (CLUT), and it acts as a type of index for the colors in the image.

You can convert to Indexed Color from RGB Color, Grayscale, or Duotone mode. In this section, you'll learn how to convert an RGB Color file to Indexed Color and edit the related color table. If your RGB Color file contains more than 256 colors, you will lose color information when you convert to Indexed Color. Although you can convert from Indexed Color back to RGB Color, Photoshop will not return the original colors to the file. Thus, you should always keep a backup copy of your original color file before converting.

OTE: *Once you convert to Indexed Color mode, Photoshop's filters and the Image/Effects submenu commands will not be available. You must execute these before converting to Indexed Color.*

Converting from RGB Color to Indexed Color

If you wish to experiment with Indexed Color, choose Revert from the File menu to return to the RGB Color version of the ModeTest file you created at the beginning of this chapter. If you wish to use another file, you can load any RGB Color file. Make sure that you use the Save As command first to rename the file, so you can later return to the original version.

The Indexed Color Dialog Box

To convert an RGB Color file to Indexed Color, choose Indexed Color from the Mode menu. In the Indexed Color dialog box, you can choose the desired number of colors, a color palette, and whether you wish to use a dithering pattern.

```
═══════════════ Indexed Color ═══════════════
┌─ Resolution ──────────────┐      ┌─────────┐
│  ○ 3 bits/pixel           │      │   OK    │
│  ○ 4 bits/pixel           │      └─────────┘
│  ○ 5 bits/pixel           │      ┌─────────┐
│  ○ 6 bits/pixel           │      │ Cancel  │
│  ○ 7 bits/pixel           │      └─────────┘
│  ● 8 bits/pixel           │
│  ○ Other: [      ] colors │
└───────────────────────────┘

┌─ Palette ──────┐  ┌─ Dither ─────┐
│  ○ Exact       │  │  ○ None      │
│  ○ System      │  │  ○ Pattern   │
│  ● Adaptive    │  │  ● Diffusion │
│  ○ Custom...   │  └──────────────┘
│  ○ Previous    │
└────────────────┘
```

Use the Resolution options to specify the number of colors in the Indexed Color file. In this case, resolution refers to the bit resolution of the image. If you choose 8 bits/pixel, 256 (2^8) colors can be displayed; choose 4 bits/pixel, and 16 (2^4) colors can displayed. If you know the exact number of colors that you wish in an image, you can enter it into the Other field. The Other field will only accept values less than or equal to 256.

The Palette options provide a variety of color choices for the Indexed Color file. Read the following descriptions; then, if you wish, take a look at what happens to your image with each Palette option. Click on a radio button and then click OK. After you've seen the effects of a palette on your image, choose Undo from the Edit menu and then test the next palette.

Exact   Use this option if the image contains 256 or fewer colors. Photoshop will build a table using the same colors that appear in the original RGB Color image. When this option is selected, no dithering is necessary because no new colors need to be simulated.

System   This option uses the Mac or Windows default system palette. If you designate fewer than 8 bits/pixel for Resolution, Photoshop replaces the System option with the Uniform option to indicate that the full System palette is not available.

🖎 *Adaptive*   This option generates a color table from commonly used colors in the image being converted. If you wish to have more control over the Adaptive palette conversion process, first select an area of the image that includes the colors you wish to retain. In the conversion to Indexed Color, Photoshop will choose colors based more upon the selection than on all of the colors in the image.

🖎 *Custom*   This option allows you to create your own custom color table for the file. When you select this option, the Color Table dialog box appears, in which you can edit, save, and load color tables. You can also choose from several predefined color tables. When you choose a predefined table or edit a table, the colors of the image on screen will change to those in the color table when it is applied to your image. The colors are applied to the image when you click OK in the Color Table dialog box. For a description of each predefined table, see the section "Viewing the Predefined Colors" that follows.

🖎 *Previous*   This option converts using the palette from the previous conversion, which is useful when you are converting several images at a time.

To the right of the Palette group are the Dither options. *Dithering* combines different colored pixels together to give the appearance of colors that are not actually in the image. Choosing a dithering option may be advisable because the color table that is created may not contain all of the colors in your image. Here are descriptions of the Dither options:

🖎 *None*   Choose None if you do not wish dithering to occur. When this option is chosen, Photoshop picks the closest match it can find in the Color Table to replace a missing color in the converted image. This usually results in sharp color transitions.

🖎 *Pattern*   This option uses a pattern of random dots to simulate a missing color. This option is only available if the System or Uniform palette option is selected.

🖎 *Diffusion*   When you choose Diffusion, Photoshop diffuses the difference between the original pixels and the pixels in the converted image to simulate the missing colors.

Viewing the Predefined Colors

There are two ways to access the Color Table dialog box in order to choose a predefined color table. If you have already converted to Indexed Color, you can choose Color Table from the Mode menu. If you haven't yet converted, first choose Indexed Color from the Mode menu, and then select Custom in the Palette group of the Indexed Color dialog box.

In the Color Table dialog box, the predefined tables are accessed by clicking on the Table pop-up menu. Here's a brief description of these tables; you may want to select each one to view the colors produced.

Black Body   This option transforms the color table based on colors produced when a blackbody radiator is heated. You'll see a range of colors from black to red, as well as orange, yellow, and white. This table can be used for scientific applications or to produce a hot, glowing effect.

Grayscale   This table produces transitional colors through 256 shades from black to white.

Spectrum   This table produces the colors in the color spectrum.

System   This table is the standard Mac or Windows color palette.

Editing the Indexed Color Table

If you'd like, you can open the color table used by your image and edit the colors. To do this, your image should be converted to Indexed Color.

Once you have an Indexed Color file on screen, select Color Table from the Mode menu; the color table for your file will be displayed. Now you can edit any color in the table by clicking on the color. After you click, Photoshop's Color Picker will appear, allowing you to change the colors. Use the dialog box options to pick a color that is not already in the color table, and then click OK. Photoshop will return to your document, where each pixel that contained the color you clicked in the Color Table dialog box is converted to the new color.

Photoshop's Indexed Color also allows you to change a range of colors in the table at one time. This can be helpful if you want to prevent the color changes in your image from being too dramatic. To change a range of colors, select Color Table from the Mode menu. In the Color Table dialog box, click and drag through a row of colors. When you release the mouse, the Color Picker will appear with the message "Select first color." Choose a color and click OK. The Color Picker will reopen with the message "Select last color." When you click OK, a gradient of colors—from the first color you specified to the last color—will appear in the color table. Click OK in the dialog box to see the effects in your image.

Saving and Loading Indexed Color Tables

If you wish to create a custom color table to use with other documents, you can return to the Color Table dialog box and click the Save button to name the table and save it on disk. When you wish to apply it to a document, use the Load button to load it. After the table is loaded, click OK in the Color Table dialog box to have the colors from the table appear in the document on screen.

 IP: *You can load a saved Indexed Color table into the Colors palette and paint with only those colors. To load the table, choose Load Colors from the Colors palette Options menu.*

CONVERTING FROM ANY COLOR MODE TO GRAYSCALE

If for design purposes you need to convert your digitized color image to grayscale or black and white, you will need to first convert your file to Grayscale mode. From Grayscale, you can convert to a Duotone or Bitmap file. (Duotones and bitmap images are discussed later in this chapter.)

Grayscale files are 8-bit images that can be comprised of up to 256 shades of gray. When a color file is converted to grayscale, all color information is removed from the file. Although the Mode menu allows you to convert a grayscale file to a color mode file, you will not be able to return the original colors to a file that has been converted to grayscale. Thus, before converting a color image to grayscale, it's advisable to use the Save As command to create a copy of your color file so that you have a backup.

If you don't have a color file on screen, load one now so that you can convert it to grayscale (try the ModeTest file that's been used throughout this chapter). Then select Grayscale from the Mode menu. An alert box will appear, warning that you will be discarding the color information in the file. After you click OK, your file will be converted to a grayscale image, and the Channels palette will display only one channel, Black.

For a grayscale image, the Colors palette displays only one grayscale slider, labeled K (Black). You can change the percentage of gray by clicking and dragging on the slider control. The lower the percentage, the lighter the shade of gray; the higher the percentage, the darker the shade of gray.

When working with Grayscale mode images, keep in mind that by default, the Dot Gain percentage in the Printing Inks Setup dialog box is automatically applied by Photoshop, based on your selection in the Ink Colors pop-up menu. The Dot Gain setting changes the display of a grayscale image to compensate for dot gain that can occur on press. Before editing a grayscale image, open the Printing Inks Setup dialog box (choose Printing Inks Setup from the File/Preferences submenu) and verify that the Ink Colors selection is correct. If you do not want the Dot Gain setting to affect the display, deselect the Use Dot Gain for Grayscale Images option at the bottom of the dialog box.

When Photoshop converts to grayscale, it uses a formula to convert the color information to gray values. Notwithstanding the formula's accuracy, you still may decide that the grayscale version needs some tonal corrections. If this is the case, you can make simple tonal adjustments using the Brightness/Contrast command in the Image/Adjust submenu. To learn more advanced techniques for making tonal adjustments to grayscale images, see Chapter 13.

CONVERTING FROM GRAYSCALE TO ANY COLOR MODE

While working with an image in Grayscale mode, you cannot add color to it. If you wish to add color to a grayscale image, convert the image to one of the color modes (RGB Color, CMYK Color, Lab Color, or Indexed Color) by selecting that mode from the Mode menu. After you convert, you can colorize the image.

Colorizing Grayscale Images

Using the computer to colorize a grayscale image is similar to the process of adding color to old black-and-white movies. Like the process of creating colorized movies, transforming a grayscale image into color allows the image's shadows and contours, and definition beneath the color to show through.

To start colorizing, you will need to load a grayscale image. (As usual, to ensure that you will be able to return to the original grayscale image, it's always advisable to use the Save As command and rename the file.) Then open the Colors palette by choosing Show Colors in the Window menu. Select the Mode menu, and convert your file from Grayscale to RGB Color or CMYK Color. This will allow you to add colors to your image.

Set the foreground color, and choose the Paintbrush tool in the Toolbox. If the Brushes palette isn't open, choose Show Brushes in the Window menu. In the Brushes palette, select a medium, soft-edged brush size, leave Opacity set to 100%, and in the Mode pop-up menu select Color as the painting mode.

Start painting the image with the Paintbrush tool. Notice the result: The portion you paint changes color, but you can still see the underlying shadows and textures. This is because you are painting in Color mode. When you paint using Color mode, Photoshop paints with only the hue and saturation of a color. This allows the underlying brightness values to show through your painting color. If you were painting in Normal mode at 100% Opacity, the opaque color would completely cover the image.

If there are large areas that you wish to color in your image, use the Pen tool or a selection tool to create a selection. Then choose Fill from the Edit menu, and set the Mode in the Edit menu to Color. After you click OK, color will be applied to your image, but again, the underlying lightness and darkness levels will show through the color.

You may wish to experiment with the Darken, Lighten, Multiply, and Screen painting modes. Lighten and Darken, in particular, can be used to add various color tones to areas already colorized. (For a review of Darken, Lighten, Multiply, and Screen, see "Painting Modes" in Chapter 5.) Also, you may wish to activate the Blur or Smudge tools to blend colors together. You can use the Sharpen tool to enhance detail by increasing contrast as well.

Using the Colorize Option in the Hue/Saturation Dialog Box

Photoshop also allows you to adjust colors from a variety of dialog boxes accessed from the Image/Adjust submenu. You'll be using these commands extensively when retouching and color correcting (in Chapter 13). Only the Hue/Saturation command is discussed here because it includes an option specifically designed to colorize.

Before experimenting with the Hue/Saturation command, select an area of your image that you wish to colorize. Choose Hue/Saturation from the Image/Adjust submenu. In the dialog box, click on the Preview check box. This lets you see the changes in your image as you colorize. Then click on the Colorize check box, and the selection you've just made will turn red. Don't worry—this is supposed to happen. Notice that the Hue setting on your screen is set to 0 degrees, as shown in this illustration; this is the value assigned to red in Photoshop's HSB Colors palette. When you turned on the Colorize option, Photoshop applied this setting to your selection.

Photoshop in Action

The white areas of the image were colored.

Artist: José Ortega

Black-and-white line art drawing

The black marker lines of the image were colored.

José began this project for New York's Metropolitan Transit Authority (MTA) by first using a marker to make this line drawing. He then scanned the image as black-and-white line art. Once the image was digitized, he removed any dust spots with the Eraser tool and closed white gaps in the marker lines with the Pencil tool.

Photoshop in Action

The white areas no longer exist.
They were filled using the
Darken painting mode.

Artist: José Ortega

Client: Metropolitan Transit Authority

The black marker lines no longer
exist. They were colored by using
the Lighten painting mode.

After the black-and-white line art drawing was digitized, José converted it to a color image by choosing RGB Color from the Mode menu. He colored the white areas of the image by using the Paint Bucket tool with different Tolerance settings and the Darken painting mode. By using the Darken painting mode, José prevented the black marker lines from being affected. After filling the white areas, he colored the black marker lines by using the Lighten painting mode.

To complete the project, he selected the entire image with the Rectangular Marquee tool and created a black frame around it using the Edit/Stroke command.

$\mathcal{N}$**OTE:** *When the Colorize option is on in the Hue/Saturation dialog box, the radio buttons for the various RGB and CMY colors, at the left of the dialog box, are dimmed. When you are color correcting an image with the Colorize option turned off, these radio buttons become accessible. They will be discussed in Chapter 13.*

Adjusting the Hue slider will change the color of the image. Adjusting the Saturation slider will change the amount of gray in a color. When you are colorizing a grayscale image, the more saturation you add, the stronger the colors will be and the less gray they will contain. Adjusting the Lightness slider allows you to control how light or dark the color will be. The Sample swatch previews the color you are creating.

Now try working with the Hue/Saturation sliders. To move through the color spectrum, drag the Hue slider control right or left. Drag it all the way to the left to −180, and you'll see the color in the Sample box change from red to magenta to blue and eventually to cyan. Drag to the right from 0 to 180 degrees, and you'll see red, yellow, green, and cyan again. If you find it confusing that you returned to cyan, think of the slider as the linear equivalent of a color wheel. When you move in a positive direction from red along the wheel, you eventually reach cyan; when you move in a negative direction, you arrive at the same color. Figure 9-1 shows how the Hue slider values and their corresponding colors would appear if arranged on a color wheel.

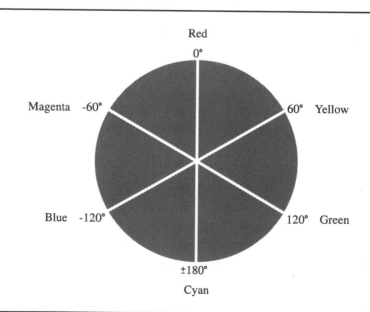

Hue slider values arranged on a color wheel

FIGURE 9-1

If you wish, you can change the Saturation setting. If you drag the Saturation slider control to the right, saturation increases; dragging left decreases saturation. Moving the Lightness slider control to the right toward 100 lightens your color; sliding it left toward -100 darkens it. With Lightness set to 100, the color changes to white; -100 changes it to black. By adjusting the Lightness slider control, you can even add color to pure white and pure black image areas.

After you decide what combination of Hue, Saturation, and Lightness you wish to apply to an image area, you can save your settings so that they can be applied to other files. Click the Save button, and a dialog box appears, allowing you to enter a name for the settings. After naming your settings, click Save (PC users: OK) to return to the Hue/Saturation dialog box. When you wish to use these color settings again, select another area of the image or open another image; then return to the Hue/Saturation dialog box and load your color settings by clicking the Load button and opening your Hue/Saturation settings file. If you wish to exit the Hue/Saturation dialog box and apply the settings now, click OK; otherwise, click Cancel.

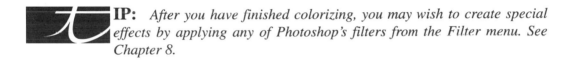

IP: *After you have finished colorizing, you may wish to create special effects by applying any of Photoshop's filters from the Filter menu. See Chapter 8.*

CONVERTING FROM GRAYSCALE TO A DUOTONE

Printing a grayscale image with an extra gray or colored ink can make it more interesting and dramatic by adding depth and dimension. These enhanced grayscale images are called *duotones*. In Photoshop's Duotone mode you can create monotones, duotones, tritones, and quadtones—grayscale images to which you add one, two, three, or four colors. This printing technique lets you create interesting images less expensively than printing four-color images.

In order to create a monotone, duotone, tritone or quadtone image, you must start with a grayscale image or convert a color image to a grayscale image. Only while in Grayscale mode can you access the Duotone mode.

In this section, you will create a duotone from a grayscale image. Start by loading any color file and converting it to Grayscale mode. If you wish, you can use the ModeTest file that was converted to Grayscale earlier in the chapter, or use the Hands file (PC users: hands.jpg) in the Tutorial folder.

1. Select Duotone from the Mode menu. In the Duotone Options dialog box, Type is set to Monotone by default. When the Monotone option is

selected, notice that Ink 1 is active. Next to Ink 1 are two squares. The square with the diagonal line represents the ink density curve. The second square is the color swatch box. This represents the color you are applying to your image. To activate another Type option, click on the Type pop-up menu and make your selection. Select the Duotone option, since that is the option most commonly used.

When you choose Duotone from the Type pop-up menu, Ink 1 and Ink 2 are active, but not Ink 3 and Ink 4. This is because duotones are composed of only two colors. The number of inks that appear depends upon the option you select in the Type pop-up menu.

 OTE: *When Photoshop prints a duotone, it prints the inks in ascending order. Thus, the darker ink is usually the first ink and the lightest ink is the last ink in the Duotone Options dialog box.*

2. Notice that for the Duotone option, you will need to pick a second ink color. Click once on the white color swatch box to the right of Ink 2. The Custom Colors dialog box appears.

In the Custom Colors dialog box, you can either pick a custom color or click on the Picker button to access the Color Picker dialog box and then enter CMYK percentages to pick a process color.

3. To pick a PANTONE Coated color in the Custom Color dialog box, click on the Book pop-up menu and choose PANTONE Coated if it is not already displayed. In the Find # field type **2645**. Notice that PANTONE 2645 CV (or PANTONE 2645 CVC if the Short PANTONE Names option in the General Preferences dialog box isn't selected) becomes the active color. Click OK to confirm the change and return to the Duotone Options dialog box.

4. To see the effects of your changes, click OK in the Duotone Options dialog box. When your image appears on screen, you will see that it contains two colors: black and PANTONE 2645 CV.

Controlling Duotone Ink

After you have selected the second ink color for a duotone, you may want to control ink density in shadow, midtone, and highlight areas. You do this by adjusting that ink's curve. Usually in duotone images, black is applied to the shadow areas, and gray or another color is applied to the midtone and highlight areas. To change the way an ink is applied to an image, follow these steps:

OTE: *Before and after you make adjustments in the Duotone Curve dialog box, you may want to open the Colors palette to see the different shades of Ink 1 and Ink 2.*

1. Return to the Duotone Options dialog box by choosing Duotone from the Mode menu. In the Duotone Options dialog box, click on the box with the diagonal line in it for Ink 1 or Ink 2. The Duotone Curve dialog box appears, containing a graph depicting the ink coverage over different image areas.

In the Duotone Curve dialog box, observe the graph on the left and the percentages on the right. In the graph, the x-axis represents the tonal range in the original image, from highlights to shadows. The y-axis represents the ink density values. The default settings of the graph are always represented by a diagonal line. The diagonal indicates that the printing ink percentage matches the gray percentage value of every pixel in the image. This means if the image contains grayscale values of 100%, they will print with a 100% density (a 100% dot of the specified ink color) for the specified ink. A 50% midtone pixel will be printed at a 50% density (a 50% dot of the specified ink). The diagonal line can be adjusted by clicking and dragging it, or by typing percentage values in the entry fields on the right. The numbers entered into the fields represent ink density. The 0% field represents highlights (the lightest portions of the image) and the 100% field represents shadows (the darkest portions of the image). The 50% field represents the midtones. Thus, if you enter 80 in the 100% box, it means an 80% dot of the specified ink will be used to print darkest shadow areas.

2. Click in the middle of the diagonal line and drag downward. When you click, a small dot (control point) is added to the curve, and a value is entered into the 50% field. (If you didn't click exactly in the middle of curve, Photoshop enters a value in the field corresponding to the point were you clicked.) The value entered is the percentage of ink density for midtone areas.

3. Try making some adjustments in the curve by clicking and dragging and by typing percentages into the fields. When you drag the curve upward, you add more of the ink to the image; drag the curve downward, and you use less ink. If you type a percentage into the field, a corresponding control point appears on the curve.

4. When you're finished experimenting with adjustments to the curve, click OK to return to the Duotone Options dialog box. Click OK again to see the adjusted curve's effects on your image.

Viewing the Duotone's Readouts in the Info Palette

Once you've examined your duotone image on screen, you may decide to make adjustments to the curve or change the color of the inks. Before you do, it's often a good idea to analyze the true colors in your image by viewing the Eyedropper's readouts in the Info palette. Viewing these readouts of the ink percentages ensures that you don't rely totally on how the image looks on your monitor.

If the Info palette is not open, select Show Info from the Window menu. If the Info palette readout does not display yoSur two inks, click on the Info palette's Options menu arrow. In the Info Options dialog box, select Show First Color Readout, and then choose Actual Color from the corresponding Mode pop-up menu. Do the same thing for the Second Color Readout. Click OK to confirm the settings. The image's actual color values in percentages for both inks will appear in the Info palette.

 IP: *For a shortcut to changing the First and/or Second Color Readout settings in the Info Options dialog box, click on the first and/or second Eyedropper in the Info palette.*

Now move the mouse pointer over different areas of your image. Notice that the Info palette displays the percentage of each individual duotone ink. This can help you judge the degree of change if you edit the curve in the Duotone Curve dialog box, as well as give you a sense of how the image will print, regardless of the brightness settings on your monitor.

Saving and Loading Duotone Settings

Use the Save and Load buttons in the Duotone Options dialog box to save duotone curves, ink settings, ink colors, and overprint colors (colors printed on top of each other). To save your settings, reopen the Duotone Options dialog box (select Duotone in the Mode menu), then click on the Save button. In the dialog box, name the file and click Save (PC users: OK). Once you have saved a setting, it can be loaded and applied to other grayscale images that you wish to convert to duotones.

***n*OTE:** *Clicking the Overprint Colors button allows you to adjust screen display so you can see how colors will look when ink combinations are output. When adjusting the overprint colors, it's best to use a printed sample of the overprint colors as a guide.*

Photoshop's Preset Duotone Curves

If you're hesitant about picking your own colors for creating duotones, you can use Photoshop's preset inks and curves for duotones, tritones, and quadtones. These ink and curve samples are loaded on your hard disk during the Photoshop installation. You can find them in the Duotone Curves (PC users: duotones) folder.

To access the sample set, click the Load button in the Duotone Options dialog box. In the Open dialog box, use the mouse to move to the Duotone Curves (PC users: duotones) folder and open it. Inside it you will see three folders: Duotones, Quadtones, and Tritones (PC users: duotone, quadtone, and tritone). Inside each of these folders are other folders for Gray, PMS (Spot Color), and Process (CMYK Color) files. Select and open a Gray, PMS, or Process file from within its folder. After you have opened a file, you will be returned to the Duotone Options dialog box. Click OK to apply the settings to your image.

Creating a Sepia

In the Process (PC users: process) folder, accessed by opening the Tritones (PC users: tritone) folder found in the Duotone Curves (PC users: duotones) folder, Photoshop has included four different sepia settings for you to use. A *sepia* is a light reddish-brown tone applied to a photograph to give it an aged effect. Try creating a sepia, using the same file you used in the previous section.

1. Open the Duotone Options dialog box by choosing Duotone from the Mode menu.

2. To load one of Photoshop's Sepia settings, click on the Load button in the Duotone Options dialog box. Then open the Duotone Curves (PC users: duotones) folder (found in the Adobe Photoshop folder), and from there select the Tritones (PC users: tritone) folder.

3. From within the Tritones folder, open the Process Tritones (PC users: process) folder.

4. In the list of files, notice BMY Sepia 1, BMY Sepia 2, BMY Sepia 3, and BMY Sepia 4 (PC users: mysepia1.ado, mysepia2.ado, mysepia3.ado, mysepia4.ado). Select and open any one of these Sepia files. Instantly, the settings appear in the Duotone Options dialog box.

5. To preview the changes to your image, click OK in the Duotones Options dialog box.

After you've previewed the settings, you may want to try another sepia setting. Just repeat the above steps to do so.

n **OTE:** *This book's color insert shows an example of a sepia (image 4). Also, in the Photoshop "Users Guide" there are printed samples of several of Photoshop's duotone, tritone, and quadtone curves, including Process Tritone BMY Sepia 1.*

After you've created a sepia image, you may wish to add other objects or images to your document that contain more colors than the ones in your tritone file. In order to do this, you must convert the tritone file to Indexed Color, RGB Color, Lab Color, or CMYK Color.

Viewing Duotone Colors in Multichannel Mode

Although duotones are one-channel images, Photoshop will let you view the duotone as if you were viewing the two printing plates involved in the printing process. It will also allow you to view tritones and quadtones as if you were viewing three or four printing plates.

In order to view the printing plates, you convert the duotone image to a multichannel image (from the Mode menu, choose Multichannel) for viewing purposes only. You'll then be able to view each duotone ink used in a separate channel in the Channels palette. Once you've examined the channels, choose Undo from the Edit menu to reconvert the image back to Duotone mode.

Printing a Duotone

Before you print your duotone (or tritone or quadtone) image, you need to specify settings for halftone screen angles, printing resolution, and screen frequency. For more information about these printing options, see Chapter 14.

To print the file, choose Print from the File menu. If you wish to print a composite image, click OK; otherwise, select the Print Separations option and then click OK.

To print a duotone from QuarkXPress or Adobe Illustrator, save the Photoshop file in EPS format, as explained in Appendix A. If you are using PANTONE colors in your image, you will need to have the same PANTONE names in QuarkXPress and Adobe Illustrator as you do in Photoshop. Since QuarkXPress and Illustrator use "short PANTONE names," the Short PANTONE Names option must be selected in Photoshop's General Preferences dialog box. (Select Preferences from the File menu and then choose General.) If the Short PANTONE Names option wasn't activated when you chose your PANTONE colors, you must return to the Duotone Options dialog box and choose them again.

If you will not be outputting your duotone (or tritone or quadtone) files yourself, consult with your prepress house or print shop to ensure that the images will be output properly.

CONVERTING FROM GRAYSCALE TO BITMAP

In order to convert an image to black and white, the image must be converted to Bitmap. In Bitmap mode, many of Photoshop's editing options are not available; thus it is often preferable to edit in Grayscale mode and then convert to Bitmap. In this section, you'll learn the different options available when you convert to Bitmap, as well as how to create a mezzotint.

Only grayscale and multichannel images can be converted to Bitmap mode. When you convert from Grayscale mode to Bitmap mode, a dialog box will appear, where you set the Output Resolution of the file and the conversion method. After you make your choices, click OK to apply them to your image. Following are descriptions of the five conversion methods.

```
┌─────────────────────────── Bitmap ───────────────────────────┐
│  ┌─ Resolution ──────────────────────┐    ┌─────────┐        │
│  │   Input: 72 pixels/inch           │    │   OK    │        │
│  │                                   │    └─────────┘        │
│  │   Output: [72    ] [pixels/inch ▼]│    ┌─────────┐        │
│  │                                   │    │ Cancel  │        │
│  └───────────────────────────────────┘    └─────────┘        │
│  ┌─ Method ──────────────────────────┐                       │
│  │   ○ 50% Threshold                 │                       │
│  │   ○ Pattern Dither                │                       │
│  │   ◉ Diffusion Dither              │                       │
│  │   ○ Halftone Screen...            │                       │
│  │   ○ Custom Pattern                │                       │
│  └───────────────────────────────────┘                       │
└──────────────────────────────────────────────────────────────┘
```

50% THRESHOLD This conversion creates high-contrast black-and-white images. When the conversion is executed, Photoshop sets the threshold level at 128 pixels. All pixel values in the grayscale image below 128 are converted to black; all pixel values of 128 and greater are converted to white.

PATTERN DITHER In this conversion, the gray levels are changed into geometric patterns composed of black and white dots.

DIFFUSION DITHER This conversion uses a diffusion process to change a pixel to black and white. This diffuses the error between the original grayscale pixels and the black-and-white pixels. The result is a grainy effect.

HALFTONE SCREEN This conversion makes the image appear as if it is a grayscale image printed using a halftone screen. Halftone Screen is typically used to print images on non-PostScript printers.

9

In the Halftone Screen dialog box, you choose a Frequency, Angle, and Shape for the halftone pattern.

Acceptable values for the screen frequency (often called "line screen") are from 1.000 to 999.999 for lines per inch, .400 to 400 lines per centimeter. Decimal values are acceptable. Newspapers often use a screen frequency of 85; magazines, 150. If you do not know the correct screen frequency, check with your print shop.

Screen angles from -180 to 180 may be entered.

Shape choices are Round, Diamond, Ellipse, Line, Square, and Cross.

Halftone Screen settings may be saved and loaded using the Save and Load buttons in the dialog box.

CUSTOM PATTERN   This conversion method allows you to apply a custom pattern to a bitmap image. This option will be dimmed unless a custom pattern is defined.

Creating a Mezzotint

A mezzotint is a black-and-white image that appears to consist of randomly shaped dots. Mezzotints are used to create special effects from black-and-white images. Traditionally, mezzotints were created with halftone screens designed to produce random or unusual dot effects. In Photoshop, composing a mezzotint is fairly easy and can be accomplished in just a few steps.

Before you can create a mezzotint, you must first define a pattern. After you convert from Grayscale mode to Bitmap mode, you apply the pattern to the bitmap image to create the mezzotint. For this exercise, load a pattern from the PostScript

Patterns folder (PC users: patterns) in the Brushes & Patterns folder (PC users: brushes).

1. Select File/Open. Mac users: Open the PostScript Patterns folder located in the Brushes & Patterns folder, and open the Mezzotint-dot file. PC users: Open the patterns folder, and load the mezzodot.ai file.

2. After you have opened the mezzotint pattern file, the EPS Rasterizer dialog box appears, containing settings for the Width, Height, Resolution, and Mode of the pattern. Click OK to accept the default settings, and the pattern will appear.

3. Choose Select/All to select the entire pattern. Then choose Define Pattern from the Edit menu and close the file.

IP: *Before defining the pattern, you might wish to use the Blur or Blur More command from the Filter/Blur submenu to blur the pattern you will be using in the conversion process, so that the edges of the pattern blend together.*

4. Load the file to which you want to apply the mezzotint. (If the file isn't a grayscale image, you'll need to convert it by choosing Grayscale from the Mode menu. If you wish, you can use the Hands (PC users: hands.jpg) file in the Tutorial folder.

5. Convert the grayscale image to bitmap by choosing Bitmap from the Mode menu.

IP: *Before you convert your grayscale image to a bitmap image, there are a few steps you can take to enhance or alter the effect of the mezzotint. Use the Brightness/Contrast command in the Image/Adjust submenu so that the converted bitmap image will display more contrast. This will produce fewer dots and more solid blacks and whites.*

6. When the Bitmap dialog box appears, select the Custom Pattern option. (It will no longer be dimmed because you defined a pattern in steps 2 and 3.) Enter an Output Resolution (the higher the Output Resolution, the better the image pattern quality). The Input Resolution is the resolution of the original file. Click OK.

You should now have a mezzotint on screen. Figure 9-2 shows an image before a mezzotint was applied (Figure 9-3).

After you've created a mezzotint, you may wish to add color to enhance the image, or create some special effects. To add color to a bitmap image, you must first convert to Grayscale and then to a color mode.

CONVERTING FROM BITMAP TO GRAYSCALE

When you convert from Bitmap mode to Grayscale mode, the Grayscale dialog box appears, allowing you to enter a Size Ratio from 1 to 16. The Size Ratio is the

multiple by which you wish to decrease an image's size. For instance, if you enter 2, the final image will be one-half its original size. Enter 3, and the image will decrease to one-third its original size.

Before creating a mezzotint (photograph by Bob Barber, courtesy of ColorBytes Inc.)

FIGURE 9-2

USING SEVERAL MODES TO CREATE A COLORED MEZZOTINT EFFECT

Here's a design tip utilizing a combination of mode changes to create a colored mezzotint effect. To produce the effect, start with a color file, then select your entire image and choose Copy from the Edit menu. Next, create a mezzotint by first defining a pattern, then converting the color image to Grayscale mode, and then from Grayscale to Bitmap mode using the Custom Pattern method. After the mezzotint is created, convert from Bitmap to Grayscale and then to a color mode.

After you've converted from Bitmap to a color mode, make sure a selection tool is activated, then paste the copied colored image. While the pasted image is still floating, use the Lighten mode in the Brushes palette to blend the black-and-white mezzotint image with the colored image.

When you paste an image with a selection tool activated and the Lighten mode selected in the Brushes palette, only darker pixels in the underlying image are pasted over with corresponding light pixels from the floating image.

Bitmap
mezzotint
effect
applied to
photograph
shown in
Figure 9-2

FIGURE 9-3

9

USING THE LAB COLOR MODE

As has been mentioned earlier in this book, Lab Color is the internal format Photoshop uses while making mode conversions. For instance, when Photoshop converts from RGB Color to CMYK Color, it first converts the RGB colors to Lab Color and then converts from Lab Color to CMYK Color.

Lab mode images have three channels: a Lightness (or luminance) channel, and two color channels designated as channel a (green to magenta) and channel b (blue to yellow). Use Lab Color mode if you wish to edit an image's lightness independent of its color values. To do this, click to activate the Lightness channel in the Channels palette. In the Lightness channel, you can edit the Lightness values of an image or even select the entire image and paste it into a new file. The copied image in the new file will be a gray version of your original because you copied and pasted only the Lightness component of the image.

As discussed in Chapter 4, Lab is a device-independent color model used to help provide consistent color on various output devices. Thus, Lab Color is also the model used for transferring files between different color systems. For instance, Kodak's Photo CD uses YCC for its images. YCC is Kodak's own version of the Lab Color model; Y is the lightness, or luminance, value, and the two C channels are similar to Photoshop's channels a and b. Thus, when you load a Photo CD image into Photoshop, there should be little or no loss of color data. Since PostScript Level 2 takes advantage of Lab's device-independent color model, Lab is the recommended mode for printing to PostScript Level 2 printers.

As you've read in this chapter, the color modes in Photoshop are vital to producing CMYK separations, duotones, and mezzotints. In upcoming chapters, you'll add alpha channels to an image in order to create masks and special effects. You'll also learn how various dialog boxes allow you to adjust colors in individual channels.

Photoshop in Action

Design Director: Michael Grossman   Art Director: Mark Michaelson

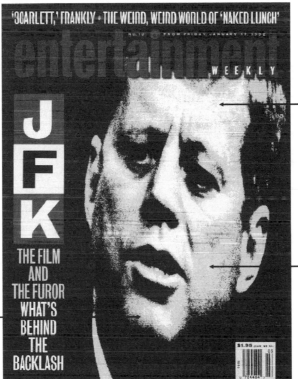

Before converting to Bitmap mode, the Brightness/Contrast command in the Image/Effects submenu was used to increase contrast in the image.

When converting to Bitmap mode, the Diffusion Dither option was chosen to create the black-and-white dot patterns.

After the image was converted from Bitmap mode to CMYK Color, it was filled with color (yellow) using the Paint Bucket tool.

Production: Carlos Lema   Client: Entertainment Weekly

9

When *Entertainment Weekly* decided to publish an article on the movie "JFK," design director Michael Grossman and art director Mark Michaelson decided to include an image of John F. Kennedy on the magazine's cover. Michael and Carlos Lema worked with a grayscale photo of JFK. To make the grayscale image more interesting, they slightly distorted it using the Skew command in the Image/Effects submenu. Carlos then converted the image to black and white by choosing Bitmap in the Mode menu. From Bitmap mode, the image was converted back to Grayscale and then to CMYK Color, so color could be added and separations created from the image.

Toto je môj dedko
a jej babička

Na strane je môj tato.

10

CREATING PATHS
WITH THE PEN TOOL

When you create objects with Photoshop's Pen tool, it's almost like being in two programs at once: a painting program and a drawing program. Unlike Photoshop's painting tools, which paint directly onto the electronic canvas, the Pen tool creates wire-frame shapes that exist *above underlying pixels.* This allows the Pen tool in Photoshop to create Bézier curves and intricate objects in much the same way as pen tools in programs such as Adobe Illustrator and Aldus Freehand. As in Illustrator and Freehand, objects created by the Pen tool are called *paths.*

ABOUT PATHS

A path can be a point, a line, or a curve, but usually it's a series of line segments or curve segments, connected by their endpoints. Because they don't lock down onto the background pixels on screen, paths can easily be reshaped, reselected, and moved. They can also be saved and exported to other programs. Thus, paths are unlike any object created with Photoshop's painting tools and unlike any selection created by Photoshop selection tools. Undoubtedly, this is one reason that the Pen tool is not included in the Toolbox and can only be accessed by opening the Paths palette.

Once you open the Paths palette, you'll see that it is not like Photoshop's other palettes. Not only does it function as a miniature toolbox just for the Pen tool, it also provides access to a set of commands that only work with paths. These commands allow paths to be filled, stroked, and turned into selections. Without these commands, the intricate and precise shapes you create with the Pen tool would be useless because most of Photoshop's menu commands and tools have no effect on paths.

Before you can begin to turn paths into artwork and into Photoshop selections, you need to learn some fundamentals. Since most paths created with the Pen tool consist of lines and/or curves, this chapter begins with an explanation of how to create straight and curved path segments, and how to join them together. You'll learn how to change a smooth corner into an angled corner, and how to change a path into a selection (and vice versa).

Then you'll be introduced to the Fill, Stroke, Make Selection, and Save Path commands in the Paths palette. Once you learn how to save paths, you'll be able to reload them when you reload your saved images. If need be, you can convert the paths to selections so that the selections can be used like *masks.* A mask allows you to protect an area on screen so that you can work within it—without affecting surrounding portions of the image.

At the end of the chapter, you'll learn how to create another type of mask, called a *clipping path.* Clipping paths are typically used to silhouette an area and mask out the background image areas, so that only the area within the clipping path will appear when the file is placed into other programs, such as Illustrator, PageMaker, and QuarkXPress.

PEN TOOL FUNDAMENTALS

In order to use the Pen tool, you must first open the Paths palette by choosing Show Paths from the Window menu.

At first glance, you may find the Paths palette a little confusing because it contains three Pen tools, not one. The first Pen tool—the one with the pen-point icon alone—creates straight or curved paths. The Pen with the plus sign is used to add points to a path, and the Pen with the minus sign is used for subtracting points from a path. The Corner tool lets you turn a smooth corner of a path into a sharp corner, and vice versa. You use the Selection pointer to select and deselect paths and points on paths.

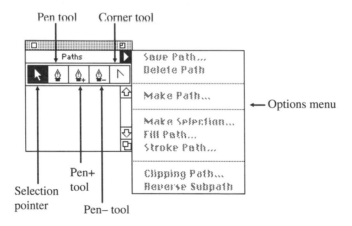

Like all other palettes, the Paths palette also includes an Options menu (PC users: Control menu). Take a moment to click on the Options menu arrow (or Control menu button) now, and examine the choices it offers. Notice the commands Fill Path and Stroke Path. When you wish to fill or stroke a path, you must access these commands from the Paths palette, *not* from the Edit menu.

Another important point to remember is that Photoshop's tools and many of its menu commands will not affect a path you create, unless you convert a path to a selection first.

Before you begin to use the Pen tool, take a look at the Pen Tool Options dialog box. Open it by double-clicking on the Pen tool (the first pen icon in the Paths palette).

The sole option in the dialog box is the Rubber Band check box.

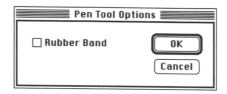

When this option is selected, a path segment trails the Pen tool after an anchor point is created. As you move the Pen tool on screen, the segment is displayed from your last mouse click to the current pen position, as if you were stretching a rubber band. If you don't turn the Rubber Band option on, each path segment appears only after you click the mouse to connect anchor points, rather than as you move the mouse.

Select the Rubber Band option now to turn it on; then click OK to close the dialog box. In the next sections, you'll see how the Rubber Band previews path segments as you create them.

Drawing Straight Paths

When you use the Pen tool to create a straight path, you first click to establish a starting point, then move the mouse to another position and click again to establish the endpoint. Each time you click the mouse to establish a starting or ending point, you create an anchor point.

In this section, you will learn how to create straight paths by connecting anchor points. To begin, create a new file, 5 inches by 5 inches. To make it easier to execute the following steps, select Show Rulers from the Window menu.

1. If the Pen tool isn't activated, click on it and move it into your document about 2 inches from the top and 1 inch from the left, then click. A small black square appears; this is the first anchor point.

OTE: *If CAPS LOCK is on, the pen pointer will turn into a crosshair. The effects of using the Pen tool are the same whether you work with the pen pointer or the crosshair.*

2. Move the Pen tool to the right, about 1.5 inches away from the first anchor point, and click. This creates a second anchor point, connected to the first anchor point with a straight path segment. Notice that the second anchor point is black and the first one is now hollow. The black anchor point is the one that is currently selected; the hollow anchor point is no longer selected.

AUTION: *When drawing straight paths, don't click and drag the mouse when you click to create an anchor point or you will create a curve rather than a line.*

3. Press and hold SHIFT while you create a third anchor point.

OTE: *If you press and hold SHIFT, this will constrain the Pen tool so that the path segments are drawn to the nearest 45-degree angle.*

The path you have just created is called an *open path*. An open path has two endpoints, a beginning and an end. As long as you have an open path and the Pen tool is activated, the Rubber Band will keep stretching from your last anchor point to the Pen tool's current position. Thus every time you click the mouse, you will be extending the open path. One way to stop Photoshop from extending an open path every time the Pen tool is clicked is to save a path or close a path. Once a path is saved or closed, you can create another path. You'll learn how to save and close paths later in this chapter.

If you make a mistake while creating your first path, press DELETE (PC users: BACKSPACE) once to erase the last anchor point. Be careful not to press DELETE (PC users: BACKSPACE) twice; if you do, you will erase the entire path. If you press DELETE (PC users: BACKSPACE) three times, all paths on the screen will be erased.

If you wish to continue experimenting with the Pen tool, move on to the next section, where you will learn how to deactivate the Pen tool in order to move a segment of a path or the entire path.

Selecting, Manipulating, Joining, and Deselecting Paths

After you have created a path, you might want to adjust it by moving an anchor point or the entire path. Or you may need to duplicate the path so you can use it elsewhere in the document.

To complete the following exercise, you will need to have a path created on screen. Either use the path from the previous exercise or create a new path. After you have a path on screen, you'll select an anchor point by first deactivating the Pen tool and then activating the Selection pointer in the Paths palette.

1. In the Paths palette, click on the Selection pointer to activate it so you can select an anchor point.

2. Position the Selection pointer over the anchor point you wish to adjust, and click to select it. The selected anchor point turns black.

IP: *If you don't see anchor points on your path, click anywhere on the path to display the anchor points.*

3. Drag the selected anchor point to a new location. When you click and drag, the path's angle and size are adjusted according to the angle at which you drag the anchor point and how far you move it. Notice that the path moves as if it were floating on another layer above the background pixels.

4. Anchor points can also be moved using the directional arrow keys on your keyboard. Try this: Press the UP, DOWN, LEFT, and RIGHT ARROW keys a few times. The selected anchor point moves in the direction of the keys you press in 1-pixel increments.

   To move the entire path as a single entity, every anchor point in the path must be selected. One technique for selecting additional anchor points is to SHIFT-click on each unselected anchor point. If the path you need to select is large, press OPTION (PC users: ALT) and click on any segment to select the entire path. You can also select an entire path by clicking and dragging over the entire path with the Selection pointer.

5. Select the entire path on your screen by pressing OPTION (PC users: ALT) and clicking on any segment of the path. All the anchor points turn black when the path is selected. Then click on any segment of the path and drag the path to a new location.

   Once a path is selected, you can duplicate it.

6. To duplicate the path, press and hold OPTION (PC users: ALT) while you click and drag the path with the Selection pointer to a new location. A duplicate of the path will appear. After the duplicate appears, release OPTION (PC users: ALT) and the mouse button.

7. Now try joining the two paths on screen. First reactivate the Pen tool. Click on the endpoint of one path, and then click on the endpoint of the second path. The two paths become one.

8. To deselect the path, activate the Selection pointer and then click away from the path. All of the anchor points will disappear. Note that the anchor points will reappear when the path is reselected.

Now that you understand the basics of drawing and adjusting straight paths, you are ready to learn about working with smooth curves, one of the features for which the Pen tool is best known. Before continuing, delete the path currently on your screen by pressing DELETE (PC users: BACKSPACE) twice.

Drawing and Adjusting Curves

The Pen tool's ability to draw smooth curves with precision makes it an invaluable aid when you need to create any curved shape or selection. Drawing a curve with the Pen tool does, however, take some getting used to. You can't just draw a curve on screen as you would with the Lasso tool or one of the painting tools. As you'll see in the next exercise, drawing curves, which slope in different directions, with the Pen tool requires a moving, "seesaw" motion with the mouse.

If you do not have a document open, create a new one now; make it a 72-ppi file, 5 inches by 5 inches. If the rulers and Info palette are not already displayed, select Show Rulers and Show Info from the Window menu to turn these features on.

1. With the Pen tool selected, move the Pen's tip about 1 inch from the left side of your screen and about 2 inches down from the top. Click (an anchor point will be created) and drag down about 1.5 inches to begin the process of creating a curve that faces down. As you drag, the Pen pointer

changes to an arrowhead, indicating that you are specifying a direction for the curve.

As you drag, a *direction line* extends in opposite directions from the anchor point, as shown in Figure 10-1. Later, you'll see that the size and angle of the direction line determine the length and slope of the curve. The two endpoints of the direction lines are called *direction points*. By clicking and dragging on either of the direction line's direction points, you can move the direction line, and thus change the shape of a curve. Once the curve is created and deselected, the direction lines and points will disappear.

2. Now create the second anchor point for the curve. Move the Pen tool horizontally to the right about 1 inch from the first anchor point. To create a curve, click and drag straight up, as shown in Figure 10-2. Notice that the curve ends at the new anchor point. As you drag, the curve takes shape and a new direction line appears. Release the mouse after dragging up about 1.5 inches.

Don't worry if you are feeling a little overwhelmed by the all of the lines, points, and other items on your screen. At this stage, the most important concept to remember is that *the curve slopes in the direction in which you drag the mouse.* The first part of the curve you drew slopes

Clicking and dragging downward starts the process of creating the lower part of the curve

FIGURE 10-1

Clicking
and
dragging
upward
creates the
upper part
of the curve

FIGURE 10-2

downward (the direction in which you originally dragged the mouse). The second part of the curve slopes upward, the direction in which you dragged in step 2.

***n*OTE:** *The curve you see on the screen is called a Bézier curve, named after the French mathematician Pierre Bézier, who defined the shape of a curve in mathematical terms with four direction points. By adjusting the direction points, you have complete control of the size and shape of the curve.*

3. To adjust the curve, you need to switch from the Pen tool to the Selection pointer. In the Paths palette, click on the Selection pointer. Then click on the bottom-left direction point of the curve and drag to the right. Now click on the bottom-right direction point of the curve and drag to the left. Notice that the curve gets more pointed. If you wish to flatten the curve, drag both bottom direction points in opposite directions.

Another way to adjust the shape of a curve is to click on the curve segment itself with the Selection pointer, and then click and drag. When you do this, both direction lines will adjust themselves according to how you move the curve. You can also change the height and depth of the curve by clicking and dragging on the direction points to make the direction line larger or smaller. Try these techniques now, in the next step.

4. Click and drag on the bottom left, then bottom right direction points to make both direction lines smaller and thus reduce the size of the curve. After you have experimented with changing the direction lines, click and drag on the direction points to return the direction lines to their original length of about 1.5 inches from the anchor point.

5. Select the Pen tool again so that you can create another curve segment.

6. To begin creating the next curve, move the Pen tool 1 inch directly to the right of the last anchor point you created. Then click and drag straight down approximately 1.5 inches, as shown in Figure 10-3.

Notice the smooth transition between the two continuous curves that you have created. The point between the two curves is called a *smooth point*. When the direction line that intersects a smooth anchor point is adjusted, the curves on either side of the smooth point change.

Besides changing the slope of a curve, you can also change its width by moving either one of its anchor points. Try this next.

Creating a
continuous
curved path
with the
Pen tool

FIGURE 10-3

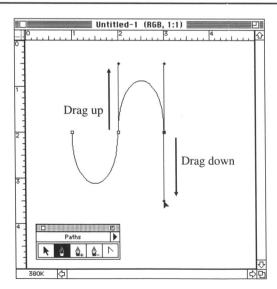

7. Before changing the width of a curve, you must activate the Selection pointer. Here's a shortcut: With the Pen tool selected, press and hold COMMAND (PC users: CTRL) to change the pen pointer (or crosshair) to the Selection pointer.

 OTE: *When the Pen tool is activated, you can temporarily activate the Selection pointer by pressing and holding COMMAND (PC users: CTRL).*

8. Change the width of the curve you just drew by clicking on the last anchor point with the Selection pointer and then dragging to the left about .5 inch. Release the mouse to return to the Pen tool.

9. Continue creating curves, alternating between clicking and dragging up, then down. To practice some more, you may want to first press DELETE twice (PC users: BACKSPACE) and delete the path currently on screen; then you can start all over again. If you create your first anchor point by dragging up, the first curve will slope upward.

 OTE: *To make the direction lines of a curve segment reappear after a path is deselected, click on that curve segment.*

10. When you are done practicing, clear the screen by pressing DELETE (PC users: BACKSPACE) twice. If you have more than one path on screen, press three times.

Drawing Scalloped Curves

You can also draw curves so that they all point in the same direction. These *scalloped curves* can be used to create curved border effects around images. Scalloped curves cannot be drawn like the continuous curves you just created. When you create scalloped curves, you create a *corner point* in order to change the direction in which the curve is drawn. As you'll see in the following exercise, the direction lines that stem from corner points do not work the same as direction lines that bisect smooth points: A corner point's direction line controls only one side of one curve.

1. To create the first curve, begin by positioning the Pen tool about .5 inches from the right side of your document window and about 2 inches from the top. The first curve you create will point upward, so start by clicking and dragging straight up about 1 inch.

10

2. Move the mouse horizontally to the right about 1.5 inches from the last anchor point. Click and drag straight down about 1 inch.

The next curve you create will point in the same direction as the first curve. To accomplish this, you need to create a corner point between the curves.

3. To create a corner point, press and hold OPTION (PC users: ALT) while you click on the anchor point that you created in step 2. Notice that one of the direction lines disappears. Continue to keep OPTION (PC users: ALT) pressed while you drag diagonally up to the right about 1 inch from the anchor point, to create a new direction line. Release OPTION (PC users: ALT). This direction line will allow you to draw the next curve in the same direction as the line you just created.

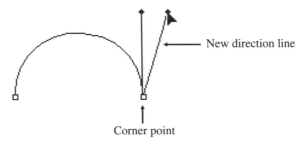

Corner point

4. To create the second curve, move the Pen tool directly to the right about 1.5 inches away from the last anchor point. This will be the endpoint of the curve that you are about to create. Click and drag straight down about 1 inch, and a curve will appear.

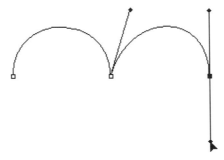

5. To create the third scalloped curve, repeat the technique in steps 3 and 4. Position the mouse over the last anchor point you created, press OPTION (PC users: ALT), and click and drag diagonally up to create a new direction line. Move the mouse about 1.5 inches to the right of the anchor point, and then click and drag down about 1 inch to create the curve.

6. When you are ready, delete the path currently on screen by pressing DELETE (PC users: BACKSPACE) twice.

Creating a corner point to control the direction of a curve also enables you to create paths in which straight segments are joined to curves, as explained next.

Connecting Curves and Straight Paths

When you are using the Pen tool and working with paths, you'll often need to connect a line to a curve or a curve to a line. Shapes made of both curves and lines are all around you: vases, bottles, paddles, and so on. When you want to trace any of these shapes with the Pen tool or create them from scratch, you'll need to master the Pen tool techniques described in the following exercise.

Start by creating a curve and connecting a line segment to it.

1. If the Pen tool is not activated, select it in the Paths palette. Position the Pen tool about 1 inch from the left side of the screen and about 2 inches from the top. To begin, click and drag straight up about 1 inch.

2. To create the curve, move the mouse 1 inch to the right from the first anchor point; then click and drag downward about 1 inch.

3. Next, create the corner point that will allow you to connect this curve to a line. Press OPTION (PC users: ALT) and click once on the last anchor point you created. Notice that the bottom direction line disappears.

4. To create a line that connects to the curve, move the Pen tool to the right horizontally about 1 inch from the curve's second anchor point, and click. Remember, if you want to create a line at an angle of 45 degrees (or increments thereof), you can press and hold SHIFT while you click. The curve is now connected to a line.

5. Now clear your screen by pressing DELETE (PC users: BACKSPACE) twice, and try creating a line and connecting it to a curve.

6. Create a line segment about 1 inch long by connecting two anchor points. If you need to review the steps to create line segments, refer to the earlier section "Drawing Straight Paths."

7. Use the OPTION (PC users: ALT) key to create a corner point so the line can be connected to a curve. Press and hold OPTION (PC users: ALT) while you click on the last anchor point you created and then drag diagonally upward to the right about 1 inch. When the direction line is created, release the OPTION (PC users: ALT) key and the mouse button.

8. Now, to create a curve that connects to the line, move the Pen tool horizontally about 1 inch to the right of the corner point. Then click and drag straight down about 1 inch. If you need to adjust the curve, use the Selection pointer.

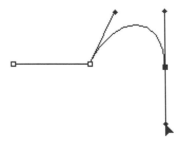

9. When you are finished practicing, clear the screen by pressing DELETE (PC users: BACKSPACE) twice. If you have more than one path on screen, press three times.

Creating a Closed Path

The next technique you will learn is how to close a path. A *closed path* is a path that ends at its starting point. Once a path is closed, you can move the pen pointer away from it and create other paths. In this next exercise, you will create a closed path in the shape of a triangle by connecting three anchor points.

If you don't have a document open on screen, create a new one, 5 inches by 5 inches. Make sure that the rulers and Info palette are displayed.

1. Activate the Pen tool in the Paths palette, and move the Pen tool up toward the top-middle part of the document. Using the ruler and Info palette as guides, position the Pen tool about 2.5 inches from the left side of the document window and about .5 inch down from the top. Click the mouse to create the first anchor point of the triangle.

2. To create a second anchor point, move the Pen tool diagonally down and left about 2 inches (in the Info palette, the x-axis is approximately 1.00 and the y-axis is approximately 2.5) and then click. This creates a line segment from the first anchor point to the second anchor point.

3. To create a third anchor point, move the Pen tool horizontally to the right of the second anchor point about 3 inches, and click. This creates a line segment from the second anchor point to the third anchor point.

4. To close the path, you must return to the starting point of the triangle. Move the Pen tool to the first anchor point. You will see a small loop at the bottom-right side of the Pen tool; this indicates that you have returned to your starting point. Click the mouse and the path will be closed.

10

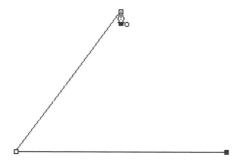

Leave the triangle displayed on your screen and proceed to the next section, which explains how adding, subtracting, and editing points on a path can change its shape.

Adding/Subtracting Points, and Switching Between a Smooth Point and a Corner Point

You've learned how to adjust a path by moving anchor and direction points. Paths can also be reshaped by adding or subtracting anchor points, and by converting smooth points to corner points, and vice versa. By combining these techniques with your Pen-drawing skills, you will be able to edit the shape of most any path.

In this next exercise, you will transform the triangular path you created in the previous section into a diamond shape, and then back to a triangle. If you do not have the triangle from the previous section on screen, create one in the middle of your document window now. You'll start by activating the Pen+ tool, which adds anchor points.

1. With the triangular path displayed, activate the Pen+ tool in the Paths palette.

2. To transform the triangle into a diamond, you need to add an anchor point to the base of the triangle. Position the Pen+ tool in the middle of the base of the triangle. Click the mouse, and a new anchor point is added to the path at the point where you clicked.

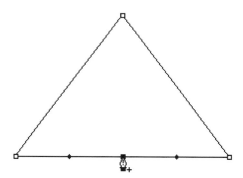

3. To move the new anchor point down to begin creating the diamond shape, you need switch from the Pen+ pointer to the Selection pointer. Rather than doing this by clicking in the Paths palette and switching tools, you can use the keyboard shortcut: Press and hold COMMAND (PC users: CTRL), and the Pen+ tool changes to the Selection pointer.

4. Once you've switched from the Pen+ pointer to the Selection pointer, click on the new anchor point you created in step 2 and drag it downward about 2 inches, so that the triangle begins to look like a diamond.

5. Notice that the new point is a smooth point. You can turn the round edge into a corner point by using the Corner tool in the Paths palette. Select the Corner tool, and then click on the smooth point, as shown in Figure 10-4a. The smooth corner point changes to a sharply angled corner point, as shown in Figure 10-4b.

OTE: *With any of the Pen tools activated, Mac users can press COMMAND-CONTROL and click to change a smooth point to a corner point, and vice versa. When the Selection pointer is activated (instead of a Pen tool), Mac users can press the CONTROL key and click to switch between smooth and corner points.*

Your diamond is now finished. Suppose, though, that you've changed your mind and want the diamond switched back into a triangle. To do this, you will need to subtract the last anchor point you created.

6. To delete the last anchor point you created, click on the Pen- tool. Then click on the anchor point you used to create the diamond. The corner point disappears, and the diamond shape immediately snaps back into a triangle.

(a) Use the Corner tool to convert a smooth point to a corner point; (b) The path after the smooth point is converted to a corner point

Corner tool ⎯⎯⎯

(a)

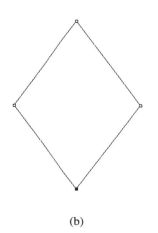

(b)

■ **FIGURE 10-4**

10

IP: *When the Selection pointer is activated, there is a keyboard shortcut for adding and deleting anchor points. To add an anchor point, press and hold COMMAND-OPTION (PC users: CTRL-ALT) while you click on a segment. To delete an anchor point, press and hold COMMAND-OPTION (PC users: CTRL-ALT) while you click on the anchor point you want to delete. Mac users: When the Pen tool is activated (not the Selection pointer!), you can also add or delete anchor points from a path by pressing CONTROL and clicking.*

The ability to convert from smooth points to corner points and corner points to smooth points allows you to quickly edit paths and change their shapes. For example, you can outline a curved object by first connecting straight segments, and then generate the necessary curves by changing corner points into smooth points.

The following exercise demonstrates how you can transform a sharply cornered wedge into a heart shape by changing corner points to smooth points. Before proceeding, delete the triangle you now have on screen, by pressing DELETE (PC users: BACKSPACE) twice.

1. Using the Pen tool, create and connect four anchor points to create a wedge shape. To make the wedge, start by creating an anchor point in the upper-left corner of your screen. Create the next anchor point at the bottom of your screen, then create another one in the upper-right corner. Continue creating the closed path so that it looks like this one:

2. Now transform the two top corner points of the wedge to smooth corner points. Start by activating the Corner tool in the Paths palette.

3. Position the Corner tool on the top-left corner point, and click and drag downward to the left until a curve is created. Notice that as you drag, the Corner tool changes to an arrowhead pointer because a direction line for the curve is being created.

4. To create a curve out of the top-right corner point, click and drag upward to the left on this corner point with the Corner tool. Stop when a curve is created.

10

5. If you wish to make adjustments to the curves of the heart, click and drag on the curves' direction points, using the Selection pointer.

6. At this point, you may wish to fill, stroke, or save the heart path that you just created. If so, turn to the section, "Filling and Stroking Paths and Subpaths" or to the section, "Saving, Loading, and Deleting Paths" later in this chapter. Otherwise, delete the heart path from the screen and proceed to the next section to learn how to convert a path into a selection.

Converting a Path into a Selection

As you work with paths, you'll often need to convert them to selections. Once a selection border is created from the path, you'll be able to use all of Photoshop's commands that affect selections.

In this exercise you'll learn how to a turn path into a selection and to merge both a path and a selection together into one selection. To start, if you don't have a blank document on screen, create a new file, 5 inches by 5 inches.

1. Start by using the Pen tool to create a rectangular *path*, approximately 2.5 inches by 2 inches.

2. Use the Elliptical Marquee tool to create a circular *selection* that overlaps the rectangular path.

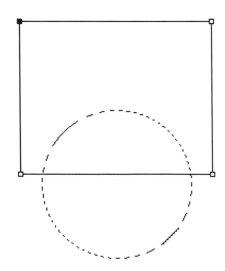

3. Open the Options (PC users: Control) menu in the Paths palette, and choose Make Selection. This opens the Make Selection dialog box, where you specify the type of selection you want to create from any paths or selections on screen.

```
══════════════ Make Selection ══════════════
┌─ Rendering ──────────────────┐   ┌─────────┐
│  Feather Radius: [0▪] pixels  │   │   OK    │
│                               │   └─────────┘
│  ☒ Anti-aliased               │   ┌─────────┐
│                               │   │ Cancel  │
└───────────────────────────────┘   └─────────┘
┌─ Operation ──────────────────┐
│  ⦿ New Selection              │
│  ○ Add to Selection           │
│  ○ Subtract from Selection    │
│  ○ Intersect with Selection   │
└───────────────────────────────┘
```

NOTE: *If a path is activated, or if you click on it before executing the Make Selection command, the path will remain on screen after Photoshop creates the selection; otherwise, the path will be deleted from the screen.*

In the Make Selection dialog box, the Feather Radius and Anti-aliased options function exactly as they do with Photoshop's selection tools. Use the Operation options to specify how you want the selection to be created. The Operations options are as follows:

New Selection Creates a selection from the path only. In the example here, only the rectangular path would be turned into a selection.

Add to Selection Adds the area specified by the path to the current selection on screen. In the example here, a selection would be created from both the rectangle and circle together.

Subtract from Selection Removes a path from a selection. In the example here, the rectangular area that overlaps the circle would be removed from the circular selection border.

Intersect with Selection Creates a selection from the area where the path and selection overlap. In the example here, the selection would be transformed into one selection, including only the overlapping areas of the rectangle and circle.

10

Try each of these options with the example on your screen. First select the New Selection radio button and then click OK. Photoshop creates a selection from the rectangle only. Choose Edit/Undo to remove the selection. Now return to the Make Selection dialog box to try out any of the other options.

 OTE: *Beginning with Photoshop 2.5.1, Mac users can convert all paths on screen into selections by pressing the ENTER key.*

Now that you've seen how Photoshop creates a selection out of a path, let's take a look at how to transform a selection into a path. Occasionally, it's easier to create a path from a selection, rather than constructing it from scratch with the Pen. For example, you might wish to create a path from an intricate Magic Wand selection that would take too much time to create using the Pen tool. To convert a selection into a path, you use the Make Path command in the Paths palette.

The following exercise demonstrates how Photoshop creates anchor points when converting a selection border into a path. You can change any selection into a path, but in this exercise you'll work with a figure eight because the path will require numerous anchor points. Begin by clearing the screen of all selections by choosing None from the Select menu. Then remove all paths by pressing DELETE (PC users: BACKSPACE) three times.

1. Activate the Lasso tool; then click and drag to create a figure eight.

2. To turn the figure-eight selection border into a path, select Make Path from the Options (PC users: Control) menu in the Paths palette.

The Make Path dialog box contains a field for setting the Tolerance value, which determines the number of anchor points the path will include. The default Tolerance value is 2 pixels; you can specify from .5 to 10 pixels. If you enter a high Tolerance value, fewer anchor points will be used and the resulting path will be smoother. Select a low Tolerance, and more anchor points will be used, resulting in a bumpier path.

```
╔════════════ Make Path ════════════╗
║                                    ║
║  Tolerance: [2.0]  pixels  ( OK )  ║
║                          (Cancel)  ║
║                                    ║
╚════════════════════════════════════╝
```

3. In the Make Path dialog box, type **1** in the Tolerance field and click OK. When the path appears, click on it with the Selection pointer (from the Paths palette) so you can examine the number of anchor points that were created. Count the number of anchor points.

4. Now try a higher Tolerance setting and observe the results. First, return to the selection on screen by selecting Undo from the Edit menu. Then reopen the Make Path dialog box. Enter **10** as the Tolerance setting and click OK. When the path appears, click on it with the Selection pointer and count the number of anchor points. Observe that the higher Tolerance value results in fewer anchor points.

CAUTION: *Converting selections to paths sometimes creates paths that are too complicated for printers to print. In this situation, your best bet is to delete some anchor points with the Pen- tool or re-create the path using a higher Tolerance setting.*

You've now learned the fundamental techniques you need to work with the Paths palette, the Pen tools, and the Selection pointer. In the next section, you'll learn how to fill or stroke a path with a color or pattern.

FILLING AND STROKING PATHS AND SUBPATHS

Photoshop allows you to fill a path with the foreground color or with a pattern, and from a Snapshot or the last saved version of the file. When you stroke a path, the stroke width is determined by the current brush size of the stroking tool.

To fill or stroke a path, use the Fill Path/Subpath or Stroke Path/Subpath command from the Paths palette's Options (PC users: Control) menu. Paths cannot be filled or stroked by Photoshop's Edit/Fill or Edit/Stroke commands.

When you fill or stroke a path, Photoshop fills or strokes underlying pixels *beneath* the path and leaves the path as a separate independent object. This means that you can move the path and execute Fill Path or Stroke Path again, or edit the path—without affecting the filled or stroked images on screen.

Filling and Stroking More than One Path at a Time

When you execute the Fill Path command from the Paths palette, every path on screen will be filled. If you select part of a path, or one path in a document that has several paths, the Fill Path menu command changes to Fill Subpath.

10

To see how Photoshop fills and strokes several paths at once, you must have several paths displayed. If you deleted the figure-eight path created in the previous exercise, create another closed path now, before beginning the next exercise.

1. Use the Pen tool to create a square path to the right of the figure eight (or any other path). To ensure that all paths will be filled, deselect any path that is currently activated or selected. To deselect a path, activate the Selection pointer in the Paths palette and click away from the path.

2. To fill all the paths on screen, open the Options (PC users: Control) menu and select Fill Path. The Fill Path dialog box will appear.

3. In the Fill Path dialog box:

   a. The Use pop-up menu should be set to Foreground Color. This pop-up menu also offers options for filling the path with a pattern, a snapshot version, or the last saved version of the image.

   b. As in the standard Fill dialog box, you can choose an Opacity setting and a painting Mode for blending. Type **50** in the Opacity field and make sure the Mode is set to Normal.

   c. As in the Lasso tool's dialog boxes, the Feather Radius and Anti-aliased options are used to soften edges. Feather Radius values can be from 0 to 250 pixels.

4. Click OK. Both the figure eight and the square path are filled according to your specifications.

Now try stroking the paths.

1. Change the foreground color to a color that will allow you to see the effects of the stroke. Make sure a selection tool is selected from the Toolbox; otherwise, the Stroke Path dialog box will not open.

2. To stroke a path, open the Options (PC users: Control) menu in the Paths palette, and select Stroke Path.

3. When the Stroke Path dialog box appears, open the Tool pop-up menu. You'll get a list of the painting and editing tools that use the Brushes palette.

4. Apply an Airbrush stroke to your path. Select Airbrush from the Tool pop-up menu in the Stroke Path dialog box and click OK.

The path is filled using the current brush size and opacity settings in the Brushes palette for the Airbrush tool. To better control how the stroke is applied to the path, you may wish to first select the tool with which you will stroke the path and choose the specific settings you want in the Brushes palette for that tool. Then choose Stroke Path from the Paths palette Options (PC users: Control) menu. Instead of opening the Stroke Path dialog box, Photoshop will automatically stroke with the activated tool in the Toolbox, using its Brushes palette settings.

Filling or Stroking a Subpath

As stated earlier, if you don't wish to fill or stroke every path on screen, Photoshop allows you to fill or stroke a *subpath.* When you click on a path, or SHIFT-click to activate more than one path, Photoshop considers the paths to be subpaths.

To see the effects of stroking a subpath, change the foreground color and make sure a selection tool in the Toolbox is selected. Then choose the subpath you wish to stroke by clicking on it with the Selection pointer. This activates the path. You do not need to select every anchor point in the path. Next, open the Options (PC users: Control) menu in the Paths palette. Notice that the Stroke Path command has changed to Stroke Subpath. In the Stroke Subpath dialog box, select a tool; then click OK. Only the path you clicked is stroked.

SAVING, LOADING, AND DELETING PATHS

After you create a path, you may wish to save it so it can be reloaded with your file, reactivated and turned into a selection, exported to Adobe Illustrator, or transformed into a clipping path.

AUTION: *Paths that have not been saved in the Paths palette are not saved with the file.*

When a path is saved, Photoshop saves all of the paths on screen, whether they are selected or not. If you edit any path after saving it, or if you add a path, the changes to the path will be saved automatically. After you save a path, you can hide it and create more paths. This ability to hide an object is somewhat similar to that of drawing programs that allow you to work in layers. But, unlike drawing programs, if you save multiple paths in Photoshop, you cannot view the multiple saved paths simultaneously.

OTE: *It's important to understand that a saved path does not receive an assigned disk filename. Rather, you provide a name for the path that will appear in a list in the Paths palette. The path names that appear in this list are only available in the document in which they were created and saved. If you wish to copy a path from one document into another document, you can use the Edit/Copy and Edit/Paste commands. The path name, as well as the path itself, will be available in the other document.*

Photoshop in Action

The background was created by scanning a rough-textured paper.

The mortarboard was created using the Pen tool.

The different pieces on the face were scanned in separately and then placed in the final image.

The diploma, hand, and jacket were created using the Pen tool.

Artist: Rico Lins   Art Director: Lucy Bartholomay   Client: The Boston Globe Magazine

Lucy had Rico create this humorous image for the cover of the *Boston Globe* magazine issue featuring an article on whether a college degree is worth the price.

Rico started the image by first scanning a rough-textured paper that was used as the background. He used the Pen tool to create the mortarboard, jacket, diploma, and hand. Once these shapes were created they were filled using the Fill Path command in the Paths palette.

All the pieces in the face were scanned in separately, selected, and then pasted into the final file.

10

In the next exercise, you'll learn how to save a path, hide a path, and then reload the path. Before you begin, make sure that you have one path displayed on screen.

1. To save the path, click on the Options (PC users: Control) menu in the Paths palette and select Save Path.

nOTE: *You don't have to select a path before you select the Save Path command. When you apply the command, all paths on screen are automatically saved.*

2. In the Save Path dialog box, you can name the path, if you wish, by typing the name in the Name field. Click OK. Notice that the name of the path now appears in the Paths palette, preceded by a check mark. If you don't see the path name, increase the size of the Paths palette.

nOTE: *Once you have saved an open path, you can create another open path in the same document.*

3. Now hide the path you just created, so that you can name and save another path. Click on the check mark to the left of Path 1 (or the name you assigned). The check mark and the path on the screen disappear, but the Path name remains.

4. Create another path.

5. Choose Save Path from the Options (PC users: Control) menu in the Paths palette. In the Save Path dialog box, Path 2 appears in the Name field; give the path another name if you wish, and click OK to save the path. The name of the path now appears in the Paths palette, with a check mark alongside.

6. With two paths now saved, you will be able to see how you can view them independently. To return to the first path, click beside the name of the path in the Paths palette. This path now appears on screen. To view the second path, click on the check mark next to the name of the path in the Paths palette.

Continue to experiment, and adjust your saved paths, if you wish. Remember, once a path is saved you can edit it without resaving because Photoshop automatically updates changes made to saved paths.

IP: *If you wish to quickly hide all paths on screen so you can create a new path, click directly below the last path name in the Paths palette.*

7. Before proceeding to the next section, delete the second path you created. First make sure the check mark is next to Path 2 (or you name you assigned to the second path) in the Paths palette. Then select Delete Path.

AUTION: *Even though a path is saved, it can be deleted by pressing DELETE (PC users: BACKSPACE) when any Pen tool or the Selection pointer is activated in the Paths palette.*

Exporting a Path to Adobe Illustrator

Exporting a path from Photoshop to Illustrator can be especially valuable after you've created a path in Photoshop by tracing over a digitized image, and want to use it in Illustrator.

To export the path so that you can integrate it into a design in Illustrator, choose Export in the Photoshop File menu. From the Export submenu, choose Paths to Illustrator. Name the file and click Save (PC users: OK). The file can then be loaded directly into Illustrator. To do this in Illustrator, just execute the File/Open command, locate the file, and open it. To activate and select the path in Illustrator, choose Select All in the Edit menu.

If you don't need to save your path, but you do want to export it to Illustrator, select the entire path and then use Edit/Copy in Photoshop and Edit/Paste in Illustrator to drop the path into an Illustrator file. To do this, you must have version 2.5 or later of Photoshop, and either Illustrator 5.0 on the Mac or Illustrator 4.0 or later on the PC.

If you wish to create a silhouette mask out of a Photoshop image and place only the masked portion in another application (such as Illustrator or a page-layout program), you must create a clipping path, as described next.

CREATING AND SAVING CLIPPING PATHS

One of the most useful features in the Paths palette is the Clipping Path command. A *clipping path* silhouettes an area, masking an image so that only the portion of the image within the clipping path will appear when the Photoshop file is placed in another application.

Figure 10-5a shows an Alaskan brown bear image before the Pen tool was used to create a clipping path. Figure 10-5b shows the results after the Bear file with the clipping path was placed in Adobe Illustrator. Only the bear was included in the clipping path, so that it could be placed on top of a new background in Adobe Illustrator.

(a) The original Alaskan brown bear image, before the clipping path was created; (b) Only the image area within the clipping path appears in Adobe Illustrator

(a)

(b)

FIGURE 10-5

The following exercise walks you through the steps required to turn a path into a clipping path and then to save the file in EPS format so it can be imported into another program.

1. Open a file that contains an image that you wish to silhouette and export to Illustrator or a page-layout program. If you don't have a suitable image, use the Frames file (PC users: frames.jpg) in the Photoshop Tutorial folder.

2. Create a path around the portion of the image that you wish to include in the clipping path.

3. Once you've created the path, choose Save Path from the Options (PC users: Control) menu. In the Save Path dialog box, enter a name for your path.

4. After the path is saved, choose Clipping Path from the Options (PC users: Control) menu in the Paths palette. When the Clipping Path dialog box appears, click on the Path pop-up menu and select the name of your saved path.

Before you can finish this clipping path exercise, you need to understand the options available in the Clipping Path dialog box.

Working with the Clipping Path Options

In the Clipping Path dialog box, you can adjust the Flatness value to *flatten*, or simplify, paths that may be too complicated to print. You can leave this field empty unless you receive a PostScript "limitcheck" error when printing the clipping path image in another application. If you do receive this error, you can try entering a number into the Flatness field. A higher Flatness value will reduce the number of straight lines that will be needed to define the curve, thus simplifying the curve. If you flatten the curve too much, however, you will alter the shape of the entire path.

10

Acceptable Flatness values are from .2 to 200 pixels. Try entering 3 in the Flatness field for low-resolution printers and 8 for high-resolution printers.

The two Fill Rule options, Even-Odd and Non-Zero Winding, in the Clipping Path dialog box allow you to specify how overlapping or intersecting areas of a clipping path will be filled when the image is placed in another program. For example, look at the star icons in the Clipping Path dialog box. If you created a clipping path in the shape of a star in Photoshop and then placed it in another program, the star may appear completely filled by the Photoshop image, or it may appear with a hole in its middle. The hole in the middle of the star would allow a background color or another object to show through.

In general, choose the Non-Zero Winding Fill Rule if you have a single path without any intersecting lines. Otherwise, choose Even-Odd Fill Rule. If you're going to be creating complicated clipping paths, here's a thorough explanation of the difference between the two options.

To understand how the Even-Odd and Non-Zero Winding Fill Rules work, you must do a little bit of calculating. First, pick a point in your image that is within the path (but not on the path). Then draw an imaginary line through any path segment(s) out to the edge of your document window. With this imaginary line in mind, you can decide whether you want to apply the Even-Odd or the Non-Zero Winding Fill Rule.

The Even-Odd Fill Rule

To use the Even-Odd Fill Rule, count the number of times a path crosses the imaginary line. If the number is even, the portion within the path where your imaginary lines starts will not be filled by the Photoshop image; this area will be transparent when it appears in the other application. If the number is odd, this area will be filled by the image area in Photoshop. For example, in the miniature icons adjacent to the Even-Odd Fill Rule option, an imaginary line drawn from the middle of each icon would strike two paths for both of the circles and the star. Thus, the middle areas would be transparent after placement into another application because an even number of paths are intersected by your imaginary line. The white areas in the icons indicate the areas that would be transparent.

Notice that the middle of the star icon is white. Assume that you created a star-shaped clipping path over a blue image in Photoshop. With the Even-Odd Fill Rule applied, the blue Photoshop image would only appear in the triangular areas of the star when the Photoshop file was placed in Illustrator. Any background color used in Illustrator would appear through the center of the star.

The circle path icons adjacent to the star icon indicate that the direction in which the paths were created will have no effect on whether the area is filled. The direction of the path is important, however, when using the Non-Zero Winding Fill Rule.

The Non-Zero Winding Rule

When using the Non-Zero Winding Fill Rule, you must also plot an imaginary line from within your path to the edge of the document window. Imagine also that you are facing in the direction of the imaginary line. Unlike the Even-Odd Fill Rule, the Non-Zero Winding option analyzes paths according to how many times the path lines intersect your imaginary line, and in what direction. When using Non-Zero Winding, as you count, add 1 each time the path strikes your imaginary line from left to right. Add -1 each time the path strikes your imaginary line from right to left. If the total adds up to zero, the portion of the path where your imaginary line begins will be transparent. If the total is not zero, the area will be filled by the Photoshop image.

To better understand how Non-Zero Winding works, it's best to start by looking at the two miniature circle icons next to the option in the dialog box. Pick a point in the middle of the circle on the far right of the Non-Zero Winding option; then imagine a line through the concentric circular paths. The arrows in the circular paths depict the direction of the paths. Since one path would cross your imaginary line from the left and one would cross from the right, you would add 1 to -1; thus the area within the path would not be filled, because 1 plus -1 equals zero. The white in the middle of the circle confirms that the area would be transparent. When the file with this clipping path is loaded into another program, any background created in that program will appear through the middle of the concentric circles.

The paths in the middle circle icon adjacent to the Non-Zero Winding Fill Rule option will produce a different result in the Illustrator file. An imaginary line from the middle of this clipping path would be struck two times from right to left, resulting in a total of -2. Thus, the middle path area will be filled by the Photoshop image, not by the background of the program you import the clipping path to.

If you have a path with no intersecting lines or overlapping lines, your best choice for Fill Rule is Non-Zero Winding. This will produce a less-complicated curve when printing to a PostScript printer. Consequently, you are less likely to experience PostScript printing errors.

Now let's finish the clipping path exercise:

1. In the Clipping Path dialog box, select either the Even-Odd or the Non-Zero Winding Fill Rule.

2. To save the path as a clipping path, click OK. The image on screen will not change. You will see the effects of creating a clipping path only when the file containing the clipping path is placed in another program.

10

Photoshop in Action

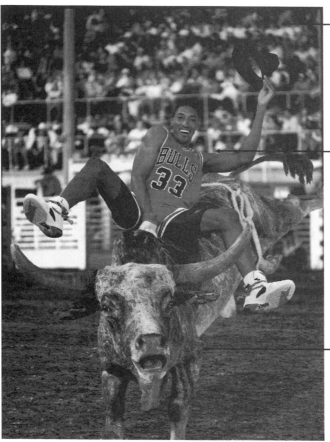

The background scene was photographed in Florida, then scanned.

Chicago Bulls star Scottie Pippen was photographed sitting on foam stairs. After the photograph was scanned, the Pen tool was used to outline Pippen. This image was later copied and pasted over the bull.

The stuffed bull was shot in California, and then scanned. Once it was scanned, the Pen tool was used to outline it. The bull was later copied and pasted into the final image.

Artist: Nik Kleinberg   Client: Sports Illustrated for Kids

Nik created this "unbelieva-BULL" image for a *Sports Illustrated for Kids* cover using photographs taken by George B. Fry III.

After all the shots were taken, they were scanned separately. First the background was scanned, then the bull, and then Pippen. After the bull and Pippin were scanned, the Pen tool was used to silhouette (outline) each image. The paths were saved and then turned into selections with the Paths palette's Make Selection command. The selections were copied and then pasted into the final image to make it appear that Pippen was having the ride of his life.

In order to use the clipping path in another program, you must save the Photoshop file in EPS format. The clipping path will automatically be saved with the file. If you are going to be creating color separations from the image masked by the clipping path, the file must first be converted to CMYK Color mode before you save it. For more information about saving in EPS format, see Appendix A.

When the Photoshop document is placed in Illustrator or a page-layout program, only the portion of the image within the clipping path will appear.

NOTE: *If you experience problems when printing a clipping path that uses the Non-Zero Winding Fill Rule, Adobe recommends the following: Reopen the file containing the clipping path, select the subpath, and choose Reverse Subpath from the Paths palette Options (PC users: Control) menu. Resave your document in Photoshop before importing it again into the other application.*

If you've followed the exercises in this chapter from beginning to end, you've progressed to a more sophisticated level of expertise with the Paths palette and the Pen tools. Now that you're familiar with the scope of the Paths palette commands, you'll want to keep the palette handy. As you become proficient at using the Pen tools, very few shapes or objects will be beyond your grasp.

10

11

SPECIAL EFFECTS WITH THE PASTE AND MAP COMMANDS

Photoshop's reputation as a powerful generator of special effects is well deserved. As you've seen so far in this book, Photoshop's special effects are sophisticated and often appear to be complicated, but many are in fact quite easy to achieve. In this chapter you'll be introduced to simple variations of the standard Mac and Windows Paste commands, as well as Photoshop's Image/ Map commands. Once you learn how to use the Paste commands from the Edit menu and Image/Map commands individually, you'll be able to use them together to produce special effects.

This chapter will show you how to use

- The Paste, Border, and Feather commands to create glowing text effects.

- The Paste command and Modes in the Brushes palette to seamlessly blend one image into another.

- The Paste Into and Paste Behind commands to paste one selection into and behind another.

- The versatile Composite Controls command to blend two images and effectively control what is included in the blend.

- The Map commands (Invert, Equalize, Threshold, and Posterize) to *remap* or reassign, the brightness values of an image. Using these commands, you can take a color image and convert it to black and white, reduce its gray levels, or quickly invert its pixels to create a negative of the original.

WORKING WITH THE PASTE COMMANDS

Like most Photoshop users, you probably use the Cut and Copy commands primarily to move a selection from one file into another. In the following sections, you'll learn that you can do much more than just paste one image on top of another.

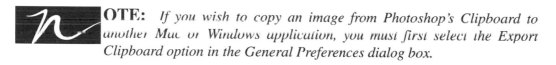

OTE: *When you use the Paste command to work with text, bear this in mind: Unlike most Mac and Windows programs, you cannot paste text from another application directly into a Photoshop document. Instead, you must paste it into the Type Tool dialog box.*

Temporarily Storing the Contents of a Selection in the Clipboard

Before you begin to experiment with Photoshop's Paste commands, you will need to understand how Photoshop handles memory when you Cut or Copy the material you want to paste. When Photoshop's Edit/Cut and Edit/Copy commands are executed, Photoshop automatically copies the contents of a selection to an area of the computer's memory called the *Clipboard.* The Clipboard is a temporary storage area for copied or cut items. Every time a selection is copied into the Clipboard, that selection replaces any existing Clipboard contents; only one item at a time can be stored in the Clipboard. When the Paste command is executed, the contents of the Clipboard is copied into the active document.

OTE: *If you wish to copy an image from Photoshop's Clipboard to another Mac or Windows application, you must first select the Export Clipboard option in the General Preferences dialog box.*

It's important to realize that when the contents of a large selection is being held in the Clipboard, there is less memory available for Photoshop to use. In this situation, you may receive an unexpected out-of-memory message. To prevent this from happening, make sure that you allocate as much RAM as possible to Photoshop and that your scratch disk storage capacity is as large as possible. Ideally, of course, the best solution is to purchase more RAM or a larger hard disk. For more information about allocating memory, RAM, and hard disks, see Chapter 1.

If you think the contents of the Clipboard is consuming too much memory (and you no longer need to store that information), there's an easy way to reduce the amount of memory used by the Clipboard. Make a small selection—even one pixel—and then select Cut or Copy from the Edit menu. Your small selection will thus replace the memory-hungry one currently in the Clipboard.

11

Handling Different Resolutions During Paste Operations

When you paste a selected area from one Photoshop file into another file with a different resolution, you may be surprised at the consequences. The contents of the selection you paste will take on the resolution of the file into which you paste. Thus, if the selection's resolution is higher than that of the target file, the selection will enlarge when pasted. If you paste a selected area with a low resolution into a higher-resolution file, the selection will shrink when pasted. To understand this phenomenon, remember that pixels in high-resolution files are smaller than pixels in low-resolution files; thus there are more pixels per inch in the high-resolution file.

If an image's size increases or decreases after pasting, you can easily resize the selection using the Image/Effects/Scale command. This command works because Photoshop automatically places the selection in float mode after the Paste command is executed.

EMEMBER: *When you enlarge a floating selection, Photoshop interpolates (see Chapter 7 for more information), so the contents of the selection may lose detail. Applying a filter from one of Photoshop's Filter/Sharpen submenus can help sharpen details after interpolation, but be careful not to sharpen too much or your image will become pixelated.*

Defringing a Pasted Image

Another design enigma you may encounter is a mysterious halo of color that sometimes surrounds a pasted selection. When you select an area with the Magic Wand or Lasso tools, Photoshop may include extra pixels along the edges of the selection; these become noticeable when the selection is pasted or moved, particularly when a light-colored image on a darker background is selected and then moved. The extra pixels are often the result of Photoshop's anti-aliasing feature, which softens selections by blurring the edge pixels. In the process, extra pixels around the perimeter are added to the selection.

With the Select menu's Defringe command, you can remove the unwanted color from fringe pixels. (This command doesn't create a special effect; rather, it allows for cleaner pasting.) Defringe replaces the colors on the fringes of a selection with a color that is closest to the fringe from within the selection. In order for the Defringe command to be accessible, the area you want to defringe must be floating. When you select Defringe, a dialog box appears, allowing you to specify the pixel width of the fringe area to be colored. The following illustration (a) shows an image that was copied and pasted without Defringe. Illustration (b) shows the same image after the Defringe command was applied.

(a)   (b)

Creating Glowing Text

In this exercise, you will learn how to create a glowing, or backlit, effect for text by copying, pasting, and using the Select menu's Border and Feather commands. The Border and Feather commands control the width and intensity of the glow.

Although this example creates a glowing background for text, you can produce the same effect on a digitized image instead of text. Here are the steps:

1. Create a new file, 6 inches by 4 inches, in RGB mode at 72 ppi.

2. You're going to create yellow text with a red glow, and you'll create the text first. Change the foreground color to red and the background color to white.

3. Activate the Type tool. Make sure that in the Brushes palette, the Opacity slider is set to 100% and the Mode to Normal.

4. Click in the center of your document. When the Type Tool dialog box appears, type **GLOW** in the text box. Set the font to Helvetica. Enter **120** in the Size field and type **-10** in the Spacing field. In the Style group, choose Bold and turn on the Anti-Aliased option. Click OK to place the text in your document.

11

*n*OTE: *The value entered in the Spacing field in the Type Tool dialog box controls the spacing between letters (kerning). Entering a negative number decreases the spacing between letters (a positive number would increase spacing). The Spacing value is in points or pixels, depending upon the measurement unit set for font size. Values can be from -99.9 to 999.9.*

5. Once the floating text is on screen, move it into the center of the document window; you can do this by pressing the arrow keys or by clicking and dragging on the text. *Don't deselect.*

6. Next you will place the text into the Clipboard so that it can be copied back into the image after you've bordered, feathered, and filled it. From the Edit menu, choose Copy, and keep the text selected.

7. Now place a border selection around each letter of the text. From the Select menu choose Border, type **20** in the Width field, and click OK.

8. To soften the edges of the newly created border, choose Feather from the Select menu. Type **6** and click OK. The 20-pixel border now has a 3-pixel feather beyond its edges. (The Feather command feathers 3 pixels within the selection and three pixels beyond the selection.)

9. Now fill the selection on screen with the foreground color, red, to start creating the glow effect. Choose Fill from the Edit menu. In the Fill dialog box, set Opacity to 100% and the Mode to Normal. You will see the soft edges of the feathered border.

10. To make the text sharper and more readable, paste the text from the Clipboard back onto the soft-edged glow. To do this, select Paste from the Edit menu. Keep the text selected.

11. Now you will fill the text with yellow; the combination of yellow text with a red feathered border will provide the glowing text effect. Start by changing the foreground color to yellow. Keep the text selected.

12. Choose Fill from the Edit menu or press OPTION-DELETE (PC users: ALT-BACKSPACE). Click away from the text to deselect. Your text is now glowing.

Photoshop in Action

The bricks intersecting the circle were created by defining a pattern and then selecting and filling the areas with the pattern.

The glowing circle was created by applying the Select/Feather command to a circular selection and then filling it with black.

The hands and arms were created in Adobe Illustrator and then placed into the final image.

The Select/Feather command was used to soften the edges of the globe and the segmented circle beneath it.

Artist: Louis Fishauf, Reactor Art + Design Limited   Client: Digital Equipment

Louis created this image for a quarterly publication for Digital Equipment. To produce the glow around the circle, he created a circular selection with the Elliptical Marquee tool and then softened its edges by using the Select/Feather command. Once the feathering was applied, he filled the circle with black.

Next, inside the glowing circle he created another circle where he could paste the face using the Edit/Paste Into command. While the face image was still selected, he applied the Spherize filter.

After the face was completed, he created the hands and arms in Adobe Illustrator and used Photoshop's File/Place command to put them into the image. To create the four brick walls, Louis selected a digitized image of bricks, then executed the Edit/Define Pattern command. He filled the four walls with the brick pattern using Edit/Fill.

If you'd like, try applying one or more of Photoshop's filters to create a more dramatic effect. Here we applied the Spherize filter:

Now continue on to the next section, where you'll see how the Paste command can be used with the Brushes palette's Mode pop-up menu to blend images together.

Blending Images Using the Paste Command and Brushes Palette Settings

Photoshop provides several techniques for blending two images together into a composite image. One method that is quick, versatile, and simple is to use the Paste command. When you use the Paste command, the pasted image is automatically placed in float mode.

When an image is floating and either the Type tool or a selection tool is activated, you can use the Opacity slider and the Mode pop-up menu in the Brushes palette to control how the pixels in the floating selection will blend with pixels in the underlying image. In this situation, the modes in the Brushes palette work much the same way as when a painting tool is activated. (To review the painting modes, see Chapter 5.) The difference, though, is that Photoshop applies the painting mode to underlying pixels based upon the pixels in the floating selection, rather than using the foreground color.

Here are some ways you can use the Mode pop-up menu in the Brushes palette to blend the floating selection with the underlying image:

To replace lighter pixels in the underlying image with corresponding darker pixels in the floating selection, choose Darken.

To replace darker pixels in the underlying image with corresponding lighter pixels in the floating selection, choose Lighten.

To blend the Hue and Saturation values of the floating selection with those of the underlying image, choose Color. The Luminosity value of the underlying image will not be affected, thus preserving the underlying image's gray levels.

To create a darker composite from the pixel values of both the floating selection and underlying image, choose Multiply. This can produce a result similar to overlaying colored magic markers.

To create a lighter composite from both the pixel values of the floating selection and underlying image, choose Screen. This often creates the effect of bleaching out colors from an image.

To create a random effect from the pixels in the floating image, choose Dissolve and use the Opacity slider to adjust the results. As you lower the Opacity, the floating selection gradually dissolves, revealing more of the underlying image.

OTE: *The Multiply and Screen commands in the Mode pop-up menu produce the same effects as Multiply and Screen in the Image/Calculate submenu. To learn more about the Multiply and Screen commands, see* *Chapter 12.*

When an image is floating *and* either the Type tool or a selection tool is activated, two additional modes appear in the Mode pop-up menu: Black Matte and White Matte. These options are used to eliminate extraneous dark or light edges that stick to a selection when it is cut or copied from a black or white background. Black Matte removes dark edges, White Matte removes light edges. The fringe pixels appear because of the softening of selection edges due to feathering and anti-aliasing.

Figure 11-1a shows a backyard scene that was pasted over the waterfall image shown in Figure 11-1b to create the composite shown in Figure 11-1c. After the backyard scene was pasted, and while it was still floating, the Darken mode was selected in the Mode pop-up menu of the Brushes palette. Remember, when the Darken mode is applied, Photoshop compares the pixel values in the floating selection to the pixel values in the underlying image. It then replaces underlying pixels that are lighter than corresponding floating pixels with the darker pixels from the floating image. Thus, in Figure 11-1c, the lighter areas of the waterfall were replaced by the darker trees and fence from the backyard scene. To make more of the underlying image visible, Opacity in the Brushes palette was lowered to 50%.

(a)

(a) Floating
selection;
(b) under-
lying image;
(c)
composite
created
using
Darken
mode and
low
Opacity in
the Brushes
palette

(b)

(c)

FIGURE 11-1

Now follow these steps to create a composite from two images using Copy and Paste and by changing Modes in the Brushes palette.

1. Select part or all of an image or some text that you wish to blend into another image. If you don't have an image to work with, you can open the Blues file (PC users: blues.jpg) in the Tutorial folder. Select the entire image by choosing the Select/All command or by pressing COMMAND-A (PC users: CTRL-A).

2. Choose Copy from the Edit menu.

3. Activate the image into which you want to paste your selection. If you don't have an image, open the Window file (PC users: window.jpg) in the Tutorial folder.

4. From the Edit menu, choose Paste. Reposition your image as desired. (If you are using the Blues and Window files, reposition the floating selection so it is flush with the top of the underlying image.) *Don't deselect.*

5. In the Brushes palette's Modes pop-up menu, experiment with different modes and opacities to create the effect that you desire.

6. When you are done experimenting, drop the floating pixels into the background image by deselecting.

Creating Composite Blends with the Composite Controls Command

Certainly you can create a variety of interesting blending effects with the Brushes palette's painting modes and Opacity settings, but the Edit menu's Composite Controls command is even more powerful. The Composite Controls command also allows you to create a blend (composite image) from a floating selection and an underlying image, but this command allows more precise control over exactly what pixels in the underlying image will be replaced by the floating image.

The Composite Controls command appears dimmed in the Edit menu until a selection is floating in a document. After a selection is put in float mode, by pasting or moving it, or by executing Select/Float, the Composite Controls command can be accessed.

11

n **OTE:** *A shortcut to opening the Composite Controls dialog box is to press OPTION (PC users: ALT) while clicking on the Paste command in the Edit menu. Be aware, however, that if you execute the command with this shortcut, you will not be able to reposition the floating image on screen before the dialog box appears. Therefore, it's usually advisable to Paste your image first, reposition it, and then choose Edit/Composite Controls.*

The following exercise demonstrates the Composite Controls command and its options. For the exercise, you will need two images: one image to be the underlying background image, and another to be the image that you will blend into the background image.

For example, Figure 11-2a shows an image of a boat that was pasted into the textured background image shown in Figure 11-2b to create the composite shown in Figure 11-2c. The Edit/Composite Controls command was used to blend the boat and the background together. The Composite Controls command allowed the lightest pixels from the boat image to be eliminated so that the textured background could show through.

The background image shown in Figure 11-2b was created by applying the Add Noise and Zigzag filters to a Linear blend. (See Chapter 8 for a review of the filter commands and Chapter 5 for a review of creating blends.) If you wish to re-create this background for the following exercise, create a new file, 4 inches by 6 inches.

After you create the new file, choose a foreground and a background color to be the starting and ending colors for the Linear blend. Once you have created the blend, apply the Add Noise filter (in the Filter/Noise submenu) with the Uniform option set to 32. Apply the filter two or three times to achieve a speckled effect. To transform the image into a rippled pond, apply the Zigzag filter in the Filter/Distort submenu. Choose the Pond Ripple radio button, set Amount to 87 and Ridges to 20.

Now that you have created the background file, follow these steps to blend this image with another:

1. Open a file that you wish to blend with the textured background you just created. If you do not have a file to use, you can open the Window file (PC users: window.jpg) in the Tutorial folder.

2. Select the entire file, or an area of it, that you wish to paste into the target background file.

(a)

(a) Floating
selection
for
composite
(photograph
courtesy of
Jonathan
Pite); (b)
underlying
image
created
with the
Gradient
tool and the
Add Noise
and Zigzag
filters; (c)
composite
image
created
using the
Composite
Controls
command

(b)

(c)

11

FIGURE 11-2

3. From the Edit menu, choose Copy, and then close the file.

4. Activate the textured background image. Choose Paste from the Edit menu. Don't deselect.

At this point, feel free to apply the Image menu commands to scale, rotate, or add other image effects. After applying Image menu commands, you may wish to apply sharpening filters afterward to sharpen the details in your image.

5. Choose Composite Controls from the Edit menu.

The Composite Controls dialog box includes several options for controlling how a floating selection and underlying pixels will blend together. These options are examined in the paragraphs that follow.

Composite Controls Sliders

The sliders let you control exactly which pixels to include and exclude from the floating selection (the top slider) and underlying image (the bottom slider). For both sliders, the black slider control affects dark areas, and the white slider control affects light areas. The range of both sliders is from 0 (black) to 255 (white).

When the Floating slider's black slider control is dragged to the right, darker pixels of the floating selection will not be included in the composite image. When the Floating slider's white slider control is dragged to the left, lighter pixels of the floating selection will not be included in the composite image. All pixel values designated in the range between the floating selection's two slider controls will appear in the composite image.

With a little experimentation, the effects of the two sliders will be more apparent to you, so let's continue with the exercise.

OTE: *Before you begin adjusting the sliders, make sure the Preview check box is selected in the Composite Controls dialog box, so you can see the results.*

Try dragging the Floating slider's black control to the right. This will remove the darker pixels from your image. Drag the white control to the left, and you remove the lighter pixels in the floating selection from the composite. The results will be more obvious if you drag the black control back to 0 before moving the white control.

Before you begin experimenting with the Underlying slider, reset the Composite Controls dialog box to its original settings. This will make it easier to see the effect of adjusting the Underlying slider controls. To quickly reset all options, press OPTION (PC users: ALT). The Cancel button will change to a Reset button; click this to reset the settings and remain in the dialog box.

Now consider the Underlying slider: When you click and drag the black slider control to the right, dark areas from the underlying image will be added into the composite. As you drag, underlying pixels with values from 0 to the value set by the black slider control will appear in the composite. Clicking and dragging the white slider control to the left will add light areas from the underlying image into the composite. As you drag, underlying pixels with the value set by the white slider control to 255 will appear in the composite image. Thus, values between the black and white controls are the pixel values in the underlying image that can be replaced by pixels from the floating selection in the composite image.

Try clicking and dragging the Underlying slider's black control to the right. As you drag, you add dark pixels from the underlying image and remove any pixels from the floating image that would have been pasted over this area. Move the Underlying slider's black control back to 0 and try moving the white control to the left. Notice that as you drag, you are adding light pixels from the underlying image to the composite and removing pixels from the floating image in the composite.

Splitting the Slider Controls

To create a smoother composite effect, you can split each individual slider control (▲) into two parts (◢ ◣). To split a slider control, press OPTION (PC users: ALT)

11

and then click and drag on one of the edges of the control. For each slider control that is split you will see two values showing the range between the split controls. The pixels in the range defined by the split slider control will only be partially colored. This can help smooth the blend between the floating and underlying pixels.

To get familiar with how your composite image will be affected by splitting the slider controls, experiment with all four of the controls on both the Floating and Underlying slider bars.

Other Composite Controls Options

The remaining options in the Composite Controls dialog box allow further possibilities and refinement when creating a composite image.

The Blend If pop-up menu allows you to control the blend based upon the color values of individual color channels. When viewing an RGB image, the word Gray in the pop-up menu indicates that the Composite Controls affects the luminance of the pixels in all channels. In an RGB image, Blend If lets you work separately in the red, green, or blue channel of the image. Thus, if Red were chosen in the Blend If pop-up menu, you could control the range of red values (from 0 to 255) for both the floating and underlying image.

You'll also find the familiar Mode pop-up menu and Opacity setting in this dialog box. By entering an Opacity value less than 100%, you can make your floating image more translucent. The Mode pop-up menu offers you the same modes that are available in the Brushes palette. These modes work almost exactly as they do when you use the Brushes palette to edit a floating selection (as described in the previous section)—with one difference: The effect only applies to the pixel values specified by the Composite Controls sliders.

Experiment with the modes and opacities in the Composite Controls dialog box until you achieve the effects you desire. Once you are satisfied with the preview of your image, choose OK to create the final composite.

Using the Paste Into Command

The Paste Into command allows you to paste images from the Clipboard into a floating selection. This special effect is often used to paste images and backgrounds into text. When you paste an image into a selection, the pasted image is put in float mode. While it is floating, you can reposition it, execute Image menu commands, apply filters, and change the opacity and painting mode in the Brushes palette.

In this next exercise, you will use the Paste Into command to paste a photograph into text to create a fashion advertisement, such as the one shown in Figure 11-3. Here are the steps:

1. Create a new file, 5 inches by 5 inches, in RGB mode at 72 ppi.

2. Click on the Default Colors icon to set the color for the text to black.

3. Activate the Type tool; then click on the image to open the Type Tool dialog box. In the text box, type **WEAR** on one line and press ENTER; then type **IT WELL** in the next line. Choose the following settings: Font, Helvetica; Size, **55**; Leading, **45**; Spacing, **–3**; and Style, Bold. Turn on the Anti-Aliased feature and set the Alignment to Center.

IP: *The example in Figure 11-3 uses Helvetica Black. If you have this font, use it instead of Helvetica. Using Helvetica Black, or any heavy typeface, allows more of the image to appear through each letter.*

The Paste Into command was used to paste an image of a model into the text (photograph courtesy of Stacy Kollar Photography)

FIGURE 11-3

11

4. Click OK to have Photoshop place the text on screen. If necessary, reposition the text in the middle of the screen. Don't deselect.

OTE: *Notice that the leading setting of 45 keeps the two lines of text close together. If the leading were larger, more space would appear between the two lines. In Photoshop, leading is measured from baseline to baseline. You can enter leading values from 1 to 1,000.*

IP: *Here's a way to quickly select a letter or group of floating letters to be moved either closer together or farther apart. While the Type tool is still activated, press COMMAND (PC users: CTRL). The Type tool changes to the Lasso tool, which you can click and drag over the floating letters to electronically "rope in" the ones you wish to select.*

5. Use the Scale command to enlarge the type to allow more of the image to show through the letters. If you wish to review the Scale command, see Chapter 7. Don't deselect.

6. Open the file that contains the image you want to paste into the text, and use the Rectangular Marquee tool to select the image, or a portion of it. If you don't have a digitized image to use for this exercise, you can open the Portrait file (PC users: portrait.jpg) from the Tutorial folder.

7. Choose Copy from the Edit menu, and then close the file. The file with the text in it is now the active window.

8. From the Edit menu, select Paste Into to paste the image into the floating text. If you wish, you can now use the Image/Effects/Scale command to resize the selection that is floating in the text. If you rescale the image, sharpen it with a sharpening filter, if necessary.

9. You may need to click and drag to reposition the floating selection. While it is still floating, you can lighten or darken the image with the Brightness/ Contrast command in the Image menu. If you wish, experiment with various Opacity settings and Modes in the Brushes palette.

10. When you are satisfied with the image's appearance, click away from it to deselect, and then save the file, if you wish.

Photoshop in Action

The moon was created by combining a photograph of a clay model of the moon and a photograph of a person.

The arcing water was created using R/GA Print's own proprietary 3-D modeling software.

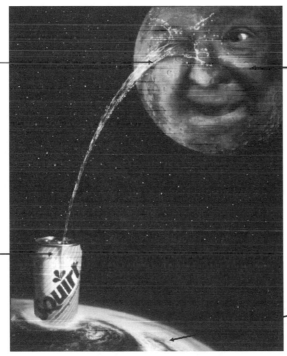

The Squirt can is a product shot. White was added with the Airbrush tool to the area around the base to create a cloud effect.

The earth image is a NASA photograph.

Artwork by: R/GA Print   Photograph by: Steve Bronstein   Client: A&W Brands/Squirt

The painting tools were used to create stars over a black background. Next, a digitized image of the earth and a product shot of a Squirt can were pasted into the file. A clay moon with the contours of a face in it was sculpted by a model maker and then photographed by Steve Bronstein. Steve then took a photograph of a person whose round visage would provide a good man-in-the-moon face. Both the moon and face photographs were scanned and combined using the Paste Into and Composite Controls commands in the Edit menu. In the Composite Controls dialog box, Luminosity mode was applied. This removed color from the face but left the gray values. Then the Rubber Stamp's cloning option was used to enhance the blending effect. The painting tools and painting modes were used to turn the man in the moon purple.

To complete the image, Steve took a photograph of water squirting out of a hose. The photo was scanned and then warped using R/GA's own proprietary 3-D modeling software. The squirt was then pasted into the final image.

11

Using the Paste Behind Command

The Paste Behind command allows one selection to be pasted behind another selection. The pasted image becomes a floating selection, so you can reposition it, execute Image menu commands, apply filters, and change the opacity and painting modes in the Brushes palette.

Figures 11-4a, 11-4b, and 11-4c illustrate the usefulness of Paste Behind. Figure 11-4a is a package design for a pretzel box; in this version, the beer stein is behind one pretzel. The text effect on the side of the box was created using the Skew command in the Image/Effects submenu. To add more pretzels to the package, the designer selected and copied the pretzels from the image in Figure 11-4b. Once the pretzels were copied, the stein was selected before the Paste Behind command was applied. Figure 11-4c shows the final package design after the additional pretzels were positioned behind the stein.

Without the Paste Behind command, there would be no efficient way to place more pretzels behind the stein after the image was created.

To complete the package design, the words *Hard Pretzels* were added. The transparency of the text was achieved by adjusting the Opacity setting in the Brushes palette while the text was selected.

Now try the next exercise, in which one image will be pasted behind a rectangle, creating the illusion that it is sandwiched between the rectangle and a square.

1. Create a new file. Then, using the following illustration as a guide, create two overlapping shapes. (Use the Rectangular Marquee tool and Edit/Fill command to create the shapes.)

2. Now you need to place an image between the two shapes. First select the rectangle on top, using the Magic Wand with a Tolerance setting of 0. Don't deselect.

3. Open any image file, and use the Rectangular Marquee to select a portion of the image for pasting behind the rectangle.

4. Choose Copy from the Edit menu, and close the image file.

(a)

(a) Original package design; (b) image used to Copy and Paste Behind original design; (c) final package design after executing Paste Behind

(b)

(c)

FIGURE 11-4

5. Choose Paste Behind from the Edit menu. When the image appears behind the rectangle, click and drag to reposition it as desired. Your image should look similar to the following illustration.

You may want to try the paste-behind technique again, using another image. To remove the floating image you have already pasted between the two shapes, just press DELETE (PC users: BACKSPACE)—but be aware that this will remove not only the pasted selection but also the selection marquee surrounding the rectangle. So you will need to reselect the rectangle before you execute Paste Behind again. If you have a complex selection, this could take some time.

One way to avoid having to reselect is to make and save a path, then convert the path into a selection. (See Chapter 10 if you need to review how to create and save paths.) In Chapter 12, you'll learn another method of maintaining selections—with the Select menu's Save Selection command.

WORKING WITH THE IMAGE/MAP COMMANDS

The Map commands in the Image menu are used to remap, or reassign, pixel values in a selection or in an entire image. The Map commands let you quickly create special

effects that drastically change the brightness values in an image—for instance, you can transform a color or grayscale image into a high-contrast, black-and-white image or invert all of the color values in an image to produce a negative of the original.

Creating a Negative Using Invert

The Image/Map/Invert command reverses your image, turning it into a negative of the original: All black values become white, all white values turn black, and all colors are converted to their complements. Pixel values are inverted on a scale of 0 to 255. A pixel with a value of 0 will be inverted to 255; a pixel with the value of 10 will be change to 245; and so on.

You may invert a selection or an entire image; if no area is selected, the entire image is inverted.

In the example in Figure 11-5, black text was entered on screen first; then the bottom half was selected using the Rectangular Marquee. When the Image/Map/Invert command was applied to the rectangular selection, the black text within the selection turned white, and the white area between the letters turned black.

Expanding Tonal Range with Equalize

The Equalize command distributes light and dark values evenly and can be used to adjust dark scans and make them lighter. When the Equalize command is executed, Photoshop remaps light and dark values over the full tonal range from black to white. The darkest areas in the images are darkened as much as possible, and the lightest are lightened as much as possible. All other values are distributed according to the new tonal range. Images will often look brighter, exhibiting more balance and contrast.

The Invert command can be used to create a reverse (negative) effect

FIGURE 11-5

Scanned image before (a) and after (b) the Image/Map/ Equalize command is applied (photograph courtesy of Stacy Kollar Photography)

(a)　　　　　　　　　　　　　　　　(b)

FIGURE 11-6

When an area is selected and you execute Image/Map/Equalize, the Equalize dialog box will appear. Choose the Selected Area Only radio button to Equalize only the selected area. If you choose Entire Image Based on Area, Photoshop equalizes the entire image based upon the lightness and darkness values of the selected area.

Figure 11-6a shows the original scanned image of a wine glass and bottle. Figure 11-6b displays the results after the Equalize command was applied.

Converting an Image to Black and White Using Threshold

The Image/Map/Threshold command converts a color or grayscale image into a high-contrast, black-and-white image. The Threshold dialog box allows you to pick a Threshold Level—a dividing line between black and white pixels. All pixels lighter than or equal to the Threshold Level value become white; all pixels darker than the Threshold Level are converted to black.

In the dialog box, you see a *histogram*, which graphically presents the brightness, or luminance, values of the pixels in the current image or selection. The histogram plots the number of pixels at each tonal level of the image. You'll read more about using histograms when retouching and color correcting in Chapter 13.

Clicking and dragging on the Threshold dialog box slider control changes the Threshold Level (dragging right raises the value; dragging left lowers it). Or you can enter a value between 1 and 255 in the Threshold Level field (the default is 128). If the Threshold command is executed at the default settings, all pixels with values greater than or equal to 128 will turn white, and all pixels with values less than 128 will turn black. If the Preview check box is selected, Photoshop will show you the results of the Threshold command.

Figure 11-7 shows the wine bottle image after the Threshold command was applied.

The results of applying the Threshold command to the image from Figure 11-6a

FIGURE 11-7

11

An Exercise Using Threshold and Paste Behind

The following exercise shows you how to create an interesting artistic effect by decreasing the number of colors in an image.

1. Open any color image. If you don't have one to use, load the Portrait file (PC users: portrait.jpg) from the Tutorial folder.

2. Select the entire image by pressing COMMAND-A (PC users: CTRL-A).

3. Choose Copy from the Edit menu.

4. Paste the image over itself by choosing Paste from the Edit menu. (The Select/Float command can also be used instead of Paste.)

5. To convert the floating selection to black and white, choose Threshold from the Image/Map submenu.

6. In the Threshold dialog box, make sure the Preview check box is selected, and then drag the slider control to choose a level that creates an attractive black-and-white image. If you are using the Portrait file, try setting the Threshold to **95**. When you like what you see, click OK.

7. To add the image's original color back into the dark areas of the image, choose Lighten in the Mode pop-up menu of the Brushes palette. (Make sure you have a selection tool activated in the Toolbox.)

   The result will be a composite image with color in what was once the darker areas, and white in the lighter areas.

8. If you wish, continue to experiment with different modes and opacities. When you are ready to continue to the next section, save it, if desired, and close the file.

Reducing Gray Levels Using Posterize

In this next exercise you will reduce the gray levels in an image using the Posterize command. This command can create some unusual special effects, because the gray contours in an image disappear and are replaced by large flat-color or gray areas.

When you select the Image/Map/Posterize command, the Posterize dialog box appears. In the Levels field, enter the number of gray levels you wish to have appear in the image or selected area. Acceptable values range from 2 to 255. The lower the number, the fewer the gray levels. When the Preview check box is selected, Photoshop will preview the results of applying the Posterize command.

For a dramatic affect, try **4** in the Levels field. Then raise the number of gray levels a few increments at a time to see the different effects. Figure 11-8a shows a scanned image of South America's Iguaçu Falls; Figure 11-8b shows the results after applying the Posterize command with Levels set to 4.

(a)

Iguaçu
Falls before
(a) and
after (b)
applying
Image/Map/
Posterize
with a
Levels
setting of 4

(b)

FIGURE 11-8

In the next chapter, you will expand your ability to create composite effects by learning how to use Photoshop's Image/Calculate commands. You'll also see how to create masks so that you can save selections that can be reloaded quickly and conveniently at any time.

12

CREATING MASKS AND USING CHANNELS

Before computers came along, the traditional method of isolating parts of an image for color correcting, image editing, and retouching was to create a mask. A *mask* is a type of stencil, often translucent, which is laid over an image to protect certain areas and allow others to be edited. Cutouts in the mask make selected portions of the image accessible for painting and editing, while the remainder of the image is protected by the stencil. Although the process of creating a mask can be time consuming, it allows work on the image to be performed precisely.

In many ways, the selections you create with Photoshop's selection tools are masks. When a selection is on screen, all the painting and editing work you do affects only the area within the blinking selection marquee. Unlike a traditional mask, however, a selection is temporary. When a new selection is created, the previous one disappears. As discussed in Chapter 10, one method of retaining a selection is to create a path with the Pen tool. Unfortunately, the Pen tool can be difficult to master, and creating intricate paths takes time. To meet the need for maintaining multiple reusable selections that are easy to edit, the designers of Photoshop developed an electronic masking capability that surpasses both the Pen tool and the traditional mask. This electronic capability allows you to save a selection as a mask in an extra channel, called an *alpha channel*, attached to your image.

Once an alpha channel is created, you access it through the Channels palette. The mask in the alpha channel is loaded on screen to serve as a selection. Using alpha channels, you can reload complicated selections and easily switch back and forth among selections while working on a document.

If the relationship between a mask, an alpha channel, and a selection sounds complicated, don't worry. The exercises in this chapter lead you gradually from creating simple masks (called Quick Masks) and working with alpha channels to sophisticated commands that let you superimpose channels and files to create exquisite effects.

As you work through the exercises, you'll see a new and powerful facet of Photoshop open up for you. You'll never have to worry about intricate selections disappearing into the digital stratosphere if you inadvertently click on the screen or close your file. Once you learn how to use masks, you'll be able to save, load, and easily edit any selection, no matter how complex. Not only will this be helpful in your day-to-day Photoshop work but you will also gain the skill to create sophisticated three-dimensional effects that require precise control over light sources and shadows.

WORKING WITH QUICK MASKS

Perhaps the easiest way to understand the relationship between masks and channels is to start by using Photoshop's Quick Mask mode, which creates a temporary mask and a temporary alpha channel. A Quick Mask is similar to a *rubylith,* the red-colored translucent film that is used as an overlay to protect parts of an image in print production.

Like a rubylith, a Quick Mask allows you to view your work through a translucent "overlay." The areas on screen covered by the overlay are protected from image editing; the cutout areas not covered by the overlay are not protected. (If desired, you can change the Quick Mask settings so that the reverse is true.) In Quick Mask mode, the shapes of the cutout areas (the unprotected areas) are easily edited with Photoshop's painting and editing tools. When you exit Quick Mask mode, the unprotected areas are transformed into selections (or one selection).

  Notice the Quick Mask mode icon in Photoshop's Toolbox: The default setting is a shaded square with a clear circle cut out of it. The shaded area represents the translucent mask; the circle cutout is the unprotected area. The Standard mode icon (beside the Quick Mask icon) depicts what you will see when you exit Quick Mask mode: The overlay is gone, but a blinking selection marquee remains on screen.

Creating a Quick Mask

In this section you'll learn how to create a Quick Mask and use it to edit a selection. If you wish to follow along, load the Bad Scan 2 (PC users: badscan2) file, an image of fruit on a plate, from the Tutorial folder. (Our example uses an image of a pork chop on a dinner plate.) You'll create the Quick Mask along the rim of the plate, so that you can add variety to it and make it look more interesting.

 OTE: *The file size of your image will increase after you create the Quick Mask because another channel has been added to your image.*

Begin by creating a small selection with the Elliptical Marquee in the rim of the plate, as shown in Figure 12-1. Don't deselect.

Clicking once on the Quick Mask mode icon puts you in Quick Mask mode; double-clicking on the icon activates the mode and opens the Mask Options dialog box as well. To view the dialog box options, double-click on the icon. Once the Mask Options dialog box appears, as shown in Figure 12-2, you'll see that a red overlay also appears on screen. If the default settings are in use, the red overlay area represents the protected area; and the area you selected is not covered by the red overlay (this is the unprotected area).

12

Selected area

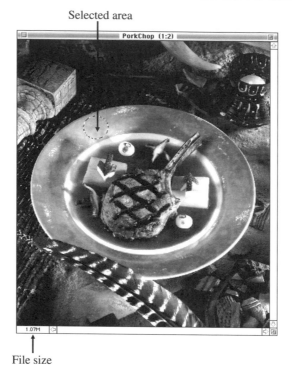

Image
before
entering
Quick
Mask mode
(photograph
courtesy of
Stacy
Kollar
Photography)

File size

FIGURE 12·1

NOTE: *If you can't see the unprotected area on screen because the Mask Options dialog box opened in front of it, move the dialog box by clicking and dragging in its title bar (on "Mask Options").*

In the Mask Options dialog box you can designate what you want the color overlay to indicate: the masked (protected) areas or the selected (unprotected) areas. By default, the Masked Areas radio button in the Color Indicates section is selected. The default color setting for the overlay is red with a 50% Opacity. With the Masked Areas radio button selected, the specified color and opacity are applied to all areas in the image *except* those that were selected before you entered the Quick Mask mode. When the Selected Areas radio button is selected, the translucent colored overlay will appear *over* your selection, rather than around it. (If this is the case now, click on the Masked Areas radio button.)

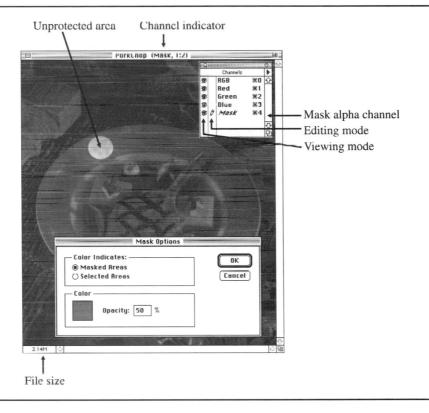

Unprotected area   Channel indicator

Mask alpha channel
Editing mode
Viewing mode

Image in Quick Mask mode with translucent color overlay (compare with Figure 12-1)

File size

FIGURE 12-2

TIP: *You can switch between the Masked Areas and the Selected Areas options without opening the Quick Mask dialog box by pressing OPTION (PC users: ALT) and clicking on the Quick Mask icon. The Quick Mask icon will change to reflect the option you have chosen.*

You can change the overlay color by clicking on the swatch in the Color section of the Mask Options dialog box; this opens Photoshop's Color Picker. If you change the percentage in the Opacity field beside the color swatch, the translucency of the overlay is adjusted accordingly. For the following exercise, leave the default Mask Options settings selected (Color Indicates Masked Areas, and the overlay color at 50% red). Click OK to continue.

You are now in the Quick Mask alpha channel overlay. Before continuing, take a moment to look at Figure 12-2 to see how your surroundings have changed. First, examine the document's title bar. You should see "Mask" rather than "RGB."

12

The Channels palette should now be open; if it isn't, open it by choosing Show Channels in the Window menu. In the Channels palette, notice that a new channel called Mask has been added (this is an alpha channel). Next to the Mask channel, the eye icon (👁) means the channel is visible, and the pencil icon (✏) indicates the channel can be edited. Notice that there are eye icons next to each of the RGB channels also, but no pencil icons. Thus, even though you can see your image on screen, any editing changes you make now will not affect it, but rather the mask only.

Editing a Mask in Quick Mask Mode

To resize and fine-tune the mask, you can paint it. This changes the unprotected and protected areas (which changes the selection marquee on screen after you exit Quick Mask mode). When you paint to edit the mask, you can only use black, white, or shades of gray. Your Colors palette is now restricted to 256 shades of gray. If the Colors palette isn't on screen, open it, and notice that all of the swatches are now shades of gray.

When you paint with white in Quick Mask mode, you add to the unprotected area (the selected area). When you paint with black, you subtract from the unprotected area (and add to the protected area). Painting with gray shades creates a type of "partial" selection when you exit Quick Mask mode. When this selection is filled with an opaque color, the result is a translucent color.

The following table summarizes the effects of painting with white, black, or gray when the Color Indicates Masked Areas radio button is selected in the Mask Options dialog box:

Painting Color	Effect in Quick Mask Mode	Effect in Standard Mode
White	Subtracts from colored overlay (protected area); adds to unprotected area	Adds to selection marquee
Black	Adds to colored overlay (protected area); subtracts from unprotected area	Subtracts from selection marquee
Gray	Adds a partial overlay	Partial selection

To see how painting in white edits the mask and changes the selection, set the foreground color to white. Select any painting tool, and click on a medium, soft-edged brush in the Brushes palette. (A soft-edged brush will produce a selection with feathered edges; a hard-edged brush will create a sharper selection.) Make sure Opacity is set to 100%.

Use the Paintbrush tool to paint around the segment of the plate's rim that you can see through the translucent overlay. As you paint with white, the translucent overlay melts away. As you remove the overlay, you increase the size of the selection that will appear when you exit Quick Mask mode.

IP: *You might want to zoom in and use a smaller brush so that you can carefully select the rim and nothing else. If you make a mistake, just paint with black to add to the overlay.*

Before leaving Quick Mask mode, take a moment to view the mask channel *without* the composite image displayed. This will give you an idea of exactly what happened in the alpha channel when you painted with white. To turn off the RGB composite display, click on the eye icon to the left of the RGB channel in the Channels palette. The RGB composite image disappears, and you will see the black mask and the white, unprotected area. When you painted with white, you subtracted black from the mask. Only when the RGB composite image and mask appear on the screen together is the mask displayed in a translucent color. Restore the RGB image by clicking on the eye icon next to the RGB channel in the Channels palette.

Now that you have isolated the rim of the plate, you are ready to return to Standard mode, where you can use the selection that the mask creates.

Exiting the Quick Mask Mode

To exit Quick Mask mode, click on the Standard mode icon in the Toolbox. The selection marquee now appears around the entire plate, as shown in Figure 12-3. Notice that "Mask" no longer appears in the window's title bar and that the file size indicator shows that the image has returned to its original size. In addition, if you opened the Channels palette, you'd see that the Mask channel is no longer listed. Thus, your selection remains, but the alpha channel containing the mask has disappeared.

OTE: *If you painted with white in several different areas in the Mask channel, several selection marquees will appear on screen when you exit Quick Mask mode.*

12

Now you can edit or color correct the rim of the plate. Try using the Brightness/ Contrast controls in the Image/Adjust submenu to increase the contrast. As you adjust brightness and contrast, only the selected area of the plate changes. When you're finished, don't deselect.

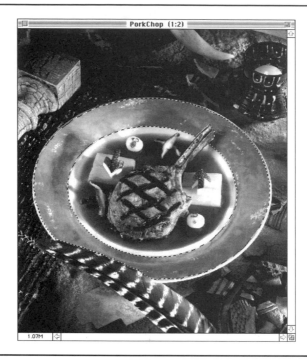

The selection reflects the area that was painted with white in the Quick Mask channel

FIGURE 12-3

As mentioned earlier, your task is to make the rim of the plate more interesting. Suppose you'd like to apply a pattern to enhance the rim of the plate. This creates a problem: You need to create a selection to define the pattern, but if you do this, you will lose the selection around the rim of the plate. The solution is to save the selection. Keep your selection on screen and proceed to the next section.

SAVING AND LOADING A SELECTION

Any Photoshop selection can be saved, whether it was created in Quick Mask mode or not. When a selection is saved, Photoshop creates a mask from the selection and places it in an alpha channel.

To try this out, make sure you have a selection on screen, then choose Save Selection from the Select menu. Notice that the Channels palette now contains a new channel, Channel #4. The selection around the rim of the plate, created in the previous section, is now stored in Channel #4 so it can be recalled after you define a pattern. (If you were in a CMYK Color file, the first alpha channel would be #5.)

Click on the eye icon column next to Channel #4 to see the mask that is stored in the Channels palette. An overlay similar to the Quick Mask overlay appears over your image. Click on the eye icon next to the RGB channel to turn it off. Without the underlying image, the mask now appears in black and white. Return to your composite image by clicking on the eye icon again, and the overlay returns. To hide the overlay from view, click on the eye icon next to Channel #4.

IP: *You can toggle back and forth between the alpha channel and the RGB composite channel by pressing* COMMAND-4 *(PC users:* CTRL-4*) to access alpha Channel #4 and* COMMAND-0 *(PC users:* CTRL-0*) to access the RGB composite.*

With your selection stored, you can safely select another area on screen and define it as a pattern. Select one of the leaves in the Bad Scan 2 file with the Rectangular Marquee tool, and choose Define Pattern from the Edit menu.

Now recall the plate rim selection by choosing Load Selection from the Select menu. The mask from Channel #4 is placed on the screen as a selection. (If more than one saved selection exists, the Load Selection command opens a pop-up menu of all saved selections. Just click on the name of the selection you want to load.)

Once the plate rim selection appears, apply the pattern using the Edit/Fill command. In the Fill dialog box, select Pattern from the Use pop-up menu. Enter **20** in the Opacity field and set Mode to Normal; then click OK. Figure 12-4 displays the results of applying a pattern (created from the feather shown in the image) with a 20% opacity to the rim selection.

DELETING A CHANNEL

Since you will not be needing the rim selection from the previous section again, your next step is to delete Channel #4. Whenever you no longer need a channel, you should delete it to keep the file size of your image as small as possible. To delete a channel, select it in the Channels palette, and then choose Delete Channel from the Options menu. Do this now to delete Channel #4, and then continue to the next section to learn about the New Channel command provided in the Options menu of the Channels palette.

12

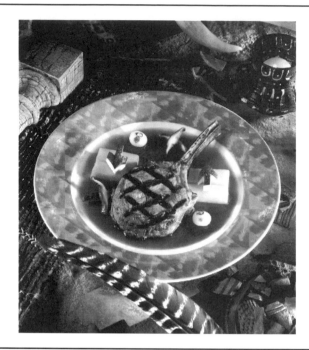

The plate,
after the
pattern was
applied to
the selection

FIGURE 12-4

CREATING AN ALPHA CHANNEL WITH THE NEW CHANNEL COMMAND

The New Channel command in the Channels palette's Options menu allows you to create an alpha channel. You can then work in the channel and create a mask from scratch using a painting, editing, or selection tool. To utilize the mask as a selection, you will need to execute the Select/Load Selection command.

In this section, continue using the Bad Scan 2 (PC users: badscan2) file from the Tutorial folder as you learn how to create and edit a channel using the New Channel command. Start with no selection on screen. If the plate rim is still selected from the previous exercise, deselect it by choosing None from the Select menu.

To create a new alpha channel, click on the Options menu in the Channels palette, and choose New Channel. A new alpha channel appears in the Channels palette, and the Channel Options dialog box opens. Name the channel; type **Plate** in the Name field. In the Color Indicates section, choose the Selected Areas radio button. This way, when you paint with black, you will be creating a selection; when you paint with white, you will be subtracting from the selection. Note that this is the opposite of what you did when you created the Quick Mask earlier in this chapter. Leave the color swatch set to red and Opacity set to 50%. Click OK.

```
╔═══════════════════════════════════════════════════╗
║                  Channel Options                  ║
║                                                   ║
║   Name: [Plate              ]      ╭─────────╮     ║
║                                    │   OK    │     ║
║   ┌─Color Indicates:──────────┐    ╰─────────╯     ║
║   │  ○ Masked Areas           │    ┌─────────┐     ║
║   │  ◉ Selected Areas         │    │ Cancel  │     ║
║   └───────────────────────────┘    └─────────┘     ║
║   ┌─Color──────────────────────┐                   ║
║   │  ┌────┐                     │                  ║
║   │  │    │  Opacity: [50 ] %   │                  ║
║   │  └────┘                     │                  ║
║   └────────────────────────────┘                  ║
╚═══════════════════════════════════════════════════╝
```

Your screen will now be white because you are in a new, empty channel, and you are viewing only the channel, not the image. Notice in the Channels palette that the pencil and eye icons appear beside the new channel (Plate), indicating it is displayed and that you can edit it. The pencil and eye icons do not appear beside the other channels.

Now you are ready to create a mask. But you'll want to see the mask in relation to the image on screen. To view the RGB image, click to activate the eye icon for the RGB composite channel. After you click, all of the channels will be visible, but only the Plate alpha channel will be editable (it's the only one with the pencil icon).

Creating and Editing a Mask in an Alpha Channel

To create a mask in the Plate channel from the previous section, click on the Default Colors icon to set foreground to black and background to white. Use the Paintbrush to paint the inside of the plate, but not the rim area. You will be painting with the same type of translucent overlay with which you worked in Quick Mask mode. If you make a mistake, you can erase the overlay by simply clicking and dragging with the Eraser. (This works because the Eraser paints with the background color, white.) If you are using the Bad Scan 2 image, also paint over the large pear in the middle of the plate.

The following table summarizes the effects of painting in an alpha channel when the Color Indicates Selected Areas radio button is selected in the Mask Options dialog box. Remember, this is the setting that is opposite to the one used when you created the Quick Mask earlier in this chapter.

12

Painting Color	Effect on Colored Mask Overlay	Effect When Selection Is Loaded
White	Subtracts from colored overlay (unprotected area); subtracts from unprotected area	Subtracts from selection marquee
Black	Adds to colored overlay (unprotected area); adds to unprotected area	Adds to selection marquee
Gray	Adds a partial overlay	Partial selection

IP: *To see the effects of painting with black, white, and gray, create a new channel in a new blank RGB file. In the alpha channel, create a blend from black to white, then return to the RGB composite and load the selection. Open one of the files in the Tutorial folder, select the entire image, copy it, then use the Edit/Paste Into command to paste the image into the selection. This will produce a fade-out effect in the image.*

After you've painted the center of the plate with the colored overlay, take a look at what appears in the Plate channel. To view the Plate channel as a separate image, turn off the eye icons in the other channels by clicking on the eye icon next to the RGB composite channel. This hides the display of the RGB channels and leaves the Plate channel on screen. Notice that you painted in black.

To load the black area on screen as a selection, first redisplay the RGB composite by clicking on RGB in the Channels palette, or press COMMAND-0 (PC users: CTRL-0). Then choose Load Selection from the Select menu. If you wish to edit the selected area, try applying the Distort/Twirl filter with a setting of 999 degrees. With the filter applied, the food turns into soup, as shown in Figure 12-5. In the Bad Scan 2 file, you'll get a similar effect. When you've finished applying the Distort/Twirl filter, delete the Plate alpha channel using the Delete Channel command in the Channels palette's Options menu.

As practice, try using the New Channel command to create an alpha channel to mask a different area of your file so you can safely edit in that area. After you're done, you may wish to save your file with the alpha channel. Proceed to the next section to learn how to do this.

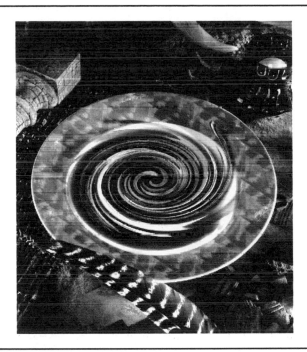

After the
selection is
loaded and
the
Distort/Twirl
filter
applied, the
pork chop
turns into
soup

FIGURE 12-5

SAVING ALPHA CHANNELS WITH A FILE

After you've created an alpha channel, you may wish to have it saved with your file
so the mask can be loaded as a selection at a later time. If you save your file in
Photoshop's native format or in PICT format, all alpha channels are automatically
saved with the file. If you save a file in TIFF format, the TIFF Options dialog box
appears. In the dialog box, make sure that the Save Alpha Channels option is selected
before clicking OK. For more information about saving in TIFF format, see
Appendix A.

Channels can also be exported into new and existing files. This can be
accomplished by executing the Image/Calculate/Duplicate command, which will be
covered later in this chapter.

Photoshop in Action

A mask of the architectural engraving was created by first selecting the engraving and then executing the Select/Save Selection command.

The sky was created by using the Blend tool.

Using the selection tools, the architectural engraving was selected and then saved to an alpha channel using the Select/Save Selection command. Once the channel was created, it was easy to isolate the building and apply color.

The architectural engraving mask was activated and the Paste Behind command was used to place the Deutsche mark behind the architectural engraving.

The stock certificate was selected and the Perspective command was used to add depth.

Using Photoshop's Feather command, the edges of the stock certificate were blurred.

Artist: Marc Yankus
Client: General Electric

Marc created this cover image for an annual report by scanning black-and-white architectural engravings, a page from the *Wall Street Journal*, a stock certificate, an American dollar, a Japanese yen, a Deutsche mark and some ticker tape. After the images were scanned, they were placed into a file and different masks were created of the images. The masks were put to use by first executing the Select/Load Selection command. After the selections were loaded, they were edited and colored.

ALPHA CHANNEL TECHNIQUES

The following sections provide exercises that will broaden your understanding of alpha channels and will send you on your way to creating sophisticated effects with them.

Using Alpha Channels to Reposition Geometric Shapes on Screen

The restraints imposed by a painting program have been emphasized throughout this book. In a painting program such as Photoshop, reselecting objects after they've been deselected can sometimes be a painstaking and time-consuming task. The following exercise demonstrates how alpha channels can be used to load selections that can then be painted with colors to make it appear as if the shapes on screen change positions.

1. Open a new file, 5 by 5 inches, RGB, and 72 ppi. Notice that the file size is 380K. This will grow every time you create a new alpha channel.

 OTE: *If you use the Pen tool to create a path, save the path so you can convert it into a selection, and your image will not grow in size.*

2. If the Channels palette is not open, select Show Channels from the Window menu.

3. In this exercise, you will create a circle, a square, and a triangle. The shapes will overlap each other as shown in Figure 12-6. Start by using the Elliptical Marquee to create a circular selection in the top-left corner of your document window. Fill the selection with green, and keep it selected.

4. While the circle is selected, choose Save Selection from the Select menu. Channel #4 is added to the Channels palette; this is the alpha channel for the circle. Notice the file size in the status bar has grown from 380K to 507K.

5. Double-click on Channel #4 in the Channels palette. The mask appears and the Channel Options dialog box opens. Make sure the Color Indicates Masked Areas radio button is selected. This means that the black region in the mask represents the protected area of the image, and the white region represents the unprotected area. In the Name field, type **Circle**. Leave the color swatch set to red and Opacity set to 50%, and click OK. Your screen should now resemble Figure 12-7.

12

Overlapping
shapes can
be
"repositioned"
using alpha
channels

FIGURE 12-6

6. Return to the RGB composite image by clicking on RGB in the Channels palette or by pressing COMMAND-0 (PC users: CTRL-0). Deselect the circle by clicking away from it or choosing None from the Select menu.

Viewing
the Circle
alpha
channel

FIGURE 12-7

7. If you wish to see the translucent overlay, click on the eye icon beside the Circle channel. The overlay appears, representing the protected area. Click on the eye icon again to hide the overlay.

8. Change the foreground color to blue. Using the Rectangular Marquee tool and the Edit/Fill command, create a square that overlaps the circle, as shown in Figure 12-6. Keep the square selected. Choose Save Selection from the Select menu to create an alpha channel. In the submenu that appears, choose New. *Be careful not to choose Circle* because this will replace the circle selection with the square selection.

9. If you don't see Channel #5 in the Channels palette, scroll down in the palette or resize it to make it larger. Double-click on Channel #5. This lets you view the alpha channel and opens the Channel Options dialog box. In the Name field, type **Square**. If you wish, change the color swatch and opacity. Click OK to activate the changes. Notice the file size in the status bar has grown from 507K to 633K.

10. Again return to the RGB composite by clicking on RGB in the Channels palette or by pressing COMMAND-0 (PC users: CTRL-0). Deselect the square.

11. Change the foreground color to yellow. Use the Lasso tool and the Edit/Fill command to create a triangle that overlaps the square, as shown in Figure 12-6. Leave the triangle selected, and choose Select/Save Selection. Then choose New from the submenu to create a third alpha channel.

12. Double-click on Channel #6 in the Channels palette to view the channel and open the Channel Options dialog box. In the Name field, type **Triangle**. Leave the other settings the same. Click OK. Notice that the file size has grown from 633K to 760K.

 OTE: *At any time, you can edit the Channel Options settings for a channel by clicking on the channel in the Channels palette, and then choosing Channel Options in the Channels palette's Options menu.*

12

13. Return again to the RGB composite by clicking on RGB in the Channels palette or by pressing COMMAND-0 (PC users: CTRL-0). Deselect the triangle.

Now suppose you want to change the order of the three objects on screen. Without alpha channels, you'd need to re-create the shapes in order to change how they overlap. But the alpha channels let you achieve this effect more quickly and easily by loading a selection for each shape and then repainting it.

14. First load the circle selection. To load it from the alpha channel, choose Load Selection from the Select menu and then choose Circle from the list. A selection marquee appears around the circle.

15. Fill the entire circle with green. The easiest way to switch colors is to activate the Eyedropper tool and then click on the green part of the circle. Once the foreground color changes to green, fill the circle by pressing OPTION-DELETE (PC users: ALT-BACKSPACE). The circle now appears to be in front of the other objects.

16. To bring another shape forward, follow steps 14 and 15 again but load a different selection and fill it with the appropriate color. For instance, to move the square to the front, load the square selection with Select/Load Selection and then fill it with another color. The square will appear in front of the other objects.

Before you close the file containing the three shapes, proceed to the next section, and learn how to save alpha channels along with a file.

Using Alpha Channels to Create Shadowed Text

Now that you possess the power to save and load selections, creating special effects becomes easier. For instance, you can easily create shadowed text, as shown in the following illustration, by utilizing the alpha channel features already covered in this chapter. In this exercise you'll create two alpha channels, one for the shadow area of the text and the other for the text.

1. Create a new RGB Color file and then open the Channels and Colors palettes if they are not already open.

2. Next use the Type tool to create some text on screen. When the text is on screen, move it into the center of your document window. Keep the text selected.

3. While the text is still selected, choose the Select/Save Selection command to create a mask in an alpha channel (Channel #4) of the text floating on screen. Don't deselect.

4. Now create another mask in an alpha channel of the text floating on screen. Choose New from the Select/Save Selection submenu. After you have a mask of the floating text in the second alpha channel (Channel #5), deselect the floating text.

5. Click on Channel #5 in the Channels palette to activate the alpha channel.

6. To offset the text in Channel #5, choose Offset from the Filter/Other submenu. In the Offset dialog box, type in the amount you want to offset the text horizontally and vertically. Type a positive number less than 10 in the Horizontal and Vertical fields to offset the shadow text to the right and down (a negative number offsets to the left and up). Choose the Wrap Around radio button in the Undefined Areas group and click OK.

7. Once the text in Channel #5 is offset, click on RGB in the Channels palette to return to the composite image.

8. Now use the Load Selection command from the Select menu to load selection #5, and then fill the selection with a dark color. Load selection #4 and fill it with a light color.

At this point, both selections are saved in two different channels. This means at any time, you can reload the #4 (the text) or #5 (the offset text) selection, change colors, or fill either selection with a blend, or apply a filter. To enhance the drop-shadow effect, reload #5 (the offset text) selection, then apply the Gaussian Blur filter to the text with a setting of 3 pixels. This is a common technique for creating a soft-shadowed look. If you want to create a more dramatic effect to make it look as though the type is jumping off the page, redo the exercise and increase the Offset values in the Offset filter's dialog box.

Creating a Three-Dimensional, Raised-Type Effect

You can create endless striking three-dimensional effects by loading and filling selections from alpha channels. You can save even a sliver of a selection that has just the look you want and reload it to be used as a light source or a shadow. The exercise in this section demonstrates how to create a raised-type, or embossed, effect by filling one selection for a light source and another selection for a shadow.

Before starting, examine Figure 12-8. Notice the raised look of the text; it is created primarily from the thin slivers of light and dark along the sides of the letters. The white slivers along the left edges create the illusion of a light source, and the dark slivers along the right edges appear as shadows. Together, they create the depth needed to produce the raised-type effect.

In the exercise, you'll create a separate mask for the light source and another for the shadow. Then the selections are filled with white and black. If you keep these steps in mind as you work through the exercise, you'll have a clearer idea of why you are executing each step. The concepts presented here can be used in other situations where a raised, recessed, or bevelled effect is needed.

1. Start by opening any file to which you would like to add raised text. If you don't have a suitable image, load the Blues file (PC users: blues.jpg) from the Tutorial folder.

2. Activate the Type tool and click on screen to open the Type Tool dialog box. Type the text to be added to your image and click OK. Once the type appears on screen, move it to the desired position. Then set Opacity in the Brushes palette to **1%**. Don't deselect the text.

"Embossed" text (photograph courtesy of Stacy Kollar Photography)

FIGURE 12-8

You're undoubtedly wondering why the Opacity value is 1%. This setting prevents the text from being filled with the foreground color. The text will be produced by light and shadows, rather than a fill color. The 1% opacity creates a marquee selection of the text that is completely transparent. Later this text selection will be transformed into the two masks for the white edge and the black edge.

3. While the text is still selected, choose Save Selection from the Select menu. After the alpha channel appears in the Channels palette, double-click on it. In the Channel Options dialog box, name the alpha channel **Black Shadow**; this is the channel you will use to create the shadow for the text. Select the Masked Areas radio button for the Color Indicates option, and click OK.

4. In the Black Shadow alpha channel, deselect the text. To lay the groundwork for creating the black shadow slivers, apply the Emboss filter to the entire channel. Choose Emboss from the Filter/Stylize submenu, and in the Emboss dialog box type **135** in the Angle field, **3** in the Height field, and **100** in the Amount field. Click OK to execute the filter.

5. Next, duplicate the alpha channel by selecting it, then copying and pasting it into a second channel, which will provide the basis for the light source for the raised text. Choose All from the Select menu, and then choose Copy from the Edit menu to copy the selection to the Clipboard.

6. While the alpha channel is still in the Clipboard, select New Channel from the Channels palette's Options menu. When the Channel Options dialog box appears, name the alpha channel **White Shadow** and click OK. When the new alpha channel appears, select Paste from the Edit menu.

7. From the Image/Map submenu, choose Invert to reverse the light and dark areas on screen.

8. Next you will isolate the white area of the alpha channel. Choose Threshold from the Image/Map submenu. In the Threshold dialog box, set the slider control to 255 and click OK. Before continuing, compare your image with Figure 12-8. Remember that white represents the image area that will become a selection.

9. Now isolate the area that will provide the black shadow for the text. Click on the Black Shadow channel in the Channels palette; when the channel is active, choose Threshold from the Image/Map submenu. In the Threshold dialog box, set the slider control to 255 and click OK. Once again, compare your image with Figure 12-8. The white area on screen

12

represents another selection that will be loaded into your image. This selection area will be filled with black.

10. Now you are ready to create the raised-type effect. Activate the RGB composite channel by clicking on RGB in the Channels palette or by pressing COMMAND-0 (PC users: CTRL-0).

11. To create the shadow portion of the text, load the Black Shadow selection. Choose Load Selection from the Select menu, and select Black Shadow in the Load Selection submenu. When the selection appears, fill it with black. To examine the shadow you just created, hide the selection marquee by choosing Hide Edges from the Select menu.

12. To create the light source for the text, choose Select/Load Selection again and select White Shadow in the Load Selection submenu. When the selection appears, fill it with white. Deselect.

This three-dimensional effect can be applied to any object or shape, not just to text. Also, if you'd like, you can reload the White Shadow and Black Shadow selections and fill them with other colors using various opacities. Try experimenting to create different effects. Fill the Black Shadow selection with white and the White Shadow selection with black, then try filling the white selection with yellow at a 50% opacity.

If you wish to create your own three-dimensional effects, start by analyzing shadow and light sources, and text or object areas. Use the Offset and Emboss filters to help create displacement effects. Use the Image/Effects submenu's Threshold or Invert commands, or the Image/Adjust/Levels command to control the brightness levels. Experiment by filling the selections with the different colors.

Now that you know how to create and use alpha channels, you may wish to explore the other commands in the Channels palette's Options menu. But before you go any further, use the File/Save As command to save your document under a new name.

Using Alpha Channels to Create and Print Spot Colors

In order to print spot colors from Photoshop, you need to use alpha channels. (Spot colors were introduced in the section "Accessing Custom Colors from the Color Picker" in Chapter 4.)

To create spot colors in an RGB Color or CMYK Color file, you first need to select the areas where you want the spot colors to be printed. To easily select the areas, switch to Quick Mask mode, then use the painting and/or selection tools to edit the mask. When you exit Quick Mask mode, these areas will be selected.

Once the areas are selected, choose Save Selection from the Select menu. Double-click on New Channel in the Channels palette to open the Channel Options dialog box. In the dialog box, enter the name of your spot color in the Name field. The Color Indicates Masked Areas radio button should be selected. Click OK to close the dialog box. On screen, the selected areas are represented by white and the unselected areas are represented by black. This creates a negative plate. If you wish to print a film positive, invert the image by choosing Invert from the Image/Map submenu.

When you wish to print, click on the channel you want to print, then choose Print in the File menu. Do this for each channel.

Video Alpha Channels

If you are producing Photoshop images for output to video, the Channels palette provides an option for copying the masks you create in alpha channels into a *video alpha channel.* Video alpha channels are often used to overlay titles and graphics in video productions.

Video alpha channels can only be utilized if a 32-bit video card is installed in your computer. These cards are often used in desktop multimedia and videotape production. As discussed in Chapter 1, 24-bit video cards provide over 16 million colors; 32-bit cards such as those manufactured by Radius and TrueVision provide an extra 8 bits that Photoshop's video alpha channel can utilize for storing graphics and titles.

Like all other alpha channels, the video alpha channel allows 256 shades of gray. The brightness values of images and text in the video alpha channel determine the opacity of the image overlaid on the video. The lighter the area, the more translucent; thus, white areas are completely transparent and black areas are completely opaque.

To use an alpha channel as a video alpha channel, choose Video Alpha from the Channels palette's Options menu. In the Video Alpha dialog box, click on the Channel pop-up menu to pick a channel, and click OK. When a video alpha channel is created, the eye icon in the Channels palette is replaced with a miniature television (▣).

12

```
╔══════════ Video Alpha ══════════╗
║              None                 ║
║  Channel: ✓ Opening Title    ▲    ║    ┌──────────┐
║              Background           ║    │    OK    │
║                                   ║    └──────────┘
║                                   ║    ┌──────────┐
║                                   ║    │  Cancel  │
║                                   ║    └──────────┘
╚═══════════════════════════════════╝
```

SPLITTING AND MERGING CHANNELS

A powerful utility offered in the Channels palette allows you to split the channels in a color image into separate files. You can edit an image's separate channels and then merge them back together. In the next section, you'll see how splitting and merging channels can be used to create a colored mezzotint effect.

To split the channels, choose Split Channels in the Channels palette's Options menu. The split documents will appear on screen as grayscale images, and the original document is closed.

You can also combine separate channels into a composite image by using the Merge Channels command. To execute this command, all channels to be merged must be open on screen. They must be grayscale images, and their width and height in pixels must be equal. You can merge Photoshop documents together using the Merge Channels command, as long as the documents meet these conditions. In the Merge Channels dialog box, you can specify the number of channels you want to merge and to what mode (RGB Color, CMYK Color, and so forth).

```
╔═══════════════ Merge Channels ═══════════════╗
║                                               ║
║   Mode:   │ RGB Color    ▼│    ┌──────────┐   ║
║                                │    OK    │   ║
║   Channels: │3▐│               └──────────┘   ║
║                                ┌──────────┐   ║
║                                │ Cancel   │   ║
║                                └──────────┘   ║
╚═══════════════════════════════════════════════╝
```

Click OK, and another dialog box appears where you specify the channels into which you want each open document on screen loaded.

```
╔═══════════════ Merge RGB Channels ═══════════════╗
║                                                   ║
║   Specify Channels:          ┌──────────┐         ║
║                              │    OK    │         ║
║   Red:   │ Book Cover.Red   ▼│└──────────┘        ║
║                              ┌──────────┐         ║
║   Green: │ Book Cover.Green ▼││ Cancel   │        ║
║                              └──────────┘         ║
║   Blue:  │ Book Cover.Blue  ▼│┌──────────┐        ║
║                              │  Mode    │         ║
║                              └──────────┘         ║
╚═══════════════════════════════════════════════════╝
```

After you click OK, a new image consisting of the formerly split documents appears in an untitled window.

Using Split Channels/Merge Channels to Create a Colored Mezzotint Effect

The Split Channels and Merge Channels commands can be used to create an interesting colored mezzotint effect. First, load an RGB Color or CMYK Color file. Then use the Split Channels command to split the image into separate grayscale files.

Next, create a custom pattern. From the Mode menu, change each file to Bitmap, and choose the Custom Pattern option in the Bitmap dialog box. Click OK to apply the pattern. Do this to every file, and then convert each file back to grayscale.

Next, use the Merge Channels command to merge the channels back together. The color image will reappear, but with a black mezzotint pattern overlaying the colors. The final effect will depend upon the pattern you choose and the colors in the original image.

WORKING WITH THE CALCULATE COMMANDS

Once you've learned the fundamentals of creating and using alpha channels, the power of Photoshop's Calculate commands will open a whole new world of design possibilities for you. These commands help you create exquisite and often striking effects by superimposing files over other files, channels over other channels, and channels over files, and vice versa. The Calculate commands will add, subtract, average, or blend the values of each pixel in an image or a channel with the corresponding pixel values of another image or another channel. The resulting, or destination, image is created from the calculations applied to the pixel values of the two original images.

It is important to understand that pixel values are measured on a scale of 0 to 255, with 0 representing black and 255 representing white. Therefore, when pixel values increase, the image grows lighter and when pixel values decrease, the image grows darker.

n **OTE:** *When working with a composite image, 0 to 255 represents brightness values of all the RGB channels. If you are a bit puzzled by the representation of brightness values in an image, think of them as a grayscale version of your image. A visual representation of an image's brightness values can be seen by choosing Histogram from the Image menu. For more information about histograms, see Chapter 13.*

All of the Calculate commands are accessed by choosing Calculate from the Image menu and then selecting the appropriate command from the Calculate submenu. Virtually every one of the commands—Add, Blend, Composite, Constant, Darker, Difference, Duplicate, Lighter, Multiply, Screen, and Subtract—allow you to create a multitude of effects.

Although each Calculate command provides its own specific results, keep in mind a few general attributes that apply to the Calculate commands. When you execute any of these commands, a dialog box appears. In most of the dialog boxes, you will be allowed to choose two *Sources,* which are the channels or images that you wish to superimpose. It's important to note that a Source image is listed in a Calculate dialog box only if its width and height in pixels are equal to other Source images; therefore, the width, height, and resolution of your Source images should all be the same.

Most Calculate dialog boxes also allow you to specify a *Destination,* where you see the results of applying the Calculate command. The destination can be a new channel or an existing channel. You can also choose whether the channel will be in an existing file or a new file.

NOTE: *The mathematical formulas for many Calculate commands are provided in this section. Undoubtedly, you won't want to keep your calculator accessory open on screen to compute pixel values before applying commands. The formulas are supplied here not so you have to do the math but to help you understand how the commands work and aid you in predicting their outcome.*

Duplicate

The Duplicate command requires no math and can be extremely useful in all areas of Photoshop work, regardless of whether you are creating special effects. It allows you to create an exact duplicate of a channel or a file and place the duplicate into an existing channel, an existing file, a new channel in an existing file, or a new channel in a new file.

Duplicate is often used to duplicate channels into new files so they can be deleted from their original file, helping to keep file size to a minimum. By duplicating the channel into a new file, the channel can always be duplicated back into the original file as a channel or a blinking selection marquee and used again. You can use the Duplicate command with any file except a Bitmap file or an Indexed Color file.

Here is the Duplicate dialog box:

```
╔══════════════════ Duplicate ═══════════════════╗
║  ┌─ Source 1 ──────────────────┐   ┌─────────┐  ║
║  │ Document: │ Untitled-1  ▼ │   │   OK    │  ║
║  │                               │   └─────────┘  ║
║  │ Channel:  │ #4    ▼ │         │  Cancel  │   ║
║  └──────────────────────────────┘  └─────────┘  ║
║  ┌─ Destination ───────────────┐                ║
║  │ Document: │ New        ▼ │                    ║
║  │ Channel:  │ New ▼ │                           ║
║  │           □ Invert                            ║
║  └──────────────────────────────┘                ║
╚══════════════════════════════════════════════════╝
```

When you execute the Duplicate command, the filename of your document will automatically appear in the Source 1 pop-up menu. If more than one document is open on screen, you need to specify which one to use as the source document. In the Destination group, use the Document pop-up menu to specify the name of the document where the channel will be placed. To place the channel in a new document, choose New in both the Channel and Document pop-up menus. To place the channel in the new document as a selection marquee, choose Selection in the Destination Channel pop-up menu.

The Invert option for the Destination is similar to choosing Invert from the Image/Map submenu. This option remaps light pixels to dark pixels and dark pixels to light, producing a negative of your image.

If you export a channel to a new document and then delete the channel from the original document, you can always use the Duplicate command to return the channel to its original document. To do this, load both the original file and the file containing the channel to be duplicated. Activate the file with the channel in it, and execute the Image/Calculate/Duplicate command. In the Source 1 Channel pop-up menu, choose the name of the channel that you are duplicating. For Destination, set the Document pop-up menu to the original file, and in the Channel pop-up menu choose New. This will duplicate the channel back into its original home and place it into a new alpha channel.

12

Add and Subtract

The Add and Subtract commands add or subtract the values of corresponding pixels from two Sources. As mentioned earlier, if an image's pixel values increase, the image grows lighter; if the pixel values decrease, the image grows darker. Thus the

Add command can be used to blend two Sources to create a lighter Destination image, and the Subtract command can be used to blend two images create a darker Destination image.

Both commands allow you to adjust the pixel values of the Destination image by entering a Scale value and an Offset value. To understand these values, let's analyze the formulas Photoshop uses to add and subtract. Here is the Add command formula:

$$\frac{(\text{Source 1} + \text{Source 2})}{\text{Scale}} + \text{Offset} = \text{Destination}$$

This formula adds the pixel values from the two Sources to produce a brighter Destination image. The Scale factor is divided into the sum of the Source pixels; thus Scale can be used to *decrease* the brightening effect. Scale can be any number between 1.000 and 2.000. If Scale is 2, the calculation will result in the average brightness of both images. The Offset factor can be a number between -255 and 255. Adding a positive Offset number lightens the image; adding a negative Offset number darkens the image. The Add command can be used to place image areas from two nonoverlapping Sources so they appear unchanged in the Destination image. To do this, execute the command with Scale set to 1 and the Offset factor set to 0.

The Subtract command formula uses the same components as the Add formula, except that the Source pixels are subtracted, as is the Offset value.

$$\frac{(\text{Source 1} - \text{Source 2})}{\text{Scale}} - \text{Offset} = \text{Destination}$$

Here is an exercise to try out the Add and/or Subtract commands using the Blues (PC users: blues.jpg) and Hands (PC users: hands.jpg) files in the Tutorial folder.

1. Load the Blues and Hands files (or any two files in which you want to Add or Subtract brightness).

    To combine these two files together using Add or Subtract, the two images must have the same dimensions in pixels. To check the dimensions and resolution of your files, press and hold OPTION (PC users: ALT) while you click on the file size indicator in the status bar. If the two files do not have the same dimensions and resolution, use the Cropping tool to adjust one of the files so that they are both the same. In this case, the Blues file is 6.75 inches by 5.5 inches at 72 ppi, and the Hands file is 6.5 inches by 5.75 inches at 72 ppi. Let's crop the Blues file so that it matches the Hands file.

2. Double-click on the Cropping tool and type **6.5** (inches) in the Width field, **5.75** (inches) in the Height field, and **72** in the Resolution field. Click OK. Then click and drag over the Blues image with the Cropping tool, and click inside the selected area to make the crop.

3. Once the two files have the same dimensions, choose Add from the Image/Calculate submenu. In the Add dialog box:

   a. For Source 1, click on the Document pop-up menu and set it to Blues. Set the Channel to RGB.

   b. For Source 2, in the Document pop-up menu choose Hands. Set the Channel to Black.

   c. For Destination, set the Document to New and the Channel to New. In the Scale field, type **1**; in the Offset field, type **30**.

```
╔══════════════ Add ══════════════╗

  ┌─ Source 1 ──────────────────┐    ┌─────────┐
  │ Document:  [ Blues  ▼]       │    │   OK    │
  │                              │    └─────────┘
  │ Channel:  [ RGB    ▼]        │    ┌─────────┐
  └──────────────────────────────┘    │ Cancel  │
                                       └─────────┘
  ┌─ Source 2 ──────────────────┐
  │ Document:  [ Hands ▼]        │
  │ Channel:  [ Black ▼]         │
  └──────────────────────────────┘

  ┌─ Destination ───────────────┐
  │ Document:  [ New   ▼]        │
  │ Channel:  [ New ▼]           │
  │   Scale:  [1    ]            │
  │  Offset:  [30   ]            │
  └──────────────────────────────┘
```

4. Click OK to execute the Add command. The results will show the Hands file lightened against a light-blue background.

5. Close the Destination file, and save it, if you wish.

12

6. Choose Subtract from the Image/Calculate submenu. In the Subtract dialog box, use the same Source 1 and 2 files as described in step 3. In the Destination pop-up menus, choose New. Type **1** in the Scale field and type **30** in the Offset field. Then click OK. This will produce the opposite results of the Add command. The blended images will be darker.

Difference

The Difference command subtracts the pixel values of one source from another source. The results of the Difference command are fairly easy to predict because the supporting equation is quite simple:

Source 1 – Source 2 = Destination

With this formula, if darker pixels (other than black) are subtracted from lighter pixels, the Destination pixels will be darker than the Source 1 image and lighter than the Source 2 image. Also, two very bright pixels subtracted from each other will result in a dark pixel. If a negative number results from the calculation, that number is used as a positive number.

Apart from creating special effects, this command can be useful in video animation to compare two video frames. When Difference is applied to two images that are different, the Destination image will show only the areas that differ between the two Source images. The results on screen can be somewhat similar to the effects of applying the Find Edges filter because the difference between the two animation frames often results in an image edge.

The image in Figure 12-9a was combined with the alpha channel containing black and white stripes shown in Figure 12-9b to create the effect in Figure 12-9c. The dialog box settings for this Difference command are shown in Figure 12-10. The Destination image shows you that when black is subtracted from the Source, no change is produced (because the pixel value of black is 0). When white, with a pixel value of 255, is subtracted from the Source, the result is a negative of those image areas.

If you'd like to see the Difference command in action, load any color image, or use the Bad Scan 2 file (PC users: badscan2) from the Tutorial folder. Once your file is on screen, select New Channel from the Channels palette's Options menu. In the Channel Options dialog box, make sure the Masked Areas radio button is selected, then click OK. In the channel, create a series of black stripes, as shown in Figure 12-9b. Then execute the Difference command. In the Difference dialog box, set the

(a)

(a) Source 1:
photograph
of Aruba;
(b) Source 2:
black-and-
white
stripes
created in
alpha
channel; (c)
image after
using the
Image/
Calculate/
Difference
command

(b)   (c)

FIGURE 12-9

Dialog box
settings for
the Image/
Calculate/
Difference
example
shown in
Figure 12-9

```
                    Difference
   ┌ Source 1 ──────────────────┐   ┌──────┐
   │ Document:  [ Aruba ▼ ]      │   │  OK  │
   │ Channel:   [ RGB   ▼ ]      │   └──────┘
   └────────────────────────────┘   ┌──────┐
                                      │Cancel│
   ┌ Source 2 ──────────────────┐   └──────┘
   │ Document:  [ Aruba ▼ ]      │
   │ Channel:   [ #4    ▼ ]      │
   └────────────────────────────┘
   ┌ Destination ───────────────┐
   │ Document:  [ New   ▼ ]      │
   │ Channel:   [ New   ▼ ]      │
   └────────────────────────────┘
```

FIGURE 12-10

12

Document in Source 1 to Bad Scan 2 (or to whatever color file you are using) and the Channel to RGB. For Source 2, set Document to Bad Scan 2 (or to whatever color file you are using) and Channel to #4. For Destination, set Document to New and Channel to New. Click OK to see the effects.

Blend

The Blend command blends two images together by adding the brightness values of two different channels. Unlike the Add command, though, Blend allows a Weight percentage to be applied to the calculation, which can intensify the effect of either of the Sources on the Destination. By experimenting with the Weight percentage, you'll often be able to create beautiful superimposition effects. High percentages make the Source 1 image more influential in the Destination, lower percentages make the Source 2 image more influential. For instance, if you are blending text into an image and wish to increase the brightness of the text in the Destination, you would make Source 1 the text image and enter a high Weight percentage.

In the Blend formula, the Source% is the value entered into the Weight field in the Blend dialog box:

$$[(Source\ 1)(Source\%)] + [Source\ 2(100\text{-}Source\%)] \div 100 = Destination$$

The Blend command was applied to the digitized image of the piano in Figure 12-11a and the alpha channel with text in Figure 12-11b to create the effect shown in Figure 12-11c. In the resulting blend, the piano is visible through the text. The dialog box settings for this Blend example are shown in Figure 12-12.

If you wish to try creating a similar effect, you can use the Window file (PC users: window.jpg) in the Tutorial folder. Once the file is on screen, choose New Channel from the Channels palette's Options menu, and name the channel **Text.** Make sure the Masked Areas radio button is selected. Click OK. Then click on the eye column next to the RGB composite channel to turn on the view of the RGB composite. This allows you to see the image in the Window file while you work in the channel.

Use the Type tool to add text to the Text channel. After the text appears, position it as desired. Then deselect the text.

Execute the Image/Calculate/Blend command. In the dialog box, set the Source 1 Document to Window and the Channel to RGB. Enter **60** in the Weight field. (Remember, the higher the Weight, the brighter the Source will appear.) For Source 2, set Document to Window and Channel to Text. For Destination, set Document to New and Channel to New. Click OK. The result will be a blend of the file image with the channel.

(a)

(a) Source 1: photograph of piano (courtesy of Stacy Kollar Photography); (b) Source 2: text created in alpha channel; (c) image after using the Image/ Calculate/ Blend command

M
E
L
O
D
I
C

R
H
Y
T
H
M
S

(b)

(c)

FIGURE 12-11

Dialog box settings for the Image/ Calculate/ Blend example shown in Figure 12-11

Blend

Source 1
Document: Piano ▼
Channel: RGB ▼
Weight: 60

Source 2
Document: Piano ▼
Channel: Text ▼

Destination
Document: New ▼
Channel: New ▼

OK
Cancel

FIGURE 12-12

12

Photoshop in Action

The Image/Map/Invert command was applied to a square selection created with the Rectangular Marquee.

Digitized images of a snail's shell and marble tile were combined using the Image/Calculate/Blend command.

The raised type was created using alpha channels, the Emboss filter, and the Image/Map/Threshold and Image/Adjust/Levels commands.

Artists: Judyann and Loren Ruderman   Client: Now, Voyager

This surreal image is a CD cover for the band Now, Voyager. The image shows how you can use both alpha channels and the Image commands to create interesting effects.

Loren started by first scanning a photograph of a snail's shell and a piece of marble. Once the marble tile and the snail's shell were digitized, they were scaled to the same size, 5.5 by 5.5 inches. After the two images were resized, they were blended together using the Image/Calculate/Blend command. The destination of the blend was a new file.

In the new file, the Rectangular Marquee tool was used to create a small section in the middle of the CD cover, then the Image/Map/Invert command was applied. This inverted the pixels from both the marble tile and the snail's shell.

Two separate alpha channels, one for highlights and one for shadows, were created to produce the raised-type effect on "Now, Voyager." By keeping the text highlights and shadows in different alpha channels, Loren was able to experiment until he achieved the perfect raised-type effect. For step-by-step instructions on creating raised text, refer to the section "Creating a Three-Dimensional, Raised-Type Effect" in this chapter.

Lighter and Darker

The Lighter command automatically compares the pixel values of two Source images. Lighter pixels from the Source images replace darker pixels when the Destination image is created. The Lighter command has a similar effect to that created by the Lighten painting mode (Chapter 5).

The Darker command produces the opposite effect: It places only the darker pixels from the two Source images into the Destination image. The effect of this command is similar to that created by the Darken painting mode (also in Chapter 5).

The Lighter command was applied to the two Source images shown in Figure 12-13a and 12-13b to achieve the result shown in Figure 12-13c. Notice that the lighter brick

(a)

(a) Source 1:
photograph
of Aruba;
(b) Source 2:
photograph
of a brick
wall
(courtesy
of D'pix
Inc.); (c)
image after
using the
Image/
Calculate/
Lighter
command

(b)

(c)

FIGURE 12-13

12

mortar pixels appear in the Destination image rather than the corresponding darker pixels from the Aruba image. Throughout much of the Destination image, the lighter texture of the bricks is also visible. Figure 12-14 illustrates the Lighter dialog box settings for this example. Had the Darker command been applied instead of Lighter, the dark trees would have been more dominant in the Destination image.

If you wish to try out the Lighter and Darker commands, load the Window and Blues files (PC users: window.jpg and blues.jpg) from the Tutorial folder. Use the Cropping tool so that both files have the same dimensions, as you did in the Add and Subtract exercises. Execute the Lighter command, and in the Lighter dialog box make the Window file the Source 1 file and the Blues file the Source 2 file. For the Destination, set Channel to New. Click OK to execute the command. In your Destination image, you will see that the darkest areas of the window panes are completely replaced by the light pixels of the Blues files. Next, apply the Darker command to the same images. The results will be just the opposite: Black window areas will be seen in the Destination file, as well as the darker blue portions of the Blues file.

Multiply

The Multiply command produces the effect of two positive transparencies placed over each other and viewed over a light table. The effect is similar to that created by the Multiply painting mode (Chapters 5 and 11).

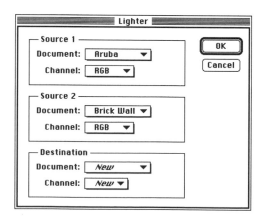

Dialog box settings for the Image/ Calculate/ Lighter example shown in Figure 12-13

FIGURE 12-14

Photoshop in Action

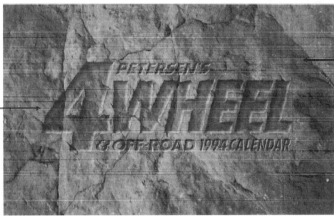

The recessed-type effect was created using alpha channels and the Image/Calculate/ Darker and Image/Adjust/ Levels commands.

The background image is a photograph of a rock that was scanned.

Artist: Daniel Clark　　　　　　　　**Client: Petersen Publishing**

Daniel started creating this calender cover by scanning a photograph of a rock into Photoshop. Next he traced the "4Wheel & Off-Road" logo in Aldus Freehand and filled it with black. In the digitized rock file, he created a new alpha channel and placed the logo into it.

While the logo was still floating, he copied and pasted it into two other alpha channels. In each alpha channel, he blurred and then feathered the floating logo. Next he deselected the logo and offset it. The alpha channel that would be used for the highlight areas of the recessed text was offset to the right by using the Filter/Other/Offset command. (The alpha channel that would be used for the shadow areas of the recessed text was offset to the left using the same filter.) After the filter was applied, the logo in each alpha channel was inverted using the Image/Map/Invert command. This produced white type on a black background.

To create a mask for the highlight area of the text, the Image/Calculate/Darker command was used. In the Darker dialog box, the digitized rock file was chosen in all the Document pop-up menus. The Source 1 Channel pop-up menu was set to the very first alpha channel (containing the text that was not offset). The Source 2 and Destination Channel pop-up menus were set to the highlight channel (the second channel). To create a mask for the shadow area of the text, the Image/Calculate/Darker command was also used. The same settings were used, except the Source 2 and Destination Channel pop-up menus were set to the shadow channel (the third channel).

Once the masks were completed, Daniel loaded each selection individually and used the Levels command to darken or lighten the selection to complete the recessed effect. For a finishing touch, he exported the file to Fractal Painter, where he used a textured airbrush tool to add cracks to the letters.

The Multiply formula multiples the two Source values and divides it by the brightness value of white (255). Thus applying the Multiply command to a dark image and a light image will produce a dark Destination image. Here is the formula:

$$\frac{(\text{Source 1})(\text{Source 2})}{255} = \text{Destination}$$

Using the Multiply command, you can easily create the effect of a portrait emerging out of dark shadows. Try an exercise using the Portrait file (PC users: portrait.jpg) from the Tutorial folder.

First open the Portrait file. Create a new channel and name it **Blend.** Make sure the Masked Areas radio button is selected. Click OK. Click in the eye icon column to activate the RGB composite channel so you can see the Portrait image while you work in the channel.

Next, using the Gradient tool, create a white-to-black radial blend in the Blend channel. Make sure the Midpoint Skew field in the Gradient Tool Options dialog box is set to at least 50%. With both the Blend channel and the Portrait file visible, you can easily create the blend in the area over the girl's face. Since you want the blending effect to occur around the girl's face, create the blend by clicking and dragging from the middle of her face to the end of your document window.

Execute the Image/Calculate/Multiply command. For Source 1, set the Document to Portrait and the Channel to Blend. For Source 2, set the Document to Portrait and the Channel to RGB. For Destination, set both the Document and the Channel to New. Click OK. Your final composite image shows darker pixels enveloping most of the Portrait image. The girl's face only appears through the very lightest areas of the blend.

Screen

The opposite of the effect created by the Multiply command is achieved by the Screen command: the effect of layering one film negative on top of another and printing the combined image on photographic paper. This is similar to what happens when you use the Screen painting mode (discussed in Chapters 5 and 11).

The more complicated Screen formula generally ensures that the resulting Destination pixel values will be greater than the Source pixel values; thus the Screen command produces an image that is lighter overall than the two blended Source images.

$$255 - \frac{(255-\text{Source 1})\,(255-\text{Source 2})}{255} = \text{Destination}$$

The Screen command was used to combine the image of the model in Figure 12-15a with the radial blend in Figure 12-15b to create the final image in Figure 12-15c. The radial blend was created in a new channel in the digitized file of the model. Then the

(a)

(a) Source 1: photograph of a model (courtesy of Stacy Kollar Photography); (b) Source 2: blend created in an alpha channel; (c) image after using the Image/ Calculate/ Screen command

(b)

(c)

FIGURE 12-15

12

Screen command settings shown in Figure 12-16 were used to blend the two images together. The resulting effect is a vignette; the Screen command used the white pixels in the Blend channel to overpower the dark pixels in the model image. It also took the pixels in the model image that corresponded to the dark part of the blend, lightened them, and placed them in the Destination image.

You can easily duplicate this vignette effect using the Portrait file (PC users: portrait.jpg) in the Tutorial folder. Follow the same basic steps that you used for the Multiply command, except this time use the Gradient tool to create a black-to-white radial blend, rather than a white to black. After you execute the Image/Calculate/Screen command (with the same settings you used when you applied the Image/Calculate/Multiply command), your final image will show that the white pixels in the blend have more influence than the darker pixels in the portrait file. If you wish to darken the effect, set the Midpoint Skew field in the Gradient Tool Options dialog box to at least 50% and the Radial Offset field to 40% before creating the radial blend. This will produce a large black area in the radial blend.

Composite

The Composite command lets you combine two images—a foreground image (Source 1) and a background image (Source 2)—with another element—a Mask, which can be a file, a selection, or a channel. The brightness values of the mask determine the strength of each Source image's appearance in the Destination file.

To help you visualize the effect of the Composite command, suppose you are creating a patriotic poster containing images of the president, the vice president, and

Dialog box settings for the Image/ Calculate/ Screen example shown in Figure 12-15

FIGURE 12-16

the flag of the United States. Let's say the president is the foreground image (Source 1), the vice president is the background image (Source 2), and the flag is the Mask. When the Composite command is applied, the foreground image appears more prominently in the lighter areas of the Mask, and the background image is more prominent in the darker areas of the Mask. Thus, the image of the president would be more apparent in the areas corresponding to the flag's white stripes, and the vice president would appear in the areas corresponding to the red stripes.

The Composite command formula is one of the most complicated of the Calculate commands. If you wish to do some math, you can see how the foreground image is more influential in the Destination image in areas corresponding to lighter Mask pixels. In the Composite formula, substitute 255 (white) for the brightness value of the Mask; this causes the background image to have no influence in the Destination image.

$$\frac{[\text{Foreground(Mask)}]}{255} - \frac{[\text{Background(255–Mask)}]}{255} = \text{Destination}$$

Figure 12-17 shows the results of the Composite command when executed with the piano (Figure 12-11a) as the foreground image, Source 1; the model (Figure 12-15a) as

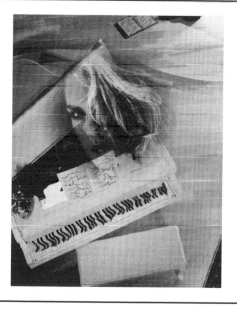

Image after using the Image/ Calculate/ Composite command to combine the piano and model images

FIGURE 12-17

12

the background image, Source 2; and a blend as the Mask (Figure 12-15b). The blend was created in a channel in the same file as the model. The Composite dialog box settings for this example are shown in Figure 12-18. When the Composite command was applied, the piano appeared in areas corresponding to the lighter areas of the Mask, and the model appeared primarily in areas corresponding to the darker part of the Mask.

If you wish to try out the Composite command, you can work with the Window and Portrait files used earlier in this chapter to create a similar effect.

1. Load the Portrait file from the Tutorial folder, and then load the Window file. Use the Cropping tool to set both files to the same dimensions.

2. In the Portrait file, create a new channel and name it **Blend.** In the Channel Options dialog box, make sure that the Color Indicates Masked Areas option is selected. Click OK.

3. Click on the eye icon column next to the RGB channel to activate it, and make sure the pencil icon is not activated. This way you can see the Portrait image while you work in the channel, but you won't affect the little girl's face.

Dialog box settings for the Image/ Calculate/ Composite example shown in Figure 12-17

Composite		
Source 1		OK
Document: Piano ▼		Cancel
Channel: RGB ▼		
Mask		
Document: Model ▼		
Channel: Blend ▼		
Source 2		
Document: Model ▼		
Channel: RGB ▼		
Destination		
Document: New ▼		
Channel: New ▼		

FIGURE 12·18

4. Before creating the radial blend, set the foreground to black and the background to white. Then double-click on the Gradient tool and set the Blend Type to Radial. Choose Normal for the blend Style, and set the Midpoint Skew value at 50%. In the Radial Offset field, type **20**. This will increase the black portion in the center of the blend.

5. To create the radial blend, click in the middle of the girl's face and drag past the end of her head, about half an inch, or so.

6. Execute the Composite command. For Source 1, set the Document to Window and the Channel to RGB. For the Mask, set the Document to Portrait, since this is the file that contains the blend; set the Channel to Blend. For Source 2, set the Document to Portrait and the Channel to RGB. For Destination, set both the Document and Channel to New.

7. Click OK to create the composite.

The results will show the little girl's face appearing through the image of the window. The effect is produced because the Window image (Source 1) is more pronounced in areas corresponding to the lighter areas of the Mask channel. The girl's face (Source 2) is more pronounced in areas corresponding to the darker areas of the Mask channel.

Constant

The Constant command is undoubtedly the simplest of the Calculate commands. It allows you to apply a gray level between 0 and 255 to an entire channel. The lower the value, the darker the gray level, and the higher the value, the lighter the gray level.

In the Constant dialog box, you can enter a gray level for your Destination Channel and Document. Once the gray is applied to your file or channel, you can then proceed to execute other Calculate commands using the gray image.

```
┌─────────────── Constant ───────────────┐
│  ┌─ Destination ─────────────────┐      │
│  │                               │  ┌────────┐
│  │  Document:  [ New  ▼ ]        │  │   OK   │
│  │                               │  └────────┘
│  │  Channel:   [ New  ▼ ]        │  ┌────────┐
│  │                               │  │ Cancel │
│  │  Level:  [128]                │  └────────┘
│  └───────────────────────────────┘      │
└──────────────────────────────────────────┘
```

12

MASKS, RETOUCHING, AND COLOR CORRECTING

You've seen in this chapter how valuable channels can be in image editing and in creating special effects. In Chapter 13 channels and masks will be used to isolate image areas so that they can be retouched and/or color corrected. You'll learn that you can color correct not just in a file's composite channel but also in each channel of the image.

13

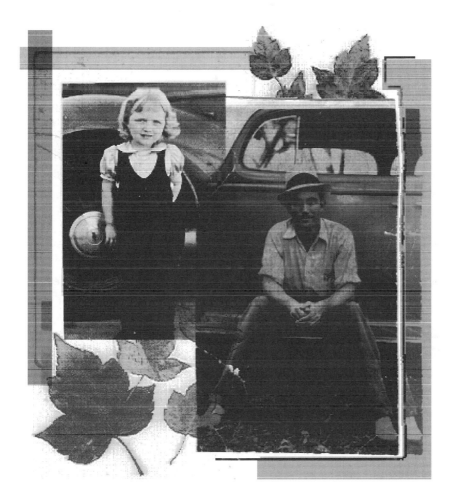

RETOUCHING AND COLOR CORRECTING

A Photoshop image frequently undergoes numerous transformations before it is finally output to the printed page, to video, or to a transparency. No matter what the project, an essential and often unavoidable step is color correcting or retouching. These steps are critical to making the final design match the Photoshop artist's vision.

Color correcting involves changing an image's hue, saturation, shadows, midtones, and/or highlights so that the final output has the most appealing appearance possible. Color correcting is often required to compensate for loss of color quality as a result of digitization. The process of translating your Photoshop image to the printed page often makes color correction a necessity as well. For instance, paper stock, resolution, and impurity of printers' inks may force you to adjust your Photoshop image's colors to produce a suitable printed version. Color correcting is important in making sure that an image's colors conform to those of the original, and may in fact be an improvement over the original. You may also need to *retouch* an image. In addition to removing imperfections, retouching can make an image appear better than real life.

For example, nature often doesn't cooperate by providing the perfect weather, the perfect setting, or the perfect face. A photo of a beach resort taken on a damp, cloudy day will show the beach and water looking brown, the sky gray, the models pale, and the picnic food soggy and uninviting. Photoshop's color-correcting tools can turn the sky and water magnificent shades of blue, make the models tan, and the sand pearly white. When reality must truly take a back seat to the needs an image must meet, you can summon the magic of retouching.

Retouching can remove little bits of litter and debris from the beach. It can smooth a few wrinkles or clear up a pair of bloodshot eyes in a tired face. Even the picnic food can be made to look more inviting. With Photoshop's Rubber Stamp's cloning option, you can even toss more shrimp on the barbecue and add more strawberries to the shortcake.

Clearly, retouching and color correcting often go hand in hand. To get you started with the fundamentals of these operations, this chapter begins with a discussion of how to improve the tonal qualities of a grayscale image. After you learn how to correct a grayscale image, you'll see how faded, damaged old photographs can be retouched. Next, you'll apply retouching techniques to eliminate wrinkles and blemishes in a face and learn how to improve outdoor scenes. The chapter concludes with the steps for color correcting images, particularly CMYK Color files.

Since both retouching and color correcting require the use of many of the tools and techniques discussed throughout this book, you may wish to review some previous chapters. For color correcting, you should be familiar with the basics of color theory (Chapter 4). For advanced color-correction work, you will need to know how to select areas using the Pen tool (Chapter 10), or isolate an area in Quick Mask mode in order to save selections to channels so they can be reloaded later (Chapter 12). For retouching, you will need to know how to use the Eyedropper, Rubber Stamp, Pencil, Paintbrush, Airbrush, Smudge, Blur/Sharpen, and Dodge/Burn tools (Chapters 5 and 6).

Both color correcting and retouching call for some artistic skills that require practice. The more experience you gain with Photoshop's color-correcting commands and retouching tools, the better your skills will be. You'll also be able to save yourself and/or your clients a substantial amount of money if you can correct images and retouch them on your desktop computer. The color examples you'll see in this chapter are from professional work created in Photoshop that in previous years would have required high-end computer workstations or dot etchers, who would edit the individual halftone dots by hand on the film separation.

BEFORE YOU BEGIN

This chapter won't just introduce you to new Photoshop commands but will also show you how to obtain the best-quality results from your work. With this goal in mind, we must again emphasize the importance of *calibration* before you commence any color-correcting or retouching project. If your monitor is not calibrated, you may well find that your final image is quite different from the one you were working with on screen in Photoshop. Be sure to follow the steps in the section on calibration in Chapter 1.

You might also want to review the File/Preferences/Printing Inks Setup dialog box, which lets you change the display of grayscale images to compensate for dot gain. Although the settings in the dialog box do not affect the display of RGB Color images, they do affect the display of CMYK Color images. For more details, see Chapter 9.

ANALYZING THE IMAGE

When you start with the best possible original and digitized image, you'll have less retouching and color-correcting work to do. If the original image is underexposed, overexposed, damaged, or has other defects, the digitized version will reflect this.

13

Thus, before digitizing, always try to obtain high-quality originals, since corrections are easier if the problems are small. Of course, correcting a bad image may not be impossible, but it could involve completely re-creating parts or most of the original image. You'll have to decide whether it's worth the time to perform major surgery.

After your image is digitized, look carefully for imperfections. Many digitized images may seem near perfect when viewed on screen at actual size, but when magnified or printed, flaws may become apparent. To properly analyze an image, zoom in to different areas and carefully check for noise or *posterization*, which is a lack of sufficient gray levels, and whether the image is sharp and crisp, or blurry and out of focus. Keep in mind that if an image looks flawed on screen, it may be best to redigitize it with better equipment or at a higher resolution before retouching and color correcting.

One of this book's authors, Adele Droblas Greenberg, worked on a project that involved correcting faded and scratched grayscale images for a Reader's Digest book. She digitized the images on a midrange scanner (Agfa Arcus) rather than on a low-end scanner. Images that had been test-scanned on a less sophisticated scanner often exhibited noise and black blotches in shadow areas. The blotches were caused by posterization. The images were eventually rescanned on the Agfa Arcus to ensure that no problems arose during the printing or tonal-correcting process.

OTE: *For more information on digitizing your images, review Chapter 7.*

Once you have the best possible digitized image, avoid the temptation to dive right in and start making changes. Take a few moments to identify your objectives. Decide carefully how you want to improve your image. Your goal is obviously to make the final image look as good as, or better than, the original; nevertheless, it should still look natural and believable.

After you've digitized your image, use the Save As command to make a backup of your original digitized image. *This is extremely important* because you may find that color correcting or retouching removes details or colors that shouldn't have been replaced. If you need to start again from scratch, or to sample part of the original image so you can clone back the detail you've removed, you can always use the backup. While working with an image, try to save different versions of it as you proceed, or use the Edit/Take Snapshot command. That way you'll always be able to return to a previous version.

Whether you are working on a color or grayscale image, start the correction process by taking readings of the image using the Info palette and the Eyedropper tool. The Info palette assists you in reading gray and color values. When you move the Eyedropper over various areas in the image, the Info palette reads out the exact color or gray values of the underlying pixels. Once you grow accustomed to reading them, you'll learn to rely on them (rather than on your monitor) as a true guide to an image's tones and colors.

*n***OTE:** *Before you begin using the Eyedropper tool to gauge grayscale and color adjustments, it's a good idea to set the Eyedropper's sample size to a 3-by-3 pixel sample rather than Point sample, which only evaluates one pixel at a time. This way, one errant pixel won't unduly influence the Info palette readout. To reset the sample size, double-click on the Eyedropper in the Toolbox and choose 3-by-3 Average from the Sample Size pop-up menu.*

CORRECTING A GRAYSCALE IMAGE

If you wish to learn how to correct the tones of a grayscale image, open any grayscale image on your screen, or open the Hands file (PC users: hands.jpg) in the Tutorial folder.

When you make tonal corrections, you increase detail in the shadows, midtones, and highlights of an image. Figure 13-1a displays a digitized photograph that will be used to demonstrate the techniques involved in correcting a grayscale image. The photograph, taken in the late 1800s, is of Medora von Hoffman de Mores, a French nobleman who came to the Dakotas to raise cattle. The problems in the photograph are numerous: Details are faded, the image is too dark, and dirt and dust spots are sprinkled throughout. Ken Chaya, art editor of the Reader's Digest book *Discovering America's Past*, asked Adele Droblas Greenberg to retouch the photograph of Medora. Figure 13-1b shows the photograph after the gray tones were corrected and the image was retouched. The final image was converted to a sepia. (The finished retouched sepia is shown as image 4 in the color insert of this book.)

Using the Eyedropper and Info Palette to Take Readings

Once you have a grayscale image on screen, open the Info palette and activate the Eyedropper. Since you are working with grayscale, all you need is one readout in the Info Palette. If you have two readouts, open the Info palette's Options (PC users: Control) menu. In the Info Options dialog box, make sure that Show First Color Readout is checked and is set to Grayscale or Actual Color. Show Second Color

13

A digitized old photograph of Medora von Hoffman de Mores in the late 1800s (courtesy of the Library of Congress), before and after tonal adjustments and retouching

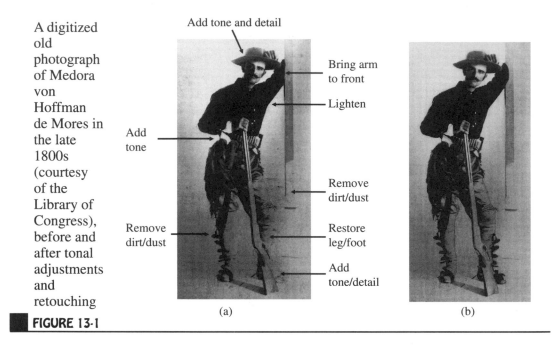

Add tone and detail

Bring arm to front

Lighten

Add tone

Remove dirt/dust

Remove dirt/dust

Restore leg/foot

Add tone/detail

(a)   (b)

FIGURE 13-1

Readout should not be enabled. Leave Show Mouse Coordinates on, and choose the measurement option of your choice. Click OK to activate the changes.

With the Eyedropper selected and the Info palette on screen, move the Eyedropper over different parts of your image. Notice that the K (black) value in the Info palette displays the percentage of black in the area touched by the Eyedropper. Your next step is to take readings of the darkest and lightest points in your image. It's important to do this because areas with less than 5% black tones will often print as white, and dot gain in printing may cause areas with over 95% black tones to look blotchy. If you are outputting to newsprint, dot gain increases, so try to keep the darkest shadow areas around 80%. In Figure 13-2, you can see that the darkest shadow area reads 99% K (black). Soon you'll see how these dark areas were diminished.

 OTE: *The paper, screen frequency, and printing press used all affect the quality of the final output. Consult your print shop if you have questions.*

Once you know the values of your darkest and lightest points, take a reading of the midtones. If the midtone areas are too light or too dark, you'll probably want to adjust these levels during the tonal-correction process.

Reading
the darkest
areas of the
image with
the
Eyedropper
tool

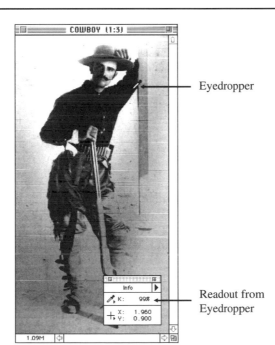

Eyedropper

Readout from
Eyedropper

13

FIGURE 13-2

Since it's impossible to take a reading of every pixel of your image by using the Info palette and the Eyedropper, it's often valuable to view a histogram of the image, as described next.

Using a Histogram to View the Tonal Range

When you open a grayscale image on screen, every pixel in the image can have a value between 0 (black) and 255 (white). Darker pixels have lower gray values; lighter pixels have higher values. A *histogram* plots the disbursement of the gray tones in an image and gives you a visual sense of an image's tonal range. To display a histogram of your image, select Histogram from the Image menu. If part of your image is selected, the histogram will only chart the selected area.

The Histogram dialog box graphs the number of pixels in relation to the tonal range of all possible gray values in an image. The horizontal (x) axis represents the possible gray values from 0 to 255. The vertical (y) axis represents the number of pixels for each tone/color. Beneath the x-axis is a gradient bar showing the actual gray levels from black to white. Dark image areas are graphed on the left of the graph, midtones in the middle, light areas on the right. The height of each vertical line represents the number of pixels for each tone on the x-axis; the higher the line, the more pixels at that gray level in the image.

If the histogram is weighted predominantly toward the right, your image is probably too light. If it is weighted toward the left, it's probably too dark. A histogram that bulges in the middle is stuffed with too many midtone values and thus may lack contrast. In general, a well-balanced image will show pixels spread over the entire tonal range.

The Histogram dialog box also displays the following precise statistics of your image:

- The Mean value represents the average brightness.

- The Std (Standard) Deviation value represents the variance of the brightness values in the image.

- The Median value represents the middle brightness value in the image.

- The value in Pixels is the total number of pixels in the image or selection.

When you move the mouse within the graph, the pointer becomes a crosshair. When you move the crosshair over the histogram, the Level, Count, and Percentile values will change, as follows:

≫ Level represents the level of grays at the crosshair location on the graph; 0 is the darkest level (black) and 255 is the lightest level (white).

≫ Count represents the number of pixels at the crosshair location on the graph.

≫ Percentile is a percentage based on the crosshair's position on the x-axis, from 0% to 100%.

Move the crosshair from left to right over the histogram. As you do, the Level and Pixels values display brightness values and a pixel count. Next, click and drag in the middle of the histogram. A blue or black bar appears above the area over which you drag, and the Level readout displays the gray-level range.

IP: *As you make adjustments to your image during the correction process, you should return periodically to the histogram to get a sense of how your changes are affecting the tonal range.*

The histogram's crosshair readout in Figure 13-3 shows that at level 255, the pixel count is 0. Thus, there are no white pixels in the cowboy image, and no need to reduce the highlights in the image. Figure 13-4 shows the histogram after very dark values were eliminated to ensure better printing of shadow areas. Notice that the histogram's crosshair readout indicates that at level 0 (black), the pixel count is 0.

Histogram
of cowboy
image,
before
tonal
adjustments

FIGURE 13-3

13

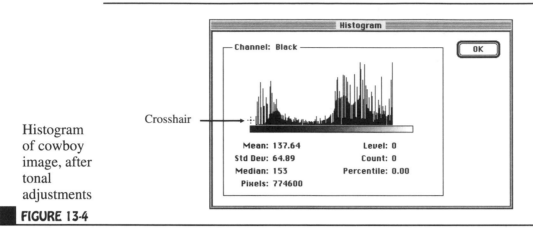

Histogram
of cowboy
image, after
tonal
adjustments

FIGURE 13-4

If you are viewing the histogram of the Hands file, notice that the image is weighted toward black pixels; otherwise, the tonal distribution is fairly constant.

When you think you are well acquainted with the tonal distribution in your image, you are ready to make tonal adjustments to that image.

ADJUSTING A GRAYSCALE IMAGE

What do you do if the shadows in your image are over 95%, the highlights under 5%, and the midtones either too dark or too light? When you make tonal adjustments, you often must increase the brightness or contrast. Sometimes you need to expand the tonal range of an image—the range from the lightest point in the image to its darkest point.

To change the darkest, lightest, and midtone areas in an image, you can either use the Levels, Curves, and/or Variations commands in the Image/Adjust submenu. (You won't use the Image menu's Brightness/Contrast command because it has no controls for adjusting shadows, highlights, and midtones.) The command you choose for adjusting these elements in your image will often depend upon the image itself and on how comfortable you are with the available tools. Sometimes you may need more than one Image/Adjust command to complete the operation successfully. Practice using these commands before you attempt to correct images in a real project.

The next three sections tell you how to use the Image/Adjust Variations, Levels, and Curves commands to improve tonal range by adjusting highlights, midtones, and shadows for grayscale images. All of these commands can be used for correcting color images as well, as discussed later in this chapter.

Using the Variations Command

The Variations command provides a simple and quick way to visually adjust highlights, midtones, and shadows, using miniature image previews—undoubtedly the most intuitive way to adjust tones in an image. Unfortunately, this method does not provide exact adjustment for the color or grayscale values in image areas. Though you can make an image's highlights, midtones, or shadows lighter or darker by clicking on the thumbnail images, you cannot specify a precise value for lightness or darkness (as you can using the Levels and Curves commands).

 OTE: *If the Variations command does not appear in the Image/Adjust submenu, the Variations plug-in has not been installed or removed from the Plug-ins (PC users: plugins) folder.*

Open the Variations dialog box by selecting Variations in the Image/Adjust submenu. The original image, before adjustments, is displayed in the thumbnail labeled "Original" at the top of the dialog box. You make your adjustments to the shadows, midtones, and highlights by selecting the appropriate thumbnail. To make image areas lighter or darker, click on a thumbnail labeled "Lighter" or "Darker"; the effects are then displayed in the Current Pick thumbnail. Generally, if you darken shadows and lighten highlights, you add contrast to your image. If you lighten shadows and darken highlights, you decrease the contrast. If you want to revert to the original image, press and hold OPTION (PC users: ALT) while you click on the Original thumbnail.

The Fine/Coarse slider allows you to specify the level of change in brightness that will occur when you click on a Shadows, Midtones, or Highlights thumbnail. When you drag the slider control to the right, toward Coarse, the difference between lighter and darker grows larger. When you drag the slider control to the left, toward

13

Fine, the difference decreases. Each increment on the slider is double the previous incremental change.

The Show Clipping option, shown in Figure 13-5, turns grayscale image areas to a white color if making them lighter or darker pushes, or boosts, the area to pure black or pure white. If you're viewing the Hands image, the Darker thumbnail in the Shadows column also reveals the results of having Show Clipping selected. Part of the image is chromed out, and this is a warning: If you darken the image, detail will be lost.

To try out the Variations command, click on one of the Shadow thumbnails and choose Lighter. This tells Photoshop to make the darkest parts of the image lighter. Notice how the thumbnails change to reveal the Current Pick. Try another variation: Click on a Highlight thumbnail and choose Darker; this will darken the lightest parts of the image. If you wish, try adjusting the Fine/Coarse slider and then examine the effects on various thumbnails.

The Variations dialog box with the Show Clipping option enabled

White areas show clipping

FIGURE 13-5

OTE: *Unfortunately, when the Variations dialog box is open, you can't move the Eyedropper over your image to gauge the degree of change as you can when the Levels and Curves dialog boxes are used.*

Be sure to cancel the adjustments you have made before exiting the dialog box if you don't want to change your image. To cancel your changes, press OPTION (PC users: ALT) while you click on the Original thumbnail.

Using the Levels Command

With the Levels command, you reduce or increase shadows, midtones, and highlights by dragging sliders. It allows more precision than the Variations command because specific values can be entered in the Levels dialog box. Another advantage to using the Levels command is that it allows Eyedropper/Info palette readings to be taken while you make tonal adjustments. The Info palette displays these readings as "before" and "after" settings.

Select Levels from the Image/Adjust submenu; the Levels dialog box displays a histogram of your image or selection. Directly beneath the histogram, along the bottom axis, is the Input Levels slider, which allows you to add contrast by adjusting shadows, midtones, and highlights. The white slider control on the right side primarily adjusts the image's highlight values. When you move the white slider control, corresponding values—0 (black) to 255 (white)—appear in the right-hand Input Levels field at the top of the dialog box. The higher this value, the brighter the highlight.

The black slider control on the left of the Input Levels slider primarily adjusts shadow values, and its corresponding values appear in the left-hand Input Levels

13

field at the top of the dialog box—the lower this value, the darker the shadow. The values for shadows, like those for highlights, range from 0 (black) to 255 (white).

The middle slider control represents the midtones, or gamma, in the image or selection. The default gamma setting, which appears in the middle Input Levels field, is 1.00. Moving the middle slider control to the left raises the gamma value and primarily makes midtones lighter; moving it to the right primarily makes midtones darker. When the gamma is set at 1, it's always equidistant from the shadows and highlights.

When you change values for shadows, midtones, or highlights in the Levels dialog box, Photoshop remaps, or shuffles, the image's pixels accordingly. For instance, if you reset the white Input Levels slider control from 255 to 230, values that were 230 are remapped to 255; highlights are thus brightened, and the total number of highlight pixels is increased. The rest of the pixels in the image are reassigned to reflect the new white value. For instance, you'll also see the midtone lightened. The exact number of pixels and how they are remapped is based upon how far you drag the slider control, so be aware that lightening the highlights can cause a rippling effect that partially lightens midtones and shadows.

When the Preview check box in the Levels dialog box is selected, the image or selection changes according to the values in the Input Levels fields. If you wish to see where the highlights and shadows begin in an image, deselect the Preview check box and press and hold OPTION (PC users: ALT). Then drag either the highlight (white) or shadow (black) Input Levels slider control. The screen will show a high-contrast view of your image, indicating the darkest and lightest image areas. (For this to work, the Video LUT Animation option must be selected in the General Preferences dialog box.)

n **OTE:**   *On the Mac, you may find that Photoshop provides a full-screen preview, even when the Preview button is off. This is caused by a Color Lookup Table that dynamically updates your screen when the Video LUT Animation option in the General Preferences dialog box is on. If the Video LUT Animation option is turned on, color and grayscale adjustments appear throughout your entire screen (in every open window) if the Preview button is not selected. For a more accurate preview, click the Preview button, which temporarily disables Video LUT. This will cause the preview to appear only in the active window.*

The Output Levels slider at the bottom of the dialog box reduces contrast by subtracting white or black from an image. Move the black slider control to the right and you will subtract shadow areas from your image, thereby lightening it. Move the white slider control to the left and you will subtract highlight areas, thus darkening your image. When the image is lightened or darkened, Photoshop remaps the pixels according to the new Output Levels values.

For instance, if you drag the white Output Levels control to the right, resetting it from 255 to 200, you remap the image so that 200 is the lightest value. Any pixels with a value of 255 are changed to have a value of 200, and all values are remapped accordingly to make the image darker. The same is true if you move the black control. If the black control is moved from 0 to 50, 50 becomes the darkest value in the image. Pixels that were 0 would now have a value of 50.

At this point, you may be somewhat confused about the difference between the Input Levels and Output Levels sliders. When you drag the left Output Levels slider control to the right, the values increase and the image lightens. But the values also increase when you drag the left Input Levels slider control to the right—yet the image darkens.

Here's the distinction between the two: Assume you change the left (black) Input Levels value to 40. This tells Photoshop to take all the shadow values between 40 and a lesser value and change them to 0 (black). Thus darker pixels are added and the image grows darker. The difference between the lightest and darkest pixels is increased; thus the contrast is increased. On the other hand, if you move the left (black) Output Levels slider control to the right to 40, you are telling Photoshop to take all pixels with values of 0 to 39 and shift them to be 40 and more. Thus darker pixels are subtracted and the image brightens, but the contrast is reduced. Also, remember that the Input Levels slider focuses on highlights, midtones, and shadows; the Output Levels slider adjusts the entire tonal range.

If the shadows in your image are too dark, try dragging the left Output Levels slider control to the right. Figure 13-6 illustrates how this was done to decrease the black areas in the cowboy image. After the blacks were decreased   with the Levels dialog box still open—the mouse pointer (which turns into an eyedropper if CAPS LOCK is not depressed) was placed over the image to measure the degree of change. Notice that the Info palette in Figure 13-6 shows the before-and-after readouts: 99% dark areas were changed to 97%. To avoid lightening midtones and highlights, the shadow areas were not reduced any more in the Levels dialog box; rather, for fine-tuning the shadows, the Curves dialog box was used, as you'll see in the next section. If the white areas in your image are too light, try dragging the white Output Levels control to the left.

If you've moved the sliders too much in your experimentation and you're unhappy with the results, you can reset the image by holding OPTION (PC users: ALT) while you click on the Reset button in the Levels dialog box. (When you press OPTION or ALT, the Cancel button changes into a Reset button.)

13

Eyedropper readouts, before and after adjustments

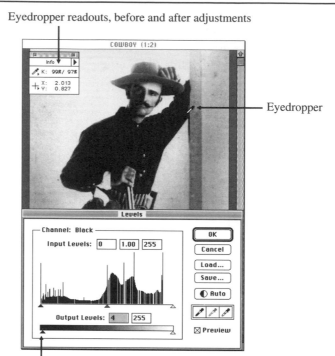

Eyedropper

Using the
Levels
dialog box
to lighten
shadows

FIGURE 13-6

Slider moved from 0 to 4

IP: *If you achieve Levels settings that you think you will use frequently, you can keep them handy by clicking on the Save and Load buttons. You can even work on a low-resolution image, save the settings, and apply them to high-resolution files.*

You might have noticed the three eyedropper icons and the Auto button in the Levels dialog box. The white and black eyedroppers can be used to automatically expand an image's tonal range, which can become compressed during the digitization process. The eyedroppers and the Auto button will be discussed later in this chapter.

Next you will investigate Photoshop's most powerful and precise tool for adjusting colors and tones: the Curves dialog box.

Using the Curves Command

The Curves dialog box is probably the most versatile and powerful of Photoshop's tone- and color-correcting utilities. It allows the adjustment of any point on an image's tonal curve. By clicking on your image when the dialog box is open, you can also find where that portion of your image is plotted on the curve.

When the cowboy image (Figure 13-1a) was corrected, the Curves dialog box was used to precisely pinpoint shadow areas that were above 95%.

Select Curves from the Image/Adjust submenu. In the Curves dialog box, you see a graph displaying a diagonal line. The x-axis (horizontal) on this graph represents an image's Input values; these are the brightness values in the image when the dialog box opens. The y-axis (vertical) represents the Output values, which will be the new values after the curve is changed. Perhaps it's easiest to think of Input values as the "before" values and Output values as the "after" values. When the dialog box first opens, since no values have been changed, all Input values equal all Output values. This produces a diagonal line because at each point on the graph, the x- and y-axis values are the same. The range of both Input and Output values is from 0 (black) to 255 (white).

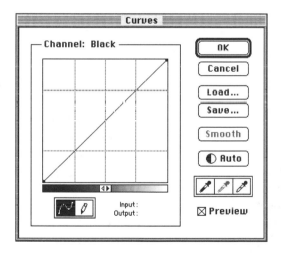

To see a readout of the points on the diagonal line, move the mouse pointer over the graph. The pointer will change to a crosshair. Click anywhere on the diagonal line and you will see that both the Input and Output values are displayed at the bottom of the Curves dialog box. Notice that both values are the same. If the dialog box hasn't been changed from its default settings, the gradient bar (under the graph) depicting the gray values of the x-axis starts at black and gradually blends to white. If the gradient bar on your screen starts at white and blends to black, click on either one of the arrows in the middle of the bar, or click on the bar itself, to reset the curve to the default settings.

13

When black is the starting point on the x-axis, the bottom-left corner of the graph—with coordinates of 0,0—plots the darkest part of the image. The upper-right corner—255,255—represents the lightest point in the image. The slope of the line represents the tonal range, with its bottom depicting the image's shadows and its top the image's highlights. The middle of the slope represents the midtones. The coordinates between the midtones and the highlights are called the *quarter (1/4) tones*. The coordinates between the midtones and the shadows are called the *three-quarter (3/4) tones*.

Since the curve allows you to change an image's tonal range, highlights are adjusted by clicking and dragging on the top part of the diagonal line in the graph, shadows by clicking and dragging on the bottom part of the diagonal line, and midtones by clicking and dragging in the middle of the diagonal line.

If you click on the arrows in the gradient bar to reverse black and white endpoints, the tone curve is also reversed, causing shadows to be represented at the top right of the graph and highlights at the bottom left. This also causes Input and Output levels to be displayed in percentages of black from 0% to 100%. You may prefer to work using percentage values, since the percentages of black correspond to the percentage values of halftone dots that make up a grayscale image. If you do work with the percentage values, remember that the curve directions will be opposite those given in this chapter.

The curve icon and the pencil icon at the bottom-left of the dialog box tell you what mode you are in. When the curve icon is active (the background of the icon is black) you are in *curve mode*; in this mode you adjust the diagonal line by setting *control points* on it and then dragging the point to move the line until it becomes a curve. When the pencil icon is active, you are in *arbitrary mode*; in this mode the pencil is used to draw new lines in the graph. The arbitrary mode is used primarily for creating special effects.

As stated earlier, the Curves dialog box is unique because it can pinpoint any area of an image along the curve's tonal range. When you position the mouse pointer over part of an image and click, a circle appears on the curve, displaying exactly where that image pixel is plotted. All image areas corresponding to that point on the curve are edited by adjusting the point where the white circle appears.

To see this powerful feature in action, move the mouse pointer outside the Curve dialog box and click anywhere in your image. Notice that the mouse pointer turns into the Eyedropper tool and the circle appears on the curve, representing the pixel's exact tonal location. Now click on any dark or shadow area of your image. The circle appears at the bottom of the curve. Examine the Input and Output values; they should reflect low numbers (0 to 60). Now click on any highlight or bright area. The circle moves toward the top of the curve, and Input and Output values increase to about

200 or greater. Click on the gray or midtone areas of your image. Now the circle is in the middle of the curve, and the Input and Output values are near 128.

To help you better understand how to use the curve to adjust shadows, midtones, and highlights, let's say you want to lighten the darkest areas of your image and darken the lightest areas. Position the pointer at the lowest point in the curve; try to get the Input and Output readouts close to 0,0. (If you don't see a readout of values, you've undoubtedly positioned the crosshair off the graph. If so, move the crosshair so it touches the graph.) Click on the diagonal line and drag upward. A dot, the control point, will appear on the line, showing the precise point were you clicked on the curve. As you drag, try to keep the Input readout at 0. Drag until the Output value is 10. As you drag, your image becomes lighter.

Dragging the curve tells Photoshop to take the darkest pixels and remap them to a value of 10. This lightens the shadow areas. But because you are clicking and dragging a curve, and not just one individual point, other Input values besides the 0 value change to new Output values. You can see this by examining the middle point of the curve; it's now higher. When you clicked and dragged on the shadow area of the curve, some of the midtone values came along for the ride. If you truly want to isolate the shadow area and keep other Input values from changing, click on the graph to establish control points to serve as anchors on the curve, as described next.

Suppose you wish to darken the highlights in your image, but you want to restrict the change from the midtones. To prevent areas other than the highlights from changing, set a control point. To set a control point in the midtone area, click about halfway along the curve. A small dot will appear, indicating that a control point exists. Create another control point at the beginning of the highlight area, at about 190 on the graph. Now position the pointer on the top area of the diagonal, and then click and drag down. Notice how the curve bends as you drag the new control point while the other control points serve as anchors. To prevent swaying in the middle of the curve, you can add more control points. If you need to eliminate a control point, click on the point and drag it off the curve.

Figure 13-7 shows the Curves dialog box being used to lighten just the darkest shadows of the cowboy image. Look carefully and you'll see control points applied at each quadrant along the diagonal line, as well as at two additional points in the shadow area. The highest control point in the shadow quadrant was used to anchor the lighter shadows so that they would barely be affected when the curve was changed. The lowest point was the one dragged upward to lighten the darkest shadows. Afterward, the mouse pointer, which turns into an eyedropper, was placed over the image to sample the change. The mouse was clicked to locate the adjusted image area on the curve, and a circle appeared in the graph to indicate the area that

13

Eyedropper readout, before and after adjustments

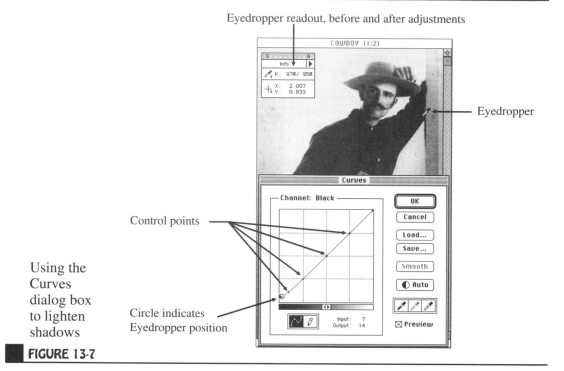

Eyedropper

Control points

Using the
Curves
dialog box
to lighten
shadows

Circle indicates
Eyedropper position

FIGURE 13-7

was clicked on. The Info palette confirmed that the image areas had been changed to the desired percentage, 95%.

To gain more of a feel for using the curves, try a few more tonal adjustments. First, reset the curve by pressing OPTION (PC users: ALT) and then clicking on the Reset button. Assume that you've already adjusted an image's highlights and shadows, yet the image is too dark. To lighten an image overall, set a control point in the middle of the curve and drag the curve upwards. If your image is too light, you can darken it by dragging in the opposite direction.

Reset the slope to the default settings again so that you can create a curve that will be used to bring out the contrast in images that are flat. This type of curve is called an *S curve*. To create it, drag the top part of the slope up to lighten hightlights; then drag the bottom of the slope down to darken shadows. This creates the *S*-shaped curve shown in Figure 13-8.

With the *S* curve created, move the mouse pointer over your image and examine the Info palette. Notice the readout that shows the before-and-after brightness values.

If you'd like, continue experimenting with the Curves dialog box, making adjustments to the highlights, midtones, and shadows in your image. Remember, if

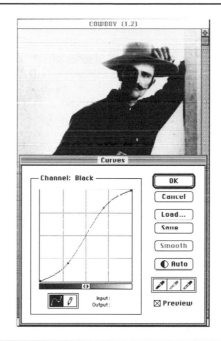

Create an *S* curve to add contrast to an image

■ **FIGURE 13-8**

you find a setting for the curve that you will need later, save it by clicking on the Save button. A curve can be reloaded by clicking on the Load button.

Using the Curves Arbitrary Mode to Create Special Effects

In both grayscale and color images, you can create special effects by clicking on the Curves dialog box's pencil icon and then dragging it over the graph to create either lines or curves. Before leaving the Curves dialog box, try using the pencil icon in the arbitrary mode. To switch from the curve mode to the arbitrary mode, click on the pencil icon at the bottom of the Curves dialog box.

One effect you can create is to posterize (reduce the gray levels) of your image. Use the pencil to create some small lines cutting through the diagonal line, as shown in Figure 13-9. The more lines and the longer they are, the greater the posterizing effect will be.

To invert your image to create a negative, click on the top-left corner of the graph; then press and hold the SHIFT key while you click on the bottom-right corner of the graph. This produces a diagonal line from the top-left corner to the bottom-right corner, thus making all black areas white and all white areas black, as shown in

13

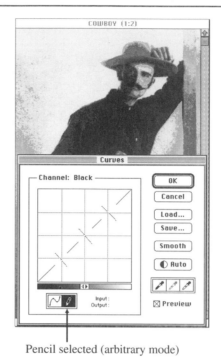

Use the pencil to draw lines along the graph in the Curves dialog box to create a posterized effect

Pencil selected (arbitrary mode)

Figure 13-10. Creating this slope produces the same effect as executing the Image/Map/Invert command, which is described in Chapter 11.

To create a *solarized* effect, which turns part of your image into a negative, use the pencil to change your graph to look like the one in Figure 13-11. To create this graph quickly, click on the bottom-left corner of the graph, then SHIFT-click in the center of the graph. SHIFT-click again on the bottom-right corner. The resulting image looks the same as if you had applied the Solarize filter from the Filter/Stylize submenu.

There are many other special effects you can create by using the pencil icon to adjust the graph in the Curves dialog box. For instance, you can use the pencil to create a few individual lines and then join them by clicking on the Smooth button.

Using the Dodge and Burn Tools to Darken and Lighten Areas

If the areas in your image that need lightening or darkening are small and don't need much tonal adjustment, you might wish to use the Dodge and/or Burn tools for the task.

As discussed in Chapter 6, the Dodge and Burn tools are used to lighten and darken, respectively, portions of an image. Take a moment now, if you need to, and review the Dodge and Burn tools, which can also be used to make tonal corrections.

Reverse the
slope to
create a
negative
image

FIGURE 13-10

Use this
graph to
create a
solarized
effect

FIGURE 13-11

13

The Burn tool was used to add tone to the pistol in the cowboy's holster, as shown in Figure 13-12. Here the Exposure value was raised to 25% to add more contrast to the lighter midtones.

RETOUCHING IMAGES

Once you are happy with the shadows, midtones, and highlights of your image, you're ready to perform any retouching that might be necessary to clean up the image or make it better than the original. Before you begin retouching, you should develop a game plan. Decide which areas you will fix first, and which ones you will do last. To get started and give yourself a better feel for your image, it's often best to begin with the elements that will be easiest to fix, and then proceed to the more difficult ones. Once you have analyzed your image and decided how to proceed, you are ready to begin retouching.

Using the Burn tool to darken the lighter midtones of the pistol handle

FIGURE 13-12

IP: *As you work, it's often helpful to have two windows open, both containing the same image but set to different magnifications. This way you can zoom into a specific area, yet view the results of your work simultaneously at actual size. To open a duplicate window on screen, choose New Window from the Window menu. Also, don't forget that when you zoom in, you can use the Toolbox's Pencil tool with the smallest, hard-edged brush to edit your image one pixel at a time.*

Now let's see how the worn and faded cowboy photograph in Figure 13-1a was retouched.

Retouching Old Photographs

Old photographs often present significant challenges in retouching. The pictures are often marred by spots and scratches, as well as being torn and faded. For very damaged photographs, be prepared to apply some painting and drawing skills to re-create entire sections in your digitized image.

Start by looking for any dust, dirt, scratches, or spots that appear in your image as a result of the digitizing process or due to a flawed original. Spots and scratches can usually be eliminated by using the Rubber Stamp's cloning option to clone background areas over the particles. If you do need to correct spots and scratches, experiment with different opacities until you achieve a soft and natural effect.

In the cowboy image, the dirt spots in the original photograph and the dust spots introduced by the scanner were cloned away with the Rubber Stamp. After the spots were removed, the hat was the next item to be retouched, since it was the simplest part of the project. A sample from another part of the hat was duplicated over the faded area.The retouching continued from the hat down to the leg and foot—the most difficult area to correct.

Follow along with the techniques used to retouch the cowboy image, and try them in the Hands file (PC users: hands.jpg) or in the image you are using. If you are working with the Hands file, you may wish to retouch the cracks and broken parts of the statue's face.

To restore the cowboy's left arm, the Eyedropper, Airbrush, Paintbrush, and Rubber Stamp tools were all put to use. First the Eyedropper was activated to change the foreground color to match the gray tone of the arm. Then the Airbrush tool was selected and used to paint a light outline to serve as a boundary that would not be

13

Photoshop in Action

Before Retouching

Jacket was too light, lacking tone.

Notice the unnatural-looking white brush strokes.

Notice the white lines and that the leg is barely noticeable.

Photograph courtesy of the Library of Congress

This picture of hobos taken in the early 1900s was needed for the Reader's Digest book *Discovering America's Past*. Years ago a retoucher began correcting the image traditionally, but stopped in the middle of the job. Notice the white brush strokes on the pants and jacket sleeve of the hobo on the right, and on the jacket sleeve of the hobo in the center. These were painted in by the retoucher. Adele was asked to finish the job so that the picture looked natural.

Photoshop in Action

After Retouching

Tone was added to jacket.

The white brush strokes were removed.

The white brush strokes are gone and the leg is more visibly defined.

Retouched by: Adele Droblas Greenberg   **Client: Reader's Digest General Books**

Before beginning to retouch the image, Adele used the Eyedropper tool to take readings of the image. Areas that were too dark (in the background) were lightened and areas that were too light (the white brush strokes and the ground) were darkened using the Levels and Curves dialog boxes. In addition, she used both the Dodge and Burn tools to lighten and darken various areas in the image that needed to be corrected.

To add more tone to the jacket of the hobo on the left, Adele used the Rubber Stamp's cloning option. Then she used the Airbrush tool with a soft-edged brush and varied the opacity setting and brush size to create a more natural-looking image. Before activating the Airbrush tool, Adele used the Eyedropper tool to change the foreground color to match the gray tones in the image.

To paint over the white brush strokes on the jacket sleeve and pants of the hobo on the right and on the jacket sleeve of the hobo in the center, Adele used the Airbrush and Rubber Stamp tools. As she worked, she used the Rubber Stamp's Clone options, From Saved and From Snapshot, to complete the retouching process.

13

painted over. The boundary line helped Adele visualize the missing limb while she worked to re-create it.

Airbrush

The area where the limb was re-created was painted using the Rubber Stamp and the Paintbrush, with a medium-sized, soft-edged brush. Although a mask could have been used to isolate the arm, it wasn't necessary. If the area beyond the boundary line were painted over, it could have been easily corrected by changing the foreground color to the correct color and painting with that color.

EMEMBER: *If you want to be cautious, or if an area is particularly intricate, you should create a mask and then work in the unprotected (selected) area bordered by the mask. See Chapter 12.*

The Airbrush tool was also used to restore detail and tone to the shotgun. The edges of the shotgun's handle were restored with a small, hard-edged brush with Pressure set at 50%.

After the simpler retouching tasks were completed, all that remained was to completely restore the lower part of the left leg. This was more difficult to repair because it required that more details be created. Several steps were involved: First, the Airbrush tool was used to sketch the left leg, as shown in Figure 13-13. Again, the outline served as a boundary line to visualize the missing limb.

Once the left leg was sketched, the Lasso was used to select the lower right leg. This selection was duplicated by OPTION-dragging (PC users: ALT-dragging) on the selection. The selection was flipped, using the Image/Flip/Horizontally command, and then the leg was cut and pasted into a new file. Remember, when you copy or cut an image and create a new file, the new file settings will be the same size as the cut or copied image.

After the right leg was duplicated, flipped, and placed in a new file, the flipped image and the original one were placed side by side so that the flipped leg could be cloned into the original file. In Figure 13-14, the crosshair indicates the sampled area; the rubber stamp pointer shows the target area where the cloning is being applied.

Using the Airbrush to create an outline for the missing part of the left leg and foot

FIGURE 13-13

Airbrush

13

Rubber stamp

Crosshair

Retouching the lower left leg by cloning the flipped lower right leg

FIGURE 13-14

Before using the Rubber Stamp's clone option, the file was saved so Adele could revert to the last saved version if necessary. As Adele worked, she used the Edit/Take Snapshot command so that she could used the Rubber Stamp's From Snapshot option to revert to the snapshot version of the file. See Chapter 6 for more information on the Take Snapshot command.

After all the retouching was finished, the Unsharp Mask filter was applied to the image to sharpen it and bring out details. Chapter 8 describes this filter.

Removing Wrinkles or Freckles from Faces

Another common task of the retoucher is to eliminate facial wrinkles and otherwise touch up images of people—particularly for advertising projects. Using the Rubber Stamp's cloning feature and the Smudge and Airbrush tools, wrinkles and blemishes can easily be removed.

In the following illustration, the image on the left shows wrinkles surrounding a person's eye before retouching; on the right is the retouched image.

Eye with wrinkles
before retouching

Eye without wrinkles
after retouching

The trick to removing wrinkles or any other facial blemish is to apply a vibrant skin color over that area of the image. Dark skin crevices can easily be blended into lighter flesh tones with the help of the Smudge and Rubber Stamp tools.

Start by using the Zoom tool to magnify the target area. Next use the Eyedropper to change the foreground color to the desired skin color. Then use the Smudge, Rubber Stamp, and Airbrush tools to blend skin tones together in the magnified area. For a gentler, softer effect, use a small-to-medium, soft-edged brush with Opacity set from 2% to 90%.

In our example, the smaller wrinkles were blended into the face using the Smudge tool. To remove the more pronounced lines, the Rubber Stamp's cloning option was used to clone the surrounding tones. The Airbrush tool was then applied to produce a more subtle blend.

If you want to try removing wrinkles from an image, practice on the left hand in the Hands file (PC users: hands.jpg). To experiment with removing freckles, open the Portrait file (PC users: portrait.jpg) in the Tutorial folder. Use the Zoom tool to magnify the girl's nose; then try using the Rubber Stamp, Airbrush, and/or Smudge tools to remove the freckles.

Retouching Landscapes

Retouching not only restores old photographs and makes people look younger and more glamorous but it is also used to transform landscapes so that they are more attractive than their real-life originals.

13

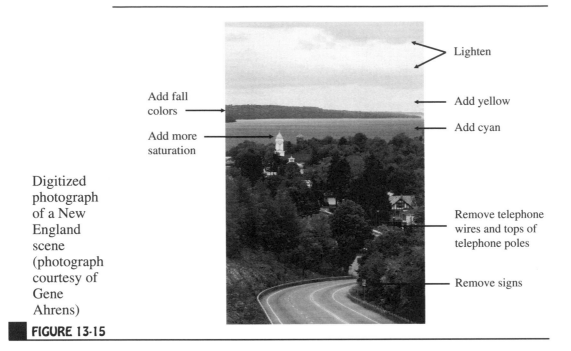

Lighten

Add fall colors

Add yellow

Add cyan

Add more saturation

Remove telephone wires and tops of telephone poles

Remove signs

Digitized photograph of a New England scene (photograph courtesy of Gene Ahrens)

FIGURE 13-15

For example, the art director of Reader's Digest General Books, Dave Trooper, wanted the scene for the cover of a proposed book, *Back Roads of America,* to look better than reality. The original image was a near-perfect photograph of a lovely New England scene. Figure 13-15 shows the image before retouching (also reproduced as image 1 in the color insert of this book).

Marring the beauty of the original image were the telephone poles and overhead wires running through the town. For the cover design, Dave wanted to put a map next to the photograph and to remove the road sign for Junction 14. The stop light warning sign, barely visible behind the trees, was also deemed a detraction and needed to be erased. Figure 13-16 shows the final retouched image (also reproduced as image 2 in the color insert of this book).

The Junction 14 sign was the first item to be retouched. The Rubber Stamp's cloning option was used to remove it, with a medium, hard-edged brush rather than a soft-edged brush. A soft-edged brush would have made the cloned area look unnatural because the leaves on the trees were sharp and crisp, not soft and faded. To maintain a natural look, a variety of different leaves from several tree areas were sampled and cloned over the sign. During the cloning process, the Brushes palette Opacity was set to varying values between 65% to 85% to blend the leaves into the trees.

—— Crosshair

—— Rubber stamp

To eliminate the stop light warning sign, part of the road was cloned over the sign, and the trees were extended into the road. The Rubber Stamp's cloning feature and the Airbrush were both used to retouch the area. Some of the railing area was re-created with the Airbrush because the cloning tool couldn't create a perfect match between the old railing and the new railing.

Proposed book cover after retouching and color correcting

FIGURE 13-16

13

Then the Rubber Stamp's cloning option was used again, this time to remove the unwanted wires. For a more natural effect, both a hard-edged and a medium soft-edged brush were used. Opacity was set to about 75% to blend the new leaves with the old leaves.

Rubber stamp   Crosshair

The next section provides an overview of how to undertake a color-correction project, and we will continue using the book cover project as an example. If you have a grayscale image on screen, close it now because you will be using a color file for the remainder of this chapter. If you wish to rename your file and create another copy of it, use the Save As command. Otherwise, close the file without saving it.

COLOR CORRECTING

Many of the same issues involved in grayscale tonal correcting also arise when you're *color* correcting. As with grayscale images, it may be possible to transform an inferior color original or poorly scanned color picture into a perfect image. Exposure and lighting defects found in many grayscale images are also the most common problems in color images. But correcting color is much more complicated than correcting grays because every pixel has the potential of being any one of millions of possible colors, rather than just 256 levels of gray.

The number of colors in an image brings up an important display issue: If your image contains many more colors than your monitor can display, color correcting that image will be difficult. With a video card that only displays 256 colors, you won't be able to accurately judge the colors of continuous-tone images by their appearance on screen. So if you are serious about color correcting, you will want to invest in a 24-bit video card, which can display over 16 million colors.

Even if your system is calibrated and you are working in 24-bit color, you still must be wary of how colors look on your screen. As discussed in Chapter 4, differences between onscreen and printed colors are to be expected. The best way to judge colors is by using the Eyedropper tool and the Info palette. If you are working on color images that will be printed, it's crucial that CMYK colors are displayed in the Info palette. This readout will display exclamation points alongside the CMYK values of any colors that fall beyond the CMYK printing gamut.

Always check the Info palette when you're analyzing onscreen colors. For instance, if an apple on the screen looks rich, juicy, and crisp, but the Info palette reading lacks a high magenta percentage, this tells you that your monitor is not displaying the correct colors. For bright red, you should see CMYK values of cyan 20%, magenta 100%, yellow 80%, and black 5%, or RGB values of red 168, green 0, and blue 61.

To see the Eyedropper and Info palette in action, load an RGB or CMYK file (if you don't already have a color image on screen). For an RGB file, you can load Bad Scan 1 (PC users: badscan1.jpg) or Bad Scan 2 (PC users: badscan2.jpg) from the Tutorial folder. For a CMYK file, load the Olé No Moiré file from the Separation Sources folder found in the Calibration folder (PC users: testcalib.jpg file from the calib folder).

If the Info palette is not displayed, open it now. If you do not see the RGB and CMYK percentages, click on the Options menu arrow (PC users: Control menu button) in the Info palette. In the Info Options dialog box, make sure that the Mode pop-up menus for First Color and Second Color Readouts are set to RGB and CMYK.

You might wonder why you should keep the RGB values displayed in the Info palette if you are working on a CMYK color file. As discussed in Chapter 4, when you *add* cyan, magenta, or yellow to an image, you *subtract* its complement (red, green, or blue). When you *subtract* cyan, magenta, or yellow, you *add* the color's complement. With both color readouts showing in the Info palette, you'll be able to judge how much of a color or its complement is added or subtracted.

Take a look at the relationship between RGB and CMYK colors in your image. Move the mouse pointer over your image, and notice that any color showing a high RGB value displays a low percentage of its CMYK complement, and vice versa. For instance, a color with a high red value displays a low cyan percentage, and a color with a high cyan percentage displays a low red value. The relationship between RGB and CMYK colors is clearly depicted in a color wheel, as discussed in Chapter 4. Before you start color correcting, you may wish to get a color wheel (such as the

13

one shown on the first page of the color insert of this book) and keep it handy. On a color wheel, each color resides between the two colors that create it. For instance, green is created by adding cyan and yellow. On the opposite side of each color is its complement; for example, opposite green on the color wheel is magenta.

Color-Correcting Tips

As you work on color-correction projects, here are a few suggestions to keep in mind:

FASHION   Work carefully with pure white and pure black fabric colors; it's difficult to hold detail and definition in pure white and pure black cloth. Too much yellow will make white look creamy. You might wish to obtain fabric samples so you can compare their real colors and materials with a color proof.

PEOPLE   Strands of hair should be as sharply defined as possible. Teeth should be white rather than dull and yellow, though pure white teeth will look unreal. Consult your print shop concerning the effects of dot gain on flesh tones. Here are some CMYK and RGB values to use as starting points: (C=20%, M=45%, Y=50%, K=0%) or (R=203, G=154, B=125) should be a satisfactory reading for Caucasian flesh tones; for black flesh tones, aim for (C=40%, M=45%, Y=50%, K=30%) or (R=123, G=106, B=93).

FOOD   Images containing a variety of food can be difficult to correct; it's often difficult to make all the food in a shot look delicious. For example, brilliant red tomatoes may look delicious, but meat that red will appear raw. Analyze or ask your client what should be the most important element in the image. Foods that do not have readily identifiable colors, such as cereals and soup, can be difficult to correct.

LANDSCAPES   Green landscapes produced with too much cyan and yellow can turn out too yellow or too blue. Magenta adds detail, but too much will turn your image muddy. Use black to make greens darker, rather than magenta. Look at the neutral grays in the landscape to make sure they are gray and aren't exhibiting color casts. When creating sky, the relationship between cyan and magenta will determine the shade of sky you are creating. For instance, by adding more and more magenta, you can go from bright blue to dark blue.

SNOW SCENES   Snow should not be pure white; otherwise, detail will be lost. Concentrate on adding detail to the highlights. Avoid losing detail in darker areas when enhancing whites.

RGB or CMYK?

A question that many Photoshop users wrestle with is whether to work in an RGB Color or a CMYK Color file. In making your decision, consider the following guidelines.

For output to slides or video, color correct in RGB because slides and video use RGB colors rather than CMYK. For output to a printing press, you may want to color correct in CMYK so you will be working with the same colors that your print shop uses for your job.

It is helpful to color correct in CMYK colors when you are adjusting blacks in your image. If need be, you can adjust only the blacks in a CMYK file by making adjustments to the black channel (with RGB colors, no black channel is available).

Since CMYK files are always larger than their RGB counterparts, you may wish to color-correct in RGB mode to work efficiently with large color images.

OTE: *If you are working with an RGB Color file with the Info palette's CMYK reading displayed, be aware that the CMYK Color equivalents change based on the settings in the Separation Setup dialog box. For more information about this dialog box, see Chapter 9.*

If you are correcting an image that was digitized on a high-end scanner, chances are that the image was saved as a CMYK Color file. If you scanned the image yourself on a low-range or midrange flatbed or slide scanner, the file will probably be digitized in RGB rather than CMYK. Digital and video cameras will digitize images in RGB rather than CMYK color.

If you wish to work in CMYK mode, you can do so by converting your RGB Color image to CMYK Color. But do not convert to CMYK without first verifying the settings in the Monitor Setup, Printing Inks Setup, and Separation Setup dialog boxes. Before converting an image to CMYK, review Chapter 9. It's important to understand that if you convert to CMYK with improper calibration settings, you may be forced to return to your original RGB file. Once you have reset the calibration options to the correct settings, you'll need to reconvert to CMYK and start color correcting again from scratch.

If your system cannot handle large, high-resolution CMYK Color files, another alternative is to work on a low-resolution color file and save your dialog box settings, or write them down. Then use the Load button in the Levels, Curves, Hue/Saturation, and Variations dialog boxes to apply the settings to the high-resolution version, and make final color adjustments as needed.

13

PROCEDURES FOR COLOR CORRECTING

When you are ready to color correct an image, your first steps should be to correct the overall tonal range of the image. Then proceed to correct specific areas.

The New England scene in the Reader's Digest book cover, first discussed in the "Retouching Images" section of this chapter, will be used here to demonstrate the steps involved in color correcting.

The image was scanned by a prepress house on a high-end drum scanner to obtain the best digitization. In the scanning process, the image was converted to a CMYK file and saved in TIFF format. Since the file was over 30MB, it was saved on a Syquest cartridge so it could be delivered to the client.

After examining a Matchprint (a proof made from film separations) from the original scan, it was decided that the clouds should be lightened so that the book title would stand out as much as possible. The decision to color correct was made not because the original image or scan was flawed but because the design of the book cover required it. The art director also decided to enhance the color of the foliage in the town. Additionally, he felt that the color of the water and church dome were a little light and wanted the saturation increased. Finally, he wanted a more autumn-like look to the hills across the bay.

Before color correcting, the colors in the Matchprint were compared to those on the CMYK Color file on the monitor. After analyzing the two, slight calibration changes were made in the Gray Balance fields in the Printing Inks Setup dialog box. (For more information on calibrating to a proof, see Chapter 14.)

Taking Readings with the Eyedropper and Info Palette

The next step in color correcting the New England image was to analyze the problem areas as well as the good areas using the Eyedropper and Info palette to carefully evaluate the colors.

Once you know the RGB values or CMYK percentages of the image areas, you can evaluate the colors that need to be added or taken out, and in what percentage. In the photograph for the proposed book cover, readings were taken of the clouds, water, hills across the bay, church dome, and foliage. The Eyedropper readings of some of the foliage showed a predominance of cyan, with little yellow and little magenta. These would obviously need to be boosted to improve the impression of autumn colors.

Using a Histogram to View the Tonal Range

After analyzing the areas that needed enhancement, the next step was to view the image's histogram. As explained earlier in this chapter, a histogram is useful for examining the tonal range of an image—from its brightest to darkest points. In a color image, a histogram provides not only a visual impression of the brightness values of the entire image but of the separate channels as well.

The histogram of the New England image before color correcting revealed that the tonal range was fairly broad, with few shadow pixels.

OTE: *If you are working with a CMYK Color file, you may wish to open the Channels palette and click on each channel to view its colors.*

To view a histogram of an RGB image, you can load the Bad Scan 1 file (PC users: badscan1.jpg) from the Tutorial folder. Or you can load a CMYK file, the Olé No Moiré file from the Separation Sources folder found in the Calibration folder (PC users: the testcalib.jpg file from the calib folder).

With the image file open on screen, choose Histogram from the Image menu. Click to open the Channel pop-up menu. If you are viewing a CMYK image, the Channel pop-up menu allows you to view brightness (luminance) values of the CMYK composite (Gray channel) and the color values of the individual Cyan, Magenta, Yellow, and Black channels. For an RGB image, you'll see a Gray channel for the composite brightness values and one for each of the Red, Green, and Blue channels.

13

If you are viewing the Bad Scan 1 file, click on the Channel pop-up menu in the Histogram dialog box, and take a moment to enter each channel to see the color values. You'll see that the image is lacking in shadow areas. If you are viewing the Bad Scan 2 file, you'll see that the image is lacking in highlight areas. In the next section, you'll learn how to stretch out the tonal range.

Setting a White, Black, and Neutral Point

 During scanning, an image's tonal range can be compressed, particularly by low-end scanners that cannot reproduce as broad a range of colors as high-end scanners. The histogram often reveals this compression: Images with compressed tonal ranges often look flat on the graph. One technique for expanding the tonal range of an image is to set a white (highlight) point and a black (shadow) point. By setting a white and black point, you specify areas in your image that you wish to have as its lightest point and darkest points. The eyedropper icons in the Curves and Levels dialog boxes, described earlier in the chapter, allow you to set these points—as well as a gray point to help eliminate color casts from an image.

The tasks of eliminating color casts and setting white and black points are often handled before an image is converted to CMYK. If your image was scanned on a high-end scanner and converted to CMYK (as the New England image was), you probably will not need to set a white, black, or gray point. On the other hand, when you work with RGB-digitized images, you should be aware of how setting these points can be helpful.

In Photoshop you can set the white and black points automatically, manually, or by setting levels in the Color Picker. As you work through the following paragraphs describing these methods, have on screen any color image; you may want to use the Bad Scan 2 file (PC users: badscan2) from the Tutorial folder.

Setting the White and Black Points Automatically

The easiest way to set the white and black points is to have Photoshop do it automatically. If you set the white and black points automatically using Photoshop's default settings, the lightest areas in an image are remapped to white and the darkest areas to black. This often expands the tonal range, providing more contrast to images that are flat and dull.

With your color image on screen, open the Levels dialog box (choose Levels from the Image/Adjust submenu). To have Photoshop set the white and black points automatically, click on the Auto button. Immediately you will see a change in your image, which is reflected in the histogram. In the histogram, you'll often see that the balance between shadows, midtones, and highlights is improved.

To ensure that Photoshop does not use only one tone when it sets the white and black points, a preset *clipping* percentage range is built in when Photoshop adjusts the image. This can prevent very light or very dark areas from overly influencing the tonal change when Photoshop sets the white and black points.

This clipping range can be changed in the Auto Range Options dialog box. To open the dialog box, press OPTION (PC users: ALT) and click on the Auto button. Acceptable values for the Black Clip and White Clip fields are from 0% to 9.99%. The value entered is the percentage that Photoshop will ignore when it automatically sets the white and black points. For instance, if you enter 9% in the Black Clip field, Photoshop ignores the darkest 9% of your image when it redistributes pixel values after you click on the Auto button.

If you are unhappy with the results of Photoshop's automatic setting of the white and black points, you can return your image to its original settings. First press and hold down OPTION (PC users: ALT); the Cancel button will change to a Reset button. Click Reset to return your image to its original settings, and then try the manual method of setting white and black points.

Manually Setting the White and Black Points with the Eyedroppers and Color Picker

To gain more control when you set the white and black points, you can use the eyedroppers in the Levels and Curves dialog boxes to pick the lightest and darkest points in your image. From these dialog boxes, you can also use the eyedroppers to access the Color Picker to set color levels for the white and black points. If you choose this method, you'll first want to take color readings with the eyedroppers to locate the lightest and darkest parts of your image. But don't click on the eyedroppers in the dialog box yet.

First locate the lightest and darkest parts of your image. Move the mouse pointer (which will change to an eyedropper) over the lightest areas of your image, and examine the Info palette readouts as you go. Very light areas will display high values of each R, G, and B component. Generally, when evaluating an image to set the white point, you should search for highlight areas with detail, not pure white areas.

Next, locate the darkest part of your image and move the eyedropper over it. Dark image areas will display low values of each R, G, and B component. When searching for the black point, look for shadow areas that are not pure black.

OTE: *With the Levels dialog box open, you can identify the lightest and darkest portions of an image by using the OPTION (PC users: ALT) drag method described earlier in this chapter.*

Now that you've found the lightest and darkest points, you're ready to set a white and a black level. By setting white and black levels, you can avoid losing detail in highlight and shadow areas when the white and black points are set.

To set a value for the white level, double-click on the white eyedropper in the Levels dialog box. The Color Picker dialog box opens; notice the words "Select white target color" at the top.

Let's assume you want to ensure that the lightest areas of your image are not pure white, not created from the absence of ink on paper. Entering the following values in the CMYK fields should provide good results: C=5, M=3, Y=3, K=0. Click OK to close the Color Picker.

Now move the Eyedropper tool over the lightest portion of your image that you identified earlier, and click the mouse. Photoshop automatically adjusts the tonal range so the lightest areas match the white point you set.

The procedure for setting a target value for the black point is virtually identical to that for setting the white point, except you use the black eyedropper. Double-click on the black eyedropper. The Color Picker dialog box opens, and you'll see the words "Select black target color" at the top. The following values should help to ensure detail in shadow areas: C=95, M=83, Y=83, K=80. Click OK to close the Color Picker.

Now move the eyedropper pointer over the darkest portion of your image that you identified earlier, and click the mouse. The tonal range is adjusted so that the darkest areas in the image match the black point you set.

If the results of setting the black and white points are not satisfactory, try setting different points in the image, or slightly adjusting the White and Black point levels in the Color Picker. If you want more practice, try setting white and black points on the Bad Scan 1 (PC users: badscan1.jpg) file in the Tutorial folder. You'll see a dramatic improvement in the contrast.

OTE: *When you are setting the white and black points of a grayscale image, you may wish to set the white point at 5% in the K field (leave the CMY fields blank) and the black point at K=95% (again, leave the CMY fields blank).*

 OTE: *If you set color levels for white and black points in the Color Picker dialog box, they will be used when you set the white and black points with the Auto button.*

After setting the white and black points, you may wish to fine-tune the tonal balance in your image by lightening or darkening it. If so, you can use the Output Levels slider in the Levels dialog box to reduce the white and dark values of your image. As described earlier in this chapter, drag the right-hand Output Levels slider control to the left to reduce the brightness in image highlights, and drag the left-hand Output Levels slider control to the right to lighten shadow areas. You may also want to enhance the midtones; do this by clicking on the middle (gamma) Input Levels slider control. As discussed earlier in this chapter, dragging left lightens midtones, and dragging right darkens them.

When you're satisfied with the tonal adjustments in your image, click OK. Your next step is to eliminate any color casts that may exist.

Adjusting for Color Casts by Defining a Neutral Tone

Color casts can be the result of several factors. Photographs taken in fluorescent light often produce pink color casts. Outdoor images taken with indoor film might display a blue color cast. Indoor scenes shot with daylight film may yield a yellow color cast. Color casts can also be introduced inadvertently during the digitizing process.

Both the Curves and Levels dialog boxes include a gray eyedropper icon that can be used to reduce color casts. Here are the steps: Click on the gray eyedropper in the dialog box and move it over your image to the most neutral, or gray, area. Click, and any color cast should disappear or be diminished. Photoshop shifts the hue and saturation values to match neutral gray (for an RGB image: red 127, blue 127, green 127) and continues to shift hue and saturation values to eliminate color casts. If you wish to specify the gray that Photoshop uses when it sets its neutral gray level, you can double-click on the gray eyedropper. This opens the Color Picker dialog box in which you enter the desired values.

13

Creating Masks to Isolate Areas to be Color Corrected

After you have adjusted the basic tonal range in your image and eliminated any unwanted color casts, you can proceed to the tasks of fine-tuning problem areas in your image. To color correct specific areas of an image, you must select them first. As discussed in Chapter 12, it is often helpful to create masks of these areas in alpha channels, since you will likely need to select them again and again. (There are various ways to create and edit a mask in an alpha channel. For more information, see Chapter 12.)

OTE: *If you wish, you can use the Pen tool to create a selection. First create a path and then save it as a selection. For more information about paths, see Chapter 10.*

In the New England image, five different masks were created in alpha channels: one for the church dome, one for the water, one for the hills across the bay, and two for different parts of the sky. These masks were created so that they could be reloaded in case more changes were needed. Because masks increase file size, only one mask was included in the New England file at a given time. The masks that weren't being used were exported into a new file using the Duplicate command in the Image/Calculate submenu. Masks of the foliage were created when needed using the Lasso tool and the Quick Mask mode. These masks weren't saved; they could easily be re-created and they didn't need to be as precise as the others.

Using the Image/Adjust Commands to Color Correct

Once all of the preparation work has been accomplished, you are ready to begin selective color correction. The same Image/Adjust commands you used to correct grayscale images are also available for correcting color images—except that more options are available. For instance, the Variations command allows saturation to be added and subtracted. The Curves and Levels dialog boxes allow you to work with the individual RGB or CMYK channels.

In color correcting the New England image, a selection was generally loaded before a dialog box was opened. As mentioned earlier, to work more efficiently, Adele had previously duplicated channels into separate files. When she needed to load the mask selection, she opened the file containing the alpha channels with the masks. Then she chose the Duplicate command from the Image/Calculate submenu to copy the channel into the New England image file. She loaded the dome selection using the Load Selection command in the Select menu and used the Variations command to color correct the dome.

Using the Variations Command

Often it's a good idea to begin correcting specific selections with the Variations command because it's the easiest and most intuitive color-correction tool to use. As described in the grayscale portion of this chapter, the Variations dialog box features thumbnails that preview how your image will be changed.

If you'd like to experiment with the Variations command, start by selecting an area of your color image, or load another selection you want to work with.

Choose Variations from the Image/Adjust submenu. When you are working with a color image, the Variations dialog box also allows you to adjust the saturation (purity) of a color, in addition to shadows, midtones, and highlights. Strong, full colors are saturated; pale colors are undersaturated; neutral tones, such as black, white, and gray, contain no saturation. In most instances, fully colored, saturated images are preferable—but too much saturation can also make an image look unreal, gaudy, or blotchy, which can also cause printing problems.

In the New England image, the Variations command was used to add a touch of yellow to the midtones of the church dome. Figure 13-17 shows the church dome selected; in the Variations dialog box, the Midtones radio button is chosen. After the midtones were enhanced, the Saturation radio button was selected, and the More Saturation thumbnail was clicked to boost saturation. The changes transformed the dome from looking flat to full-bodied.

Using the Color Balance Command

The next step in correcting the New England image was to add fall colors to the foliage in the town using the Color Balance command. This command allows you to mix colors together to improve the color balance in an image. If you have a sense of color theory, you will find the Color Balance dialog box to be very intuitive.

Before the Color Balance dialog box was opened, Eyedropper/Info palette readings of various selections of the foliage were taken and written down. During

13

Using the
Variations
dialog box
to adjust
the
saturation
in the
church's
dome

FIGURE 13-17

the correcting process, the Lasso tool and the Quick Mask mode were used to isolate the background trees that would be corrected.

Choose Color Balance from the Image/Adjust submenu. In the Color Balance dialog box you will see radio buttons for selecting Shadows, Midtones, and Highlights, and three color sliders. The first slider ranges from Cyan (on the left) to Red (on the right). The second slider ranges from Magenta to Green, and the third ranges from Yellow to Blue. If you move a slider control to the right, you add that slider's RGB color to your image. Move the slider control to the left, and you add that slider's complement (a CMYK color) to your image. By clicking and dragging the slider controls, you can move through the range of each RGB color and into the color range of its CMYK complement. RGB values go from 0 to 100, and CMYK colors are measured in negative numbers from 0 to -100.

In the New England image, the various selections of trees were made to look more autumn-like by adjusting the Color Balance sliders and selecting the Shadows, Midtones, and Highlights radio buttons. Most selections required adding more magenta and yellow and decreasing cyan. As the colors were changed, the

Eyedropper tool and Info palette were used to compare the old CMYK values to the new settings to ensure that they were the right color.

After the foliage was corrected, the hills selection was loaded to receive the same color correction. Red, magenta, and yellow were added to the shadows, midtones, and highlights. Besides providing fall color, the change also enhanced the detail in the hills. Figure 13-18 shows the selected hills and the red, magenta, and yellow values added to the midtones.

Using the Levels Command

The next step in color-correcting the New England image was to add cyan to the water. To do this, the Image/Adjust/Levels command was used because it allows more precise control than the Variations command. The Levels dialog box, like the Curves dialog box, gives you access to individual color channels for color correcting.

To add more cyan to the water, the Cyan channel was selected from the Channel pop-up menu in the Levels dialog box. The right-hand Output Levels slider control was dragged to the left to 236, as shown in Figure 13-19. This took the lightest cyan value over 236 and remapped it, making the cyan level darker; all values over 236 were remapped accordingly. (If the left-hand slider control had been dragged instead of the right, cyan would have been subtracted and red, cyan's complement, would have been added.) Notice that the Info palette in Figure 13-19 shows that when cyan was increased, the level of red in the RGB display in the Info palette decreased.

Using the Color Balance dialog box to add fall colors to the hills across the bay

 FIGURE 13-18

Eyedropper

Using the Levels dialog box to add more cyan to the water

FIGURE 13-19

Cyan increases

Red decreases

Slider moved from 255 to 236

If you'd like to try your hand at color correcting, open the Bad Scan 1 file (PC users: badscan1.jpg) in the Tutorial folder. Select a red area on screen; then open the Levels dialog box and switch channels in the Channel pop-up menu to Red. Click and drag on the left-hand Output Levels slider control. Notice that as you drag to the right, red is added. If you drag the right-hand Output Levels slider to the left, cyan is added. For each RGB and CMYK channel, the sliders will move from one color to its complement. The left Output Levels slider control is always an RGB color and the right Output Levels slider control is its CMYK complement. The left Input Levels slider control is always a CMYK color and the right Input Levels slider control is always an RGB color.

Using the Curves Command

The next step taken in the New England image was to lighten the clouds in the sky using the Image/Curves command. The Curves dialog box allows a specific area to be corrected precisely by pinpointing the area on the curve, and so it was the best tool to use to correct the clouds. Before the correcting process began, the cloud selections were loaded as needed with the Load Selection command.

Like the Levels dialog box, the Curves dialog box allows entry into channels for correcting. When working with a CMYK color file, if a channel is chosen in the Channel pop-up menu, dragging downward on the curve will add the channel's color (when the gradient bar is set for dark to light); dragging upward will add its complement. If you click on the gradient bar so that it changes from light to dark, the directions for dragging the curve are reversed. When the gradient bar is set for light to dark, the Input and Output Levels are measured in CMYK percentages, rather than in values from 0 to 255. When working with an RGB Color file, if a channel is chosen in the Channel pop-up menu (and the gradient bar is set for dark to light), dragging downward on the curve will add the channel's complement color; drag up, and you add the channel's color.

Since the easiest way to lighten the dark clouds in the New England image was to remove black from the selection, the Black channel was chosen in the Curves dialog box. Next, the Eyedropper was used to click in the middle of the dark area in the cloud selection. A circle appeared on the curve showing the precise point that represented the cloud's color. To lighten the image, the part of the curve where the circle appeared was dragged upward and to the left. This lightened all areas in the same tonal range within the selection that corresponded to the curve value.

After the blacks were reduced in the cloud area, the Cyan channel was selected so that cyan could be reduced in the darkest parts of the clouds. To reduce cyan and add a bit of red, the part of the curve representing only the darkest part of the cloud was dragged upward. The Info palette in Figure 13-20 shows the change in the cyan (14% to 8%) and red (224 to 237) after the Eyedropper was clicked to resample the

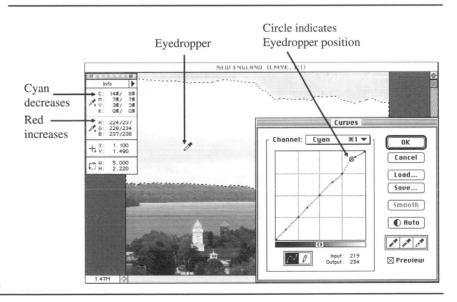

Using the Curves dialog box to reduce cyan and add red to the clouds

FIGURE 13-20

corrected area. When cyan was reduced, its complement, red, was added automatically.

To complete the correction of the clouds, a sensation of sun and warmth was added by adjusting the Yellow channel's curve downward.

After each of the above corrections, the Eyedropper was used to sample areas that were changed. By keeping an eye on the Info palette, it was possible to gauge the amount of each change.

Once all color correcting was done, the Unsharp Mask filter was applied to sharpen the image. (For more information on the Unsharp Mask filter, see Chapter 8.) The image was then saved on a Syquest cartridge and delivered to Reader's Digest General books, and from there to the prepress house that had scanned the image. From the retouched and color-corrected image file, the prepress house produced a Matchprint, which was used as a proof before printing the image. A color print of the final image is reproduced as image 2 in the color insert of this book.

Using the Hue/Saturation Command

Even though the Hue/Saturation command was not used to color correct any part of the New England image, this dialog box can be very helpful when you wish to focus on changing the hue, saturation, or lightness values of colors. The Hue/Saturation dialog box features a color sample that helps you focus on exactly how a color is being changed.

If you want to test the Hue/Saturation color-correction controls, first use the Eyedropper tool to click on a color that you wish to adjust. This changes your foreground color to the image color that will be displayed in the dialog box. Next, choose Hue/Saturation from the Image/Adjust submenu.

In the Hue/Saturation dialog box you will see color swatches representing the additive (RGB) and the subtractive (CMY) colors. The Sample swatch at the bottom of the dialog box indicates the color that you clicked on with the Eyedropper. The sliders adjust the hue, saturation, and lightness of an image.

When you select the Master radio button, the Hue slider will move you through the colors on a color wheel, letting you adjust all of the colors in an image. If you click on a radio button for a particular color (rather than Master), you can change the hue, saturation, and lightness of the color by clicking and dragging on the appropriate slider control. Try clicking on the R (red) radio button. The Hue slider will change, showing an endpoint for M (magenta) and for Y (yellow). You can adjust the red levels by dragging the slider control to add and subtract magenta or yellow. In many respects, this is a linear representation of the color wheel: On the color wheel, red is between magenta and yellow. When you click and drag with the R (red) radio button selected, you change only the red values in your image.

Here is a list of the Hue/Saturation radio buttons and how the sliders change when you click on the buttons:

Radio Button	Slider Colors
R (Red)	M/Y
Y (Yellow)	R/G
G (Green)	Y/C
C (Cyan)	G/B
B (Blue)	C/M
M (Magenta)	B/R

Try selecting one of the radio buttons, and then click and adjust the Hue slider control to see how it changes the color. Try clicking and dragging on the Saturation and Lightness slider controls, too, to see how changing these settings affects your color. Drag the Saturation slider control to the right and the colors get more intense; drag to the left and the image becomes grayer as you remove saturation. Drag the Lightness slider control to the left and the color becomes darker.

If you select the Colorize check box option, the colors in the image change to one color. In this case, adjusting the slider controls lets you tint the image with the color controlled by the Hue slider. To review image colorization using the Hue/Saturation dialog box, turn to Chapter 9.

As you've seen, Photoshop provides enormous possibilities and many different options when you need to retouch or color correct an image. As you gain more experience with retouching and color correcting, you'll be better able to predict how changes in the relevant dialog boxes will affect your image on screen. You'll also be better able to judge the best retouching and/or color-correcting tool for the job at hand.

13

CALIBRATION AND OUTPUT

No matter how exquisite your Photoshop images, all of your design and image-editing work may be in vain if the final printed (or other) output does not match the onscreen image. To get sharp and vibrant printed images, you need to have a clear understanding of how they are produced and how system calibration affects output quality.

This chapter focuses on two subjects: the printing process and system calibration. Most Photoshop users do not need to have a thorough knowledge of the printing and calibration processes because the prepress house or print shop will take care of these complicated issues. On the other hand, even if you don't output your own proofs and film separations, and even if you don't have to set screen frequency in the Halftone Screens dialog box, understanding the prepress concepts covered in this chapter will make for a smoother and more efficient production process. With that goal in mind, this chapter provides an overview of the printing process, explains how proofs can be used to predict color accuracy, and shows you how to calibrate your system to a proof. It concludes with step-by-step instructions for printing separations, and a brief look at how to output to produce slides, chromes, and video images.

Once you grasp the printing process, you'll understand how output resolution, screen frequency, paper stock, and halftones effect the output quality of your images.

THE ROLE OF HALFTONES IN IMAGE OUTPUT

When an image is printed on a printing press, it consists of many small dots called *halftones*. The size and shape of these dots and the angle at which they are printed create the visual illusion of continuous grays or continuous colors. In traditional printing, halftones are created by placing a glass or mylar screen containing a grid of dots between an image and the film or negative paper on which the image is printed. This photomechanical process re-creates the image as a pattern of dots. Dark areas have large dots, and light areas have small dots.

In color publishing, cyan, magenta, yellow, and black screens are used in the traditional halftone process. The print quality depends on how close together the lines are. The finer the lines, the better the quality. The final result also depends upon the screen angles at which the halftones were created. Specific angles must be used in order to provide clear and consistent color. The traditional screen angles are 105 degrees for cyan, 75 degrees for magenta, 90 degrees for yellow, and 45 degrees for black. When screen angles are not corrected, a mottled and undesirable pattern, called a moiré, may appear. (An example of a moiré pattern can be seen in Chapter 8, Figure 8-1a.)

Commercial printers use the halftone screens to create plates for each of the four process colors. In the printing process, paper is printed with patterns of different-sized cyan, magenta, yellow, and black dots to create the illusion of countless colors. Take a magnifying glass and look closely at a printed color image, and you'll see the pattern of dots in various colors and sizes.

Digital Halftones

As in traditional printing, digital images that are output to a printer or imagesetter are also separated into halftone dots. The output device creates the halftone dots by turning groups of smaller dots, often referred to as pixels, on or off.

If the output device is an imagesetter, it can output to film as well as paper. An imagesetter producing output at a resolution of 2,450 dpi creates over 6 million dots per square inch. At 300 dpi, a standard laser printer creates images with 90,000 dots per square inch. The more dots an image has, the better its resolution and the higher its printed quality.

It's important to remember that these pixels are *not* the halftone dots. In the printing process, the pixels are organized into a system of cells, and it is within these cells that the halftone dots are created. For instance, the dots from a 1,200-dpi imagesetter might be divided into 100 cells per inch. By turning the pixels off or on inside each cell, the printer or imagesetter creates one halftone dot.

The number of halftone dots per inch is called the *screen frequency*, *screen ruling*, or *line screen* and is measured in lines per inch (lpi). A high screen frequency, such as 150 lpi, packs the dots very closely together, producing sharper images and distinct colors. When the screen frequency is low, the halftone dots are spread out and produce coarser images with less refined colors.

 EMEMBER: *For the highest-quality reproduction of digital images, image file resolution generally should be twice the screen frequency. To review the relationship between image resolution and screen frequency, see* Chapter 7.

Calculating Gray Levels

The number of pixels that the imagesetter turns off or on to create a halftone determines the maximum number of gray levels that can be printed in an image. The number of gray levels determines the quality of continuous tone images, and whether a gradient blend prints properly. If you print at a screen frequency of 150 and a resolution of 2,450 dpi, you produce output with the maximum number of grays possible (256). Most continuous-tone images require at least 150 shades of gray for acceptable printed results.

IP: *To help eliminate banding due to insufficient gray levels in a blend, apply the Add Noise filter to each channel containing color in your CMYK Color image. Filters are explained in Chapter 8.*

In order to ensure the image quality you desire, you can calculate the number of gray levels (including white) that will be printed, using this formula:

$$\text{Number of Grays} = (\text{Output Resolution} \div \text{Screen Frequency})^2 + 1$$

On an output device printing at 1,200 dpi and with a screen frequency of 100, each cell is a 12-by-12 matrix of pixels (1,200 ÷ 100 = 12). Each cell produces one halftone dot. In this 12-by-12 cell, the different combinations of pixels being turned on or off produce 145 levels of gray ($12^2 = 144 +$ white = 145).

Figure 14-1 illustrates how a halftone is created from pixels, and how the number of pixels in the cell determine the number of gray levels. (Although the pixels are represented in Figure 14-1 as square, they are actually round.) In a 5-by-5 cell, 26 combinations of gray ($5^2 +$ white) are possible. White is created when no pixels are truned on, 50% black is created when half the pixels are turned on, and 100% black is created when every pixel is turned on.

Conversely, if you know your output resolution and the number of grays desired, you can compute the required screen frequency with the following formula:

$$\text{Screen Frequency} = \text{Output Resolution} \div \sqrt{\text{Number of Grays}}$$

If more grays are desired, the screen frequency can be reduced. For instance, if the screen frequency drops to 80 lpi and the resolution remains at 1,200 dpi, the

Cell containing
a halftone dot

Cell containing
a halftone dot

Pixel turned off —

Pixel turned on —

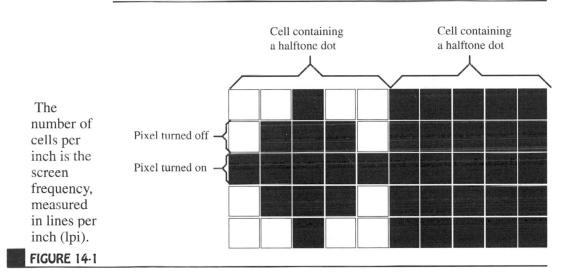

The number of cells per inch is the screen frequency, measured in lines per inch (lpi).

FIGURE 14-1

halftone cell size is increased to a 15-pixel square ($1,200 \div 80 = 15$), which produces 226 grays ($15^2 + 1$). This can create a dilemma: the greater the number of grays, the lower the screen frequency; the greater the screen frequency, the sharper the image; yet, the fewer the gray levels. The simple solution to this predicament is to always print at the highest resolution with the highest screen frequency, assuring sharp images, crisp colors, and 256 shades of gray.

On the other hand, printing at the highest possible resolution and screen frequency may not always be possible, because of two factors: paper stock and printing presses. Not all printing presses can handle high-screen frequency output, and not all paper is suitable for high-screen frequency printing. For instance, when you print at a high screen frequency on newspaper stock, it absorbs the dots, causing too much ink to spread and produces a muddy output. Thus, paper stock is often the determining factor in deciding what screen frequency to use. Magazines printed on coated stock often use a screen frequency of 133 or 150 lpi. A glossy magazine or art book may be printed at 200 lpi. Newspapers are usually printed at 85 lpi.

Resolution, screen frequency, and paper stock are all issues that should be discussed with your print shop, prepress house, or service bureau. You should also decide whether you want your output on paper or film. Although film is more expensive than paper, it provides sharper output, which is especially important at screen frequencies over 100 lpi. This is the reason color separations are output to film.

14

If you are producing color separations, the imagesetter will produce four different film separations. The four pieces of film will not be in color, but rather four monochrome versions of the cyan, magenta, yellow, and black components of your image. The print shop will use the four pieces of film (for each of the four process colors) to create plates for use on a printing press.

PRINTING PROOFS OF YOUR IMAGES

Before you actually go to press with a Photoshop project, you should view a printed sample, or *proof,* of your image. The proof will help you judge the anticipated quality of the final printing job. Proofs can warn you that colors will not print correctly, that moirés may appear, and tell you the degree of dot gain to be expected. (*Dot gain* is the expansion or contraction of halftone dots usually due to ink spreading on paper.)

If you are printing a grayscale image, you may feel that your 300- or 600-dpi laser printer output is sufficient as a proof. If you are creating color images, there are a variety of choices available for color proofs: digital proofs, off-press proofs, and press proofs.

 OTE: *No matter how good your proofs look, various problems can occur onpress that affect the quality of your images.*

Digital Proofs

A *digital proof* is output directly from the digital data in your Photoshop file. Most digital proofs are created by printing to a thermal-wax printer, color laser printer, dye-sublimation printer, high-end inkjet printer such as a Scitex IRIS, or other high-end printers such as the Kodak Approval Color Proofer. Digital proofs are often very helpful as the design process proceeds.

Because digital proofs are not created from an imagesetter's film, color output is often not highly accurate. Commercial printers generally will not accept a digital proof as a *contract proof* that they will contractually agree to match.

 OTE: *If a service bureau will be creating a digital proof of your image, you may be asked to save your file in EPS format. For more information, see Appendix A.*

Off-Press Proofs

These proofs are created from the imagesetter's film that will eventually be sent to the print shop. Thus, an off-press proof is considered more reliable than a digital proof as an indicator of how the image will print. The two major types of off-press proofs are *overlay proofs* and *laminated proofs*.

The overlay proof comprises four different images exposed on acetate sheets that are overlaid. An overlay proof is generally considered not as accurate as a laminated proof, where each colored layer is developed and laminated to a base material. Apart from providing a reliable indication of color, laminated proofs can be very helpful in predicting if moirés will appear in your final output. Dupont's Chromalin and 3M's Matchprint are two well-known laminated systems. When analyzing a Matchprint, be aware that it can make colors look more intense than actual colors produced by inks on a printing press.

Press Proofs

A press proof is considered the most accurate proof because it is made from the actual plates the printer will use, and it is printed on the stock that has been chosen for the job. Thus, the press proof will be a good indication of dot gain, as well as provide an accurate assessment of final color.

Bear in mind that press proofs are often printed on sheet-fed presses, which may be slower than the press used for the actual print job. The cost of creating printing plates and inking the press make the press proof the most expensive proofing process. For this reason, most clients opt for off-press proofs.

WHY YOU SHOULD CALIBRATE YOUR SYSTEM

Of course you will want to proof your images as often as possible during a project—the earlier you catch problems with color and design, the easier and cheaper it is to fix them. Another way to avoid problems in attaining color accuracy is to properly *calibrate* your monitor and system. Calibration helps ensure that the image you see on screen portrays your final output as accurately as possible. Calibration is necessary because monitors, scanners, printers, and printing presses vary in the way they render color.

Monitor Calibration

Calibration is discussed in several places in this book. In Chapter 1, instructions for monitor calibration were included to emphasize the importance of calibrating your monitor as soon as possible before you start using it for color image work. Ideally, you've been working through the exercises in this book with your monitor already calibrated and the options in the Monitor Setup dialog box properly set.

Nonetheless, before you incur any printing expenses, you should ensure that your monitor is properly calibrated. If you don't, you may be working with onscreen colors that are tainted by color casts. Images may appear lighter or darker on screen than they will print. Also, don't forget that the settings in the Monitor Setup dialog box are used when Photoshop converts from RGB Color to CMYK Color.

If you have not calibrated your monitor or selected appropriate options in the Monitor Setup dialog box, return to Chapter 1 now and follow the instructions there, or refer to the Photoshop "Users Guide" before continuing. Once your monitor is calibrated, you can fine-tune it further using a printed proof as a guide.

CALIBRATING TO A PROOF

The Photoshop "Users Guide" recommends that you use a press proof to fully calibrate your system. If you can't afford a press proof, it's still advisable to calibrate using an off-press proof, such as a Matchprint. The following sections give an overview of calibrating a system to grayscale and color proofs. If you have questions regarding calibration, consult your prepress house—many use Photoshop every day and may be able to help out.

Calibrating to a Grayscale Proof

If you are printing a grayscale image, calibrating to a proof is quite simple. When calibrating, you can compensate for dot gain that occurs "on press." (As mentioned earlier and discussed in detail in Chapter 9, dot gain is a change in the size of a halftone dot, usually caused by ink absorption. Dot gain may also be caused by a miscalibrated imagesetter.)

Your first step in calibrating to a grayscale proof is to obtain a proof of a grayscale image that is printed at the resolution, screen frequency, and (hopefully) on the paper stock you will use for printing. Try to use an image that spans a large tonal range from highlights to shadows. You might wish to add an 11-step gray bar in an area in the image. Also, be sure to have your prepress house or commercial printer output the image with a grayscale calibration bar, which steps through grayscale levels. For more information about printing calibration bars, see the section, "The Page Setup Dialog Box" later in this chapter.

When you are ready to calibrate to the proof, open the grayscale image from which the proof was created. To compensate for dot gain, you use the Printing Inks Setup dialog box, accessed by selecting Preferences from the File menu and then choosing Printing Inks Setup. From the Ink Colors pop-up menu, choose the printer or inks that you will be using, and a corresponding percentage is automatically entered into the Dot Gain field. Make sure the Use Dot Gain for Grayscale Images check box is selected. This means that the display of your image on screen will reflect the Dot Gain percentage specified in the dialog box. Click OK to see the effects in your image.

EMEMBER: *For a grayscale image, the settings in the Printing Inks Setup dialog box only affect screen display when the Use Dot Gain for Grayscale Images check box is selected. This will not affect the data in the grayscale image itself.*

If the image on your monitor is lighter or darker than the proof, you may want to reopen the Printing Inks Setup dialog box and change the percentage in the Dot Gain field so that the display matches your image. Before you make changes, however, be sure to consult with your commercial printer and find out if Photoshop's default Dot Gain setting is sufficient. If you do wish to change the value in the Dot Gain field, entering a higher percentage will make your screen display darker, and a lower percentage will make it lighter. Click OK to see the results in the image on screen. Once your screen image matches the printed proof, click the Save button so that you can name and save your Printing Inks Setup settings.

14

When you work on a grayscale image, load the saved Printing Inks Setup settings. Then use the Image/Adjust command's Curves and Levels dialog boxes to lighten or darken your image. Since the Printing Inks Setup settings only affect screen display in a grayscale image (when Use Dot Gain for Grayscale Images is enabled), changes in the Curves and Levels dialog boxes will compensate for dot gain. (To review the Curves and Levels dialog boxes, see Chapter 13.)

Calibrating to a Color Proof

For printing a color image, the calibration process is a bit more complicated. If you will be converting images from RGB Color to CMYK Color, your calibration settings will affect the color data in the CMYK Color file. As discussed in Chapter 9, when you switch RGB Color to CMYK Color mode, Photoshop utilizes the settings in the Monitor Setup, Printing Inks Setup, and Separation Setup dialog boxes to create the color data for the CMYK Color image.

When you calibrate to a color proof, you attempt to match screen colors in a CMYK image to printed color output. To begin the calibration process, use a CMYK Color image as your proofing image—it should not be an image that you converted to CMYK Color from RGB Color. The Photoshop "Users Guide" includes instructions for creating a proofing image from CMYK color-swatch combinations, but it's probably easiest to use the calibration file that is provided with Photoshop. This is the Olé No Moiré file in the Calibration folder (PC users: testpict.jpg in the calibrat folder).

Once your prepress house or commercial printer creates the proof, load the image from which the proof was created on screen. Your first step is to make adjustments to compensate for dot gain.

Compensating for Dot Gain

To compensate for dot gain, open the Printing Inks Setup dialog box (File/Prefer-ences/Printing Inks Setup). In the Ink Colors pop-up menu, shown in the following illustration, choose the correct printer or ink colors. The Dot Gain percentage will change according to your choice for Ink Colors, and represents expected dot gain in image midtones. Photoshop uses the Dot Gain percentage to create a dot gain curve for the entire image's tonal range, from highlights to shadows. (As mentioned earlier in this chapter, the Dot Gain field in the Printing Inks Setup dialog box changes the image display to compensate for dot gain on press.)

Custom...
Other
HQ-LITHO (Newsprint)
Canon Color Laser Copier
Eurostandard (Coated)
Eurostandard (Newsprint)
Eurostandard (Uncoated)
NEC Colormate® PS
Océ Graphics Color PS
QMS ColorScript 100 Model 1Q
QMS ColorScript 100 Model 30
SWOP (Coated)
SWOP (Newsprint)
Ink Colors: ✓SWOP (Uncoated)
Tektronix Phaser II PX/PXi
Tektronix Phaser III PXi
Toyo Inks (Coated)
Toyo Inks (Newsprint)
Toyo Inks (Uncoated)

Adobe recommends that you use a densitometer to take a reading on the proof's calibration bar (a color bar of CMYK colors and CMY combinations). A *densitometer* is a device that measures densities of colors and can provide a precise reading of dot gain. If you don't want to incur the expense of purchasing a densitometer or don't know how to use one, your next best choice is to adjust Dot Gain so that the image on screen looks like the proof. The higher the percentage you enter in the Dot Gain field, the darker the image will become. Click OK to see the results on screen. Once you have found the best setting, return to the Printing Inks Setup dialog box so that you can name and save your settings. To save your settings, click the Save button.

OTE: *If you are uncertain about the effects of changing the Dot Gain setting, consult your commercial printer.*

As mentioned earlier, dot gain can also occur because of a miscalibrated imagesetter. Photoshop allows you to compensate for miscalibration in the Page Setup dialog box. On the other hand, when dot gain appears in film separations due to miscalibrated equipment, compensating for it is probably better left to service bureau or prepress professionals. See the "Transfer Functions" section later in this chapter.

Adjusting for Custom Ink Colors

In addition to adjustment to Dot Gain, the Printing Inks Setup dialog box allows you to adjust for custom ink colors. This might be necessary when you use ink sets that do not appear in the Ink Colors pop-up menu.

To adjust for custom inks, choose Custom from the Ink Colors pop-up menu. An Ink Colors dialog box will open. The values you see for the different CMYK color combinations are x and y coordinates based upon internationally defined standards (the captial Y stands for lightness). The Photoshop "Users Guide" suggests taking a color reading of your proof using a *colorimeter* to enter the correct values. If you do not have color reading equipment, you can click on the color swatches and adjust the colors to match your proof. When you are finished, click OK. Save your settings in the Printing Inks Setup dialog box by clicking the Save button, and then click OK to exit.

	x	y	Y		
C:	0.1673	0.2328	26.25		**OK**
M:	0.4845	0.2396	14.50		**Cancel**
Y:	0.4357	0.5013	71.20		
MY:	0.6075	0.3191	14.09		
CY:	0.2271	0.5513	19.25		
CM:	0.2052	0.1245	2.98		
CMY:	0.3227	0.2962	2.79		
W:	0.3149	0.3321	83.02		
K:	0.3202	0.3241	0.82		

Ink Colors

Your next calibration step is to adjust for possible color casts, which may appear when one of the process inks produces a higher dot gain than the others. Color casts can also be caused by incorrect screen angles and the order in which the different plates are printed.

Examine the gray areas of your proof for color casts. If you spot one, you can compensate by adjusting color levels. To do this, select Image/Adjust/Levels to open the Levels dialog box. Drag the Input Level slider's gamma control to adjust the screen display until it matches the proof. Adjust the gamma level for each channel, as necessary. (Refer to Chapter 13 for details on using the Levels dialog box.) After you adjust the gamma levels, write down the value for each channel, because you will use it to change the entries in the Gray Balance fields in Printing Inks Setup dialog box. Once you have recorded the channel values, click Cancel. (Since these settings are for a systemwide correction, you do not need to click OK, which would change the gamma levels for the proof image only.)

Return to the Printing Inks Setup dialog box so you can enter the numbers that you recorded for each color channel into the appropriate Gray Balance fields. If the value in a Gray Balance field is not 1, take the number that appears there and multiply the gamma setting by it; then enter this number in the Gray Balance field. Raising the value in any of the fields will decrease that color's percentage on screen; lowering the value will increase the color on screen. After you have entered the Gray Balance values, save the Printing Inks Setup settings and then click OK. When you wish to work with an RGB Color image that you will be converting to CMYK Color, load these saved settings.

REMEMBER: *As discussed in Chapter 9, changes made in the Printing Inks Setup dialog box do not affect the color data in a CMYK file, but only the screen display of the image; the settings are used when Photoshop converts from RGB Color to CMYK Color. The settings in the Printing Inks Setup dialog box do not affect the display of RGB Color images.*

Saving Separation Tables

Now that you have compensated for dot gain and adjusted for custom ink colors, your system is calibrated. If you need to convert an image from RGB Color to CMYK Color, your next step is to ensure that the proper settings are entered into the Separation Setup dialog box. Once the information in the Monitor Setup, Printing Inks Setup, and Separation Setup dialog boxes is correct, you can save the settings as a separation table. Open the Separation Setup dialog box (with the File/Preferences/ Separation Tables command), and click on the Save button; name your table after Photoshop creates it. When you wish to use the separation table, open the Separation Tables dialog box and load the table by clicking on the Load button. Photoshop will use this table when you convert from RGB Color to CMYK Color.

For more information about using the Separation Setup and the Separation Tables dialog boxes, see Chapter 9.

Calibrating with EfiColor for Photoshop

If the previous sections on calibration seem somewhat daunting, you may wish to investigate using a color-management software package to aid in calibrating your

14

system. EfiColor for Adobe Photoshop, by Electronics for Imaging, Inc., is designed to provide consistent color based upon the color properties of specific output devices. It includes a pack of core color tables for various output devices and a color table for color monitors. Calibration is handled in a few simple steps.

Once the EfiColor software is installed and Photoshop is opened, you load the Efi Calibrated RGB monitor table by selecting the Load button in Photoshop's Monitor Setup dialog box. Next, you load a separation table for a specific output device using the Load button in Photoshop's Separation Tables dialog box. Efi's core pack comes with tables for digital printers and color separation standards, such as SWOP (Coated), SWOP (Uncoated), and Euroscale. You can purchase other tables, too, in case your output device is not accommodated in the package. Once the separation table is loaded, you can convert from RGB Color to CMYK Color using commands in the Mode menu. The following illustration shows the Separation Tables dialog box, after loading Efi's SWOP-Coated separation table.

TRAPPING IN PHOTOSHOP

When calibration is completed and you are ready to produce your output, your next consideration is whether you'll need to correct for registration problems that might occur during the printing process. Photoshop's Image/Trap command can help.

As paper passes through a printing press, misalignment or movement of the printing plates may cause thin white gaps or color halos to appear around adjoining areas of colors. *Trapping* fixes these discrepancies by slightly overlapping the colored areas so that the gaps won't appear during on-press printing.

When Photoshop traps, it spreads lighter colors under darker ones. Pure cyan and pure magenta, however, spread equally under each other.

OTE: *Before you begin to adjust trap settings, bear in mind that trapping is primarily needed when solid tints adjoin. Since most Photoshop images are continuous tone-images with gradual color transitions, trapping is usually unnecessary.*

To trap, you must be in a CMYK Color image. After consulting with your print shop on the width of the trap adjustment, select Trap from the Image menu. In the Trap dialog box, select a measurement unit from the pop-up menu, and in the Width field enter the width for the trap.

Here's an example of how trapping works: Suppose you entered a value of 2 pixels for the trap width. When a portion of an image with a high percentage of yellow adjoins a dark color, the yellow (because it is the lighter color) will spread out 2 pixels. Thus, if a gap existed between the two plates that was 2 points or less, the yellow ink would fill the gap.

If you wish to see the Trap command in action, create a CMYK file with a swatch of a dark color overlapping a swatch of yellow. Execute the Trap command. Then use the Channels palette to view only the yellow channel. To see the difference—before and after applying the Trap—use the Edit/Undo command.

AUTION: *Discuss trapping issues with your prepress house, which may use a specific software package to trap before outputting your image to film.*

PHOTOSHOP'S PRINTING OPTIONS

Now that you have an understanding of the printing and calibration processes, you'll probably want to explore all of the options available in Photoshop's Page Setup and Print dialog boxes. The Page Setup dialog box provides numerous output features, several of which fall into the realm of the prepress house or service bureau. If you are not printing to a color printer or imagesetter, you may never need to access these options; nonetheless, getting familiar with them will help complete your knowledge of the printing process.

The Page Setup Dialog Box

As discussed in Chapter 2, the Page Setup dialog box allows you to specify whether labels, registration marks, and crop marks will be printed on a page. As you'll see in this section, this dialog box also contains prepress options that govern screen frequency and halftone angles.

Figure 14-2 shows a composite output of an image with a label, crop marks, registration marks, calibration bars, a caption, and a 1-pixel-wide border around the image.

To access the Page Setup dialog box, choose Page Setup from the File menu. PC users will choose a printer from the Page Setup dialog box. Mac users will pick a printer

The Page Setup dialog box lets you print calibration bars, labels, a caption, a border, and registration and crop marks with your image

Gradient tint bar

Label

Santa Fe Mailboxes

Border

Progressive color bar

Crop marks

11-step gray bar

Photograph by Stacy Kollar

Caption

Registration marks

FIGURE 14-2

using the Chooser in the Apple menu; the Chooser cannot be accessed while the Page Setup dialog box is displayed.

Here is an overview of the Page Setup dialog box:

✎ For both Mac and PC users, the Paper and Orientation settings work much the same as in any Mac or Windows program.

TIP: *In Photoshop, it's faster to use the Image/Rotate command to rotate an image before printing, rather than changing orientation when printing.*

✎ *Labels* Select Labels to print the document name and channel name on the page with the image.

✎ *Crop Marks* Crop marks indicate where paper should be trimmed. Turn on Crop Marks to print these marks at the edges of your image.

✎ *Calibration Bars* This option prints an 11-step gray bar, a progressive CMYK color bar and CMY gradient tint bar (if the image is a CMYK Color image) on each page. The calibration bars are used to match a proof to the screen image; you can see how closely screen grays or colors match the printed output. The gray bar on the page prints from 0 to 100% gray in 10% increments. The progressive CMYK bar prints the following colors or color combinations: yellow, magenta-yellow, magenta, cyan-magenta, cyan, cyan-yellow, and black.

14

Registration Marks   Registration marks are used to align pieces of film for printing color separations or duotones. Turn on Registration Marks when you want these marks printed around the edges of the image. Choose from marks such as bull's-eyes and stars.

Negative   Negatives are often used for film output. Most commercial printers in the United States require a film negative to create plates, although other countries create plates from positives, rather than negatives. Ask your printer whether a film positive or negative is required. If you are printing to paper, do not select the Negative option.

Emulsion Down   Both film and photographic paper have a photosensitive layer called *emulsion*. When examining film, the emulsion side is the dull side. When the emulsion side is up in a film negative, type will be readable and not reversed. Your print shop may require the emulsion to be up or down. Usually, printing on paper is Emulsion Up; this is Photoshop's default setting.

Interpolation   Some PostScript Level 2 printers can improve the appearance of low-resolution files by interpolating pixels when printing. If you do not have a PostScript Level 2 printer, this option will not change output quality.

     The Page Setup dialog box also includes buttons that open up additional dialog boxes with more printing options; these buttons are described in the paragraphs that follow.

Printing with a Border

Select the Border button if you wish to have a black border printed around your image. In the Border dialog box, you select a unit of measurement and a width for the border.

```
┌─────────────────────── Border ───────────────────────┐
│                                                       │
│   Width: ┌──────┐  ┌─────────────┐   ┌─────────────┐ │
│          │      │  │  points  ▼  │   │     OK      │ │
│          └──────┘  └─────────────┘   └─────────────┘ │
│                                      ┌─────────────┐ │
│                                      │   Cancel    │ │
│                                      └─────────────┘ │
│                                                       │
└───────────────────────────────────────────────────────┘
```

Printing with a Caption

Select the Caption button to add text that will print below your image. Captions can be up to six lines long, and will print in Helvetica 9-point. In the Caption dialog box, type the text that you wish to use as a caption.

Printing with a Background Color

If you are outputting to slides, you may wish to have a colored background printed to fill in the area surrounding the image. When you select the Background button, Photoshop's Color Picker will appear. Choose the color that you wish to have as your background and click OK.

Transfer Functions

As mentioned earlier in this chapter, when an image is output to film, dot gain can occur due to miscalibration of the imagesetter. The Transfer Functions are used to compensate for this.

In the Transfer Functions dialog box, you enter compensating values in fields that correspond to the dot gain percentages in the image. For instance, if dot gain is higher than it should be, you subtract the desired dot value from the dot gain caused by the miscalibration, then enter the value in the appropriate field. Here's an example: Assume that an imagesetter is printing halftone dots at 60%, when they really should be printed at 50%. The difference between the two figures is 10%. Subtract 10% from 50% and you get 40%. Thus, you enter 40 in the 50% field of the Transfer Functions dialog box (shown on the following page).

NOTE: *If you check the Override Printer's Default Functions option in the Transfer dialog box, and you export an EPS file with the Include Transfer Function selected in the EPS Format dialog box, the transfer information is used in the exported file.*

CAUTION: *Don't change any of the settings in the Transfer Functions dialog box without first consulting your service bureau.*

Setting Halftone Screens

The Screens button presents a Halftone Screens dialog box, in which you can specify elements such as screen frequency, screen angle, and halftone dot shape.

AUTION: *Before changing the default settings in the Halftone Screens dialog box, consult with your service bureau or print shop.*

Ink pop-up menu If you are working with a CMYK Color image, click on this pop-up menu to select the channel. Enter the screen frequency and angle for each channel. If you are printing color separations, the angle for each screen must be set properly to prevent the appearance of moiré patterns.

Auto button If you wish to have Photoshop calculate the screen angles, click the Auto button. In the Auto Screens dialog box, enter the printer resolution and screen frequency. Click OK to have Photoshop calculate the best screen angle for all four halftone screens.

Shape pop-up menu This pop-up menu in the Halftone Screens dialog box offers a list of custom halftone shapes that you can select from to create various printing effects.

Use Accurate Screens option If you are sending output to a PostScript Level 2 printer or an Emerald controller, turn on this option.

Save and Load buttons Use these buttons to store and use your halftone screens settings. If you wish to change the default settings, press OPTION (PC users: ALT), and the Load and Save buttons will change to Default buttons. To create new default settings, click the ->Default button; to return to the original default settings, click <-Default.

Use Printer's Default Screens option If you select this option, any dialog box settings are overridden, and output will be based upon halftone screen settings built into the printer.

14

The Print Dialog Box

After you have selected all the desired options in the Page Setup dialog box, your next step in printing an image is to open the Print dialog box by choosing Print from the File menu. Most of the options in the Print dialog box will be familiar to Mac and Windows users, except for the options at the bottom of the dialog box. These options vary depending upon the image mode (RGB, CMYK, etc.). The following options are important to understand when printing Photoshop images:

- *Encoding*   Some networks and spoolers will not process binary data. If this is the case for your spooler or network, select ASCII. Bear in mind that an ASCII file is twice as large as a binary file, so transferring data to the printer will take longer. (This option is always available no matter what image mode your file is in.)

- *Print Selected Area*   If you wish to print an area you have selected on screen, choose Print Selected Areas. (This option is always available no matter what image mode your file is in.)

- *Print In Gray, RGB/Lab, or CMYK*   If you have a PostScript color or Quickdraw printer, you can print a CMYK or Grayscale version of an RGB Color, Lab Color, or Indexed Color file. To print a Grayscale version of your image, select the Gray option. Select RGB or Lab if you wish to print neither a Grayscale nor a CMYK version of your image (if you are in a Lab Color image, there will be a radio button for Lab rather than RGB). When you choose CMYK, Photoshop will convert the colors to produce a CMYK composite version of the image. For proper colors, make sure your system is calibrated. The following illustration shows the Print dialog box when you are using an Indexed Color or RGB Color file.

Print Separations Select this option when you are printing separations. This option will only be available when you are working with CMYK Color or Duotone images. The following illustration shows the Print dialog box when you are using a Duotone or CMYK Color file.

OTE: *Photoshop will only print one image per page. However, NIQ's Image Up printing software allows multiple Photoshop images to be printed on a page.*

PRINTING SEPARATIONS

This section leads you step by step through the process of a printing a CMYK separation. Even if you're producing output to a 300-dpi laser printer, you may find it educational to see the separation process in action.

To print separations, you will need a CMYK Color image or an RGB Color image converted to CMYK Color. When converting, Photoshop uses the settings in the Monitor Setup, Printing Inks Setup, and Separation Setup dialog boxes. Before you convert an image from RGB Color to CMYK Color, make sure these settings are correct. And always use the Save As command to rename your file before converting, so you'll have a copy of your original image. After converting to CMYK Color, apply the Unsharp Mask filter to clarify your image. For a complete discussion of converting from RGB Color to CMYK Color, see Chapter 9.

Suppose you want to print your CMYK Color image with registration marks, the image's file name, and crop marks. Follow these steps:

1. From the File menu, choose Page Setup.

14

2. In the Page Setup dialog box, select the Registration Marks, Labels, and Crop Marks check boxes. Click the Screens button.

3. In the Halftone Screens dialog box, click the Auto button to have Photoshop automatically set the halftone screen angle.

4. In the Auto Screens dialog box, enter your printer's resolution. If you are printing to your laser printer, type **300**. Enter **53** as the screen frequency, make sure lines/inch is set in the corresponding pop-up menu. If you are using a PostScript Level 2 printer, select the Use Accurate Screens option. Click OK to return to the Halftone Screens dialog box.

5. Select the Use Same Shape for All Inks option. Click OK.

6. In the Print dialog box, select Print Separations and click OK.

When the separations print, four images will be output, one for each of the CMYK colors.

PRODUCING OUTPUT TO A FILM RECORDER

Film recorders are RGB devices and will not output CMYK files. Thus, if you are producing output to a film recorder for slides or chromes, do not convert RGB Color images to CMYK Color.

For images that will be output to a slide recorder, the gamma of a film recorder is higher than that of the standard gamma setting of 1.8 for images that will be printed. Since the gamma of most film recorders is 2.2, Mac users should recalibrate their monitor with this setting, using the monitor calibration Control Panel device discussed in Chapter 1. Both Mac and PC users should change the Gamma setting in the Monitor Setup dialog box, accessed from the File/Preferences submenu.

When working with a service bureau that outputs transparencies, ask the service bureau for the resolution used by the film recorder. Film recorder resolution is measured by the width and height of the pixels in an image. Many film recorders can output at various resolutions; for instance, two typical resolutions of a film recorder would be 2,048 by 1,366 pixels and 4,096 by 2,732 pixels. When you output to a film recorder, the pixels in your image should fit within the film recorder's grid of pixels; otherwise, the image size will be reduced. Remember to consult your service bureau about the resolution you should use when creating your Photoshop file.

Photoshop in Action

A linear blend from dark to light violet was created with the Gradient tool.

To create the spheres, the Elliptical Marquee tool, Gaussian Blur filter, Fill command, and an alpha channel were used.

A scanned photograph of the World Trade Center was selected with the Elliptical Marquee tool. Then Kal's Power Tools were applied to create the fisheye effect. It was then copied and pasted into the final image.

The New York city skyline was created in Adobe Illustrator and then placed into the final image in Photoshop.

Artist: Loren Ruderman   Client: The Port Authority of New York and New Jersey

Loren created this image for the panels in the Observation Deck elevator in the World Trade Center in NYC. He started by making a selection with the Rectangular Marquee tool, filling it with a blend using the Gradient tool, then duplicating it twice. After all three linear blends were completed, he proceeded to make the largest shaded sphere by creating a circular selection with the Elliptical Marquee tool in a black alpha channel. After the circular selection was created, he filled it with white. He then created a smaller circular selection in the top-left side of the circular selection and filled it with black. Then the Gaussian Blur filter was applied before filling the circular selection with black. Next, the spherical selection was loaded onto the final image and filled with black using a low opacity setting. In order for the sphere to have four rings (four levels of shading), Loren repeated these steps three more times, but each time he increased the size of the circular selection and increased the opacity value. By duplicating the large shaded sphere five times and scaling each duplicate, Loren created the smaller shaded spheres. The final step was to apply the Add Noise filter to each channel in the file to compensate for banding.

If you are designing in Photoshop for clients, find out if they will accept your completed work output on a 4-by-5-inch or 8-by-10-inch chrome from a film recorder. Your client can then have the transparency digitized on a high-end scanner and separated into a CMYK Color file for printing.

PRODUCING OUTPUT TO VIDEO

If you plan to output your Photoshop images to videotape for multimedia presentation, Photoshop images can easily be exported into animation and video programs such as Adobe Premiere, Macromedia Director, and Avid VideoShop. To calibrate your monitor to video, Gamma should be set to 2.2. See the previous section, "Producing Output to a Film Recorder" for instructions on changing gamma.

Adobe Premiere, Macromedia Director, and Avid VideoShop will all accept Photoshop files saved in PICT format. Photoshop files can be loaded directly into Premiere without changing file formats. From Premiere, images can be output directly to videotape by choosing the Print to Video command from the File/ Export submenu. As discussed in Appendix A, (Premiere) filmstrip files can be opened, edited, and resaved in Photoshop. Premiere accepts image resolutions of 72 ppi; thus, if your images are intended for video, there generally is no need to create large files in Photoshop at higher resolutions.

For information about importing Premiere files into Photoshop, see Appendix A.

ON YOUR WAY TO THE PHOTOSHOP FUTURE

This chapter has shown how Photoshop allows you to enter into a technical realm once open to prepress professionals only. Undoubtedly, many Photoshop users would rather not worry about calculating gray levels, compensating for dot gain, and choosing between GCR and UCR (covered in Chapter 9). Although these prepress tasks can be avoided to some degree, you'll find that the more you work with Photoshop, the less daunting they will become. If you establish good relations with prepress houses and commercial printers, you'll have an easier time overcoming problems and getting your questions answered.

Whether you're a novice, intermediate, or advanced Photoshop user, stick with it. We hope this book has truly opened up the wonders of the Photoshop world to you. Now that you've worked through the chapters, examined the beautiful images in the Photoshop Portfolio color insert, and studied the excellent Photoshop in Action examples, you'll have learned that Photoshop offers you almost unlimited design choices. We hope that you've already begun to use the examples in this book as a springboard for your own creativity and design ideas, and are planning projects that might once have seemed difficult or even impossible. We're sure that you already agree that after you've experienced the magic of Photoshop, you'll never want to turn away from it. And the future's more powerful computers and improved versions of Photoshop are sure to be even more exciting and enticing. We hope this book will help bring you into that future.

If you have comments about the book, or suggestions for subjects and/or artwork to be included in future editions, please write us at this address:

Fundamental Photoshop
P.O. Box 3117
Westport, CT 06880

We hope you've enjoyed your journey through *Fundamental Photoshop.*

Adele and Seth

IMPORTING AND
EXPORTING FILES

Y ou will often use Photoshop as part of a team of graphics applications. This appendix discusses file formats and the techniques for exporting files created in Photoshop to other programs, and importing files created in other programs into Photoshop.

THE FILE/SAVE AS COMMAND

When you need to save a file in another format, you can use either the File/Save or the File/Save As commands. If you've already saved the file, you must use File/Save As to switch formats. The Save As dialog box allows you to pick a specific format from the Format pop-up menu, shown in Figure A-1. (PC users will choose from Save File as Format Type menu.) After you click the Save button (PC users: OK), a file format dialog box often appears, which allows you to specify conversion options.

WORKING WITH EPS FILES

The EPS (encapsulated PostScript) format is widely accepted by graphics and page-layout programs in Mac and PC environments. The format was originally created as an output format for printing graphic images. If you need to output your

In the File/Save As dialog box, choose a file format for the saved file, and enter a filename

FIGURE A-1

files to programs such as QuarkXPress, Adobe Illustrator, or Aldus PageMaker, you can use the EPS format.

The EPS format is often used to export CMYK separation files from one computer application to another. If you are producing your file to be output by a service bureau, you may need to convert your file to EPS format.

Saving an EPS File

To save a file in EPS format, you choose Save As from the File menu. So that you don't overwrite the previous version of the file, rename the file. In the Format pop-up menu (PC users: Save File as Format drop-down list), choose EPS. (PC users will see the filename extension change to .EPS.) To continue the conversion process, click the Save button (PC users: OK).

Photoshop next opens the EPS Format dialog box. The dialog box that appears depends upon the mode of the file you are exporting (CMYK Color file, RGB Color file, and so forth). If you are exporting a CMYK Color file, for example, the EPS Format dialog box you see is like this one:

```
┌─────────────────────── EPS Format ───────────────────────┐
│                                                           │
│  ┌─ Preview ─────────┐  ┌─ Encoding ──┐   ┌─────────┐     │
│  │ ○ None            │  │ ○ ASCII     │   │   OK    │     │
│  │ ○ 1-bit IBM PC    │  │ ◉ Binary    │   └─────────┘     │
│  │ ○ 8-bit IBM PC    │  └─────────────┘   ┌─────────┐     │
│  │ ○ 1-bit Macintosh │                    │ Cancel  │     │
│  │ ◉ 8-bit Macintosh │   ☐ Include Halftone Screens       │
│  └───────────────────┘   ☐ Include Transfer Functions     │
│                                                           │
│  ┌─ "Desktop Color Separation" (5 files) ─────────────┐   │
│  │ ◉ Off                                              │   │
│  │ ○ Master file: No composite PostScript             │   │
│  │ ○ Master file: 72 pixels/inch grayscale            │   │
│  │ ○ Master file: 72 pixels/inch CMYK color           │   │
│  └────────────────────────────────────────────────────┘  │
│                                                           │
└───────────────────────────────────────────────────────────┘
```

Many programs, Adobe Illustrator included, allow previews of the EPS file. If you choose the 1-bit option (IBM PC or Macintosh) in the Preview box, the preview image will be black and white. The 8-bit choices (IBM PC or Macintosh) allow 256 colors or shades of gray. Mac users can create previews for both Mac and PC environments. PC users can create previews for PC files only.

The Encoding radio button options allow you to choose whether the EPS file will be a binary or ASCII file. A binary file is more compact than an ASCII file.

Photoshop provides both formats because some applications, such as Aldus PageMaker and Freehand, cannot read the binary format.

In general, you will want to avoid using the Include Halftones Screens and Include Transfer Functions check box options; both of these options may override the settings of an imagesetter or a page-layout program. *Check with your service bureau before you turn on these options.* Here is what they do:

With Include Halftone Screens enabled, Photoshop sends the halftone screen angles and screen frequency settings that are entered into the Halftone Screens dialog box (accessed from the Page Setup dialog box). Enabling this option may override an imagesetter's or other application's halftone screen settings.

With Include Transfer Functions enabled, Photoshop sends its Transfer Functions information to the EPS file. The Transfer Functions dialog box (accessed from the Page Setup dialog box) allows you to specify dot gain settings to compensate for miscalibrated imagesetters. A well-run service bureau keeps its imagesetters properly calibrated, thus, any Transfer Functions settings you make can adversely affect the quality of the final color separations.

The EPS Format dialog box shown in the previous illustration allows you to create five separate EPS files for use with programs that utilize Quark's Desktop Color Separation (DCS) format. When you use this format, Photoshop creates a file for each CMYK component. The fifth file, called a master file, contains a preview of the file in PICT format discussed later in this appendix. The EPS Format dialog box allows you to choose what type of master file is created. If you want the best possible preview file, choose the 72 pixels/inch CMYK color option. If you choose No composite PostScript, you cannot print a color composite from the file. Note that all five DCS files must be in the same folder if you wish to reload the composite file.

OTE: *IN SOFTWARE's Platemaker is a Photoshop plug-in that allows you to export DCS files that can include channels for spot colors, varnishes, foil stamping, or even embossing plates.*

OTE: *If you wish to export a clipping path, the Photoshop file must be saved in EPS format. For more information about clipping paths, see Chapter 10.*

Opening an EPS File

This section tells you how to open an Adobe Illustrator file into Photoshop. Photoshop's EPS format is designed to read files created by Adobe Illustrator and Adobe Dimensions. If you are using Aldus Freehand, you can convert your files to an Illustrator format by using Altsys' file conversion program, EPS Exchange.

1. To open an EPS file created in Adobe Illustrator or Dimensions, choose Open from the File menu.

2. Select the file you wish to open. Notice that the file format displayed in the File/Open dialog box is EPS. Click OK.

   The EPS Rasterizer dialog box that appears next aids you in converting from a drawing or vector program to Photoshop's pixel-based or raster format. In the dialog box, you can change the image's Width, Height, Resolution, and Mode. You can also choose whether to use anti-aliasing. If you want Photoshop to soften the edges of the imported file, click the Anti-aliased check box.

   Turning on the Constrain Proportions option ensures that Width and Height will remain at the same ratio in the converted file. When Constrain Proportions is enabled, a change in either the Width or Height measurement forces a proportional change in the other dimension.

3. When you're ready to load the file, click OK. In a few moments, the file opens into Photoshop.

   Although the EPS file is now open in Photoshop, it has not been converted to Photoshop's native format. If you intend to edit the file and save and reload it, it's best to convert (save) the file to Photoshop 2.5

format. Otherwise, you will be met by the EPS Rasterizer dialog box each time you load the file.

4. To save the file in Photoshop format, choose either Save or Save As from the File menu. Before continuing to save the file in another format, Mac users should rename the file; this prevents overwriting the previous file on the disk. (On the PC, when you change file formats, Photoshop changes the filename extension of the file to .PSD; thus, the original file is not overwritten. It's a good idea to rename the file anyway, however, to avoid confusion between versions.) To switch to Photoshop 2.5 format, choose Photoshop 2.5 from the list in the Format pop-up menu. Click Save (PC users: OK) to execute the conversion.

Placing an EPS File into a Photoshop Document

At times you may want to place an Adobe Illustrator document into a file that is already open in Photoshop. If you want the image to be anti-aliased, select the Anti-alias PostScript check box in the General Preferences dialog box. This dialog box is accessed by choosing General from the File/Preferences submenu.

Here are the steps to place an Illustrator EPS file into a Photoshop file:

1. Open the Photoshop file into which you intend to place the Illustrator file.

2. From the File menu, choose Place.

3. From the list of files that appears, select the file that you wish to place, and click Open (PC users: OK).

4. The Illustrator file appears as a boxed, floating selection on screen. If you wish to move the imported image, position the mouse pointer on the border of the floating box. (The selection pointer should be the arrow pointer.) Click and drag the image to the desired location.

5. If you wish to resize the image and change the width-to-height (aspect) ratio, press and hold down COMMAND (PC users: CTRL) while you click and drag the mouse. If you wish to change the image size but maintain the aspect ratio, press SHIFT and then click and drag the mouse.

6. Once you are satisfied with the size and placement of the imported image, position the mouse pointer over it; when the pointer changes to a gavel icon, click to lock the image down.

WORKING WITH TIFF FILES

The TIFF format is frequently used for both Mac and PC graphics files. TIFF stands for "tagged-image file format" and was introduced by the Aldus Corporation as a format for saving scanned images. Although the format is used by most page-layout programs, it is not accepted by all drawing programs.

TIFF files can be loaded directly into Photoshop. When you save a TIFF file in Photoshop, a TIFF Options dialog box appears:

Here you can specify whether the document is for the Macintosh or IBM PC-compatible computers. Just choose the appropriate radio button under Byte Order.

One valuable feature of exporting files in TIFF format is that TIFF files can be compressed. In the TIFF Options dialog box is a check box you can select to enable LZW (Lempel-Ziv-Welch) Compression. LZW is a "lossless" compression format; the file is compressed without removing image data from it. Most page-layout programs can read compressed TIFF files.

If you have created alpha channels in your Photoshop file, the TIFF Export dialog box lets you export the alpha channels with the file. Alpha channels are generally used to save selections, as explained in Chapter 12.

WORKING WITH PICT FILES (MACINTOSH ONLY)

PICT is one of the most common data-file formats available on the Macintosh. Most Macintosh graphics applications, such as MacDraw and MacDraw Pro, can save files in this format. Some PC programs, including CorelDRAW, also accept the format. Both PICT and PICT2 (colored PICT) images can be loaded directly into Photoshop.

When saving nonbitmap files in PICT format, a PICT File Options dialog box appears, which allows you to designate the Resolution (pixel depth) of the image. The dialog box you see will depend on whether you are saving a grayscale or color file.

A

```
┌─────────────────────────────────────────────────┐
│ ═══════════════ PICT File Options ═══════════════│
│ ┌─ Resolution ──────────────────┐   ┌─────────┐  │
│ │  ○ 16 bits/pixel              │   │   OK    │  │
│ │  ● 32 bits/pixel              │   └─────────┘  │
│ └───────────────────────────────┘   ┌─────────┐  │
│                                      │ Cancel  │  │
│ ┌─ Compression ─────────────────┐   └─────────┘  │
│ │  ● None                       │                │
│ │  ○ JPEG - low quality         │                │
│ │  ○ JPEG - medium quality      │                │
│ │  ○ JPEG - high quality        │                │
│ │  ○ JPEG - maximum quality     │                │
│ └───────────────────────────────┘                │
└─────────────────────────────────────────────────┘
```

✎ If you are saving a grayscale file, specify 2 bits/pixel for 4 colors, 4 bits/pixel for 16 colors, and 8 bits/pixel for 256 colors.

✎ The choices for color images are 16 bits/pixel (approximately 65,536 colors) or 32 bits/pixel. If you are exporting a 24-bit color image, choose the 32 bits/pixel option. This 32-bit option appears because the Macintosh includes an extra 8-bit channel (an alpha channel). Most software and video cards do not use this extra 8 bits of information, so if you are not using 24-bit color in Photoshop, choose the 16 bits/pixel option; this keeps file sizes smaller.

When QuickTime is installed, the Compression section allows you to reduce file size with JPEG compression. (See the section, "Compressing Files Using JPEG" later in this appendix.)

Importing PICT Images Using the Anti-Aliased PICT Command

Although PICT images load directly into Photoshop using the File/Open command, you may prefer to use the File/Acquire command to import PICT images. With File/Acquire, you can select the Anti-Aliased PICT option; this activates a plug-in that offers options similar to those in the EPS Rasterizer dialog box. (See "Opening an EPS File" earlier in this appendix.)

```
┌─────────────────────────────────────────────────┐
│ ═══════════════ Anti-Aliased PICT ═══════════════│
│                                                  │
│  Image Size: 2.2 Mb              ┌─────────┐     │
│                                  │   OK    │     │
│     Width:  [1024▾] (pixels)     └─────────┘     │
│                                  ┌─────────┐     │
│     Height: [768  ] (pixels)     │ Cancel  │     │
│                                  └─────────┘     │
│                                                  │
│  Mode:              ⊠ Constrain Proportions      │
│     ○ Gray Scale                                 │
│     ● RGB Color                                  │
└─────────────────────────────────────────────────┘
```

The Anti-Aliased PICT dialog box lets you change Width and Height proportionally and choose to open the document as a Gray Scale or RGB Color file. When you execute the Acquire command and import the PICT file, Photoshop uses anti-aliasing to soften image edges.

COMPRESSING FILES USING JPEG

The JPEG file format is used to compress files to make them smaller. JPEG (Joint Photographic Experts Group) is a "lossy" standard, which means information is removed from the file during the compression process. Usually the absence of the subtracted information is not noticed if the image is compressed using a high-quality setting. When the file is reopened, the lost information is not returned to the file. If you've opened any of Photoshop's tutorial files, you may have already worked with JPEG files. JPEG files can be opened directly into Photoshop.

When saving a file in JPEG format, use the File/Save As command and choose JPEG from the Format pop-up menu. A dialog box appears that contains an Image Quality slider, allowing you to click and drag the control to specify Fair, Good, or Excellent. The better the quality of the compressed file, the larger the file will be.

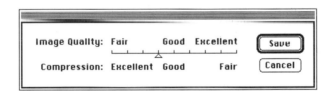

Exporting and Acquiring Files with Storm JPEG

If you've purchased a Photoshop accelerator card, it may have been bundled with Storm Technology's JPEG Plug-in, which offers additional compression settings and options. The plug-in is accessed through the File/Acquire and File/Export submenus. You can specify different compression settings for selections. It also creates thumbnail previews of the images that you compress.

OTE: *If you wish to export an EPS file using JPEG compression, choose Export from the File menu, then select Compress EPS JPEG (PC users: EPS JPEG Export).*

SCITEX CT FILES

Scitex workstations are often used at prepress houses for image editing and color-correction. Files created by Scitex workstations using the Scitex CT (continuous tone) format can be loaded directly into Photoshop.

Only Grayscale and CMYK Color Photoshop files may be saved in the Scitex CT format. If you have a Scitex system, you need special utilities created by Scitex to complete the transfer process.

PHOTO CD FILES

Photo CD files can be opened directly into Photoshop. Version 2.5.1 of the program includes Kodak's CMS CD plug-in, which was designed to increase the color range and fidelity of Photo CD images that are loaded into Photoshop. The plug-in helps color reversal or slide film formats look similar to their appearance when viewed on a light box.

You can open Photo CD images from the Open dialog box. If the File/Open As command is used, choose Kodak CMS Photo CD from the Format pop-up menu before selecting the file.

After you execute the Open command, a dialog box appears. You'll need to make the following settings:

 Specify the desired Resolution for the file to be imported.

 Click on the Source button to open a dialog box where you can choose a Precision Transform option for conversion—Ektachrome (color reversal/slide); Kodachrome (color reversal/slide); or Photo CD Color Negative. If the film "term" is not known but the medium is color reversal/slide, choose Ektachrome. Choose Kodachrome only if K-14 film processing was used to create your negatives. Click OK to accept the Source setting.

Photoshop in Action

The 3-D shapes were created in Infini-D.

The icons were created in Aldus Freehand.

The pattern was created in Adobe Photoshop.

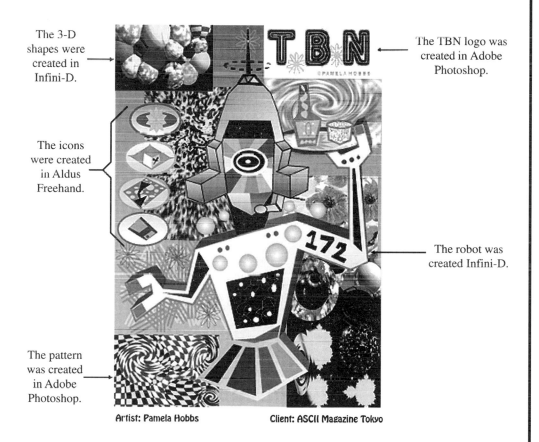

The TBN logo was created in Adobe Photoshop.

The robot was created Infini-D.

Artist: Pamela Hobbs   Client: ASCII Magazine Tokyo

Pamela created this magazine cover using Adobe Photoshop, Aldus Freehand, and Infini-D (a 3-D program). She started by creating the TBN logo and patterns in Photoshop. Once these images were completed, she saved the files as EPS images so they could be placed into Aldus Freehand.

The 3-D shapes in the top left-hand corner of the cover and the robot were created with Infini-D. Once these images were completed, she saved the files as EPS images and placed them into the final image in Aldus Freehand. With Freehand, she created the icons on the left side of the cover.

To specify the Destination color space, click the Destination button to open another dialog box. In the Device pop-up menu, select Adobe Photoshop CIELAB if you wish to have images opened in Lab color mode. Images that will later be converted to CMYK Color should be opened in this format. To open an image in RGB Color mode, select Adobe Photoshop RGB. You will see the words "RCS to Adobe Photoshop" or "RCS to Adobe RGB." Don't be confused by the abbreviation RCS, which stands for Reference Color Space. This is an interim color space used in the conversion from Photo CD color space to the destination color space. When you're ready, click OK to accept the settings.

To load the image, click OK in the dialog box.

If you are working on images that will be converted to CMYK, check with Kodak to see whether you can use one of their profiles that converts a file from Photo CD's color space (Photo YCC) into a CMYK color file. Kodak sells a starter pack for about $150, with monitor and output-device profiles that may suit your proofing and printing needs.

For more details on using Photo CD technology with Photoshop, refer to Chapter 7.

OTE: *Photoshop cannot save files in Photo CD format.*

FILMSTRIP FILES

Filmstrip files are used in animation programs such as Adobe Premier. Filmstrip files can be loaded into the Macintosh version of Photoshop and resaved using Filmstrip format. You cannot, however, convert a file created in Photoshop into a Filmstrip file.

FROM MAC TO PC AND BACK AGAIN

If you are using a Mac and wish to load a Photoshop file created on the PC, or vice versa, you need only use the standard File/Open command. No special conversion procedures are necessary to load and save files between these two platforms.

To use a PC file on the Mac or to save a file on the Mac for use on the PC, you need to save the file on a medium formatted for the PC (a disk or removable hard drive). Several utility programs, including Dayna's DOS Mounter, Insignia's Access PC, Dataviz's MacLink Plus, Apple's PC Exchange, and Apple

File Exchange, allow PC files to be displayed on the Mac. If you are using DOS Mounter or PC Exchange, Adobe recommends saving the file first to your Mac's hard drive and then drag-copying the file to the DOS-formatted medium. This has proved more reliable than saving directly to a DOS disk from Photoshop.

 OTE: *Many Macintosh computers manufactured earlier than the Mac IIcx are not equipped with drives that read DOS-formatted disks.*

If you are saving a file on a Mac that will be loaded onto a PC, you must give the file a name that is no more than eight characters long and contains no spaces. When you name the file, include a period at the end, followed by a two- or three-letter filename extension. The extension is a "code" that alerts Photoshop for Windows what file format to expect. The following is a list of acceptable file formats and their filename extensions.

 OTE: *To open an Adobe Photoshop 2.0 file in Photoshop for Windows, you must first save the file as a Photoshop 2.5 file.*

Format	Filename Extension
Amiga	.IFF
CompuServe Graphics	.GIF
Encapsulated PostScript	.EPS
Illustrator/ASCII EPS	.AI
JPEG (Compressed)	.JPG
MacPaint	.MPT
PC Paintbrush	.PCX
Photoshop standard	.PSD
Pixar	.PXR
PixelPaint	.PXI
Raw	.RAW
Scitex CT	.SCT
Targa	.TGA
TIFF	.TIF
Windows Bitmap	.BMP

The following is a list of PC-compatible filename extensions for palettes and settings:

Palette/Setting	Filename Extension
Arbitrary	.AMP
Brushes palette	.ABR
Color table	.ACT
Colors palette	.ACO
Curves	.CRV
Custom filters	.ACF
Displacement maps	.PSD
Duotone options	.ADO
Halftone screens	.AHS
Hue/Saturation	.HSS
Levels	.ALV
Printing inks	.API
Separation setup	.ASP
Separation table	.AST
Transfer functions	.ATF
Variations	.PSV

Saving PC Files on Mac Disks

Many service bureaus accept data on Syquest removable hard disks. If you use Photoshop for Windows and need to format disks in Mac format, use a formatting utility such as Pacific Micro Electronics' Mac-in-DOS Plus for Windows. This program will format both Syquest cartridges and disks.

INDEX

D